T0328395

# Media Management

*Media Management: A Casebook Approach* provides a detailed consideration of the manager's role in today's media organizations, highlighting critical skills and responsibilities. Using media-based cases that promote critical thinking and problem-solving, this text addresses topics of key concern to managers: diversity, group cultures, progressive discipline, training, and market-driven journalism, among others. The cases provide real-world scenarios to help students anticipate and prepare for experiences in their future careers.

Accounting for major changes in the media landscape that have affected every media industry, this Fifth Edition actively engages these changes in both discussion and cases. The text considers the need for managers to constantly adapt, obtain quality information, and be entrepreneurial and flexible in the face of new situations and technologies that cannot be predicted and change rapidly in national and international settings.

As a resource for students and young professionals working in media industries, *Media Management* offers insights and guidance for succeeding in contemporary media careers.

**C. Ann Hollifield** is Thomas C. Dowden Professor of Media Research at the University of Georgia.

**Jan LeBlanc Wicks** is Professor and Vice Chair in the Department of Journalism at the University of Arkansas.

**George Sylvie** is an Associate Professor at the University of Texas at Austin.

**Wilson Lowrey** is Professor and Chair in the Department of Journalism at the University of Alabama.

# Routledge Communication Series

Jennings Bryant/Dolf Zillmann, Series Editors

Selected titles include:

# Media Management

## A Casebook Approach
Fifth Edition

C. Ann Hollifield, Jan LeBlanc Wicks, George Sylvie, and Wilson Lowrey

 Routledge
Taylor & Francis Group

NEW YORK AND LONDON

Fifth edition published 2016
by Routledge
711 Third Avenue, New York, NY 10017

and by Routledge
2 Park Square, Milton Park, Abingdon, Oxon, OX14 4RN

*Routledge is an imprint of the Taylor & Francis Group, an informa business*

First edition published by Routledge 1993
Fourth edition published by Routledge 2007

*Library of Congress Cataloging in Publication Data*
Hollifield, C. Ann, editor.
  Media management : a casebook approach / C. Ann Hollifield, Jan LeBlanc Wicks,
George Sylvie, and Wilson Lowrey. — Fifth edition.
    pages cm — (Routledge communication series)
  Includes bibliographical references and index.
  1. Mass media—Management—Case studies.   I. Wicks, Jan LeBlanc, editor.
II. Sylvie, George, editor.   III. Lowrey, Wilson, editor.
  P96.M34M4 2016
  302.23068—dc23
  2014045615

ISBN: 978-1-138-90101-8 (hbk)
ISBN: 978-1-138-90102-5 (pbk)
ISBN: 978-1-315-70033-5 (ebk)

Typeset in Sabon
by Apex CoVantage, LLC

*To my husband, Lee Becker, my best friend and partner in a lifetime of adventures, both intellectual and in the far places of the earth.*

*—Ann Hollifield*

*To Mom and Dad who cultivated my love of writing, and to Rob and Ian who continue to nurture it.*

*—Jan LeBlanc Wicks*

*As always, to my wife, Mary Kathleen Looney Sylvie, my best friend and inspiration: Thank you.*

*—George Sylvie*

*Thanks to Mary-Loyd for her support over the years, and to my generous colleagues at The University of Alabama.*

*—Wilson Lowrey*

# CONTENTS

# PREFACE TO THE FIFTH EDITION

The fifth edition of *Media Management: A Casebook Approach* represents a new approach and focus, manifested by the change in leadership and approach to writing the book. Those who write media management books typically serve in management positions, meaning their demanding jobs require them to give up old tasks, such as writing this book. Thus we bid a fond farewell to Steve Lacy and Ardyth Sohn, two of the original authors. We are proud to add Wilson Lowrey to the team, whose research includes a variety of media management topics and issues including blogs, online news, the Internet, and convergence. His contributions are welcome additions to this edition. Ann Hollifield, George Sylvie, and Jan LeBlanc Wicks remained on the authorship team. On this edition, we also had the assistance of an extremely talented editorial assistant, Stephanie Stevens, a graduate student at the University of Georgia.

In the few short years since the publication of the fourth edition, dramatic changes have overtaken media industries. The trends toward a decline in print media and an increase in multiplatform media, digital and mobile distribution of content, social media, and social marketing have accelerated, while entirely new types of media such as location-based content have emerged and gained traction in the market and social media has established itself as a serious content provider in competition with more traditional media forms. Even more importantly, a major restructuring of media labor markets occurred. The Great Recession of 2008 spurred legacy media companies to dramatically cut their permanent workforces through layoffs and attrition and increase the number of contract and freelance workers they hire. The changing nature of media employment combined with the opportunities made possible by new ideas and new technologies have created a wave of media entrepreneurship. This edition actively engages these changes in both discussion and cases.

We also took a new approach to writing the book. Ann and Jan served as co-first authors to bring two perspectives to all chapters and revisions, viewing the book through the eyes of a media management/economics/media in economic development lens, along with an advertising and integrated branding/social issues/self-regulation lens. Future media managers must consider problems and solutions from a variety of viewpoints and have expertise in a number of areas. We felt it was important to take a multidiscipline perspective in writing and revising the book as well. We collaborated with Wilson and George to present a fifth edition that retains the coverage of major management concepts and research while introducing new technologies, new types of media messages, entrepreneurship, and international issues to the book. As ever, we seek to join the important knowledge from the past to the future knowledge needed by our students.

While the fifth edition is significantly changed from the fourth edition, important concepts are retained. Chapters that were kept but significantly revised include Leadership, Motivation, Planning, Innovation, Market Analysis, Marketing Research, Law, Regulation, and Ethics, and two completely new Extended Cases. The chapter on decision making has been folded into the Leadership chapter. Similarly, the discussion of workforce issues, which was included in the Leadership chapter in the last edition, has now been given an entire chapter of its own. The Workforce chapter will allow professors and students to more thoroughly engage in discussion of media career paths in the new industry environment and the challenges of managing an increasingly multicultural and impermanent workforce. The Planning chapter has been revised to include a strong focus on project planning and management because, in the try-fast/fail-fast business environment of today, media content, business, and technological innovations are often developed through structured projects. The Global Media Management chapter was eliminated as a separate chapter and folded into Planning because overseas expansion often is managed as a project. Finally, we developed a new chapter on Entrepreneurship in recognition of the fact that many of our students will eventually start their own media companies—or be charged with developing entrepreneurial projects within established companies.

A few major themes permeate the fifth edition. We examine how managers must constantly adapt, obtain quality information, and be entrepreneurial and flexible in the face of new situations and technologies that cannot be predicted and change rapidly in national and international settings. Nowadays the title "media manager" refers to roles ranging from the CEO of a media conglomerate to director of a small agency with a handful of employees to the sole proprietor of a for-profit blog, a technology startups, or your own business as a freelancer. Regardless of the scope of his or her media operation, a media manager today must be a leader, visionary, negotiator, operations manager, supervisor of human resources, trainer, expert in promotions, public relations, marketing and branding; and knowledgeable not only about content production and distribution, but also about audiences and audience behavior. Finally, he or she must be able to apply all that to domestic markets, overseas markets, or some combination of both. On top of all that, the entrepreneurial manager also needs skills in finance and investor or donor management.

Consequently, we address the topics above as well as social media, other new forms of media messaging, change, entrepreneurial journalism, and international topics and issues. We emphasize current trends in management to allow professors and students to consider both established theories and new concepts in management and apply both to contemporary and changing problems faced by media managers. The emphasis on entrepreneurship throughout the fifth edition provides conceptual and skills training in self-sufficiency and initiative, which future leaders in the field must have, especially if they start their own media outlets or firms. The emphasis on international topics and examples throughout this edition reinforces the importance of diversity found in this and earlier editions, while adding research and issues regarding international management.

Here is a short summary of the perspective each author had in each chapter.

## CHAPTER 1—LEADERSHIP

Understanding leadership and having leadership skills is imperative for media professionals in a global labor environment where more work is done via freelance or temporary contracts, or in one's own media startup. A manager must be able to manage and strategize for oneself, as many work outside the structure of a formal organization, so more senior and experienced leaders will not be there to help. Although there are many different leadership approaches and styles, true leadership depends on vision and the ability to adapt your style and approach to the characteristics of the people around you and the situation in which you find yourself. Even young professionals provide leadership in the turbulent digital market and competitive environment, participating in change management due to their new ideas and approaches, creativity, and lack of organizational socialization as to "how it should be done."

## CHAPTER 2—MOTIVATION

It is especially important to understand how to motivate employees during turbulent, uncertain times where traditional media jobs are disappearing, many employees freelance or manage their own jobs or outlets, many positions are converged whereby professionals must use varied skills and knowledge in multiple formats, and digital technologies mean a local outlet now has an international audience. The modern employee's search for positive self-identity and the increasing levels of exhaustion that convergence have wrought make the manager's job more challenging and uncertain than ever before. Managing in media involves analyzing complex human behavior in evolving positions and situations, often produced in rapid cycles by creative personnel who enjoy autonomy. The major theories and concepts regarding motivation are retained, while current examples and research include the changing media industries, diversity, gender, technology-employee match, teams, and convergence in a recession.

## CHAPTER 3—WORKFORCE

Media work has always been rife with uncertainty, but recent economic turbulence and technological changes have made the environment especially precarious for workers, who have been faced with fewer traditional jobs, many new specialties and converged roles, stagnant salaries, and a need to pursue entrepreneurial opportunities. The traditional, stable, routine work that dominated media fields for decades is harder to come by. The data on emerging labor trends in media markets suggest that career tracks in media are changing and that media managers will need to adjust in response to those changes. Managers need to be flexible and seek diversity in their hiring, keep an eye on change while not neglecting their operation's core, and be sensitive to burnout—both in workers and in themselves.

## CHAPTER 4—ENTREPRENEURSHIP

The odds of success for entrepreneurs are long, but they can succeed if the entrepreneur finds a supportive and collaborative—even familiar—environment, and plans rigorously. Being in the right place, at the right time, with the right amount of money, the right background knowledge, and the right business connections can be more valuable than having a "light bulb" moment. Well-defined niches, collaborative relationships, and diversifying revenue streams are important to successful entrepreneurships. Working as an entrepreneur includes taking new perspectives: For example, rather than focusing solely on financial pay-offs, it can be extremely satisfying just to be in control of your work.

## CHAPTER 5—PLANNING AND PROJECT MANAGEMENT

Planning is a synonym for strategic planning, the central focus of management research and training. Planning includes long-term, mid-range, and short-term planning. In today's turbulent business environment, planning has become more difficult and even somewhat risky. In media companies, however, an increasingly important area of planning is project planning and management. Media innovations, new products, and even major content productions such as films, albums, and video games are created as "projects." Overseas expansion or investment also is often managed as a project within media companies. In the digital media environment, global expansion is frequently critical if a company is to keep control of its ideas and content. But once a company crosses national borders, management becomes an even more complex and challenging process. Challenges range from cultural differences in content preferences and tastes to varying national laws and policies.

## CHAPTER 6—INNOVATION

Media industries have and will continue to change rapidly, so one must understand how to manage and promote innovation in national and international markets. Managers must determine how well an innovation serves its purpose, its effect on the people who use it, its strategic ramifications so one's organization may take full advantage of it, as well as what the next innovation will be or when and how each innovation may be replaced to ensure the long-term health of one's organization. In other words, leaders provide a strategy for adopting an innovation and the vision to inform and shape the strategy. Beyond organizational factors, media managers must consider and attend to consumers' opinions of innovations, whether they are local, national, or international consumers. Consequently, the chapter covers classic and contemporary research on innovation and includes branding, the audience as information searchers, and international examples of innovation.

## CHAPTER 7—MARKET ANALYSIS

In an age of hyper-competition, independent production, and media entrepreneurship, understanding market analysis is a required skill for every media employee. Market analysis is the ability to understand what your product is, who your audience/customers are, what their needs are and why they use, or don't use, your content/product. It also means understanding who your competition for those audiences/consumers is and what they offer as a substitute for what you offer. Contemporary media professionals also must understand that *they* are products in the media labor market; thus market analysis skills are key to positioning oneself in the desired labor pool. Media professionals must constantly and consciously analyze the talents and skills they offer compared to their competition, and actively construct themselves as a media talent "brand" that an employer can successfully market in order to attract and retain customers.

### CHAPTER 8—MARKETING AND RESEARCH

A strong grounding in marketing and research is fundamental to a successful media entrepreneur or professional who changes jobs over a career. You cannot successfully define your own or your organization's benefits and sell them effectively unless you understand how advertisers and marketers evaluate products. You cannot obtain quality information on your product or audience unless you understand the appropriate ways to answer various questions and develop projects to obtain that information. While the chapter introduces students to major research concepts and the major types of research, it also addresses analytical techniques used by advertisers, trends, and resources for learning ethical research standards.

### CHAPTER 9—LAW, REGULATIONS, AND ETHICS

It is simply not enough to understand the legal aspects of media firms and media management. Certainly major legal concepts, issues and trends regarding diversity, gender equity, social media, and digital devices are reviewed in the chapter. But ethics and law are presented as interrelated: Laws define what a manager must do, and ethics defines what he or she should do. Media professionals operate in the court of public opinion, so a manager's integrity and reputation transcend any one position. Entrepreneurs who start media outlets must develop and maintain trust and respect among their communities, markets, donors, advertisers, employees, and audiences. Ethics, moral reasoning, and media ethics codes are discussed to show future managers how to develop their own ethical beliefs, behaviors, and standards.

## EXTENDED CASES

The extended cases encompass all chapters as well as the major foci of this edition: entrepreneurship and global management.

### Extended Case Study 1: Changing Leaders and Direction in Dallas/Fort Worth

Extended Case 1 allows professors and students to analyze and apply all the chapters and major concepts of the book. EC1 also enables students to learn and use entrepreneurship skills, one of the major foci of this edition, in many of the ways they would if they were developing or repositioning a startup. Students also learn how to find and use quality and relevant information to make important decisions associated with entrepreneurship. In essence, EC1 teaches students to consider all key managerial functions and activities across one firm, to provide a comprehensive understanding of how one outlet functions. The goal is to teach students what is involved in developing, running, and funding a startup.

### Extended Case Study 2: Solving Crises at South Asian Entertainment

Extended Case 2 allows professors and students to tackle serious crises in an international setting. The primary manager in the case is the senior manager of a "small," fictitious conglomerate located in one region, South Asia. However the "small" South Asian Entertainment is part of a large, worldwide fictitious conglomerate, Vizcacha International. Therefore, students must consider problems from the perspective of a senior regional manager, who supervises other managers who run other firms or media outlets encompassed by that regional firm, yet answers to the overall top manager of the entire media conglomerate. In addition, cultural, political, and interracial issues are raised in the context of local, regional, and worldwide firms. In essence, EC2 teaches students to consider major managerial functions and activities across several firms of varying sizes in different countries, and how problems in one firm affect others in the same media conglomerate. The goal is to educate students about various cultures and countries while appreciating the perspective of a top manager facing personal and professional crises across several firms and countries.

In our rapidly changing and expanding world of media, we believe that every media professional is, by default, a media manager. As media enterprises large and small innovate, restructure, and struggle to find business models that will allow them to survive in an increasingly fragmented and competitive market, every member of the organization will need to understand the media business and actively strategize ways to succeed. That's the very definition of management. Some say that the media industry is in crisis. We believe that every crisis creates new possibilities. We hope you will find this fifth edition of *Media Management: A Casebook Approach* a valuable and thought-provoking addition to your exploration of the extraordinary challenges and opportunities that await.

## Preparing for and Using the Case Method

A case study tells the story of a problem or problems to be solved based on actual events or decisions concerning firms and managers, or a composite of various events or problems, in an industry. In case analysis, students assume the role of the manager or managers featured in the case to learn about situations they are likely to face on the job. It is especially suited to disciplines where theory, research, and principles are applied in the real world.

The case method allows students to (a) gain experience in making decisions and solving problems; (b) learn to identify, analyze, and research complex problems; and 3) integrate theory and prior knowledge to life-like situations (Chandy, 2004). Hoag, Brickley, and Cawley (2001, p. 52) said that the case method of experiential learning "stimulates the same skills managers use: analysis with intuition, integration, decision-making, self-initiative and persuasive communication." Zbylut, Brunner, Vowels, and Kim (2007) said the case method allows students to apply theory or abstract lessons to the concrete situation described in a case, stimulates critical and creative thinking, and provides a glimpse into real-life situations from the safe and controlled structure of a classroom.

Zbylut et al. (2007) reported that the discussion component of case method instruction is important, as the question–and–answer process encourages students to actively participate in the learning process. Discussion of case concepts compels self-examination and evaluation of the arguments of others, triggers a reflective process requiring students to reevaluate and reorganize their views, encourages students to process the case material at a deeper level, and develops interpersonal and communication skills. The professor "facilitates group discussion to elicit specific points, challenge student assumptions, and engage in problem-solving and analytical skills" (Zbylut et al., 2007, p. 1). Participating in multiple case discussions over the course of a semester can help students learn about the advantages and disadvantages of group decision making and its processes (Preparing an Effective, 2005b).

Aylesworth (2008) said when students and teachers discuss cases effectively, the managerial techniques and knowledge from the case are learned and internalized by students. "A good case discussion is indeed a partnership between the students and also between the students and the instructor, in which all the players strive together to reach not only a resolution of the case issue, but also a shared understanding of the 'lessons' of the case. It is in the effort to find that resolution and shared understanding that learning occurs" (Aylesworth, 2008, p. 107).

Students accustomed to lecture classes must learn that the case method requires extensive reading, preparation, and discussion on their part. Students' work in case method courses is evaluated in terms of the quality and quantity of contributions to case discussions; simply talking is not enough. Students must offer relevant contributions using independent thought based on material in the case. Rather than saying "I think," "I believe," or "I feel," students should learn to think and respond objectively, saying "My analysis shows" (Preparing an Effective, 2005b, p. 1). The goal is to use logic and reason to solve management problems, rather than relying on emotions or feelings.

Learned (1980, in Christensen, 1987, p. 13) suggested students could prepare to discuss or write about a case by answering the following questions about it. Students are asked "why" they answered the way they did, which encourages them to dig for the underlying logic and reason:

1. "What, in your opinion, is the most fundamental, crucial or urgent issues or problems—or issues and problems—before the company? Why do you think so?
2. "What, accordingly, if anything, should anyone do? Who? When? How? Why do you think so?
3. "How will you communicate your ideas to the top management of the company? Why?"

(Learned, 1980, in Christensen, 1987, p. 13)

Often professors may expect more extensive preparation from students. The following suggestions from Foran (2002), Wertheim (2006), and Preparing an Effective (2005a, 2005b) are integrated to provide a more rigorous method for students to read a case and prepare for class:

1. Read the case once to get a quick sense of the whole case. Then read it again and consider steps 2 through 7.

2. Identify the who, what, where, when, and how of the case. Who is/ are the important decision maker(s)? What is the major problem and/or decision to be made? Who are the important persons in the case? Why? What is the background and important information about the firm? What are the key issues in the case? What important information is lacking? If you could ask questions of the case's main characters, what would you ask?

3. Define the problem(s). Where is the problem and why is it a problem? What type of problem is it (e.g., group, leadership, motivation, etc.)? Which chapters in this book address the type of problem? How urgent is the problem? What are the consequences if the problem isn't solved? What information is lacking that is needed to help solve the problem? Find and list all indicators in the case that something is wrong or not as desired or expected. Distinguish between symptoms and the problem. Symptoms are indicators of problems that reveal something is not as it should be and help you to identify the problem. Problems are the situations or conditions that require a solution before performance can improve. So your focus should be on figuring out the problem's actual causes.

4. Identify the goals. What is the organization's mission statement? What do the overall goals of the manager(s) involved seem to be? What are the important statements made by the managers or others in the case that reveal what is important or motivating factors? Are the goals of firm(s) and individual(s) similar or not? Why or why not?

5. Conduct the analysis. Reread the relevant chapter(s) you identified in section 3 above. Identify the theories, models, ideas, or research that is helpful. Apply these to the situation. As you learn more through research and discussion, review the relevant chapters and concepts again.

6. Diagnose the problem. Identify the primary goals of the organization and individuals. Think about how they relate to the problem. Unless your professor tells you otherwise, select the most important goal and consider alternative solutions to enable the performance of managers and employees to achieve that goal. Think about short-term, intermediate, and long-term actions or steps to be taken to solve the problem. What are the possible alternative solutions? What are the resources needed for each alternative? What constraints or problems are associated with each alternative? What are the likely short- and long-term consequences of these alternatives? Identify the criteria that are crucial to identifying and solving the problem (unless your professor assigned such criteria).

7. Develop an action plan and defend your decision. Identify the criteria used to select an alternative and develop an action plan for that alternative. Decide upon the best alternative or course of action to solve the problem. Explain why it is the best alternative, identify what resources are needed. Identify what the primary manager or important characters in the case must do and how they should change, and identify how or why the firm should change, etc. Be sure to develop a contingency plan where you select an alternative that allows future action or plausible alternatives should the first course of action fail to solve the problem. Identify what the best plausible alternatives are and explain why they are implemented next.

Not all cases or assignments require each step. Your professor may ask you to use a completely different approach for class discussions or when writing your assignment. But these steps provide a good approach for reading cases and preparing for class discussion. Like life, you will never have enough information, you will never have as much time as you would like, you cannot always be certain you have identified the real problem, you will face ambiguity, you will realize there is rarely one right answer, and you likely will not have a perfect solution (Foran, 2002; Preparing an Effective, 2005a, 2005b; Wertheim, 2006). Unlike a lecture, conducting a case analysis allows you to feel the frustration and face the difficulty of making hard decisions with imperfect information in difficult and complex situations where the wrong decision could ultimately cost you your job or put your employees out of work.

Cases often present ambiguous and complex problems and provide misleading and incomplete information, so you experience these realities. Students often feel overwhelmed when working on a case for the first time. Managers have these same intellectual and emotional experiences, so what you learn can be applied to business situations after graduation. More suggestions for students are available from sources such Christensen (1987), Foran (2002), Preparing an Effective (2005a, 2005b), and Wertheim (2006).

Applying the case method teaches you to read a case carefully, research it, evaluate it, and defend your decisions in class. You learn effective strategies and techniques for dealing with real-life problems on the job. You learn how to analyze problems and find information to create solutions that are more likely to alleviate the problem. You learn how to find good evidence to support your arguments to other managers and employees on how to solve a problem. And as you are learning all these helpful skills and techniques for your career, you're also learning about the major types of management issues you may face, the theories and best practices of management, and how to manage a diverse workforce in national and international settings. Finally, in considering and discussing cases and issues, you develop your own ethical beliefs and moral compass to become a principled manager who is respected for integrity in making career and life decisions.

# CHAPTER 1

# Leadership

What defines a great leader? Why are some people great leaders and others not? Are leadership and management the same thing? Why are some people excellent leaders at one point in time or in one situation, but complete failures as leaders at other times? Are leaders born, or can they be made? What does "leadership" mean if one is an entrepreneur or working freelance?

These are just some of the many questions about leadership that historians, political scientists, psychologists, and, of course, management experts have wrestled with for centuries. Leadership remains one of the continuing mysteries of human experience. All of us have observed leaders throughout our lives, whether the leaders were our parents, teachers, the class president, our boss, or any one of the dozens of other leaders and leadership situations we encounter daily. But despite the fact that examples of leadership are all around us, there is still much about it that we don't understand. Nevertheless, in this chapter, we will explore what we do know about leadership and, more importantly, how we can use that knowledge in today's media management. Probably at no time in the history of the modern media industry has leadership been more important than now.

Over the past quarter century, a combination of technological and market forces has completely disrupted media industries. Today, media executives face the need to reinvent almost every aspect of their businesses: media business models, production processes, distribution channels, audience measurement methods, demand forecasting, and human resource management. Equally importantly, changes in traditional media industries have opened new opportunities for entrepreneurs and shifted many media and journalism jobs from staff positions with established media companies to freelance and contract positions. Entrepreneurs and independent contractors are, by definition, both leaders and managers. After all, they have no one but themselves to turn to for the vision, organizational skills, strategic thinking, and discipline that separate success from failure in a highly competitive, rapidly changing market.

In short, then, the time for strong and visionary leadership in media industries is *right now*, and the most important leader in your media career must be *you*.


## THE FOUNDATIONS OF LEADERSHIP

*Management is doing things right; leadership is doing the right things.*
—Peter Drucker (2001)

*My job is not to be easy on people. My jobs is to take these great people we have and to push them and make them even better.*
—Steve Jobs (quoted in Morris, 2008)

*As we look ahead into the next century, leaders will be those who empower others.*
—Bill Gates (quoted in Kruse, 2012)


### Leadership Traits and Skills

One of the perennial questions about leaders is whether they are born or made. Today, experts in leadership acknowledge that some people are "natural" leaders, gifted with a confidence and charisma that is difficult for others to learn or imitate. If you think of the "great" leaders in history, most possessed such natural abilities. Moreover, research has suggested there is a correlation between media Chief Executive Officers' (CEOs') backgrounds and personal characteristics, and their likelihood of adopting nontraditional leadership approaches and strategies (Shaver & Shaver, 2006). However, whether natural leaders or not, people can learn the fundamentals of leadership and become more effective in leadership roles. This chapter will lay out some of skills and dynamics of successful leadership.

Early studies of leadership focused on leadership traits (Northouse, 2010; Parry & Bryman, 2006; Redmond & Trager, 2004; Stogdill, 1974). Traits are personal characteristics that people have. In some cases, they can be developed, and in other instances, developing a trait may be more difficult. Research has identified a long list of traits common to effective leaders. As the word "trait" suggests, many of these characteristics come more naturally to some people than others, although most individuals probably can improve at least somewhat in these areas with effort.

Although individual lists of traits vary, common characteristics include intelligence, ambition, self-confidence, expertise, charisma, creativity, perseverance, flexibility, commitment, integrity, the ability to inspire and motivate others, social and emotional intelligence, and the ability to envision what the future ought to be (Northouse, 2010; Stogdill, 1974; Zaccaro, Kemp, & Bader, 2004).

Many students of leadership argue that of all of these characteristics, vision is most important (Redmond & Trager, 2004; Sashkin, 1989). Vision is the ability to think creatively about the future and the opportunities it holds. Visionary leaders also must possess the ability to inspire others to adopt their vision and work toward its achievement.

It is not enough, of course, just to have vision. Successful leadership demands that leaders transform their visions into realities. Executing a vision is where most leaders fail because a new vision represents change (Johnson, 2004), and managing change is one of the most difficult of all management challenges. Any attempt to introduce change to an organization will bump into traditions, differing viewpoints, and established interests. Thus, for the leader, bridging the gap between vision and reality requires planning (see Chapter 7) and leadership skills. Unlike leadership traits, leadership skills are abilities that can be developed with training and effort.

Central among the critical leadership skills experts have identified are (a) communication and listening skills, (b) empowerment, (c) coaching, (d) delegation, (e) assertiveness, (f) decisiveness, (g) problem solving, (h) goal setting, (i) conflict management, and (j) negotiation (Harris, 2002; Hughes, Ginnett, & Curphy, 1999; Northouse, 2010). Communication, which includes listening skills, is arguably the single most important skill a leader must have (Harris, 2002). Leaders must communicate their vision, goals, and instructions clearly and in terms that motivate and inspire. Some managers cling to the idea that information is power and, thus, communicate as little as possible with subordinates. Employees who constantly receive partial or misleading information quickly stop trusting the boss. Skilled leaders communicate effectively through formal channels, such as memos, e-mail, speeches, and meetings, and informally in casual conversation and social settings. Regardless of the channel, failure to communicate leads to misdirection, misunderstandings, inefficiency, and lost trust. Nonverbal communication is another important element of leadership communication. How leaders dress, carry themselves, and interact with others communicates much about their power, self-confidence, and expectations for their employees (Harris, 2002). Research shows people read nonverbal cues as more accurate and reliable than verbal messages, particularly where relationship quality is concerned (Hickson & Stacks, 1985; Malandro & Barker, 1983), and some scholars have argued that nonverbal communication is the most important form of communication in organizations (Richmond, McCroskey, & Payne, 1987). Managers who fold their arms when talking with subordinates communicate defensiveness and lack of openness (Kurien, 2010). The bosses who give their full attention to male subordinates but don't look up when female subordinates talk to them communicate a dismissive attitude toward women. In short, we cannot *not* communicate because everyone around us constantly interprets our nonverbal displays (Harris, 2002). The leader who fails to monitor his or her nonverbal messaging is likely to quickly encounter communication problems with colleagues and subordinates.

Listening skills are no less important than communication skills; effective leaders are active listeners (Harris, 2002; Johnson & Bechler, 1998), giving the speaker full attention and ignoring cell phone, e-mail, or other interruptions. They ask questions, take notes, and rephrase back to the speaker what was said to make sure they understood correctly. More importantly, they act on advice and suggestions from employees. When managers tell employees, "My door is always open," or "I really want to hear what you think," but never act on the input they get, staff quickly come to see the boss's claim of openness as a sham.

Communication and listening skills play a role in other leadership skills such as empowering, coaching, and delegating. Leaders empower subordinates by seeking their input on important decisions, trusting them to succeed at critical tasks without constant supervision, and permitting them to find their own ways to accomplish goals as long as the goals are accomplished. With such trust, managers can delegate some of their responsibilities. Delegation allows the leader to refocus on tasks that can't be shared (Hughes et al., 1999). However successful delegation requires that subordinates be expert enough and professionally mature enough to handle the delegated authority (Hersey & Blanchard, 1969).

Assertiveness and decisiveness also are key leadership skills (Hughes et al., 1999; Stogdill, 1974). Leaders and managers must be comfortable confronting problems; advocating for their own, their organizations', and their employees' needs; and telling people when they don't meet expectations. Decisiveness is equally important: An editor who dithers in a breaking-news situation or a leader who avoids dealing with problems because he or she can't make tough decisions loses subordinates' confidence. However, decisiveness does not mean refusing to change course once the chosen course appears wrong. Effective leaders constantly seek and evaluate new information and admit when they've made a mistake.

Decisiveness does not equal blind stubbornness, the fear of admitting mistakes, or the illusion of personal infallibility, all of which can afflict people in leadership positions—often with disastrous consequences.

Assertiveness enters into conflict management, negotiation, and problem solving, which all are important leadership skills (Hughes et al., 1999). Conflict is a natural part of any organization and can be a healthy and creative force. Fear of conflict creates a passive, change-averse environment that may slow development and excellence. On the other hand, uncontrolled conflict is a destructive force, causing good people to leave a company and encouraging the survivors to focus on defeating their internal rivals rather than on achieving mutual success. A leader has to manage conflicts at organizational and individual levels, allowing differences to surface, be aired, and to contribute to change and development, but not allowing them to evolve into running feuds or disruptive outbursts. In the very public, high-pressure, ego-driven world of media professionals, conflict is inevitable. Assertiveness and conflict-management skills are particularly important for media leaders.

Successful conflict management requires negotiating skills. Skilled negotiators focus on win-win solutions allowing all parties to save face and gain something. Effective negotiations focus on the interests at stake, not the positions the parties take (Fisher, Ury, & Patton, 1991). Well-managed negotiations serve everyone's interests to some degree and leave relationships undamaged.

Finally, problem solving, motivation, strategic planning, and goal setting are the core of every leader's responsibilities. Most of a leader's activities involve problem solving at some level, and many of the problems they need to solve involve these other core leadership functions. So important are the ability to motivate, plan, and set goals to a leader's success, that those subjects will be addressed in detail in later chapters.

**Leadership Styles**

Leadership experts argue that successful leadership depends on combining the style and skills of the leader, the styles and skills of the followers, and the specific conditions of the situation the group is addressing (Fiedler, 1967; Hersey & Blanchard, 1969; House & Dessler, 1974; Hughes et al., 1999). In other words, even the most gifted leaders will fail miserably if their traits and styles do not match their followers' or the circumstances. On the other hand, even the most unlikely leaders may succeed if they develop their leadership skills and understand their followers and the situation.

Leadership style refers to the way a leader works with subordinates and superiors, including how much autonomy subordinates have, how much emphasis is placed on subordinates' personal goals and development, and whether the leader makes accomplishment of the task more important than maintenance of collegial relationships. Most leadership theories argue that there is no "best" style of leadership, despite what you may have heard or read about the importance of *humanistic* and *transformational* leadership. In reality, successful leadership requires leaders to respond to their followers and the situation.

There are different ways of looking at leadership styles. Some experts have focused on how organizational structures and working conditions create an organizational leadership style, and others have examined the personal leadership style of individual leaders.

### Effects of Organizational Structures on Leadership Style

Theories X, Y, and Z comprise one of the more common frameworks for understanding differences in leadership styles and explain the connection between organizational structure, culture, and leadership.

Theory X refers to a top-down, authoritarian style in which supervisors command and subordinates obey (McGregor, 1960, 2006). Theory X leadership typically exists in highly structured, hierarchical organizations where members' status derives from their job title, and lines of authority are clear. Subordinates may have some input in Theory X environments, but when a decision is made, compliance is expected. The military is the most obvious example of this style; other examples include police and fire departments and airline and ship crews. These types of organizations use Theory X because it is most effective when people work in changeable, potentially dangerous, or extremely time-pressured conditions. For those reasons, news organizations often exhibit elements of Theory X leadership style.

Experts often describe Theory Y leadership as a "humanistic" or "human-needs-oriented" style (McGregor, 1960, 2006). Theory Y leaders strive to create harmony between the organization's and employees' goals. Generally found in more decentralized, horizontally structured organizations, Theory Y leaders give workers some power and autonomy. The approach assumes most people are self-motivated and produce better results if they control their own work and if the work fits with the employee's personal goals and values. Media workplaces also widely use Theory Y, particularly in the creative industries and new media.

Theory Z leadership (Ouchi, 1981), often referred to as "Japanese-Style Management," first attracted attention in the 1980s when Japanese companies became major global competitors to U.S. and European industries. Theory Z combines elements of X and Y. Theory Z organizations tend to be hierarchically structured, with the expectation that employees at the hierarchy's bottom will be consulted by senior management on issues within those employees' expertise. In return, workers take personal responsibility for the quality of the product and the success of the organization.

Theory Z management requires a high level of trust, loyalty, and mutual respect across all levels of the company. It works well in organizations where managers and employees expect workers to stay with the company for most, or all, of their careers. In today's competitive economy where employment security has eroded and many companies, particularly in the media industry, are replacing employees with contract workers, Theory Z leadership is becoming harder to find—even in Japan.

For those who might wonder why these approaches to leadership are called Theories X, Y, and Z, the terms don't have any special significance. The author of Theory X and Theory Y designated them as such simply to "avoid the complications introduced by a label" (McGregor, 1957, as cited in McGregor, 1960, 2006, p. 341). Theory Z, which came later, was so named by its author (Ouchi, 1981) because it built on McGregor's earlier work.

Other aspects of organizational structures such as centralization, unity of command, span of control, division of labor, and departmentalization also affect a leader's style and effectiveness (Hughes et al., 1999). Centralization refers to the number of people in the organization who control power or, said another way, the degree to which power is shared in the organization (Andrews, Boyne, Law, & Walker, 2009). Highly centralized organizations tend to be more authoritarian or Theory X, while decentralized organizations tend to be more participative. Unity of command refers to how clearly the lines in the chain of command are drawn. Historically, organizational theorists argued that clear chains of command that had each employee reporting to one, and only one, supervisor were associated with better firm performance and more satisfied employees (Rizzo, House, & Lirtzman, 1970). In media organizations, however, authority often is very diffuse. Journalists may work with several different editors on a story, while in entertainment media, creative teams often are responsible for production. In entrepreneurial organizations and settings where new products are being developed, authority usually is highly decentralized.

Span of control refers to the number of people and projects managers supervise (Ouchi & Dowling, 1974). A wider span of control makes it more difficult to keep track of individuals and details. Widespread consolidation in local media since the 1990s has meant that many broadcast managers and newspaper publishers now run multiple media outlets, sometimes spread across hundreds of miles. As span of control increases, a manager's ability to closely supervise and direct employees and to simultaneously develop strong personal relationships with them declines.

Division of labor refers to how specialized staff members' roles are in the production process and was identified by Adam Smith (1776) as an important factor in economic efficiency. Some organizational scholars have argued that in this century, technology will cause ever-increasing division of labor in most industries, until specific jobs are "atomized" (Malone, Laubacher, & Johns, 2011). In the media industry, however, the opposite is occurring. Digital technologies have significantly reduced divisions of labor. Smaller digital cameras and laptops make it possible for reporters in converged operations to create and edit video for broadcast, extract a still shot for the newspaper and Web, and rewrite the story for all three platforms. In a transmedia environment, writers and videographers are expected to write and shoot narratives appropriate to screens ranging from smartphone screens to 70-inch high-definition home theaters—and everything in between.

Departmentalization refers to the internal structure of an organization and whether people with similar or complementary jobs work together and report to the same managers (Koontz & O'Donnell, 1964). Typically, highly departmentalized organizations also are more centralized. Conversely, as divisions of labor blur, so do unity of command, centralization, and departmentalization, while managers' spans of control increase.

In the 21st century media environment, the need to produce and distribute content for multiple screens and formats is forcing an organic restructuring within media companies and industries. Film producers and directors now work closely with video game developers in developing game-friendly narratives and visualizations for future films. Screenwriters are called upon to extend storylines from episodic television series to webisodes, mobisodes, and gaming formats for wider distribution and marketing. No longer, as was the case only a few years ago, are the journalists producing for the newspaper or magazine's print edition or evening newscast working in one room, while the online department sits in another (Powers, 2006; Singer, 2003, 2008). In the digital newsroom, the print and broadcast journalists *are* the online journalists, and also the photographers and videographers (Roderick, 2012). Journalists today are expected to produce news stories for multiple platforms—broadcast, print, online, social media, and mobile devices, using text, audio, and video. They also often work with fewer support staff such as copyeditors and designers to assist them or double check their work. The fading distinctions between print and broadcast distribution are reducing demand for specialization and increasing demand for multiskilled, multitasking generalists.

### Individual Leadership Styles

In addition to the leadership styles shaped by organizational structures, individuals bring their personal style to the Leader-Follower-Situation equation. Leadership experts have identified many different individual leadership styles ranging from autocratic to hands-off (Northouse, 2010; Redmond & Trager, 2004). Most people probably use more than one leadership style, and individuals' styles often change with time and experience. However, at any given time, an individual is probably more comfortable with some of these styles than with others (Fiedler, 1967).

### LEADING FOLLOWERS

Leaders do not operate in a vacuum. They accomplish their goals primarily through followers' activities. Effective leaders understand the strengths and weaknesses of the people working around them and adjust their leadership style accordingly.

Leading a staff of media professionals can be challenging; as a rule, media professionals are highly educated and self-motivated (Weaver, Beam, Brownlee, Voakes, & Wilhoit, 2003). Media production is a creative activity, so "artistic personalities" abound. On the news side, journalists make their living by asking tough questions, skeptically evaluating answers, and pointing out nonsense as publicly as possible. Journalists are no more likely to swallow the "company line" from their boss than they are from the city's mayor.

The Situational Leadership Theory (SLT) (Hersey & Blanchard, 1969) maintains that an effective leader approaches leadership by understanding the followers' task and psychological maturity. Task maturity refers to an employee's education, experience, and technical skills relative to a task. Psychological maturity refers to the individual's task-related self-confidence, attitude, and motivation. Task and psychological maturity are not necessarily related. The production intern may lack experience but have tremendous enthusiasm, while the senior producer may be burned out and alienated.

SLT encourages leaders to match their leadership style with subordinates' "followership" styles. According to the theory, an authoritarian approach works best with followers without job skills and motivation. Consultative or inspirational leadership would work better for those who, like the senior producer, have the skills but lack motivation or confidence. Coaching would help develop the highly motivated but inexperienced intern, while leaders blessed with highly skilled and highly motivated followers should empower them through delegation.

A second theory of leadership, Fiedler's (1967) Contingency Theory, assumes that leaders tend to be less flexible than the Situational Leadership Theory posits. Thus, the problem is to choose the right leader for the specific followers and situation, rather than ask the leader to be adaptive.

A third important approach in leadership studies is the Path-Goal Theory (Evans, 1970; House & Dessler, 1974). The Path-Goal Theory holds that a leader's primary job is to motivate followers. The theory predicts that followers' behaviors depend on whether they think their work will help them achieve their own goals. Two other factors shape followers' behaviors: (a) their perception of whether the leader's behavior will contribute to their personal satisfaction, and (b) their perception of their own self-efficacy. Followers who see themselves as powerful and in control of their own destiny prefer consensus leaders, while followers who see themselves as at the mercy of fate prefer more authoritarian leaders (Mitchell, Smyser, & Weed, 1975).

Another important element of leadership style is task-relationship orientation. Originally identified in the 1940s and 1950s (Hughes et al., 1999), leaders' orientations toward tasks and relationships have worked its way into many leadership theories. The task-relationship orientation basically argues that some leaders are more concerned about job-related tasks, while others focus on maintaining good relationships with colleagues. Whether one approach is more effective than the other is debated among leadership scholars, but several theories suggest the answer depends on the combination of the organization's followers and the situation (Fiedler, 1967; Hughes et al., 1999).

The task-relationship dichotomy also comes into play in leader-follower relations. Most people relate best to those most like themselves in task-relationship orientation, while differences can lead to tension. When relationship-oriented people spend time chatting with colleagues, their task-oriented coworkers are likely to see them as time-wasters. When task-oriented people brush off efforts at small talk, their relationship-oriented colleagues may see them as cold, arrogant, and unfriendly. In reality, good relationships among coworkers help organizations work more smoothly, and building good relationships requires time and non-task-focused communication. Conversely, a strong task focus gets things done. Managers need to recognize the valuable contributions both types of employees make to organizational effectiveness and take care not to try to force everyone into the same mold. Observing each coworker's task-relationship orientation and then matching it when interacting with that individual helps improve working relationships.

## LEADERSHIP STYLES FOR DIFFERENT SITUATIONS

Many leadership theories also suggest that the organizational environment impacts leadership effectiveness. For example, unlike the Situational Theory of Leadership, which assumes the ability of leaders to adapt their style to their followers, the Contingency Theory of Leadership (Fiedler, 1967) holds that leadership effectiveness rests on choosing the leader whose style is appropriate to the situation. Fiedler identified several situational factors that predict leader success: (a) the quality of leader-follower relations, (b) the degree of task structure or uncertainty, and (c) the power of the leader in relationship to the followers. Tests of the Contingency Theory of Leadership suggest that task-oriented leaders are more likely to be successful when these factors are extremely favorable or extremely unfavorable, while relationship-oriented leaders are more likely to succeed when conditions are more moderate.

In a startup media company, for example, the tasks will be fairly unstructured. Leaders and staff alike will be learning what needs to be done to keep the business running. The staff usually will be small, new to the organization, and enthusiastic about the chance to build a business from the beginning. Individuals will have a high degree of professional autonomy since the organization will be making things up as it goes along. In such circumstances, a task-oriented leader probably will be successful because that person will be more likely to focus on making sure that things happen and details get covered. Conversely, in an established organization going through disruptive change, a people-oriented leader probably will be more successful because he or she will focus more on the human dynamics of the situation.

When leader-follower relations are either very good or very bad, relationship maintenance efforts are not likely to matter. Similarly, highly structured or highly unstructured tasks benefit from a strong task-focus, while the leader's possession of either a lot of power, or very little, may be more important to task accomplishment than to relationship maintenance. Where conditions are not clear cut, the relationship-oriented leader may have more success navigating the ambiguities (Hughes et al., 1999)

## LEADING SMALL GROUPS AND TEAMS

In the media industry, teams or small groups commonly perform work. The word *team* refers to a small group working toward a shared goal with a high level of interdependence (Hughes et al., 1999). Groups generally are less cohesive, and members may have different reasons for belonging to the group and different objectives for the outcome. Media, film, television, newspaper, and music production, among others, require teamwork.

Leading teams and small groups is a complex process. Teams and groups develop their own internal identities and cultures and, like other organizations, are affected by size, task structure, and member relationships. Teams and groups have the advantage of harnessing the ideas and efforts of multiple people, but they have the disadvantage of requiring more time and effort to manage because of the need to negotiate between members. Many leadership issues affect teams' success. These include (a) domination by the leader, (b) poor relationships between members, and (c) the team's or group's perception of itself and its relationship to the outside world (Bormann & Bormann, 1992; Hughes et al., 1999; Janis, 1982).

A dominant leader negates most of the advantages of teams and groups because generally only the leader's view is heard. Even if a leader does not actively dominate group interactions, if the person is powerful, group members may engage in self-censorship and offer only ideas they think will be acceptable. That curtails the group's range of ideas and actions. Effective group leadership in such cases requires that the leader withdraw, appointing someone else to head the group.

Relationships between team members also can affect teamwork. If a group divides into factions or cliques, consensus may be impossible. If two members dislike each other, disruptive bickering and mutual sabotage can result. In media professions, where many projects require teamwork, such bickering can have negative consequences for both work efficiency and quality.

Another team leadership problem that arises is one almost every student knows from first-hand experience: the free rider—the team member who doesn't contribute. This occurs primarily in groups where rewards, such as grades, will be equally distributed. As long as at least one person works for the group's success, others can afford to free ride. Free riders demoralize productive members and encourage them to also start underperforming (Kerr, 1983; Olson, 1965). When free riders are spotted, they should be confronted and, if necessary, removed from the group.

Identity and perception issues also can hinder team success. In their earliest stages, teams and small groups build a shared identity and understanding of the group's relationship to the organization and to other groups—a fantasy theme (Bormann & Bormann, 1992). It develops almost unconsciously during the social interactions in the first few meetings. Once the group's identity or fantasy theme takes root, it is hard to change, and members who challenge that identity become outsiders.

A group identity can be positive or negative. For example, members of a newly formed company may be convinced that they're going to create the next big thing. On the other hand, they may decide among themselves that the boss's idea is dumb and the company doesn't stand a chance. In either case, the group's fantasy theme is likely to become a self-fulfilling prophecy (Bormann & Bormann, 1992). Leaders should monitor the development of fantasy themes during the group's formation stage, and actively counter negative themes that emerge.

## LEADING CREATIVE PROJECTS AND PEOPLE

Media are fundamentally creative businesses. Managing creative people—and managing people in a way that encourages creativity—are important leadership responsibilities. Creativity requires divergent thinking—i.e., thinking in unusual, unconventional, and unexpected ways. Creativity's nature makes it hard to understand and predict, but some people clearly are more creative than others. Even though there is an element of talent or genius in creativity, media managers can help enhance creativity in themselves and their organizations.

Research suggests that the recipe for creativity includes a certain amount of expertise mixed with a dose of naiveté (Kuhn, 1996), a steady infusion of new ideas, adequate but not excessive resources, and an organizational structure and culture that empowers individuals and rewards risk taking (Küng, 2004). Studies of scientific revolutions suggest that truly revolutionary ideas tend to come from relative newcomers to a field—people who have some expertise in an area, but whose ideas about how things work have not yet become fixed (Kuhn, 1996). Steve Jobs's development of Apple computers in the 1970s, Jerry Yang and David Filo's invention of Yahoo!, and Mark Zuckerberg's success with Facebook are only some of the recent examples of this phenomenon.

Creativity also requires constant exposure to new ideas, images, and information. Creativity-focused organizations often surround workers with bright colors and creative visual spaces. They seek diversity in their employees because variety in life experiences, knowledge, and perspectives fuel new ideas. Most people can enhance their personal creativity with simple exercises—going into a different neighborhood to shop, reading books and magazines they normally wouldn't open, worshipping with people of a different religion. The key is to constantly seek new experiences and information and to keep an open mind.

Studies of highly creative media companies such as Pixar Studios, BBC News Online, and HBO found that they shared some characteristics (Küng, 2004): teams handled creative activities; teams were given autonomy; and members had appropriate expertise and they received adequate, but not excessive, resources to encourage inventiveness with the resources they had. Leadership also played a key role. Company leaders developed a vision for the company that represented a challenge to members' creativity, provided the resources to meet that challenge, and then got out of the way, having little direct involvement in daily activities.

These findings in media organizations parallel those in other studies of creativity. Fostering creativity requires an organization to develop a culture that gives employees a high level of autonomy in their work, rewards risk taking, and permits failure. If managers constantly monitor, critique, and control creative work, or if employees believe they'll be penalized if something they try fails, workers will strive for risk-reducing conformity, not creativity.

## LEADING CHANGE

The idea that the only constant in the media industry today is change has become a cliché. But it also is a reality. Thus next-generation media managers must be prepared to lead their organizations through constant change processes.

Leading change is difficult. Change creates tension and uncertainty in organizations and has been shown to reduce job satisfaction and organizational commitment and to increase the likelihood that staff will quit (Brockner, Grover, Reed, DeWitt, & O'Malley, 1987; Wanberg & Banas, 2000). In a talent-based industry such as media (Reca, 2006), such losses can be costly. Media are talent products, whereby their quality depends heavily on the producers' individual talent, knowledge, experience, and reputation. James Cameron, Mark Zuckerberg, and Ariana Huffington cannot just be replaced, if they leave a project, with no impact on the organization or outcome. Thus, it is critical that media companies and projects recruit and retain the most talented people. Finding and inspiring top people is the essence of leadership.

Even when led by people with extensive training in change management, change is hard on organizations. In a study of newspapers led by editors who had completed a change-management training program, Gade (2004) found that editors and newsroom employees had very different views of how newsroom changes had been handled. Managers felt they had communicated a clear vision for change and included newsroom professionals in the change processes, while journalists felt left out of the process and confused about why the changes were necessary. The differences in perception were so large that Gade said, "it was hard to understand the two groups are sharing the same experiences" (2004, p. 40).

Other studies of change have had similar findings. Employees tend to view most changes negatively, at least initially, and older employees are more change resistant than younger employees (Daniels & Hollifield, 2002). Among journalists, changes that are perceived to harm the quality of journalists' work are most likely to meet resistance (Daniels & Hollifield, 2002; Weaver & Wilhoit, 1991), a finding that probably also applies to other groups of creative professionals. Change appears to be a long-term problem for managers. While staff members' attitudes toward changes improve over time, research shows they continue to believe they were happier before the changes were made. Moreover, the staff's view of management after a period of change improves even more slowly than their attitudes toward the changes (Daniels & Hollifield, 2002).

Despite the resistance managers can expect to encounter, there are things effective leaders can do to make change easier for everyone. Leaders should seek employees' input on the changes and respond to that input as much as possible. Identifying staff members who are influential with their colleagues and involving those individuals in the change-management process often helps colleagues become more accepting of the changes. Regular and open communication about the changes, and paying special attention to older and long-term employees will help, as will clearly communicating how the changes will occur, what the future will look like, and how the changes relate to the company's long-term goals and survival (Beckhard & Harris, 1987; Cummings & Worley, 1993; Miller & Monge, 1985). Research suggests good leaders can successfully offset some of the negative effects of change on organizations and the people in them (Cummings & Worley, 1993; Nadler, 1987; Powers, 2006; Wanberg & Banas, 2000).

## LEADING ETHICALLY

American businesses, government, and media are in the midst of an ethical crisis, and the media industry has not been immune. Scandal follows scandal: In one month in 2012 alone, NBC fired several people over the editing of an audio tape that strung together different parts of a 911 call in a way that gave a misleading impression of what had happened (Bond, 2012; Stelter, 2012); Yahoo's Chief Executive Scott Thompson was accused of having embellished his resume (Chang, 2012; Roose, 2012); and Rupert Murdoch, chairman and CEO of the media giant News Corp., was found by a committee of the British Parliament to be "not a fit person" to lead a major international corporation because of the extensive phone hacking conducted by journalists working for News Corp. subsidiaries (Sabbagh & Halliday, 2012). While that month may have seemed a low point for media ethics, it was followed in 2013 and 2014 by a steady parade of stories about profoundly offensive and often factually questionable comments by media anchors and commentators using outrageousness to attract attention and audiences; recurring instances of plagiarism at major U.S. news organizations; and questions about media complicity in multiple countries in covering up illegal government activities done in the name of "national security."

Such a train of ethical scandals is not exactly a performance designed to inspire public confidence in the media industry or the information it provides. Perhaps most troubling of all is that ethical scandals—in the media and other major industries and institutions such as banking, politics, and religion—have become so commonplace that they are losing their ability to shock and outrage.

Although ethics are discussed in great detail in Chapter 9, it must be noted here that at their core, ethics are a leadership issue. Honesty and integrity have been considered necessary attributes of true leaders since at least the time of Aristotle. Only the leader can set the ethical tone for an organization, and the failure of ethics in an organization is the failure of leadership. Thus, even if a leader is not directly involved in widespread illegal or unethical behavior, he or she is responsible for the development of a corporate ethos that allows such behavior to flourish.

Ethical leadership in media industries goes beyond content decisions and adherence to the law. Leaders and managers also have a responsibility to deal honestly with regulators and the public, and fairly with their employees. Corporate leaders owe workers safe and reasonable working conditions, fair wages, and adequate resources to get the job done. In this age of pervasive connectivity in which personal information is distributed and collected with nearly every click of the mouse, media executives need to insist that their organizations respect the privacy of sources, news story subjects, and audience members. Similarly, when communication professionals are virtually tied to always-on communication devices, media managers need to respect employees' right to have a life outside of work.

Media leaders' ethical responsibilities rise above those of many other industries. Media are a critical societal infrastructure. The media's performance in providing high-quality, responsible, professional journalism affects the integrity and transparency of government, the functioning of democracy, and the health of the economy (Islam, 2002).

Consider, for example, how the nature of government differs between those countries where there is an independent press and those where the media are controlled by the government. It is because of this critical role in society that media are the only industries given special protections by the U.S. Constitution. In their selection, production, and framing of news and entertainment content, media leaders shape our perceptions of our world (Lippmann, 1922). Few any longer dispute that media content has long-term effects on society, both positive and negative. This places a special responsibility on media leaders to consider the effects of their work on society and strive to lead their organizations responsibly, ethically, and with personal integrity.

## LEADING YOURSELF

In an era when more and more media professionals are becoming entrepreneurs or are working permanently in freelance or contract positions, skilled leadership has become, if anything, more important. Those working outside of a formal organization must be prepared to lead themselves. The vision, self-discipline, confidence, assertiveness, decisiveness, communication skills, flexibility, adaptability, creativity, ability to work with a wide range of other people, and integrity that a young professional might look to a supervisor to help him or her develop—must be self-supplied by the entrepreneur or freelancer.

Furthermore, clients and employers look for those characteristics in the contract workers they hire. No one wants to hire someone who doesn't communicate well, lacks self-confidence, or is change-resistant or indecisive. A freelancer, contractor, or entrepreneur who doesn't possess significant leadership skills is unlikely to survive long in the highly competitive market for media-contract services.

Similarly, those employed in media companies also will find themselves working more often with freelance colleagues. Leadership of an ever-changing list of employees or colleagues creates its own challenges.

You will know less about the people around you. Your professional relationships will be less stable and less committed. As a supervisor or colleague, you will have fewer incentives to work out problems with temporary employees and less interpersonal leverage to resolve those problems. Long-term planning will be more complex because you will be less able to count on having specific people with specific skills and abilities to help you realize the plan. More time and resources will be absorbed by what economists call "transaction costs," in this case, the constant cycle of the negotiations and bureaucracy required to hire, terminate, or continue the employment contracts of an ever-changing cadre of temporary workers.

The shift in media industries to greater reliance on temporary workers combined with the economic upheavals and layoffs that have affected media organizations in this century have other implications for media leadership. As research has shown (Daniels & Hollifield, 2002), organizational change, in general, and changes in personnel, specifically, erode employees' long-term commitment to their organizations. That, in turn, changes relationships between media leaders and their colleagues. One of the major leadership challenges for media professionals in the 21st century will be to develop new and creative approaches to leading an increasingly transitory, independent, and entrepreneurial workforce.

## SUMMARY

In the media industry, the need for strong, gifted, and visionary leaders who can find and inspire talented professionals has never been greater. The critical changes the industry faces demand flexible, knowledgeable, innovative leadership capable of navigating the fast-changing, uncertain media environment. The talent-based nature of media makes it critical that media leaders be able to manage not only tasks, but also people. Media leaders today must be insightful, adaptable, and strategic in their actions. Leaders succeed when they match their leadership style to their followers and to the dynamics of the situation in which they are working. Successful leaders work constantly to strengthen their natural leadership traits and develop their leadership skills.

The rapidly changing structure and nature of the media industry makes the job of leading media organizations exceptionally challenging—and exceptionally exciting. The next generation of media leaders will captain the industry into a new era, making their mark on the future of the industry no less than did the pioneers who led the development of early television. However, succeeding in today's uncertain industry conditions will require strong leadership traits, exceptional leadership skills, and the ability to manage change, foster creativity, and lead ethically.

---

### CASE 1.1 LEADING IN A NEW DIRECTION

Amy Johnson, editor of the *Southtown Daily*, leaned back in her chair and sighed. *Southtown Daily* and the company that owned it were in serious financial trouble. The company's owner had borrowed heavily to buy other small-city daily newspapers across the South in the late 1990s, expecting the new century to bring growth opportunities to the newspaper industry. Instead, the rapid drop in newspaper circulation and ad revenue caused by the digital information revolution of the 2000s had left the company unable to meet its debt payments and teetering on the brink of bankruptcy.

Over the past decade, the reporting staff of *Southtown Daily* had been cut from nearly 50 reporters, editors, and photographers to just 10. The news hole had shrunk from 20 pages per day to 6, and most of that space was filled with wire copy. Despite the shrinking product, the company had repeatedly raised the newspaper's subscription price in an effort to increase revenue. That, in turn, had caused more and more subscribers to cancel the paper, which encouraged local advertisers to demand lower advertising rates because the newspaper reached fewer and fewer readers every day.

From Amy's seat as editor, the situation looked like a death spiral.

In her search for ways to improve the situation, one idea Amy had hit on was to try to generate a dependable supply of high-quality User Generated Content (UGC). If the digital revolution had given readers alternatives to the newspaper for getting the information they wanted, it also had made it possible for every news consumer to become a news producer. The success of YouTube suggested that people enjoyed user-produced content, and by tapping into a city-wide network of engaged citizens, *Southtown* could effectively expand its reporting staff. Better yet, experiences with UGC showed that many people would produce and contribute content without asking to be paid.

The challenges of UGC would include attracting high-quality content that people would want to read or watch, and developing a dependable supply of submitted content that *Southtown* could count on daily. The other challenge would be getting *Southtown*

*Daily*'s professional journalists to accept UGC as part of the paper's content.

*That* wasn't going to be easy. When Amy had suggested in a staff meeting several months ago that the paper encourage UGC contributions, there had been an uproar. *Southtown*'s editorial staff argued that such contributions were amateur and would harm the quality of the newspaper and the staff's professional reputations as journalists. The journalists pointed out that UGC content had to be edited and overseen, and that would take at least some of the few remaining journalists on staff away from local reporting and professional content production.

It also had been clear from the tense discussion that the remaining staff feared that Amy's UGC proposal was just another attempt to cut the few remaining editorial jobs at the paper. The two senior reporters—Susan and Bill—who also were the most respected and influential members of the staff—had been the most vocal in their opposition. They both had been adamant that they would have nothing to do with user-submitted content.

Nor were *Southtown*'s journalists alone in feeling this way. Amy had talked with other editors around the country and found that most journalists were deeply skeptical—or totally hostile—to the idea of making UGC part of the newspapers' regular content. The common feeling was that content submitted by "citizens" was biased, inaccurate, and amateurish.

But now Amy felt *Southtown* had reached the point where it *had* to start using UGC. Figuring out how to convince her colleagues, and organizing the process so that it didn't completely drain the paper's remaining journalistic resources, were going to be a tremendous challenge.

**Assignment**

You're a change-management consultant that Amy brings in to advise her how to lead this change process.

1. Research the status and problems that are associated with User Generated Content, which sometimes also is called "Citizen Journalism." Prepare a professional report for Amy that summarizes other media leaders' experiences with UGC and some of the solutions that already have been developed for managing it.

2. How accurate are the staff's criticisms of UGC? What might Amy suggest that the paper do to ensure that the UGC *Southtown* uses does not further harm readers' perceptions of the newspaper's quality?
3. Advise Amy on how to lead the change process so that her colleagues will accept UGC as part of their newspaper and actively work to make it a valuable part of their content mix. Suggest processes and strategies that she might use to reduce the staff's resistance to UGC.

---

**CASE 1.2. ANALYZING LEADERSHIP BEHAVIORS**

Select a dramatic film, television program, or documentary that takes place in an organizational setting. Do not use a comedy for this assignment.

Watch an episode or lengthy scene and use it as a case-study observation of leadership behavior. How is the leader's style portrayed? What about the followers' styles? What environmental conditions are they dealing with in the organization or situation?

Include as many of the leadership elements discussed in this chapter as you can: verbal and nonverbal communication, conflict management, negotiation, change, creativity, organizational diversity, organizational structure, etc.

Position yourself as a management consultant to the organizational leader portrayed in the program and write a detailed analysis of the interactions that occurred in the episode. Make recommendations for improvement, as appropriate.

---

**CASE 1.3. PERSONAL OBSERVATION OF MEDIA MANAGEMENT**

Contact a media or communication company in your area. Arrange to spend several hours shadowing either the senior executive or a departmental manager.

During your visit, carefully observe the manager's leadership style and staff members' "followership" styles. Note the environment and situation and how the manager and staff work together.

Look for indicators of task and psychological maturity, and task-relationship orientations. Observe small-group interactions, if you have the chance to sit in on meetings.

Watch the manager's approach to encouraging or discouraging creativity, managing conflict, managing change processes, negotiating issues, communicating and listening, and establishing or enforcing standards, rules, and ethics.

Are there points of conflict in the organization? Do there seem to be differences in how people are treated based on their age, race, or gender? Be sure to carefully observe nonverbal communication behaviors by the manager and staff. These include not only body language, but also dress, movement, vocal tones, and even how they decorate their workspaces.

Note: If you write a case study or description of your visit or discuss your experiences in class, it is important that you protect the privacy of your hosts. Be sure to change the names of the company you visited and of all the people you observed. Alter any descriptions of the company or its operations so that readers and listeners won't be able to identify the company or any of its employees, and never discuss your visit with anyone but your professor.

---

**CASE 1.4. A STUDY OF LEADERSHIP**

Identify a media company or organization that is widely considered to be innovative and successful. Develop a case study of the history and leadership of that company that includes both research using public documents and news stories and extensive interviews with managers and staff of the company. Answer the following questions:

1. How has the leadership of the company evolved from start-up to now?
2. What is the chief executive's vision for the company?
3. What are the leadership traits of the chief executive?
4. What is the personal leadership style of the chief executive?
5. What is the organizational structure of the company and how does that shape the leadership culture in the company?
6. What is the organization's level of centralization, division of labor, departmentalization, and the managers' spans of control?

7. What levels of psychological and task maturity are exhibited by key employees?
8. How is communication between leaders and staff handled in the company?
9. What does the company produce, and how is that related to the company's organizational structure and leadership style?
10. What is the company's "situation" relative to its market, technologies, and competitors?
11. What have the company's leaders done to encourage innovation in the company?
12. What did the company's leaders do to manage the company through change? What processes did they use? Who did they involve?

Conclude by summarizing the lessons learned from your case study observations.

# CHAPTER 2

# Motivation

You enter the room unnoticed. Everyone's busy. No one looks up from their computer screen. When people do see you, they seem to be sizing you up, trying to figure whether you've "earned" the right to be here. Muted televisions scattered around the room feature cable news or talk shows, eye candy for passersby. Phones ring sporadically, amid the soft, dull clatter of typing. Your excuse for a desk occupies a corner, next to two frumpish 40-somethings. So you wanted to work *here*? You should have known *something* was up when you got hired after months of getting rejection letters.

You don't know it, but across the room, behind a glass wall, someone eyes you. "Poor kid," she mutters to her boss sitting behind the desk.

"Feeling sorry for the troops?!" he growls. "Don't. At least he's still got a job."

"Yeah, but you don't have everybody staring darts at you," she says, adding, "You don't have to figure out how to get him past that layoff-survivor's guilt."

"Who says you *have* to? You've been reading too many management blogs."

Two people, different jobs, same anxieties. The manager behind the glass wall wants to understand. A newsroom mainstay ever since college, she was the first female to win major reporting awards and when she finally got promoted to management, her bosses touted it as "a long time in coming" and said she was a role model for the other females in the newsroom. (So far, however, there hadn't been much time for mentoring the other females.) So she feels insecure to some extent, not so much afraid to make a mistake as concerned about looking as if she's "mothering" her reporters. Talent can't be rushed and younger reporters don't respond to yelling and bullying, she believes, but she can't show weakness, either. How can she motivate others to improve, she wonders, without seeming as if she's trying to manipulate someone into doing what she wants them to do and without a budget that allows raises or travel for training? Also, she doesn't want to be seen as taking advantage of the specter of looming, additional budget cuts.

At first glance, however, the latest recruit isn't thinking motivation so much as wanting to blend in. And yet peer pressure and success themselves are motivating forces. The young journalist doesn't realize that motivation involves more than something you want to do. In fact, motivation may at times seem to constitute *who you are*.

Media managing (and understanding media managing) requires knowing, comprehending, and appropriately analyzing complex human behavior. Motivation is complicated, and managers must understand it in context (Fink, 1993), if they are to successfully deal with employees. The media workplace with its rapid, cyclical nature of change and production often presents unusual, demanding, and sometimes chaotic circumstances for managing. The media manager needs a strategic framework for viewing motivation and motivational opportunities.

This chapter emphasizes motivation in terms of how a typical editor or news director regards it, with many of the media-specific circumstances. The chapter examines media employees' motivation from two perspectives: as individuals and as groups, while exploring the application of various theories. A discussion of common motivational concerns and current trends in the media workplace follows.

## MOTIVATING INDIVIDUALS
### Common Needs and Influences

Mass media require many tasks of their employees. A TV newsroom requires anchors to write and report, think critically, be skeptical (even cynical), aggressive, curious, know how to manage time, coordinate and collaborate, and develop a sense of community and civic duty. In the online world, the work is faster, requires more with less, and mandates no sacrifice of quality while under endless pressure to publish 24/7. In doing so, employees experience emotions that may range from humor or compassion to outright apathy. Therefore, *goals* are imposed on a recruit by the mere fact of being hired.

Often managers can simply look at motivation as a basic process of *needs* (in this example, job requirements) producing *drives or motives* that then lead to goals being achieved. Abraham Maslow (1954) classified needs into a five-tier hierarchy: (a) physiological (food and water, sleep, health), (b) safety (shelter, security), (c) social (acceptance, belonging, group membership, love), (d) esteem (recognition, prestige, success), and (e) self-actualization (self-fulfillment of potential). Depending on the individual, job mandates may affect one or all of these needs. However, Maslow theorized only one level of need motivates a person at any given time. Needs, according to Maslow, are satisfied in order, from lowest (physiological) to highest (self-actualization), as illustrated in Figure 2.1.

Clayton Alderfer (1972) said that an employee's needs may be partially but not completely met, or that anyone may be motivated by two or more needs simultaneously. For example, the new recruit may be concerned about his salary (safety) and his need to grow as an investigative reporter (esteem). If higher order needs are met, such as a reporter's need for journalistic prestige, then he may become frustrated and regress to being motivated by a lower level need.

Alderfer would say that any manager would do well to analyze an employee's complaints about the employee's salary. Yet if that is, indeed, a reporter's goal and it is not reached, it logically follows that maybe there was no drive or motive stimulus to action. The drive, in this case, could be manifested in a decision to excel in another area, perhaps in making deadlines. The manager must know and understand an employee's needs and goals. In addition to job mandates, other factors must be considered.

Some management experts (e.g., Straub, 1984) believe that effective employee selection is a prerequisite for successful motivation. In this chapter's opening scenario, the manager behind the glass wall needs to know whether the recruit is psychologically capable, that is, capable of carrying out the tasks required of reporters, and whether the recruit's values and skills match the position. But most media managers generally lack the time and tools to perform such an analysis and, instead, usually try to develop effective motivational techniques that appeal to most employees.

Motivating people requires forethought and strategy. Besides the previously mentioned need to achieve, most people want to influence others (*power*) and be liked (*affiliation*). Psychologist David McClelland (1961) developed this typology and suggested that one of these needs usually dominates. For example: To effectively motivate, managers must recognize all such needs and try to determine which is dominant for each employee. For example, a good editor knows that many young reporters have a need for power (what beginning writer doesn't want to make an impact?). A reporter's need for affiliation probably is less clear, although her complaints of newsroom isolation could be evidence of concern for

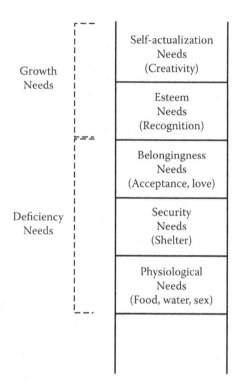

**Figure 2.1**   Maslow's Hierarchy of Needs

being liked. The manager probably also has a high need for power and achievement, which influences the assumptions made about a reporter's performance or lack of achievement. Yet knowing which need dominates or holds the key to reporter/employee motivation/performance is only part of the battle. The manager must then know what to do with that knowledge and what results to expect.

For example, people generally repeat behavior that is rewarded or reinforced and avoid behavior that is punished. Such conditioning falls into two general categories: classical and operant. Classical conditioning tries to generate involuntary, reflexive, or semi-instinctual actions through unconditioned stimuli. For example, when reporters writing stories notice they have 10 minutes before deadline, they experience an adrenaline rush, a quickened pulse, and other symptoms indicating heightened anxiety. So the repeated experiencing of an impending deadline results in the same physiological changes each time this type of stress is encountered.

With operant conditioning (Skinner, 1971), depicted in Figure 2.2, reinforced behavior is repeated voluntarily and behavior not reinforced is less likely to be repeated. Reinforcement can be positive (as when the news director rewards the anchor for the desired behavior of producing high ratings by giving him or her a raise), negative (as when the news director rewards a quiet producer who keeps legitimate complaints about the newsroom's functioning to himself by increasing his pay), punishing (as when the news director rewards the assignment editor's undesired complaining with the negative consequence of firing him), or extinctive (as when the news director eliminates the unwanted complaining by not rewarding it). Regardless of how the news director attempts to condition the employee, he or she should be aware of options and their consequences.

A modern-day, managerial twist on Skinner's thesis (Haidt, 2006) suggests that—in rapidly changing environments—obtaining the desired behavior on the employee's part also requires a series of steps. Using the metaphor of an elephant and its rider, this concept views the rider as controlling the reins and in control—except when the elephant disagrees! The key to getting somewhere or having the elephant doing what you want—or, organizationally speaking, accomplishing a task—is knowing what drives the elephant toward that task. In the case of change—or resistance to it—the rider must understand that the elephant is the one that has the energy and drive to make the change effort succeed. Also, the rider must know which direction in which to point the elephant; so rider *and* elephant are both key to the attempt to change (Heath & Heath, 2010).

So, obviously, motivation often relies on employees' beliefs rather than on what is observable or true. While the previous theories mainly focus on how managers (and other factors) manipulate motives, suggesting an element of control, people can influence their own drives via their beliefs of *personal efficacy* (Bandura, 1997, p. 2): Unless people believe

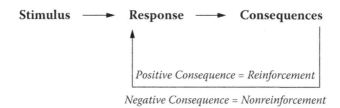

Stimulus ⟶ Response ⟶ Consequences

*Positive Consequence = Reinforcement*

*Negative Consequence = Nonreinforcement*

**Figure 2.2**  Operant Conditioning

they can produce desired effects by their actions, they have little incentive to act. This refers to beliefs in your capability to plan and take action to produce a desired effect (not to be confused with self-esteem, which involves judgments of self-worth). Managers might use caution in gauging such efficacy, however, since editors show higher levels of efficacy than their subordinates (Reinardy, 2011b).

Reporters can believe in their abilities and still dislike themselves, although reporters usually develop abilities or perform tasks that make them feel good about themselves. Self-efficacy beliefs regulate motivation by determining goals and the results a person expects for his or her efforts. For example, a reporter with fairly high self-efficacy probably would be more willing to try to meet a challenge to improve his or her skills. Such performance concerns will be discussed in the next section.

### Differences and Job Performance

Aside from job requirements and the needs they generate, managers also should note the interaction between job and employee. Doing so will broaden the manager's perspective and thus provide another decision-making tool. First, managers should know the motivation process. Three theories—equity theory, expectancy theory, and goal-setting theory—address this idea. In equity theory (Adams, 1963), the key assumption is that inequity is a motivator. When employees feel they have been unfairly treated, they will attempt to achieve a sense of equity. If a reporter's unhappiness stems from inequity (let's say she sees comparable reporters earning more), she could become happier by changing how much she works, attempting to increase her pay (or asking for a raise), reassessing how she compares herself, distorting the comparisons to make herself compare more favorably, or quitting.

Expectancy theory (Vroom, 1964) asserts that people will act in a way that will produce the desired outcome if given the freedom to do so. Figure 2.3 depicts how motivation is the product of the interaction among expectancy (a person's belief that working hard will enable various work goals to be achieved), instrumentality (a person's belief that various work-related outcomes will occur as a result of doing the job), and valence (the value the person assigns to those work-related outcomes). The motivational appeal of a reward (e.g., higher salary) is drastically reduced whenever expectancy, instrumentality, or valence together or alone nears zero. For example, a reporter's motivation to earn a pay raise will be low if she feels she cannot do the work needed to earn the

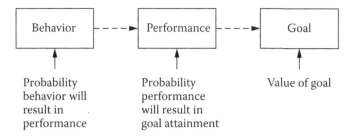

**Figure 2.3**  Expectancy Theory

raise, or if she's unsure that the extra work will result in the raise, or if she places little or no value on getting a raise.

Meanwhile, goal-setting theory says that employees behave the way they do because it helps them reach their goals (Locke, 1968), with goals' difficulty and specific nature particularly important. For example, planning to win an Emmy Award sufficiently motivates many TV writers to achieve excellence in writing. But if a new writer sets such a goal in her first year of work, the goal can be too difficult and lead to frustration. If the writer modifies and specifies the goal (e.g., winning an Emmy in 5 years or attempting to have a certain number of ideas or scripts produced in one year), then she enhances the chance for honest evaluation of the goal and proper assessment of her writing. It is important for her manager to know what goals she has set and how that affects her behavior.

In the case of our new recruit, the recruit needs to know the editor's goals, assess their difficulty, and identify their realistic qualities. This helps the recruit know whether and how to help the editor meet those goals and develop strategies to do so. If the recruit believes the goals are set too high, he or she should discuss them with the editor to help adjust the editor's expectations.

Managers, meanwhile, also may look at job–employee interaction through the lens of job satisfaction. For example, most managers assume that a satisfied employee is a productive one. Yet sometimes satisfaction does not cause performance—it may be the reverse. An employee who performs his or her job is a satisfied employee (Greene, 1972). So knowing how employee satisfaction works will help managers more completely understand motivation.

Alderfer (1972) stressed the role of frustration in terms of unmet needs. Recognizing the frustration factor implies that a manager can positively react to the frustrating item and help satisfy the employee.

Frederick Herzberg and his colleagues (Herzberg, Mausner, & Snyderman, 1968) developed the dual-factor theory, illustrated in Figure 2.4, which suggests that satisfaction and dissatisfaction are not related—but rather, they are affected by different needs and motives.

Herzberg contended that hygiene or preventive factors do not produce motivation, but can prevent motivation from occurring. Preventive factors, such as money, status, security, working conditions, work policies, supervision, and interpersonal relations are sometimes viewed as environmental influences. If a manager attends to these items, he or she helps keep employees from being highly dissatisfied. However, job-related motivators such as achievement, challenging work, increased responsibility, recognition, advancement, and personal growth provide true motivation when combined with hygiene factors. Herzberg's theory has not always been supported (Griffin & Moorhead, 1986), so media managers should note the important exceptions and nuances within the satisfaction concept.

For example, a major, national, 2002 study (Weaver, Beam, Brownlee, Voakes, & Wilhoit, 2007) found that journalists differ by medium and by individual characteristics as to how satisfied they were. Journalists at news magazines were below the average, while those at radio stations and news services reported above-average satisfaction; men reported more satisfaction than women, while—in terms of age—those 25 to 34 reported less satisfaction than their older and younger peers. Also, higher job autonomy and perceived newsroom influence were more likely to increase journalists' job satisfaction (Weaver et al., pp. 108–109) Finally, recall from Figure 2.3 that goals also factor; the same survey showed that of the key goals that the journalists perceived important to upper

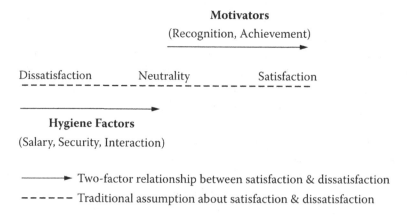

**Figure 2.4**   The Two-Factor Theory of Motivation

management, job satisfaction strongly correlated with securing high morale and producing above-average journalism (p. 111).

But studies also show the difficulty of managing for satisfaction. First, editors and reporters view satisfaction from different lenses (Beam, 2006); the latter lean toward believing their companies focus more on large profits and less on journalism, while editors don't believe that as much (p. 181). Second, managers might consider waging this battle on two fronts (Reinardy, 2009a): When Herzberg's dual-factor theory is introduced, work-family conflicts and job demands predict *dissatisfaction*, while organizational and social-support predict *satisfaction*. Third, satisfaction sources change with time, as do people. At one time in smaller newspapers, how well journalists believed the paper informed the public would determine how satisfied the journalists were (Bergen & Weaver, 1988); a decade later, the size influence disappeared. Perceptions about effectiveness in informing the public and frequency of managerial comments about work predicted satisfaction levels for journalists at newspapers of all sizes. In the 1980s, older journalists in small- and medium-sized papers were most satisfied; by the 1990s, the older journalists in small and large papers were most satisfied (Kodrich & Beam, 1997).

This difficulty in managing satisfaction rings especially true in the face of the rapid corporatization of news media. For example, journalists working for organizations that they perceive as valuing good journalism are more satisfied (Beam, 2006). When news organizations emphasize making high profits, journalists—predictably, because of their natural suspicions of nonjournalistic operational motive—say they are less satisfied than they would be otherwise (p. 180). As already noted, news supervisors don't see this issue as clearly, given that they probably are more accustomed to dealing with profit orientations. This blindspot could then affect how they manage their subordinates—particularly in newspapers, where editors believe that organizational integration (i.e., communicating the values of the rest of the organization to the newsroom, working in cross-departmental teams and being an "organizational team player") is desirable (Gade, 2005). Such managers tend to perceive higher levels of organizational support and, as a result, tend to manage for change more confidently (p. 29), albeit in direct conflict to the way many of their newsroom subordinates view change (Sylvie & Witherspoon, 2002).

So managing becomes a matter of how the manager uses various kinds of information. Individuals differ, although, typically, *different* has meant *difficult* or hard to handle. For example, media managers traditionally grapple with how to treat exceptional, or *star*, employees whose work performance sets them apart, often resulting from a unique, talented job approach stemming from their personalities (e.g., Khan, 2005). Because such employees tend not to respond to typical motivational methods, their supervisors may have to seek alternatives for myriad problems, such as fairness (less talented employees are watching), appropriate rewards (stars do not always respond to money or promotions), evaluation (what is an appropriate work standard?), as well as recruiting and retaining stars (see this chapter's discussion of common problems).

Self-efficacy theory offers help in this situation. The concept states that believing in your capability to plan and take action to produce a desired effect correlates with your actual capabilities to do so (Bandura, 1997). In this context, *different* becomes a personal matter requiring individually tailored solutions or approachs. High self-efficacy, then, becomes a goal or quality that an editor wants to groom in as many subordinates as possible. For example, many older or veteran employees present a challenge in their frequent need to be engaged or presented with growth opportunities to remain motivated. So such programs as professional development, training, or job rotation may help—but the manager must ensure the opportunities exist. Unfortunately, not every manager adequately promotes such opportunities (Cleary, 2005).

Still, *different* has increasingly evolved into *diverse*. More and more studies have highlighted numerous factors that increasingly diverse workplaces introduce to the satisfaction equation. For example, journalists of color were less likely than other journalists to say they were satisfied with their jobs (Weaver et al., 2007); African American journalists, in particular, were less likely to say they would be working in the news media in 5 years and more likely to rate their organization's success at informing the public as low. Another study (Woods, 2005) showed that media employing minorities ages 35 years of age or younger must be proactive and provide more feedback and training to retain such employees. Also, in U.S. newspapers, women reported more exhaustion and lower professional efficacy than did men (Reinardy, 2009b). This disconnect extends into management; minority news directors were less likely than nonminority news directors to say training was offered to their staffs (Cleary, 2005), while additional evidence suggests that women managers do not negotiate as persistently as male managers and, thus, need to change their styles (Arnold & Nesbitt, 2006). So motivating and understanding managers themselves is no easy task either.

Technology affects individual motivation. When management introduces a technology to employees, the consequences usually vary along three dimensions: direct or indirect, desirable or undesirable, and anticipated or unanticipated. Yet to enhance motivation, the manager needs to ensure a good technology–employee match. That means working to help employees see the technology as: (a) better than its predecessor, (b) compatible and consistent with existing values, (c) compatible and consistent with past experiences and employee needs, (4) relatively easy to understand and use, (5) experimentally friendly, and (6) capable of an observable job impact (Rogers, 1983). Trouble arises when employees' personal values clash with a technology's purpose, often unbeknownst to management until after it introduces the technology. So a manager's prior knowledge of subordinates should influence what approach he or she uses.

Unsurprisingly then, the news media move toward technological convergence—whereby journalists use multiple formats (e.g., broadcast, online, and print) to produce news—has accelerated the need for alternative motivational strategies and created managerial uncertainty (Lowrey & Gade, 2011). Convergence often means more work for the employee. For example, a local sports columnist typically appears on a daily talk-radio show, writes a daily column for the newspaper, produces a blog that includes items not in the column, records a video to accompany the online version of the column, and investigates a new story for the next day's edition. As employees experience new technologies, they learn new skills, develop new ways of thinking about their jobs, and thus require new methods of motivation (e.g., Covington, 1997) and pose new management problems (Killebrew, 2003). Some employees will lose their jobs because of convergence, creating a deflated, somewhat depressed environment for the manager to navigate and motivate (Sylvie & Gade, 2009).

Convergence set against the recession of 2008 also has prompted researchers to examine what happens to those who keep their jobs in such circumstances. For example, a study of newspaper layoffs (Reinardy, 2011a) showed that highly satisfied survivors had trust and morale reservoirs, and saw their jobs as having a high quality and themselves as possessing high organizational commitment. Those with lower satisfaction saw themselves as lower on such qualities and reported greater intentions to leave journalism. Meanwhile, a secondary analysis (Hinsley, 2012) of national survey data on newspaper journalists used social identity theory, which assumes that people's desire for a positive self-image prompts a search for, and a sense of belonging with, others who share traits they find desirable (Tajfel & Turner, 1986). The study found that while front-line journalists and editors hold strong ties to the newspaper profession, frontline workers (primarily reporters, photographers, copyeditors, and designers) do not feel as connected to their news organizations. Further investigation implied that managerial disruption of treasured journalistic routines—which may occur through convergence and layoffs—further negatively impact those workers' organizational commitment.

It's not that journalists don't see clear advantages in new convergence policies—i.e., as a career booster, the enjoyment of working with colleagues whose strengths differ from their own, and subsequent respect for people in other parts of the news organization (Singer, 2004a). But group cultural and technological differences in approaches to newsgathering and dissemination—as well as a lack of training to alleviate concerns about the perceived complexities of new media formats—may create fears about technological complexity and concerns about lack of accompanying rewards. A detailed discussion of how a manager should approach this and other technologies is in Chapter 6.

As to the new employee mentioned in the beginning, you might think that he needs to learn to "manage up," i.e., build a good relationship with his supervisor—something managers also need (Marshall, 2005)—and understand motivation from the other side of the coin. You've heard this before: To be a good employee, be receptive to your supervisor. Know your supervisor's goal and try to deliver it. Don't be afraid to work in groups or ask questions, if you're not clear on directions or goals. In short, motivate your supervisor to provide you with the things and resources that help you both to succeed. But knowing the values and decision-making styles of your boss can be a challenge. For example, one U.S. survey (Sylvie & Huang, 2006) of frontline newspaper editors found that although their personal value systems correlated with their decision-making styles, the editors used more than one style. Male editors were more likely than female editors to use an avoidant style—i.e., trying to evade decision making—as well as a more spontaneous style (usually by trying to decide as soon as possible). Other differences centered on the length of the job experience and how much they valued occupational culture and journalism.

So successful managers and savvy employees should recognize what each other brings to the job. Each person's perception is selective or each person emphasizes those aspects of a situation that reinforce or appear consistent with that person's beliefs, attitudes, and values. The situation evolves further in groups.

## GROUPS

Media organizations are composed of groups such as committees, task forces, cliques, and entities that help the firm accomplish its objectives.

This means that to effectively motivate, managers must understand groups and group influences, especially occupational groups: collections of people sharing values, standards, and views that apply to the workplace and beyond. These groups confer, vie, and compromise with each other, functioning as "major players" in organizational decisions. So when your boss places you in a group, it carries an implicit obligation to learn the forces driving the group. So the manager behind the glass wall in our introduction to the chapter also must view the new recruit within the context of his or her group memberships.

### Groups and Cultures

Group members often get their identities or self-images from their occupational group roles, take group members as their primary reference group, and frequently socialize with group peers (Van Maanen & Barley, 1984). Groups develop along two basic forms: formal and informal.

Managers create formal groups when authorizing two or more people to devote time to a task via such forms as committees, task forces, project teams, or departments. Organizations cannot function without these groups, which often may gain considerable power. Managers can directly control groups through selection of members (and, in some cases, leadership), definition of purpose, and performance oversight—and thus determine a group's level of motivation. For example, placement in prestigious or powerful groups fulfills certain needs for some, and omission or removal can provide either positive or negative motivation for others. So managers can use formal groups as a structure-based motivation tool.

Informal groups pose a more complex issue. As opposed to formal groups, informal groups develop directly or indirectly from several possible influences, ranging from something as simple as physical proximity to something as complex as the common values their jobs (and backgrounds) instill. These groups primarily originate to serve their members and may, or may not, serve managerial purposes, depending on circumstances. The key for the manager is to recognize the by-products of informal groups.

As mentioned earlier (Tajfel & Turner, 1986), groups also provide an identity of sorts for their members. Television news anchors closely identify with each other based on shared experiences and visions of what it is to be a news anchor: witty and acerbic at times, or conversationalist with an eye for news and a sense of how to entertain and accommodate TV viewers on their way to dinner or bed. Anchors may befriend other anchors at the station or in the community. They may wear similar clothes, speak the same job-related jargon, cut their hair similarly, and carry themselves the same way in public. All media employees conform in some way to other employees' tacit or overt values. Their jobs likely bring many of them together socially, creating a bond.

This is particularly true of journalists and their editors: Many see themselves as journalists first, human beings second. Journalism encourages distinct patterns of beliefs, values, norms, and interpretations. Not only do journalists learn the values of news, they learn to be skeptical, cynical, critical, detached, and analytical. This requires the adoption of a particular lifestyle. For instance, women journalists are less likely than male journalists to be married. More journalists read *The New York Times* than do members of the general public. It is not uncommon for journalists to see their politics as slightly left of center and to be unable to completely discard the journalistic lens on their environment. Journalists often speak with pride of dangerous, ordeal-like career experiences called *war stories*. Their passion for news also takes a toll on their leisure time and lifestyle, leaving little time for nonjournalistic pursuits and fostering close relationships with other journalists, resulting in similar ideas about what constitutes news. But even journalists in the same organization differ, especially if their jobs differ markedly. For example, online journalists tend to be more isolated from news sources than are other journalists, but more attuned to audiences (Weaver et al., 2007).

Groups also place pressure on their members (Kiesler & Kiesler, 1969). As members attract each other, they acquire shared norms and values, become cohesive, attract other members, and form allegiances. The greater the attraction and loyalty to the group, the more likely the members conform to group norms and values. A culture exists within occupational groups when they share a set of basic world assumptions, which in turn determines their perceptions, thoughts, feelings, and certain overt behaviors (Schein, 1985). Recurring success in implementing certain beliefs and values helps entrench them within the group (Schein, 2004). Sometimes, members avoid confronting or debating these "theories-in-use," making these norms resistant to change. That means any supervisor trying to change those norms must overcome sizeable anxiety within the group (Argyris & Schön, 1974).

The group attempts to dissuade members from violating group norms. The pressure to conform can be enormous depending on the stray member's will and attachment to the group. The group exerts such pressure in order to survive and further its self-interests. The pressure can be subtle, often through joking or gossip. For example, two northeastern U.S. newspapers' newsrooms were merged, meaning different individuals with similar jobs in the two papers often got appointed to new positions. Others in the newsroom began informally discussing those reassignments, often evaluating their reassigned colleagues' "character, skills, and likely proclivities" in the new structure (Fee, 2007, 75). Each communication, regardless of its tone, tried to set limits for members. So the alert media manager had three decisions to make: What is best for the group? What is best for the threatened employee? What is best for the company?

Sometimes, an action has positive and negative ramifications for all concerned, albeit not immediately. Again, in the example of the two merged newspaper staffs, the newsroom copy desk—as the final arbiter of content and writing style—stood out for many reasons (Fee, 2007). Ambiguity and anxiety as to who was in charge eventually solved itself when one of the two desk chiefs verbally deferred to the other in certain disputes, saying, "It's your call, chief" (p. 76). Among their subordinates, however, cliques arose, some trying to ignore the new chief (p. 77). At other times, a change or management initiative gets so out of control that an individual is terminated, as Jack Kelley was by *USA TODAY* for plagiarism. A secret managerial investigation into the accusations against Kelley, combined with his "star" status and managerial flip-flops on how to handle the fallout from the scandal hurt management's credibility and led not only to Kelley's departure, but to that of the editor as well (Sylvie & Moon, 2007). Sometimes the response is gray, as in the case of the Tampa Bay TV reporter Don Germaise, who was "disciplined" for apparently agreeing to answer questions from a white separatist in exchange for the separatist's cooperation with his own story (Deggans, 2006). In each case, group pressure—however subtly—was used to produce the desired result.

Media settings also play host to another informal group phenomenon when innovation and creativity come into play. Media constantly generate new ideas; the journalistic media do so daily. Media managers facilitate creativity without thinking about it, using incentives such as bylines (in print), video stand-ups and standard out cues (in broadcasting), and merit pay—in short, incentivizing through content and organizational administration. Creative media employees also naturally share the determination, eccentricity, curiosity, and experience required of ingenuity (Straub, 1984). Much innovation depends on the organizational or group culture in place and the degree to which employees feel involved with the organization. For example, interviews with creative specialists at one large advertising agency showed the firm had an unwritten, "creative code"—a comprehension of their common values that they developed, using a variety of internal and external sources, formal and informal

(Stuhlfaut, 2011). The code varied by timing, client, and project format, and drove managerial decision making as well.

Yet informal groups also need consistently shared meanings, adaptability to the external environment, and a shared vision (Denison, 1990). These shared items are not easily found when two informal groups suddenly merge, as often occurs in the ongoing age of technological and corporate convergence and, as noted above, in the case of the northeastern newspapers (Fee, 2007). This is especially true when examining convergent environments, which require constant contact between and among groups to avoid conflicting viewpoints (Killebrew, 2003). As a result, researchers (notably, Schmitz Weiss, 2007) are beginning to see newsrooms in general as "communities of practice" (CoP) as a way of understanding how groups communicate (Wenger, 1998). A shared repertoire—linguistics, habits, and other behaviors—is one of the ways such groups communicate. For example, a study of four online newsrooms (Schmitz Weiss & Domingo, 2010) showed that each CoP, through discussion and collaboration, adapted to technological changes—essentially learning from each other—to the point that they forgot about the change and consensually developed skills that became their shared repertoire. The ever-constant deadline pressure of the online news cycle, for instance, prompted a greater sense of urgency as to how to quickly present news in multiple platforms and, in the process, led to forming new schedules and routines.

Still, groups conflict with other groups. Their growing cohesiveness leads members to identify closely with each other, enhancing the potential for group self-direction (Sherif, 1962) and the search for some way to distinguish itself from other groups in the same organization (Deutsch, 1949). Media groups are no different. For example, editorial and business departments in Dutch newspapers often fought (Achtenhagen & Raviola, 2007). Similarly, anchors and other newsroom staffers at U.S. TV stations often don't see eye-to-eye: Anchors feel as if they are being micromanaged in their writing and in their on-air performances. They believe management to be isolated and deaf to attempts at input. They feel insulted at not being consulted regarding major changes. They believe the newscast producers and associate producers drive the journalistic car and don't want anchors' opinions when it comes to day-to-day station management. In short, many anchors believe that the no-buy-in option that management offers them determines how they do their jobs, prompting a "do what I do and don't worry about it" model to follow.

Part of the problem lies with modern organizations that continue to add more tiers to their hierarchies to lengthen chains of command. The chances for communication distortion, and thus conflict, increase. As a result, productive media managers need to understand groups and cultures, especially the ingroup communication networks (Collins & Guetzkow, 1964) that are becoming increasingly prevalent in convergent and inno-vative organizations (Küng, 2008; Lowrey, 2011). In doing so, managers gain a grasp on information flow and decision-making dynamics.

## COMMON PROBLEMS

Media firms inevitably run into motivation-related struggles. The follow-ing section deals with a common and an emerging complication, followed by a discussion of some applicable strategies.

### Retention

The ultimate motivational problem is turnover, when an employee quits—even when the motivation to do so is less, as in a recession such as the economic downturn that started in 2008. Reasons vary, from dis-satisfaction to stress about being the next cutback victim. Turnover rates in media can range as high as 50% annually, so in a year, up to half a company's employees may leave. The reasons for the high-turnover are complex: Media companies' resources and management styles vary, depending on whether they are public or private or local or regional, or whether their market is volatile or stable. Timing, too, plays a part, depending on whether advertising is up or down, and is dependent on cyclical events, such as elections. Regardless of the reasons, high turnover means managers have to recruit, select, and train replacements, while some remaining employees worry about whether they're next to go, secretly plan their own exits, or experience career-changing events.

Turnover is an inconsistent foe of media managers because not every-one quits at the same time. Yet, turnover represents a continuing prob-lem, particularly with African Americans and women, who make up a disproportionate share of departures and from whom managers often expect help in diversifying content. For example, up until 2002, jour-nalists were becoming slightly happier with their jobs (77% vs. 74% in 1992). Although that trend continued among those who said they were more likely to leave journalism within 5 years (there were fewer), women still were more likely than men to say they planned to do so (21% vs. 16%). Almost a third of African American journalists—nearly double the rate for any other group—said they'd like a new career in 5 years (Weaver et al., 2007). Another study (Reinardy, 2009b) examining women newspaper journalists found that women who said they were planning to change careers reported significantly higher levels of burnout than was true for men who had similar intentions. Too, consider that journalists with the least experience—particularly those who did not major in journalism in college—were more likely to leave the profession within 5 years than veteran journalists (Weaver et al., 2007).

To combat this expected employee exodus, managers should be smart about how they approach newsroom psychology. For example, Figure 2.5 illustrates the historical factors that have produced stress in journalists (based on Fedler, 2004). Knowing these issues, managers probably should explore how they influence the three areas important to all employees (Weaver et al., 2007): editorial policies, the chance to help others, and job security (p. 205). A closer look showed, for example, that minority employees were more likely than the majority to rate analysis of complex issues and developing the public's intellectual and cultural interests as extremely important (pp. 208–209). A deeper look at these and other factors (Beam, 2006) showed that how much journalists perceive their organizations as profit-driven also plays a role in job satisfaction levels. But managers must not be quick to overgeneralize and must realize that many things—such as who owns the organization—often are beyond their control. Instead, managers should concentrate on factors over which they exercise some influence: Morale, informing the public, pay, autonomy, and feedback all positively relate to job satisfaction (Weaver et al., 2007).

Influence, in fact, may boil down to something much simpler for managers. As media firms head toward greater convergence levels, one

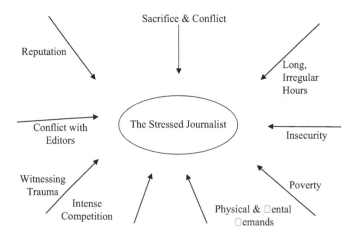

**Figure 2.5**   The Factors that Historically Create Stress in Journalists

aspect will only loom larger in terms of employee retention and satisfaction: temporary or freelance workers, about whom little is known. Technology and the post-2008 recessionary era likely will force many additional media outlets to consider either outsourcing work or contracting with independent parties, such as bloggers (Doctor, 2010). Whereas one study (Massey & Elmore, 2011) indicated freelancing women are happy with their jobs, another report (Ryan, 2009) showed that television freelancers—despite being happier than staffers were about pay and ethical conditions of the job—were not happier overall.

### Change and Challenge

Media employees crave the ability to create, to react constructively, or to see the meaning of their work. A happy journalist or one contemplating leaving the profession can be interested in a new challenge (Weaver et al., 2007). The last 10 years or so have witnessed an assault on these assumptions.

The coming together of technology, staffs, products, and media—better known as convergence—and the need for the news media to replace or adjust to declining revenue has presented the media manager with a difficult task in helping employees relocate their inspiration. Often working more than 40 hours a week, journalists in a 2011 survey told the Poynter Institute (an independent U.S. school dedicated to teaching journalists and their supervisors) that staff cuts and shortages were beginning to create work-life imbalances, to the point that two of every five respondents had seriously considered leaving journalism (Geisler, 2011). Additionally, many managers have acknowledged their lack of preparation in dealing with convergence and its related issues (Lowrey, 2006), often relying on routines and convenience (Lowrey, 2005).

A structural byproduct involves employee autonomy, which—because of convergence's requirement for multiplatform reporting and frequent collaboration—introduces additional supervision (one supervisor for each platform) and diluted independence for many reporters, creating confusion and discomfort (e.g., Singer, 2004b). Group culture also enters the frame because many journalists, assigned to cooperate with journalists from other media, have to overcome bias against such groups (Filak, 2004). Autonomy is cited throughout this chapter as a crucial factor in motivation. Organizational size plays a large role when it comes to autonomy (smaller organizations grant less) as does work assignment (having a beat beats not having one) (Weaver et al., 2007). So convergent-minded media managers must anticipate these battles, especially when combating the widely held employee perception that convergence is no more than a management plot to save money (Silcock & Keith, 2006). Winning strategies might involve increasing managers' influence in other departments (Gade, 2008), enhancing intergroup coordination (Dupagne & Garrison, 2006), and appropriate, culture-centric framing (including a feedback outlet) of the message of the coming change (Sylvie & Moon, 2007)—all while trying to meet journalists' professional expectations for their work (Kunelius & Ruusunoksa, 2008).

The wisest course involves planning for these contingencies. Wiser still is organizing and structuring policies, procedures, and programs that prevent morale problems from arising, while also fostering a healthy corporate culture. It's important to address turnover problems throughout the employment process.

Even if a manager examines the peculiarities of the job and the idiosyncrasies of the employee with respect to motivation, the combination of the job and the person brings with it a completely new set of issues for the manager to consider. The manager behind the glass wall in the introduction should carefully reconsider the interviewing process when new employees are hired. Interviews are not just negotiations for salary, benefits, and production expectations. They should reveal how the job fits the person seeking employment.

In the case of creativity and autonomy, media managers often complain that managing creative employees is difficult because these employees want more autonomy than their perhaps less-talented peers. It becomes an issue of whether the manager or employee has control. It is not uncommon in media organizations for employees to become stars of some kind. Managers must balance pleasing employees and their adoring public, behaving fairly (to stars and nonstars), maintaining the indirect revenue stream the star may help generate, maintaining credibility, and perhaps maintaining self-respect.

Managers must be patient and realize their job requires pursuing and choosing the best options. One such option is to establish strong loyalty within stars because loyalty can stem turnover, which is caused by lack of challenge or autonomy. Many creative employees lack an initial strong commitment to an organization because their creativity and confidence in that creativity allows them mobility, making job security less of a need. So the media manager needs to establish trust in star performers (after all, as stars, they could argue they merit stronger consideration than most employees). Many news directors and editors have found that the participative management style constitutes a good way to do so.

This is especially evident in the growth of teams, team building, and formal work groups. But whereas some teams develop into the basic unit of design for organizing work (Kolodny & Stjernberg, 1993), news media adoption of teams has struggled for acceptance because of the media's long dependence on individual innovation and creativity, and other negative attitudes (Gade, 2008). Despite such concerns, teams are beginning to blossom in media, particularly with the growth of multimedia newsrooms (McLellan & Porter, 2007). More proactive managers see teams as a collective way to manage the uncertainties of change that beset media. Still, teams garner mixed reactions; e.g., in South Africa, journalists are less enamored of teams than are their managers (Steyn & Steyn, 2009)—whose lack of experience with teams, inability to share some team responsibilities, and stinginess on team-related rewards might have influenced those evaluations. Despite these less-than-sterling results, however, some online teams have been shown to work (Schmitz Weiss, 2008) and teams probably will need more time than other approaches (Bourgeon, 2002; Fee, 2007).

## SUMMARY

As the workforce continues to change and the economy becomes more global and constrained, motivation grows larger as a key to successful media management. Media organizations are too complex for any manager to get by without some understanding of human needs and desires.

An effective first step: Gain firsthand knowledge of the work context, such as what employees bring to the job, what the job requires, and how they interact. This requires familiarity with motivation theories and concepts, but also sensitivity in applying those theories to the workplace. In other words, for the new recruits of the world, the reluctant supervisors need to know that each action happens for a reason; second-guessing never works.

Management requires a deep appreciation for diversity—intellectual as well as demographic—as regards each employee's idiosyncrasies and unique traits. Women and people of color bring experiences that white male media managers do not understand and perhaps fear. Yet proper motivation must be a fearless goal. Social wallflowers need not apply for management positions because dealing with people constitutes the bulk of managing.

Finally, the media have their share of potential psychological bombshells in their workforce. Most people do their jobs and need no external motivation. However, the efficiency orientation of the increasingly corporate, under-resourced, and converging workplace requires managers to know how to solve problems and act quickly.

This chapter should motivate the media manager to become a better manager, an incentive to help plan and structure systems that properly and adequately recognize and reward employees. Motivation can be understood, managed, and planned. So the manager has to structure such a plan according to the needs of the workplace. Without this perspective, managers will see motivation as a problem rather than an opportunity.

---

### CASE 2.1 CHARLES AND MAE

After covering everything from the courthouse to city hall to local schools, Mae Tyler, the 28-year-old, 6-year veteran of the newsroom took the 5 p.m. (solo anchor) and 6 p.m. (co-anchor) slots a month ago. Her promotion came after the station laid off several people, including Bob Herbert, beloved across the city and notorious in the newsroom for dragging his feet in joining The Digital Age (he refused to blog or Tweet). Mae says she is happy, but Charles Gaines, the news director and her immediate boss, thinks he sees symptoms of the opposite. She used to smile a lot, but lately she's been all business. She's been avoiding her former buddies/correspondents and doesn't even look her fellow anchors in the eye.

She even tried to convince Charles that her salary (about $75,000) was too *high*—arguing that making the same salary as co-anchor Mark Vigar, older and more experienced, wasn't fair to Mark. Charles practically had to beg her to take the pay raise, arguing it would worry the other anchors that their pay might be cut. The 5 p.m. ratings were down 15% from the last ratings period when she was promoted, but Charles believes the show's market share (second only by a half share) will increase because Mae will pull a younger demographic and more men overall.

He wants to understand. Mae has been a rising star since she joined the staff. She was the first female to win major reporting awards at the station; when she finally got promoted to anchor, station General Manager Anthony Llorens touted it as "a long time in coming" and said she was a role model for the other females at the station and across the city.

Mae prides herself on being a good wife and mother as well as a professional, although she has secretly struggled to find balance.

The promotion, for some strange reason, has made her feel simultaneously guilty (for Herbert losing his job) and pressured because he always made a point of saying that "Anyone who's also doing digitally is likely doing diddly overall." She used to enjoy blogging, but now she wonders if she should cut back.

Lately Mae's attitude, like a yawn, has been contagious. Three younger colleagues, fresh from college and cheap replacements for the three laid-off correspondents, seem to be imitating her. All three have concentrated on their broadcast work at the expense of applying their online expertise, partly for which they were hired. Mae has focused particularly on coverage issues such as story angles and source selection as it pertains to gender and race. Mae thinks Charles is sexist and, perhaps, unintentionally racist

Mae is the only Asian American on the staff. There have been other Asian American staffers in Charles's 10-year tenure as news director, but all left for more money elsewhere. Mae feels as if she is being singled out for her race. Charles has made a point of telling everyone how great she's performed, particularly in the last 6 months, as if to say, "Hey! How about our model minority, huh guys? Wish they all were like her!" Yet Mae feels Charles also is sexist, primarily because, when she started to change her hairstyle, Charles told her he did not like it. She has seen how he treats Mark (they joke around a lot) and how differently he criticizes the anchors: He is direct and blunt with her and almost apologetic with Mark. He also usually comments about her looks. He tells her, "That's a nice dress," every few days. Last week during the budget meeting, he rambled for 5 minutes about anchor makeup with her as the focus. Still, he usually ignores her ideas for news features about schools and health, usually asking "for some hard numbers" before he'll consider them.

Mae asked Charles for a meeting. She wants to challenge her evaluation and find out whether Charles has a problem with women and Asian Americans and stories about them. She thinks the problem extends to his handling of the layoffs, too. In preparation for the following questions, review the chapter guidelines.

### Assignment
1. If you were Charles, show how you would you prepare for the meeting with Mae.

2. Which factor—job mandates or employee potential—seems to be the most influential in this case? Is autonomy a factor at all? Which idea or concept in the chapter most influences your opinion and why?

3. Assign one student to play Charles's role, another to play Mae's. Have the two conduct their meeting. Afterward, (a) analyze the discussion to determine which psychological theory—equity, expectancy, or goal-setting—plays a major role in each person's approach to the conversation; and (b) determine Charles's next most logical course of action.

4. In relation to No. 3, how big a factor do the race and gender of each participant play in the meeting? Conduct some research in your library (especially on media and minority retention) to show whether Charles should consider Mae's race or gender in how he approaches the meeting and in how he devises a solution. Be prepared to defend your answer.

---

### CASE 2.2 OLD KID IN TOWN

Put yourself in the shoes of a friend of the person that the new recruit (mentioned at the beginning of this chapter) replaced. Assume you have been in the newsroom for 20 years, working your way up from cop-beat reporter to the same level of job occupied by your now-departed friend. The only difference between you is that you weren't afraid to shoot video and create podcasts.

Deona Laurent, the manager who's been eyeing the new recruit from behind the glass wall, has been working in the newsroom 5 years. She is the go-between for you and the metro editor. She was a local government reporter prior to her current position, which she has held for 9 months and in which—unfortunately—she often has been argumentative when it comes to the stories you file. Often she'll make you go back and ask additional questions or order you to write a blog item on top of everything else. The metro editor doesn't know any of this.

You were an editor at your college paper, so you think you know a little bit of how she feels, but you have your own worries concerning this place.

**Assignment**

1. What kind of preparation should you do before deciding whether to complain to Deona?

2. What kinds of things should you know about Deona's role in the newsroom? How does her role affect her approach toward motivation and how would that approach differ from a metro editor's approach?

3. What are your prime motivators as a veteran reporter? In what ways do those motivators conflict with your perception of Deona's approach to motivation?

4. Go to the Poynter Institute's website (and at least one other respected industry source) to find additional information about motivation. Report to the class your formal advice about motivation tailored to the needs of a new recruit fresh out of college vs. the motivational strategy for the older employee mentioned above.

5. Go to the same two sites you used in No. 4 above and evaluate motivational tools. Report to the class at least three motivational tools that Deona can use to help her discover the recruit's concerns without her actually having to talk to the recruit.

6. What kinds of things should a veteran reporter say to the new recruit about succeeding in the newsroom? How much should the veteran mention the friend that the new recruit replaced?

---

**CASE 2.3 MOTIVATING CONVERGENCE I**

"Convergence" is coming to your newspaper newsroom. You are a city editor and you've been asked to prepare yourself and your staff. These are the issues you face:

1. As part of the convergence process, your newsroom will be partnered with KRUM, a local TV station. You have always felt the station had an objectivity problem, and you've made it no secret among your reporting staff.

2. Another component of convergence will mean integrating the station's online staff with the paper's online crew. Broadcasting's bread and butter is immediacy, breaking news, delivering content as it happens, but you've got to figure how to make the merger work and whether to keep the two staffs in separate buildings.

3. People—how are they going to adapt to the new structures that Nos. 1 & 2 above will require? There's Jamie Morris, your star veteran known for his investigative work. Jamie detests blogs for the way they blur news and opinion, but—he doesn't know it yet—the boss wants him to do one. How do you convince him of its journalistic value? Then there's Carol Conant, your online news director, who constantly worries about quality control on her site (stories go through only one edit) combined with the station's breaking news brand. Carol's worries are warranted, especially considering newspapers typically edit stories at least three to five times before publication. But your reporting staff thinks Carol is timid and—thanks to the fact that she's the only woman on the online staff—a "wuss" when it comes to making decisions.

4. Then there's training. No one on the station's reporting staff has a clue about newspapers or the Web or how each works. They've heard talk about "forgetting old boundaries" in an even greater push to market stories that people want, rather than what they need.

### Assignment

1. What should you do to make things better between your staff and the online staff? Between your staff and the TV staff?
2. Assign students to role-play the respective heads of the converging groups. Set up a meeting to discuss organizational concerns.
3. Describe the needs the following theorists would identify in this situation: Maslow, Alderfer, McClelland, Skinner, and Bandura. Whose theory would be most appropriate to your job as convergence motivator and why?
4. What group cultural concerns are at play in this situation? How will you use them to your advantage to motivate employees to converge successfully?

### CASE 2.4 MOTIVATING CONVERGENCE II

You run the newsroom of a nonprofit newspaper, *The Voice of Smallville*. Your organization relies on advertising and small grants from local, state, and national foundations. Because of the continued recession and a dismal forecast for those kinds of funds, upper management decided to make budget cuts by about $125,000.

Yesterday, on a cold, gray, December morning, you announced to the staff that you were laying off technology reporter André Coe, schools reporter Lianne Fridriksson, online arts reporter Mike Quinn, and videographer Evonne Whitmore. CEO James Tankard said there likely will be further reductions, adding, "Life isn't fair." You battled to shield the four from the cuts. You've been pretty mum in terms of giving advice to the remaining staff so far, and it's shown: You haven't slept well for the past week, and you are beginning to develop a tic in your eye.

Today, your online editor Bob Jeffrey has come to you, seeking advice on how to quell the fears of his remaining staff. "Don't give me any of that crap about 'The show must go on,' either," he says. "I don't know if we can trust Tankard anymore," he adds.

Unknown to Jeffrey, Tankard tipped you off that the cuts probably will be short-lived, until about mid-year when things pick up because the "snowbirds" return from Florida and home construction picks up again. He's asked you to plan on replacing the four with "some bright young college kids with better social-media savvy," and to especially keep your eye on the performance of current unpaid interns Red Gibson and Lori Eason the next couple of months. "Maybe even give them a Twitter beat or music blog or whatever they can do in that regard; see how they handle it," Tankard advised.

## Assignment

1. Draw up a plan dealing with survivor's guilt for the remaining staff.
2. Develop 10 things you can do to rebuild trust—in upper management and within your staff.
3. How would you handle the online staff vs. the print staff?
4. Would it be OK for you to show some emotion to your subordinates in dealing with the fallout?
5. How would you prepare the current staff for the possible young replacements? Would you?

# CHAPTER 3

# Workforce

Fueled by a passion for creative storytelling and dreams of fame, grounded in ethical obligations to society, and buffeted by unpredictable cultural undercurrents, media work is distinct in many ways from work in other industries. A key distinguishing factor is the intense uncertainty that "culture industry" workers face. Uncertainty is inherent to the creative process, but it is also a consequence of the need to understand shifting attitudes and preferences of audiences. This is a daunting challenge, which media producers don't always meet. They may instead respond to images of the audience in their heads, or to templates that have worked before, rather than to concrete feedback (Lowrey, 2009; McQuail, 2010).

Uncertainty shapes production processes across all media industries, but the level of uncertainty in the task varies, and so the corresponding nature of production must vary with it. Media work is organized in different ways across different media sectors. In some sectors, tasks have been traditionally accomplished by hiring individuals or teams of workers for temporary projects, as with books, films, and TV show pilots. In other sectors, workers have been recruited for long-term careers—a "staff track" compatible with the bureaucratic mass production found at daily newspapers and TV news operations, and large advertising firms.

Why this split between temporary and staff? According to traditional organizational contingency theory, when an organization's product is not standardized, then workers' tasks become more uncertain. For example, no two movies are exactly alike, requiring innovation each time a movie is produced. There is no highly specific "How to Create a Movie" rule book, and so film companies rely on professionals and craft workers with unique areas of expertise, hiring a different crew of such experts for each production, depending on the unique needs of the film. The flexibility of the production crew helps the company absorb the uncertainty and risk

(Donaldson, 2001). The video game industry also exemplifies this flexible "project" approach in the production of single game prototypes. It's not efficient to pay individuals continually for the occasional production of games, and so managers hire temporarily organized teams of workers.

In contrast, when the nature and the rate of output is known, media production tends to be more standardized, and formalized work roles themselves can become more important than the individual workers who fill the roles, regardless of unique knowledge or expertise (Donaldson, 2001). We see this in the regular, daily production of newspapers and local TV news, where most work tends to be continuous and assembly line, requiring a more predictable employer-employee relationship. Of course, even in these more standardized industries, professional knowledge and expertise play a role. In fact, many media industries are hybrids of the staff and temporary approaches, including magazines, long-running TV series, and some advertising and PR project work. For example, popular print and online magazines are produced on a regular schedule, but their production requires tracking uncertain trends in popular culture, and this demands flexibility and variation in employees' talents and expertise.

According to structural contingency theory from the study of organizations, changes in a company's environment—for example, shifting market demand, competition, and resource availability—shape decisions about the type of production and, therefore, about the nature of work (Donaldson, 2001). This means that even traditionally stable industries that produce continuously may sometimes need to adopt flexible, teams-based approaches. For example, standardized media industries are finding that uncertainty in the economy and changing technologies are disrupting routines and requiring experimentation. National Public Radio has been a leader in digital innovation, as it has expanded its Internet operations, continually seeking new avenues through which to distribute its content and interact with audiences. And book publishers are emphasizing interactive digital components for their texts, as well as new formats for websites, mobile phone devices, and digital tablets.

These companies often create separate units that push innovation and are decoupled operationally from the main operation. The innovation divisions in Advance Publications' newspapers offer a good example. Divisions consist of teams of four or five individuals who help their news operations adapt to changing audiences and changing technologies (a) by seeking new ways to distribute content, whether through social media outlets such as Twitter and Google Plus, or through applications for iPads; (b) by encouraging interactivity with readers, from tracking audience use online to encouraging conversation over news stories in social media;

and (c) by working with the business side of the company to identify marketing opportunities for single products—for example, apps for local events that resonate on a national scale.

Collaboration and teamwork are key in these efforts. The innovation team must collaborate informally with newsroom reporters to enhance their stories through social media; they must collaborate with the revenue side of the company in order to fund and promote stand-alone products; and they also must strive to interact with audiences. Flexibility is also important. The division must be ready to jump at opportunities for the production and sale of new products, and they must be in tune to the ebb and flow of news and how it resonates with audiences in order to successfully push stories through social media. But despite these changes, the company needs to recognize that most revenue still flows from advertising tied to daily content—and so traditional, daily news coverage is still key (personal communication with Stacy Brooks, *Birmingham News*, November 18, 2011).

Such changes present new opportunities and new roles for media workers, and they also present challenges to the managers who hire. Constant changes in technology, cultural tastes, and areas of expertise demand flexible staffing and an emphasis on broad and merging roles. Emerging skills and knowledge areas include the ability to work across different media platforms, design skills that help audiences navigate complex and interactive media interfaces, and skills for tracking and interacting with online audiences. Also highly valued is the ability to think creatively and flexibly about new opportunities, the ability to work collaboratively with a wide range of talents and personalities, and a curiosity about changing technologies and media forms. Yet, despite all these new demands, managers cannot forget core skills: reporting and writing for journalism, storytelling for TV and film, and brand management for advertising.

From movie making, to journalism, to video game production and book publishing, media work and its environments are complex and varied, and are becoming more so. The markets and workforce across these industries are as complex and diverse as the culture itself. The next section details the changing employment levels, demographics, and salaries of the media workforce, the ways these changes reflect disruption in the media's environment, and what these changes imply. This section is followed by a discussion of the shifting nature of media work—namely, decreasing stability, the erosion of commitment that employees feel toward media organizations and vice versa, and the rise of temporary project work—and what these changes mean for staff and management.

## THE CHANGING MEDIA–WORK LANDSCAPE

The turmoil and uncertainty in the media environment is directly reflected in the disorder and frailty of media job markets, demonstrated by the employment and salary numbers in this section. The traditionally stable, routine work that dominated media fields for decades is harder to come by. In recent years, graduates have found fewer and fewer footholds for starting their careers, even as a growing number of employees across most media fields have lost jobs and faced the choice of patching together part-time work, starting their own media operation, seeking further education, or leaving the media profession altogether (Becker & Vlad, 2011). Of course the flipside to instability is freedom. At no time in recent years have young media professionals had so many opportunities to chart their own paths, from starting up their own media businesses to influencing changes within existing media companies as these companies experiment and innovate.

However you look at it, recent changes in media job markets have been considerable. While not universal, the media labor force generally saw declining employment opportunities in the first decade of the new millennium, with some bounce back since 2010. The percentage of BA recipients of journalism and mass communication schools reporting full-time jobs declined from 75% in 2000 to 58% in 2010, but then rebounded to 65% in 2013. In 2000, more than 80% of BA recipients of JMC schools reported receiving at least one job offer, compared to 65.8% in 2010 and 73.8% in 2013. (Becker, Vlad, & Simpson, 2013).

In general, the job market was stronger for work related to strategic communication (PR, advertising) and online work, and weaker for news work, such as print and TV journalism. Hiring freezes in news industries were common in the mid-to-late 2000s, making it difficult for reporters, writers, editors, and news directors to find jobs.

Recently, the tightest job market has been in the field of print news, particularly newspapers, and the financial struggles of the newspaper industry are well known. Both newspaper circulation and advertising revenue began sliding steeply in 2006 and 2007, though losses let up a bit in 2010 and 2011. These losses have been a response to volatility in technological and economic environments. News is becoming an overabundant resource online, leading to dilution of ad dollars. In addition, news companies took on too much debt in the 1990s and 2000s, even as stock prices for publicly traded media companies tumbled and a global recession took hold.

The result? Full-time newspaper newsroom employment in the United States fell by 11,000 staffers from 2007 to 2009 before leveling off in 2010 and 2011 at around 41,500 (American Society of News Editors [ASNE], 2010; Edmonds, Guskin, & Rosenstiel, 2011). Nearly three-quarters of graduates of JMC schools with a "news editorial" specialty reported full-time employment in 2000, and this declined dramatically to around half in 2010 before rebounding somewhat to 65.5% in 2013 (Becker et al., 2013). According to reports by the U.S. Equal Employment Opportunity Commission (EEOC) (2012), publishers of large U.S. newspapers (papers with more than 100 employees) employed a total of 257,893 in 2007, and only 143,548 in 2012.

The magazine industry has struggled as well, though the situation improved in 2010, as both circulation figures and number of ad pages flattened out, following severe drops the previous year. Elite specialty magazines like the *Economist* and the *Atlantic* have been financially healthy even as mainstream news magazines have suffered (Matsa, Rosenstiel, & Moore, 2011). Employment at large magazines dropped from 66,151 in 2007 to 44,543 in 2012 (EEOC, 2012).

The job market in telecommunications has also tightened. According to EEOC reports, the number of full-time employees working for large TV broadcasting companies has failed to grow significantly, as there were 87,128 employees in 2007 and 87,874 in 2012. Radio has seen a decrease, from 44,357 in 2007 to 32,976 in 2012. With the exception of cable and public radio, these industries have lost audiences as well. Audience numbers have declined for both national network news and local TV news since the mid-2000s, though this drop began leveling off for local news in 2011. Advertising sales rebounded somewhat for local TV news in 2010, an election year (Guskin, Rosenstiel, & Moore, 2011; Potter, Matsa, & Mitchell, 2011). Among TV networks, ABC suffered the most significant staff cuts, losing 25% of its news staff in 2011.

Technological and workflow changes have paved the way for some of the cuts in telecom. "Solo journalism," reporting, where one person shoots and reports a story, has replaced the traditional reporter/videographer teams at many stations (Hemmingway, 2008). Skype interviewing has become more prevalent, and networks have reduced staff at bureaus around the world (Guskin et al., 2011). Cable news, however, is a different story. Fox News and MSNBC generally gained viewership, while CNN's numbers have been somewhat uneven, dipping recently. Investment in news gathering at these networks is expected to grow (Holcomb, Mitchell, & Rosenstiel, 2011). Radio news has been a mixed bag. Commercial radio earnings grew 6% in 2010, but news operations cut staffs in 2009. Meanwhile, National Public Radio continues to grow audience and staff (Olmstead, Mitchell, & Rosenstiel, 2011).

The job market for advertising and PR work has tightened somewhat over the last 5 to 10 years, though not as dramatically as in the print news and telecom fields. The market has fared better since 2010. Among recent JMC graduates with an advertising specialty, more than 78% were employed full-time in 2000, compared to 72% in 2010, and 76.8% in 2013. According to EEOC statistics, large ad firms (more than 100 employees) employed 66,465 in 2007, and this dropped slightly to 64,414 in 2010 before climbing again to 70,306 in 2012. Among JMC graduates with PR specialties, 82% were employed in 2000, compared to 63% in 2010 and 68% in 2013 (Becker et al., 2013). Employment at large PR agencies declined from 11,162 in 2007 to 9,885 in 2010, but then climbed again to 11,302 in 2012 (EEOC, 2012).

However, there were signs of increased hiring by large ad and PR firms starting in 2010, as the media business in general began to improve (Bush, 2011), and PR and advertising jobs remained the most sought after media jobs. According to the 2013 survey of JMC graduates, 29.3% reported seeking work with PR agencies and 29.3% with advertising agencies. TV jobs were the next most popular, at 25.9%, followed by 20.6% seeking online/Internet jobs, and 18.7% seeking daily newspaper work. Just less than 16% sought radio jobs (Becker et al., 2013).

Changes in the news media workforce also varied by occupational specialty, and in general, traditional specialties in news work such as reporting, photography, and videography declined in numbers. This suggests a shift to new specialties and to merging roles—combining reporting and camera work, for example. According to Bureau of Labor Statistics estimates, the number of reporters and correspondents declined from 52,920 in 2005 to 48,460 in 2013, while the number of photographers declined from 58,260 in 2005 to 54,830 in 2013, and the number of camera operators declined from 22,350 to 16,860 during this same time (Bureau of Labor Statistics, 2005, 2013b).

However, specialties in technical fields generally fared better, again reflecting the shift to new specialties. Technology is increasingly important in the merging of specialized work. The number of broadcast audio and video technicians rose from 83,800 in 2005 to 97,720 in 2013 (OES Tables, 2013; 2005). Recent graduates of JMC programs reported increased opportunities in digital online work. Close to three times as many reported writing, editing, and designing for online media in 2013 than in 2004. There was also an increase in work with video, audio, photo, and graphics for online media, and a sizable increase in the percentage saying they work with social media, blogs, and with Web management. The most dramatic was a jump from 23.9% in 2008 to 52.9%

in 2013 for those working with "social network sites" (Becker et al., 2013). These findings reflect recent decisions by companies such as Advance Publications to emphasize their digital products and social media presence.

Employment for strategic communication roles also has increased in recent years. Although large firms lost staff, the number of all PR specialists rose substantially, from 191,430 in 2005 to 202,530 in 2013, as did the number of graphic designers, from 178,530 in 2005 to 194,360 in 2013 (OES Tables, 2013; 2005). Becker and Vlad (2011) found that graduates of PR programs were much less likely to find jobs with organizations in their own fields, indicating that PR workers are more entrepreneurial, more flexible, and less organizationally bound than workers in other media fields. This may put them in a better position in a media environment that is becoming more fluid, temporary, and project based.

## HIRING AND DIVERSITY

Culture industries both reflect and shape our culture and society, and these industries have made efforts to reflect society's diversity both in media content and in the makeup of staff and management. Yet efforts and results have been mixed, sometimes seeming more ceremonial than substantive.

Early on, news industry management targeted hiring quotas to meet the legal and normative expectations for equal opportunity. In the 1990s and 2000s, as organizations emphasized change, development, and "learning," managers embraced the idea that diversity fosters learning and innovation. There was a sense that diverse media personnel would produce diverse, creative content that represented a pluralistic society (Sylvie, 2011).

Yet for various reasons, media companies' diversity efforts often have led to modest or fleeting changes. Hiring is full of risk for managers, and so the urge to reduce uncertainty in hiring is strong. Managers tend to hire those who are similar to themselves, despite formal pressures for employment equality and diversity. High turnover and temporary, project-based work result in less stable, informal labor agreements, which tend to go hand-in-hand with more personal, less formal hiring arrangements. "Word of mouth" recommendations from employers' acquaintances become even more influential; like tends to hire like, and diversity efforts founder (Becker, Lauf, & Lowrey, 1999). Meanwhile, minority employees in media organizations tend to feel isolated, and many report less job satisfaction and commitment to their organizations than their white counterparts. Black journalists have cited race as an obstacle to advancement into management, as well as a reason for being pigeonholed into covering "black issues" (Sylvie, 2011).

What explains the likelihood that a media company will hire minorities? Group ownership is one explanation. Becker, Vlad, Daniels, and Martin (2007) found that corporate chains with a range of organizational sizes could hire and retain minorities more effectively because they had control over promotion across organizations within the chain. Other explanations for minority hiring include minority ownership, demographic diversity, and the size of the media outlet's community (Hollifield & Kimbro, 2010). ASNE data on minority hiring shows that newspapers in southern cities, which have the nation's highest percentage of blacks on average, are much more likely to have higher percentages of black staff than papers in other areas of the country (ASNE, 2011).

### Numbers on Hiring of Minorities and Women

According to EEOC figures from 2005 to 2012, the percentage of employees who were minorities increased slightly in some media fields, from 18.4% to 19.8% in magazines, 23.2% to 26.9% in TV, 22.2% to 27.3% in radio, and 18% to 23.1% for ad firms. However, diversity hiring in the most recent years has slowed, as trends generally showed a dip in the rate of minority hiring in 2010 and 2011 relative to nonminority hiring. Across all kinds of communication work, the gap between the percentage of nonminority JMC graduates and minority JMC graduates who found jobs grew from 11.7% in 2009 to 17.7% in 2013 (Becker et al., 2013). According to an ASNE 2014 study, staffs of newspaper newsrooms were 13.3% minority, though minorities make up 36% of the U.S. population. While this is a substantial increase since the 1980s, it represents no change since 2005 (13.4%), suggesting that news managers are still ignoring fundamental changes in the social and cultural makeup of society. As ASNE President Milton Coleman said, "This is an accuracy and credibility issue for our newsrooms" (ASNE, 2011).

The percentage of black employees decreased across all media from 2005 to 2012. Advertising and PR firms have the lowest percentage of black employees among all media industries. Black employees make up 5.9% of ad firms and 6.4% of PR firms, compared to 11.1% for newspapers and 9.9% for TV (EEOC, 2012). A 2009 study found that blacks were "often excluded from 'general market' [advertising] agencies and find work only in agencies specializing in 'ethnic markets'" (Bendick, 2009). There is some evidence that ad firms are hiring more Hispanics (Bush, 2011).

Across industries, the gap between the percentage of minorities employed and the percentage working in management persists, but it has narrowed somewhat in recent years. Minorities accounted for 11.3% of all newspaper newsroom supervisors in 2014, a figure that remains largely unchanged over the previous four years (ASNE, 2014). According to EEOC reports, from 2005 to 2012, the percentage of all minorities in management grew in TV work from 16% to 21.8%, in magazines from 10.7% to 13.3%, and in advertising agencies from 11% to 16.6%. However, relative to all minorities, black employees have not fared well. The percentage of blacks working in management generally dipped from 2005 to 2012: 7% to 6% in TV, 4.5% to 4.2% in magazines, and 6.9% to 5.4% in newspapers. The percentages of blacks in management increased in PR and advertising, but both were at a meager 3.5%.

Over the last 25 years, the media field as a whole has become increasingly female. According to the 2010 survey of JMC school graduates, the ratio of male to female job-finding success in the late 1980s was dead even, but in 2013, 70.4% of female graduates had full-time employment, compared to 65.9% of male graduates (Becker et al., 2013). However, this ratio differs across specific media industries. According to 2012 EEOC reports, the PR, advertising, and magazine industries were predominantly female: 64% in PR agencies, 56% in advertising agencies, and 57% in magazines. But the percentage of women employees fell to the low 40s for newspapers, TV, and radio. These percentages have held steady since 2005, with the exception of newspapers, which declined from 49% to the low 40s, and PR, which increased from 59% to 64%.

Generally, women have been less likely to serve as managers then men, though the disparity is not nearly as great as between nonminorities and minorities. Only in the magazine, PR, and advertising industries has the percentage of female managers roughly equaled the percentage that is male. A recent study by the Public Relations Society of America national committee found that the percentage of women who "are enacting the role of manager"—as opposed to a "technician" or "specialist"—is roughly the same as the percentage of men for the first time since 1979, the year these data were first collected (Knight, 2011b). The percentages of managers who were women were especially low in newspapers and radio, at 37% for newspapers and 36% in radio. Percentages across all industries changed little from the mid-to-late 2000s.

In general, trends in diversity hiring are troublesome, though this is more the case in some fields than in others—for example, the extremely low rate of black employment by ad firms deserves attention. Though increased minority hiring does not guarantee more diverse media content—after all, organizational and professional routines strongly influence content—there is some evidence of a relationship (Campbell, 1995; Zoch & van Slyke Turk, 1998). Equally troubling is the isolation and low job satisfaction that minorities feel within media organizations, partly because of their low numbers. The disparity in management between nonminorities and minorities, and between men and women, deserves watching. These numbers seem to be trending toward parity, though black employees are an important exception, as the gap between blacks and nonminorities in management positions continues to widen. Also worth watching is the "feminizing" of fields such as magazines, PR, and advertising. Prior research has shown that when a work area begins to be perceived as predominantly female, salaries and promotion opportunities tend to decline (Bielby & Baron, 1986), though perhaps the wider culture is changing enough to thwart this historical tendency.

## SALARIES

Overall, salaries across media fields tend to decline during a recession, though they have held fairly steady in constant dollars since the late 1980s. For JMC school BA recipients, annual salaries (in 1985 dollars) across media fields declined from $16,400 in 2000 to $14,400 in 2013 (Becker et al., 2013). Inadequate pay has dogged the news industry especially. Years of pay freezes and staff cuts reportedly have top performers leaving their organizations and, in some cases, leaving the occupation altogether (Edmonds et al., 2011).

Salary figures varied widely across individual media industries. According to the 2013 survey of recent JMC graduates, online, advertising, and PR positions had the highest median full-time nominal salaries (not adjusted for inflation) at $35,000 each, followed by $32,500 for cable TV and production companies, and $30,000 for radio and weekly papers. Daily papers offered $29,600, TV offered $29,000, and consumer magazines offered $25,000. Government agencies actually offered the highest median salaries for recent JMC graduates at $37,000 (Becker et al., 2013). In median salaries, specialized communication majors in these fields outperformed their humanities counterparts, English majors, by about $2,000 (Moos, 2011).

Salaries also varied by occupational specialty. According to the U.S. Bureau of Labor's 2013 report on salaries for all employees in large firms (more than 100 employees), technical work and work related to strategic communication commanded some of the highest salaries. Film/video editors made an average of $69,490 per year, sound technicians made

$56,610, and PR specialists made an average of $63,020. Salaries for reporters and correspondents have remained stagnant, with the average nominal annual salary of $44,360 in 2013 and $43,470 in 2005. Radio and TV announcers earned an average nominal salary of $41,800 in 2013, which is up a bit from $35,600 in 2005 (OES Tables, 2013; 2005).

## HIRING STRATEGIES

At the time this chapter was being written, media industries generally found themselves in an employer's market, though this was not true of all media. Small community news organizations, for example, have traditionally struggled to attract job applicants (Rossow, 2009). But in general, there has been a high ratio of potential job candidates to positions open.

Nevertheless, diligence in recruiting and hiring processes is as important as ever. Of all the trials that managers and their companies endure, employee turnover is one of the most draining—on finances, time, energy, and emotions. So while attracting a large pool of candidates is helpful, attracting a pool of high-quality and diverse applicants is even more important, as is the ability to close the deal with top picks. The following are just a handful of tips for employee recruitment and hiring.

- Hire with the future in mind, and don't think too narrowly about the candidate's fit with particular tasks or technologies, as tasks and technologies change continually. Today's uncertain times and converging roles demand an eagerness to work hard, an ability to learn new tasks and knowledge areas, and an ability to collaborate with grace and flexibility.
- Consider candidates' abilities in "core" areas of the profession. Gauge the candidate's understanding, sophistication with, and appreciation of core principles and responsibilities in the field: for example, an appreciation and facility for accuracy and detail in reporting positions and an ability to think creatively in entertainment professions.
- Recruit for diversity. Managers, most typically male and white, must look beyond their own socioeconomic groups and not rely too heavily on word-of-mouth from similar peers. Advertise positions in venues targeted at minorities and look to recruit minorities as interns. Working in a diverse environment on a daily basis helps managers see past the hidden biases to which they are blind, and which blind them in turn.

- Recruit via diverse outlets, including social media. Many PR and ad agencies work with recruitment firms, but others are relying more and more on social media such as Facebook, Twitter, LinkedIn, or their own websites (Bush, 2011). Some are moving away from headhunting firms because of the quality of applicants gained via social media. In addition, employers gain a lot of information from social media that they can't get on a few pieces of paper—links to a variety of work, profiles of applicants' social connections, and a clearer sense of candidates' ability to present themselves. However, it's important to double-check information gained from social media sites for liability purposes, and to make sure information gained through social media is relevant to hiring purposes (Rossheim, 2011). Chapter 9 details guidelines for using social media for recruiting and hiring without creating later liability problems for managers.
- Enable others on the leadership team to hire effectively. It's impossible to know when a valuable candidate may cross one's path, and so recruitment should be in the back of hiring managers' minds as well as the minds of other key managers (Herrenkohl, 2011).

## CHANGE AND THE MEDIA WORKFORCE

Economic slowdown, rapid changes in media technologies and media forms, and changes in ownership structures, market patterns, and media use add up to an unstable, fluid media landscape. It's a landscape conducive to temporary labor arrangements, job hopping, and entrepreneurial activity.

There is no doubt that media careers have destabilized in recent years. The percentage of recent JMC school graduates working part-time increased from 10.1% in 2005 to 14% in 2013, and the percentage with full-time work declined during that time from 69.9% to 65%. As might be expected, part-time workers are generally far less satisfied with their jobs. In 2013, 42.4% of full-time workers reported being satisfied, compared to 14.8% of part-time workers (Becker et al., 2013). A growing number of recent graduates since 2000 say they are taking jobs merely because of availability rather than because the job is what they want to do. And a slightly higher percentage of full-time workers are pursuing freelance work: 20.3% in 2013, compared to 18.5% in 2007.

Interestingly, media workers' commitment to their media organizations is fairly strong, according to the JMC graduate survey, with 49.8%

of respondents reporting they are "very committed" to their company, compared to 44.2% in 2009 and 40.2% in 2000 (Becker et al., 2013). Perhaps those fortunate enough to have full-time work are clinging to their jobs in harsh economic times, whether they like their jobs or not.

While conditions became especially unstable in the late 2000s, media work has always been contingent and unstable relative to other industries. Media consumers' preferences are unpredictable, and for the media workers trying to meet these preferences, it is difficult to define success (Ettema, Whitney, & Wackman, 1987). For these reasons, the media labor market is at least partly controlled through "craft administration" rather than through "bureaucratic administration." In other words, media workers are often guided by the standards and principles of their craft (or profession) rather than by management rules. The concept of craft administration comes from a classic 1959 study of the construction industry, a field that is not strongly guided by rigid management rules ("bureaucratic control") because conditions are hard to predict. Instead, decisions, which are "part of the craftsman's culture and socialization," are "made at the level of the work crew" (Stinchcombe, 1959, p. 180). Workers deal with strong uncertainty in their environment by working flexibly, according to standards of the craft, rather than according to standardized rules. Below, Deuze (2007) describes similar turbulent conditions in news work:

> Employers in the news industry traditionally offered most of their workers permanent contracts, included pension plans, healthcare and other benefits. . . . Today, the international news industry is contractually governed by . . . 'atypical work', which means all kinds of freelance, casualized, informal, and otherwise contingent labor arrangements that effectively individualize each and every worker's rights or claims regarding any of the services offered by employers in the traditional sense as mentioned. This, in effect, has workers compete for (projectized, one-off, per-story) jobs rather than [having] employers compete for (the best, brightest, most talented) employees.
>
> (p. 316)

This may be overstating the case a bit, but clearly, a lot of media work lends itself to Stinchcombe's model. Worker-level decision making seems to be growing in importance, at least for daily decisions. This is not to say that media workers are necessarily feeling more autonomy in their work. A 2007 survey of U.S. journalists found that fewer journalists perceived managerial constraints on their autonomy, but more said they felt "commercial constraints" due to the industry's economic struggles (Beam & Meeks, 2011).

## TURBULENCE AND INSTABILITY AND THEIR IMPACT ON MEDIA WORKERS

Increased flexibility also leads to problems, such as unpaid overtime and inadequate time off after completion of large, life-eating projects. The trend of workers shifting from stable work at large firms to contingent work at smaller companies or multiple jobs also has led to weakened benefits (Deuze, 2007). Benefits for full employment have been worsening as well. Among recent JMC school graduates, 17.5% reported in 2013 that their employer paid all of their basic medical benefits, compared to 33% in 2000. Just 37% said their employer paid part of their medical benefits, compared to nearly half in 2000 (Becker et al., 2013).

Increasingly, careers have weak boundaries. More media workers pursue a "portfolio worklife," a combination of temporary projects, freelance work, multiple jobs, and part-time positions, with less allegiance to a particular workplace. The freelance market for such media professionals as artists, designers, IT workers, writers, and editors is healthy, evidenced by the recent explosion of online job aggregation sites for freelancers (Briggs, 2012). But as mentioned, those who presently have full-time media employment are clinging to their current jobs despite eroding job satisfaction.

Though these changes in media work may offer more control because it is now easier to move from job to job instead of being shackled to one company, this may not lead to work satisfaction. The flip side of freedom is instability and uncertainty, and burnout rates have been high in media work. According to a 2002 survey of U.S. journalists, stress, burnout, dissatisfaction with pay, and growing job insecurity were top reasons for journalists wanting to quit their jobs (Weaver, Beam, Brownlee, Voakes, & Wihoit, 2007). In his study of journalists' job stress, Reinardy (2011b) found "high levels of cynicism and climbing rates of exhaustion." Journalists were "moving closer to reaching burnout" (p. 45), and this was especially true of younger journalists, who also reported less commitment to the profession.

Changing technologies, changing media forms, and staff cutbacks have added to uncertainty about workers' roles within media organizations. Tasks are converging, and "job enlargement" is a consequence.

Media workers are not only performing the traditional roles of writing, shooting, editing, and planning, etc., but also are interacting with audiences or customers via social media. They are spending time "adding value" to media products through multimedia and mobile formats (Beam & Meeks, 2011), and converting traditional formats to the Web, such as videos via YouTube and Web-based mixing programs (Media executive H. Prado, personal communication, November 11, 2011). Across media industries, personnel are doing more with less and working additional tasks for which they've had little or no training. As one newspaper journalist said, "I am now doing parts of five different people's jobs . . . I've had to drop parts of the job that I actually got into this field to do, things that I like to do" (Reinardy, 2010, p. 13).

At the same time that roles are converging, media content is moving toward niche specialization. Ad resources are shifting not only to the Web, but also to media aimed at niche and elite audiences that can and will pay for such content. Specialized audiences will more likely attract elite advertising (Beam & Meeks, 2011; Picard, 2009), and content with a narrow focus is less vulnerable to substitution in the marketplace (Meyer, 2004). News outlets such as Bloomberg's and Reuter's Thompson are offering "focused, professional content—sold to a relatively small client base, usually bundled with data, for extremely high rates" (Freeland, 2010, p. 36). Content specialization goes hand in hand with the creation of audience identity and community. This trend has been evident in magazines for years (titles like *Wired, Creative Knitting, Swimmer's World*, etc.), and we're now seeing finer specialization in magazines, in music (myriad obscure genres—e.g., acid jazz, minimalism, and Neo-Folk), and in video production, with tens of millions of YouTube channels.

The simultaneous trends toward content specialization and role convergence seem to support predictions from several years ago that media workers would be jacks-of-all-trades and that tasks would be less differentiated—for example, leading to "backpack journalists" or "mojos" (mobile journalists) in news work. Mobile technology has made this vision a near reality. As Singer (2011) has said, "the bulky kit has been reduced to a size that fits cozily in a jacket pocket," with devices that offer "compact versatility in capturing, organizing and transmitting information of various kinds, from text to sounds to images, both still and moving" (p. 218). The flipside of this convenience is the job enlargement it encourages, potentially followed by stress and potential burnout.

## TURBULENCE AND INSTABILITY AND THEIR IMPACT ON MEDIA MANAGERS

Creeping burnout and eroding commitment present challenges to media managers, who must deal with weary, disgruntled staff while staving off their own personal burnout. Managers need steady, reliable hands in their shops to handle day-to-day responsibilities. They need employees who are experienced and knowledgeable in their crafts and professions: Excellence in journalism requires detailed understanding of the subject matter, and excellence in entertainment media requires expertise with creative content creation. However, an increasing number of workers are juggling their daily work tasks with freelance or part-time work, and ongoing job searches, and this presents a challenge to workers' ability to attain expertise in their craft or profession. Workers are spending more time learning new and rapidly emerging skills and knowledge areas. Also, managing workers who are more likely to come and go makes it difficult for managers to plan for the long-term.

As mentioned, more and more employees are choosing to make a living by freelancing, even as more companies are choosing to rely on freelancers, stringers, and part-timers who do not demand benefits. Employers must be increasingly savvy about scouting for talented and reliable freelance or "stringer" work. There is in fact a worldwide freelance market that is accessible online, via such websites as eLance.com, Odesk.com, and RentACoder, where employers post opportunities, browse samples of possible freelancers, and wait for bids. The website Craigslist is another venue for finding freelancers, particularly if employers seek local help (Briggs, 2012).

Employers also should be aware of "intrapreneurial" activity within their own organizations, such as employees' blogs and social media pages. Controversies have erupted over media employees, or former employees, posting information about the workplace on their personal sites. Such postings can reveal information the company would like to keep competitors from seeing, and can damage the company's reputation. Having a formal policy on blogging and other online media use is a good idea, but employers should ask employees to help them write such a policy. This will likely lead to a more reasonable and widely embraced set of guidelines, and encourage employee buy-in (Markel, 2009). Although laws and regulations in this area are changing rapidly, Chapter 9 offers examples of policies on social media that are not so broad as to infringe on employees' rights as private individuals.

Of course, all this instability in the work environment has direct effects on managers' own careers as well. Buyouts have become customary for managers—2 weeks of pay for each year of service has been a common buyout deal for daily newspapers (McGinley, 2008). Retirement benefits have been diminishing for both managers and staff, a trend that does little to encourage managers to stick with companies over the long haul. Among recent JMC graduates, just 10.6% report having retirement benefits fully paid by their employer, down from 17.3% in 2000. Only 36.9% say their employers pay part of their benefits, compared to more than half in 2000 (Becker et al., 2013). A noticeable change for executives is a gradual move by companies away from defined benefits plans, such as pensions, which are based on years of service and final salary, and toward defined contribution plans, where employees contribute part of their salaries and take on the risk of making investment decisions (Hay Group, 2011).

The problem of "job hopping" employees was cited earlier—however, moving across companies may enhance an executive's career, if the moves are wise and not too frequent. "Optimal occupational choices and inter-firm mobility decisions" are much more likely to increase salary than is acquiring additional skill and knowledge within a single company (Sullivan, 2010, p. 313). This tends to be even truer for well-educated executives; less-educated employees do better to seek promotion within a company (Rubb, 2013).

However, media companies are countering managers' job hopping with the increasingly prevalent noncompete clause. By signing a contract with such a clause, typically at hiring, an employee promises not to pursue jobs with a company's competitors for a specified period of time, should the employee leave the company. The intent is to wrap up key executives and top talent, preventing rivals from hiring them away and keeping company secrets close. Noncompete clauses traditionally have been prevalent in the broadcasting industry, which is vulnerable to star talent leaving for other outlets and taking audiences with them (Malone, 2007; Zuckerman, 1982). But these clauses are becoming more common across all media for both managers and staff because of increasing competition and mobility of workers (Grimm, 2011; Packer & Cleary, 2007). Executives typically wait months before moving to other firms within the same market (Consoli, 2007; Mcilroy & Wentz, 2008), while on the other end of the spectrum, the "deal-of-the-day" website Groupon briefly required freelancers to sign noncompete clauses before attending its writing seminars (Flores, 2011). The competitive nature of today's media industry can induce employees to sign noncompete clauses, despite the fact that these contracts are not typically in the employee's best interest, and courts have usually ruled against employees (Packer & Cleary,

2007). Noncompetes are often signed by young hires—frequently, talent and young executives—and these clauses can later restrict their professional advancement, putting employees "in the position of indentured servants" (Zuckerman, 1982, p. 12).

The issue of the noncompete clause springs from the more fundamental question of who owns the knowledge and skills employees gain during employment. This is a more controversial issue in times of labor market instability. Employees tend to see growth of their own skills ("human capital") as a job benefit and, in fact, the decision to take a job can be based partly on the potential to grow knowledge and skills. But employers argue that any knowledge and skills gained are company property (Packer & Cleary, 2007).

## SUMMARY

One of the distinguishing aspects of the "culture professions" is the especially high level of uncertainty workers face. Partly, this uncertainty stems from the nature of the production process, and partly it stems from the fact that ongoing cultural and social changes strongly influence decision making about media products and the society itself. Today, media industries are trying to cope with change by switching to flexible, teams-oriented approaches that emphasize collaboration between divisions within organizations and between media workers and audiences.

As a consequence of media industries' financial struggles and technological shifts, the media labor force overall saw declining employment opportunities from 2000 to 2013. This was especially true in news work, while the PR, advertising, online, and cable media fields fared somewhat better. A growing number of potential full-time entrants to the media workforce pursued part-time work and self-employment. Salaries have stagnated since the recession, and purchasing power has declined. The suffering has been more pronounced in news industries and less severe in PR, advertising, and technical and online work.

Hiring of minorities generally leveled off or decreased across the 2000s, though there were slight increases in some fields. The percentage of minorities hired into management increased somewhat, but the percentage of managers who are black generally declined over the decade. Over the last quarter century, media fields have become increasingly female. In general, the percentage of managers who were women stayed level during the 2000s, and women managers were more common in the advertising, PR, and magazine fields.

Despite the stagnant job market, managers need to remain diligent and creative in recruiting and hiring. Rapid, unpredictable changes in technology and types of tasks require managers to seek smart, hard-working, and adaptable workers who know core areas of the profession.

Media personnel are working more than one job to make ends meet, and rapid turnover and short-term projects demand they spend time researching job opportunities and learning new skills because of the changing technologies and converging tasks. Managers must deal with stressed staff while handling their own sense of burnout, reduced benefits, and stagnant pay. Pursuing opportunities with other companies is one avenue toward career enhancement, but such changes can be disruptive and taxing. Increasingly, managers are being asked to sign "noncompete" clauses to discourage such movement.

Though the tough times are not over, conditions for managers and staff began improving—or at least the erosion slowed—for most media industries at the end of the decade. The media employees who seem to be having the most success are working in PR and online media, where work is less likely to be bound to traditional organizations within these same fields, and more likely to be flexible, specialized, and entrepreneurial. But whether such characteristics are harbingers of the future state of media or are merely temporary characteristics of fields in transition remains to be seen.

### CASE 3.1: THE JOB SEARCH

The job ads below are typical for recent postings for media positions. Consider the skills and knowledge these companies are seeking, and assess your own strengths and weaknesses relative to the job description that best fits your specialty area. What skills and knowledge areas do you have now that would help you land these jobs? What skills and knowledge would you need to gain?

#### Posting 1: News Editor

We are looking for an aggressive, disciplined journalist to assign, edit, and write stories in a deadline-conscious newsroom in a small community newspaper. Must be able to work with reporters of all experience levels. Will help plan and edit content for the newspaper, as well as several magazines. The ideal candidate will be a team player flexible enough to cover various coverage areas, and who has a passion for community journalism. Staff must also be able to shoot their own photos, and so photography experience is a plus. The job also emphasizes digital media, including producing content for our website, and the candidate must be fluent in social media, including Facebook and Twitter.

### Posting 2: Communications Specialist

The Regional Hunting and Fishing Safety Association seeks a Communications Specialist who will put in place a comprehensive communications plan that integrates existing programs with social media with the purpose of serving the members of our association more effectually and growing demand for the association's programs. Responsibilities include developing a communications plan that integrates social media with existing programs and establishes a continuing social media presence for the association. The communication specialist will produce a blog, update the association's website, prepare monthly news for members, write and distribute news releases, develop printed material promoting the association, put together annual reports, and help in coordinating workshops and annual banquets.

### Posting 3: Video Journalist

A local TV station seeks a video journalist who would be responsible for the production and reporting of local news. The job candidate must be able to develop and maintain source contacts for stories and help in covering stories that impact the local area. The candidate must be able to enterprise, shoot, write, and edit stories that are clear, concise, relevant, and attention grabbing. The position requires the ability to interact effectively with anchors, reporters, and technical staff. The ideal candidate would also be able to give live or on-scene reports from sites of events or from mobile broadcast units, and fill in as anchor if needed. The candidate would also need to occasionally represent the station at events.

## CASE 3.2: HIRING DECISIONS

You are a manager at Morphis Media, a company that owns and operates 36 local radio stations and four local TV stations, all in small- to mid-sized markets. Morphis also recently purchased three websites that focus on popular music. You are in charge of hiring a "Digital News Editor" who would oversee both the production of news content and the online distribution of this content for a Web platform that serves all Morphis-owned radio stations in your state, as well as the three music websites.

The Digital News Editor's job will involve performance of traditional journalism tasks such as reporting, writing, and editing news stories on a variety of topics, in addition to a number of Web-oriented tasks such as tracking online audience statistics, producing and assigning multimedia elements, improving the sites' "search-engine optimization" (increasing the likelihood that the site will be found via Web searches), and working with social media.

Below is a draft of an ad for the position, which you will post on various job-search websites. Is there anything you would change in the ad?

JOB POSTING: Morphis Media seeks a Digital News Editor to report, write, and syndicate stories on a variety of subjects, including music and entertainment, business, technology, and general lifestyle. Morphis owns and operates 36 local radio stations in the southwestern United States, as well as several popular music websites that reach over three million unique visitors each month. The position requires extensive experience writing and editing news copy, fluency with Web analytics and social media, and an ability to work with video and sound. Familiarity with the music industry is a plus. The Digital News Editor will create, assign, and edit news content for all radio stations' websites as well as the music websites, and will distribute this content through social media. The Digital News Editor also will be responsible for increasing audience traffic to the websites.

The job requires:

- The ability to generate compelling stories
- Strong reporting and writing skills
- Strong editing skills
- The ability to write in many voices and handle a variety of subjects

- Knowledge of search engine optimization and limited technical knowledge
- The desire to take on multiple projects. Multitasking is a desired characteristic
- Ability to develop content based on audience demand and search data
- The ability to distribute news content across the Web and grow the audience
- An understanding of online audience statistics (analytics) and how to analyze them
- Ability to strategize ways to increase site audience and engagement
- In-depth understanding of how the social media world interacts, when they interact, and what content interests audiences
- A willingness to adapt to a changing work environment

The search has been narrowed to three candidates, profiled below. Rank these three candidates, and write a justification for the ranking. In your justification, address the following: What information led you to your decision? Which type of information did you consider to be more important? Less important? Justify your ranking by explaining how the job candidate information corresponded with details in the job posting.

### Candidate 1: Dylan Jackson (photo would show white male)

- BA, State University, May 2007: journalism major, political science minor, GPA = 3.3
- City Editor, *Newtown News Journal* (circulation 46,000), February 2010 to present
- Reporter, *Newtown News Journal*, January 2008 to February 2010: Covered local government, schools, and police
- Skills: Daily experience reporting, writing, assigning, and editing community news stories; regular use of Twitter for updating news stories, regular use of Web

analytics software to gather data on site traffic for presentation at daily news meetings

### Candidate 2: Shelley Neuzil (photo would show white female)

- BA, Liberal Arts College, May 2004: music major, journalism minor, GPA = 3.7
- Instructor, Journalism Department, Southwest State University, August 2008 to present: Teach classes on TV and radio broadcast journalism and production.
- Morning cohost, production director, and writer, WZZZ Christian Broadcasting, August 2005 to May 2008: Generated show ideas, identified guests, wrote news for TV, radio and website, and cohosted weekday morning radio show.
- Production Assistant, Tones Music Studio, June 2004 to August 2005: Contracted music talent, scheduled studio time, set up and operated studio and recording equipment
- Skills: Daily experience producing and hosting radio shows, experience working with video and audio equipment, extensive experience and connections in the music business, experience writing and updating stories for the Web.

### Candidate 3: Gary Burrell (photo would show black male)

- MA, Northern University, May 2008: computer science, GPA = 4.0
- BA, Northern University, May 2006: journalism major, computer science minor, GPA = 3.9
- Software engineer, WebGear Industries, May 2007 to present: Designed and tested software programs, social media websites, and applications for the Web
- Reporter, *Smallburgh Daily,* July 2006 to May 2007: Covered lifestyle, entertainment, and technology
- Skills: Computer languages (Java, C++, PHP, Python, SQL, HTML); extensive use of Web analytics programs (Omniture, Google Analytics); extensive experience with SEO and social media

**CASE 3.3: HIRING DECISIONS, TAKE 2**

Consider the choices from Case Study 2 again, but from the context that Morphis Media recently has experienced a steady decline in audience share in its traditional media properties (its radio and TV stations). Efforts to increase this share have been relatively futile, and so management has decided to make up lost revenues through its websites, and to ramp up innovative products for mobile and tablet devices. Consider the chapter's discussion of companies' responses to uncertainty in the environment. How might the job posting in Case Study 2 be rewritten? Would the three candidates be acceptable? If they would be acceptable, would the ranking change? Why or why not? If these candidates would not be acceptable, what new skills would you look for?

# CHAPTER 4

# Entrepreneurship

If we're not living through mass media's most disruptive age, it's certainly disruptive enough. Media companies have hemorrhaged ad revenue in recent years and have responded with severe staff cuts. This has been especially true in journalism, as the size of the U.S. news workforce decreased about 25% during the first decade of the 2000s (Mitchell & Rosenstiel, 2012), but employment levels dipped in telecom, PR, and advertising as well (Bureau of Labor Statistics, 2013). Around three-quarters of those who received undergraduate degrees from U.S. journalism and mass communication schools reported working full-time in 2000, compared to 65% in 2013 (Becker, Vlad, & Simpson, 2013).

Some who lost media jobs left for other professions, but far more stayed: Loyalty to the craft is unusually strong in media work (Deuze, 2007). What does this mean for media work and media workers? For one thing, it means more frustrated and disillusioned workers, as the ranks of the underemployed have swollen. The percentage of recent JMC school graduates working part-time rose from 9% in 2007 to 14% in 2013, and part-time workers are typically less satisfied with their jobs than full-timers (Becker et al., 2013).

The decrease in full-time employment has also corresponded with an increase in the number of entrepreneurial startups. According to the Kauffman Foundation's annual report, entrepreneurial activity is growing across occupations: "During the Great Recession, more Americans have become entrepreneurs than at any time in the past 15 years . . . [and the] economy and its high unemployment rates may have pressed more individuals into business ownership" (Weitekamp & Pruitt, 2011). This seems to be the case in media fields, and the trend is substantial, if not dramatic. According to the Bureau of Labor Statistics, the number of self-employed in journalism, broadcasting, and PR jobs rose from around

375,000 in 2000 to around 450,000 in 2013, a 20% increase out of all persons employed in these areas (Bureau of Labor Statistics, 2000, 2013).

Is this a good time to start your own media business? School offers a temporary shelter from unemployment, but given skyrocketing tuitions and mounting college loan debt (Lewin, 2011), starting a business venture may make more sense. Certainly, barriers to entering the market are low—starting a website is cheap and easy. However, it's important to appreciate the harsh realities of startups: Odds of success in any field are long. Roughly 60% of new ventures reach "fledgling status" (Aldrich & Ruef, 2007), and half of all entrepreneurs go back to work for someone else within 7 years. Support is hard for media ventures to come by, as investors are typically spooked by high uncertainty and limited growth potential (Picard, 2011). Few entrepreneurs get rich. According to a 2005 study, a third of all owner-operated businesses make more than $10,000 annually, the median income for those self-employed for 10 years is 35% less than income earned working for someone else, and amount of earnings vary widely, adding an element of uncertainty (Shane, 2008). Of the ventures that succeed, nearly all remain small, and growth is usually a result of acquisition or merger (Aldrich & Ruef, 2007).

That's sobering information, but think of it as a challenge rather than an obstacle. Understanding the changing, treacherous lay of the land can enhance chances of success. Arguably, we live in an especially favorable time for entrepreneurship, as a number of seismic shifts in our society have opened opportunities: technological disruption, the rise of social networks, the increasing pursuit of affordable luxury, the greening trend, and an aging population, among them (Siegelman, 2010). Certainly, many startups do succeed, and at any rate, there is more than one way to define success. The satisfaction that comes from calling the shots is worth it for many, even when the financial payoff is modest.

## ENTREPRENEURS: NATURE OR NURTURE?

What are the ingredients of successful entrepreneurship? Early studies of entrepreneurship focused mostly on the individual characteristics of entrepreneurs, who were generally found to be achievement-oriented, risk taking, gregarious, and self-confident (Aldrich & Ruef, 2007). An owner's personality may matter more in new companies than in established companies, as new firms tend to be small with few management levels, making owners more accessible (Beaver, 2003). But later studies found that traits such as self-confidence and risk taking may trip up entrepreneurs. The confident risk-taker may rely too much on intuition and ignore research and help from others (Shane & Venkataraman, 2000).

Studies of entrepreneurship have tended to focus on high-growth and high-risk ventures. Partly, this is due to the influence of social theorist Joseph Schumpeter's pioneering work on entrepreneurship. Schumpeter (1950) saw revolutionary innovation as the heart of new business ventures, and he believed innovation was found in recombining existing ideas. For Schumpeter, innovation grew from the ashes of the "creative destruction" of established businesses that have depended heavily on traditional processes and technologies (Baum, 2001). Schumpeter's ideas seem especially relevant today. Technological, demographic, global, and ecological shifts have destroyed business institutions while clearing fertile ground for innovative upstarts. One example among many is the disruption of the photo film industry. Despite taking steps in the 1990s to relearn its practices and prepare for the coming of digital imaging, the industry was unprepared for the speed with which new technology made their core processes, knowledge areas, and connections obsolete. Paper, film, and chemical production became irrelevant, and disastrous financial loss followed, as photo companies such as Polaroid and Agfa went belly up. New digital imaging companies surfaced in the wake of the disruption, and electronics companies like Sony and Samsung entered the industry, having merged ideas from the innovation wings of traditional photo companies with ideas from the electronics industry (Sandstrom, 2008).

This is not to say that the more innovative an idea is, the more likely it will be to succeed. Would-be entrepreneurs too often obsess on the genius of a "big idea." Timmons (2004) calls this the "mousetrap fallacy," borrowing from Ralph Waldo Emerson's famous line: "If a man can build a better mousetrap than his neighbor . . . the world will make a beaten path to his door" (p. 31). As the photo industry example shows, knowledge of shifting environments, ability to respond flexibly, and ability to borrow ideas from others are key.

Being in the right place, at the right time, with the right amount of money, the right background knowledge, and the right business connections can be more valuable than having a "lightbulb" moment (Chell, 2007). Some tough questions need asking. Is there evidence of a need for the venture? Is there a large and growing, but not overcrowded market? Are there relationships with other organizations that offer expertise the entrepreneur doesn't have? The defunct startup "Wesabe," an online personal finance site, learned the hard way that both collaboration and accurate assessment of the market can be critical to survival. Wesabe's founder Mark Hedlund blamed the startup's failure on (a) the venture's decision to aggregate customers' financial data on their own rather than collaborate with an experienced outside company (which their competitor did) and (b) their misread of the consumer market. Their successful competitor automatically categorized consumers' data, "making them do no work," while Wesabe gave consumers self-help tools. Hedlund admitted he pursued this path because he personally thought consumers would be better off in the long run, and not because market research suggested it—a fatal error, as it turned out (Hedlund, 2011).

In contrast, the Qcitymetro news site in Charlotte, North Carolina, was nurtured by a partnership with the Charlotte *Observer* newspaper, and improved through audience research. Glenn Burkins, the site's founder and a former Charlotte-area journalist, identified upscale African Americans as a target audience. Through personal and professional experience, and through Web traffic data, he found this to be a community that was underserved by increasingly spotty news coverage. He benefited from the traffic and legitimacy his partnership with the *Observer* generated, and the advice he received. The site grew from an average of around 5,000 unique visitors per month in late 2011 to around 12,000 in spring 2012 (G. Burkins, personal communication, September 15, 2012).

The context of one's peers is important too. Any new idea needs test-driving, and by concealing the idea, the entrepreneur can't swap notes with other entrepreneurs. Wesabe and Qcitymetro again serve as good examples. Wesabe's owner says their successful competitor benefited by adjusting for the mistakes Wesabe made in pioneering their field, while Qcitymetro "went to school" on the experiences of nearby citizen-news pioneer DavidsonNews.Net, which at that time had gained national prominence. Waiting too long to launch can deprive an entrepreneur of valuable feedback, and this is especially true of online ventures, highly visible by nature. Also, new ventures have negative cash flows early on, and the perfectionist entrepreneur who tweaks and delays will watch revenues dwindle. In short, an entrepreneur should jump early, but not be the first one in. Online entrepreneurs talk of bypassing extensive beta testing and instead taking a "minimum viable product" to market. It's best to launch quick, gather online audience data, and collect feedback via social media or informal interviews. Formal surveys and focus groups can come later. Entrepreneurs then engage in "loop refinement": constantly assessing and changing the product based on ongoing feedback (Siegelman, 2010).

## CRADLES OF ENTREPRENEURSHIP

How do you know "opportunity" when you see it? Cognitive psychology tells us we are more likely to recognize and successfully process phenomena we have already experienced and become familiar with (Lang, 2000), and this applies to entrepreneurs. Most new ventures are incrementally innovative, based on prior knowledge, spun off from previous jobs, and started in areas where similar ventures exist, with an established network of suppliers and purchasers. Having strong connections with other businesses within one's field opens avenues to resources, and the learning curve for a new venture is less steep when the processes and products are familiar (Shane & Venkataraman, 2000).

The author's own research on changing news forms in urban areas demonstrates this. News startups that had staying power were most often started by former employees of major news outlets. These entrepreneurs were well known by local institutions, giving them some advantage over their rivals. However, this advantage aided news gathering more than revenue gathering, especially in already crowded markets. As a publisher of a startup print/online weekly said: "It's been harder on the business side, . . . regardless of the credibility [and] history we bring on the editorial side" (Lowrey, 2012). This may be partly a consequence of the lay of the land in the digital era, where news of opportunity is quickly available to all. It's hard to find an advantage, and the "field of opportunity" created by low barriers to entry can be uninviting to new growth. Urban "hyperlocal" news startups—those online outlets that serve boroughs and neighborhoods—offer a good example. It would be difficult to find a phenomenon in journalism that has generated as much online buzz as hyperlocal news ventures. But hyperlocal ventures rarely survive for any length of time (Mutter, 2011) as these media proliferate, copy one another, and seek small niche audiences that offer scant sustenance.

It's also the case that adopting the processes, routines, and forms of well-known ventures or types of ventures aids legitimacy and saves money (Campbell, 1992; De Clercq & Voronov, 2009). This is what Mint did to Wesabe, and what Qcitymetro was able to do with DavidsonNews.Net. Likewise, recent research on advertising company startups has shown that mimicking the practices, personnel titles, and client types of existing New York "Madison Avenue" style ad firms (even to the point of building one's shop near Madison Avenue) is beneficial to a new company. But embarking into uncharted waters, while innovative, is risky (Khaire, 2005). While the practices of other companies may be copied, the environmental context of these practices often can't be. What works here may not work over there. The tendency to mimic blindly can lead to "a world of fad-like waves of adoption and abandonment" by would-be entrepreneurs (Strang & Macy, 2001, p. 162). A major criticism of the failed online hyperlocal news venture Backfence.com was its "one size fits all" model, with similar design and similar approaches across its sites in multiple communities—for example, a tendency to report in a top-down way rather than engage in conversations unique to particular communities (Potts, 2007a).

Many startups incubate within larger firms. Startups are typically born at the point that employees decide the risk of staying in a firm and continuing to receive "wage labor" is higher than the risk of setting out on one's own (Campbell, 1992). Knowledge "spillover" from a firm's research and development efforts is important: "Opportunities are created when incumbent firms invest in, but do not commercialize, new knowledge" (Acs & Audretsch, 2009, p. 17). Launching a venture from the platform of an existing firm—becoming a "midnight CEO" (Dailey, 2011)—improves one's immediate position in the resource network: "High accomplishment new organizations are more likely to form ties with high-status partners" (Hallen, 2008, p. 710). Qcitymetro is a good example, as the owner's past and ongoing relationship with Charlotte's most prestigious news organization has served as a support.

Entrepreneurial ventures within a company's external environment can encourage the company to interact with, and even acquire, these ventures, leading to experimentation. For example, acquisition of independent ventures can help major music studios find new talent (Dubini & Provera, 2008), and a news organization's partnering with community bloggers can open up advertising opportunities at the hyperlocal level (Lowrey, 2011). However, the sluggish pace of innovation by large media firms is legend, and employees' frustration with it is common. We see this across media industries, from the news industry, where it is common to hear of young, technology-savvy employees chafing at the rigidity of a traditional management (Stepp, 2007), to the gaming industry, in which indie company game developers find they can't tolerate the "cold business" culture and diminished autonomy of the large companies that inevitably buy them out (Kuchera, 2011). Typical is the experience of PR practitioner Michael Pazyniak, founder of Lighthouse Creative Works, a PR company that plans corporate events. During the economic downturn of the late 2000s, Pazyniak said his former company "clung to more traditional ways of generating business," stifling innovation. He decided to embark on his own venture. The work of his new company is very similar to his old, with many of the same clients, except that he's now charting his own course (Dailey, 2011).

## THE MEDIA ENTREPRENEURIALISM LANDSCAPE

While there is no one database that reliably tracks the number of new media ventures, several organizations are tracking new journalism startups. The Knight Community News Network at the University of Maryland's J-Lab is assembling a list of websites that offer "any original reporting, analysis, commentary, reviews, photos, audio, video or other content on local news, events or issues, created by individuals not employed by professional news organizations" (Knight Community News Network, 2014). Content is gathered by J-Lab staff and is also submitted directly by site creators. As of 2014, 1,334 sites are listed, and around half are business ventures: Roughly half have sought profit and reported paying staff. But nearly half are inactive, despite the fact that nearly all started in the mid-to-late 2000s, showing the fragility of new media ventures (Knight Community News Network, 2014).

In 2010, Columbia Journalism Review established the "Online News Startups" database, which seeks and publishes in-depth information about entrepreneurial media that the CJR staff judge to be journalistically sound. The database listed 300 sites at the time this chapter was written. Two-thirds of these launched between 2008 and 2014, and most are business ventures, with 171 reporting they seek profit. Advertising generates most of the revenue, with 167 sites accepting local advertising and 119 accepting national advertising. Many of the sites are also experimenting with other revenue streams: 103 accept (usually corporate) sponsorships, 100 accept donations, 94 have received grant money, 40 hold events for revenue, 32 syndicate content, 27 sell subscriptions, 22 sell merchandise, 19 sell training services, 17 solicit paid memberships, and 8 have obtained venture capital (Columbia Journalism Review, 2014).

The entrepreneurial media movement's growing legitimacy is signaled by an increasing number of schools that offer programs in entrepreneurialism, including CUNY, Missouri, Northwestern, and American University. And there's an explosion of schools offering entrepreneurial media courses: Minnesota, UC-Berkeley, DePaul, Texas, NYU, South Florida, Georgetown, Memphis, Arizona, UMass, Washington, Columbia, Ithaca College, Nevada-Reno, Florida, Penn, and Temple are among them. Clearly this indicates a budding knowledge base in the area of entrepreneurial media, as well as growth of institutional support.

It's important to remember that entrepreneurialism as a practice is fragile, and it's tough reseeding media fields on a large scale during turbulent, crowded conditions: Note the high number of startups listed in the Knight database that already have become inactive. Yet, many media providers stay in the market despite crowded markets and diminishing revenues, attracted by the low cost of operation, love for the profession, and the status that can come from high-profile media work (Hollifield, 2006). For some, it is a "lifestyle business," measured on metrics other than (or in addition to) revenue, like social impact, status, or simply personal satisfaction (Siegelman, 2010). Former journalist Mike McKisson's TucsonVelo.com is a good example. He started his bicycle website because he loved cycling and "missed doing journalism." His busy full-time work and his inclination for doing journalism over doing business keep the site a "side project" with modest revenues, but he says he has no intention of quitting (M. McKisson, personal communication, April 6, 2012).

### TIPS FOR MEDIA ENTREPRENEURS

Research shows that entrepreneurialism is a steep challenge (Aldrich & Ruef, 2007; Bygrave, 2004; Shane, 2008), and as the data above indicate, most online news ventures do not last beyond 5 years. This does not necessarily mean starting your own venture is a bad idea. Conditions are ripe, with staff cut-backs at large firms, and low barriers to entry online. And there are a growing number of lessons learned from pioneering entrepreneurs who have been through the wars. Some lessons learned and tips follow.

*Get a firm grasp on the venture's purpose and the market niche.* Marketing research and analysis, which are discussed in detail in Chapters 7 and 8, are needed to clarify the goal of the venture, the potential customer base, and the nature of the competition. The entrepreneur must have a firm grasp on the venture's goal, purpose, and niche, as these guide decisions and make it easier to communicate the core idea in a concise, effective way to potential investors, advertisers, and staff.

*Create a business plan.* One study of media entrepreneurship showed that some 30% of new media ventures have no business plan at all (Briggs, 2012). A business plan is not a must if no venture capital is being sought, but it's still a good idea. The process of putting together a plan forces the entrepreneur to identify key aspects of the venture—the primary purpose, target audience(s), resource availability, competitors and collaborators, the specific steps and target dates of the revenue plan, and pricing strategy. If investment capital *is* sought, a business plan is a must, and it should be clear and pithy enough to grab potential investors immediately. The following business plan to-do list is not comprehensive, but it covers the major components. See the reading list at the end of the chapter for more detailed information about business plans.

*Create an executive summary.* An executive summary may be all that is needed at the start, as the entrepreneur vets ideas early on (Briggs, 2012). Entrepreneurs can send potential investors an "expanded executive summary" of 6 to 10 pages, which provides an overview of the business plan. The formal business plan can then include a brief version of the executive summary—no more than a page or two. Most investors will read only the executive summary and/or the expanded summary, using the detail in the report as an appendix (Ellis, 2009). An executive summary includes the problem or opportunity and exactly why the product/service addresses it well, the target market, an overview of the field and why the proposed venture offers a better solution than the competition, and the collaborations and resources available. A concise version of one's purpose, niche, and strengths should roll off the tongue when talking about the plan with investors, advertisers, customers, staff, and collaborators (Siegelman, 2010).

*Know the product well and the entrepreneur's fit with that product.* Entrepreneurs need to evoke "authenticity" when discussing their product. The entrepreneur must be *the* credible expert, especially when it comes to discussing the fit between the problem or need and the solution the product offers (Siegelman, 2010). Can the product address a core need, or is it merely something some people might find interesting or mildly helpful? And is the product something that fits well with the entrepreneur's own interests, talents, and previous connections (so these can fuel the effort)?

*Know the likely customers or audiences.* The entrepreneur should be able to name particular buyers, advertisers, or customers who have expressed interest. For a media product, that means knowing specifically what audiences are being targeted, and what potential audiences are looking for in the product. It's a good idea to canvass potential audiences, even starting with friends and acquaintances:

- Do you currently use the product/service offered? If so, how?
- What other products/services have you considered, and how does ours compare?
- What qualities do you look for in this product/service?

*Demo the product or service.* Ask customers how much they like the product or service, how likely it is they would use it, and how much they would pay, if anything. Also gather demographic information and final comments (Ali & Seiders, 2004).

Questions could be tailored to the specific product and market. If, for example, the product were a local news site, potential customers in the area could be asked how they currently get their news, and what kind of information and ads they attend to (Briggs, 2012). Also find people who have tried something similar and failed. Being able to explain how your product will avoid a similar fate can impress potential investors (Ellis, 2009). Later, if the venture will be online, mining analytics data is a must (see the discussion on analytics later in the chapter). These data help reveal where customers live, how they use the Web, and with which online communities they identify.

*Detail the competition.* As discussed earlier, most successful new enterprises take root in a field where similar enterprises already have been operating and have helped clear the way ahead. Recall the examples of Mint learning from Wesabe, and Qcitymetro learning from Davidson-News.Net. However, entrepreneurs want to avoid overcrowded fields, and they want to distinguish their startups from similar others. They should "[f]ind a niche and attack it in a way that no one else can" (Briggs, 2012, p. 168). Entrepreneurs may create a "competitor matrix" grid that rates the five closest competitors according to a list of characteristics that customers find important (on a one-to-five scale for each characteristic). If competitors are online, information about their site traffic is a click away, via compete.com or quantcast.com (Briggs, 2012; Zacharakis, 2004). Note that entrepreneurs are commonly advised to aim for large, growing markets with no clearly dominant players. In such a market, substantial revenue may be earned by capturing just a small percentage of the market, thereby not threatening large competitors (Siegelman, 2010; Timmons, 2004). This advice is less relevant to media entrepreneurs who want to make money but who may also be content with modest earnings, doing what they love to do. Startup funds needed for such outlets are minimal, and seeking a narrow, popular niche may be a more achievable path to success.

*Name possible collaborators.* Collaboration means partnering with others whose skill sets differ from, but complement, the entrepreneur's. Is there a sales expert who might work on commission? Can a relationship with an IT (information technology) expert be established? Many IT workers may be attracted to media work, even on a volunteer basis. Partnerships with existing companies can help a startup reduce risk (Picard, 2011). Arguably, Wesabe's decision to aggregate their own data rather than partner with a data aggregating company sped their demise; while in contrast, Qcitymetro's partnership with the city's daily paper benefited both. Such partnerships are found in other fields as well. In the gaming (Kuchera, 2011) and music industries (Dubini & Provera, 2008), firms may seek partnerships with independent ventures to gain access to new audiences and cheap labor.

*Know the promotion strategy.* Entrepreneurs need to know how to present themselves, craft their image, and publicize their services. Strategies for promotion and costs for these should be listed. Don't forget social media strategies, which are increasingly important for media ventures (see the discussion on social media later in the chapter).

*Detail the finances.* Entrepreneurs should create a credible "worst case" financial outlook for themselves and for potential investors. From where will revenue come? What are the direct costs and overhead? Is start-up capital needed? Create a balance sheet and clarify cash flow, with projected yearly income and expenses (Zacharakis, 2004). (See section on revenue sources later in the chapter.) Cash flow is critical for any startup: Ad revenues from a big sale may be on the horizon, but these won't help if the venture runs out of cash because of immediate costs such as rent or payroll (Ellis, 2009). Other assets may be listed as well, such as access to databases or proprietary technology (Briggs, 2012).

*Know the long-term details.* Create a development timeline for potential investors, collaborators, and advertisers. Is there a plan in the event of failure?

*Find the right niche.* A narrow, well-defined niche means a well-defined audience, demographically, economically, and geographically; a budding community; and a shelter from competitive pressures (Picard, 2011). Once a specialized area has been identified, the entrepreneur should aim for "narrow comprehensiveness" in order to "own" the specialized area (Briggs, 2012). There are many opportunities for journalists to become reputable experts and build loyal communities of readers in specific areas: a narrowly defined locale; a particular political issue; a particular celebrity; a sport, hobby, or activity. Niche is important in other media fields as well. Independent musicians identify with highly specialized genres, and independent producers of online shows seek strong audience identification with a narrowly targeted age group (e.g., via YouTube channels). Finding a niche also goes hand in hand with the opportunity to be creative. Big firms and their big investors tend to be risk averse to extreme creativity, but this is less so with smaller operations built by individuals or highly focused teams (Deuze, 2007).

*Seek start-up capital.* Media ventures are often unpopular with investors because of the high uncertainty and historically low payoff, though there are exceptions. A well-known example is AOL's purchase of the Huffington Post in 2011 for $315 million (Parr, 2011). Most media ventures are funded out of the entrepreneur's personal or family resources. However, a growing number of foundations are offering support for new media ventures. Notable is the Gannett-affiliated Freedom Forum foundation, as well as the Knight Foundation, which invested some $300 million in the first decade of the 2000s (Lewis, 2011). There are an increasing number of "new media incubators" in the United States and Europe that fund and help develop new ventures (Picard, 2011). For example, Knight started the media incubator Project Liberty to help develop innovative media ventures in Philadelphia. Selected entrepreneurs undergo a 6-month residency program with free rent, office equipment, and operation support (Bracken & Frisby-Greenwood, 2012).

Though investment funds are hard to come by, diligence and a wide net may pay off. Jeff Israely, who started the international news site "Worldcrunch" noted the importance of holding on to the core "gem" idea of his venture. He said that as he met with possible investors, it was easy to cater to the "flavor of the month" (i.e., social media, mobile apps), which seemed to generate more buzz and enthusiasm for those who might part with their money. He said he was ultimately glad he fought these temptations (Israely, 2011). Israely hung on to his core mission and demonstrated "entrepreneurial authenticity." Given the likelihood that investors will find a hole in your project, it's critical to be the expert in your core area—and not just expert about media content, but also about unmet audience needs and preferences, the competition and how you'll fit audience need better than they can, and reasons for prior failures by others (Siegelman, 2010).

*Network.* No single entrepreneur can know everything. It's important to know and admit the holes when meeting with possible investors. Hooking up with like-minded others online or through professional groups can help an entrepreneur gain valuable collaborators with new ideas and areas of expertise—about legal issues, technology, and business operation, for example. Most cities have professional associations for media entrepreneurs (Ellis, 2009). For example, Qcitymetro's involvement with an informal group of Charlotte-area media entrepreneurs led to valuable advice from peers about operating a business.

*Budget wisely.* This is important for any business, but it is critical for new ventures. Entrepreneurs should have low overhead and minimal ownership of capital assets. They should seek low or deferred rent, and they should seek volunteers for content production, IT help, and even for legal advice. Immediate cash flow and quick payment are in some ways more important than income level. Once positive cash flow can be generated, much of it goes back into operating costs (and debt). Planning for the lean periods of business cycles is also important. For example, magazine publishers receive most of their ad revenue during certain months, and so must put some revenue away (Picard, 2011).

*Be familiar with the legal stuff.* The high profile nature of media brings legal risks. Hiring a lawyer may be necessary at some point, but lawyers are expensive, and free information for entrepreneurs can be found online from sites such as the Digital Media Law Project, The Startup Lawyer, and Startup Law 101. Forms and documents for establishing business, for taxes, and for freelance contracts can be found online, and completing them can limit the time spent on a lawyer's clock. Also, a lot can be learned by talking with other entrepreneurs (Digital Media Law Project, 2014).

One of the first legal decisions an entrepreneur faces is choosing a business form. The most critical factors to consider are exposure to personal liability, administrative costs, tax issues, and control and autonomy (Mandel, 2004). The following are pros and cons for the common business forms. (a) A *sole proprietorship* is a form owned by an individual, with no other owners. It's the simplest and easiest form to deal with for daily management and taxes, and it's cheap in many ways; however, the owner's personal resources will have scant protection in the event of a liability lawsuit against the business; (b) an *informal arrangement* allows daily operation without adoption of a specific form—again, this is easy and inexpensive on the front end, but liability and tax consequences may lay in wait; (c) a *formal contractual partnership agreement* demands lower up-front costs and offers tax benefits; (d) a *limited liability corporation (LLC)* involves some up-front costs and hassle, but combines tax benefits of a formal partnership with the limited liability of a corporation; (e) a *corporation* greatly reduces liability, but has tax disadvantages and involves a lot of complex, costly paperwork and record-keeping; and (f) a *nonprofit* offers tax benefits and limits liability, but constrains the organization's purposes and activities, and requires time-consuming tax filing (Briggs, 2012; Digital Media Law Project, 2014; Mandel, 2004).

Another important legal issue is the selection of the venture's name. The wrong name can lead to trademark and copyright violations (Mandel, 2004). Check the availability of a potential name by doing a basic Internet search, searching "fictitious" or "assumed" business names in a state's database of such names, and at a county clerk's office for no cost. If the venture is online, also search for and register a domain name: GoDaddy.com and Google Apps offer domain registration, as does the hosting services DreamHost.

*Don't dither—go ahead and launch.* The planning stage can string out too long, as entrepreneurs hide their ideas away without reaping the benefit of feedback from others. Don't get caught up in the plan's "big idea" and the perception that prying eyes must not peek (Timmons, 2004). Increasingly common advice for online media entrepreneurs is to launch a site early, even before it's complete. Online feedback from interested others can be valuable, helping to focus the venture's purpose and ensuring that it is tailored correctly to the market and audience. Also, rather than waiting for one big investor, it may be more realistic to pursue a "bootstrap" approach to fundraising. Jeff Israely (2011) of Worldcrunch said he found success launching early, playing it by ear, and keeping costs to a minimum. He says there is "a vast territory between no funding and fully funded."

*Track customers and audiences.* When operating a new venture, it's critical to know the changing behavior patterns of customers or audiences. For new online ventures, following Web analytics is essential. Analytics can be used merely to make a website more functional, but they can also drive revenue forecasts (McKelvie & Picard, 2008, p. 6). Below are a handful of fundamentals, but see the list of online and print sources at the end of the chapter.

- Know the key metrics. The *pageview* is the fundamental unit of measurement of audience site use. It measures a visit to a single site page, and *page views per visit* can get at the depth of a user's site experience during a single journey through a site's pages. The *unique visit*, or *unique*, is counted each time someone on a different computer enters a site. Number of uniques indicates the site's ability to generate new audiences.
- Level of user involvement or *engagement* with the site correlates with loyalty and with behavioral activity such as clicking on ads and purchasing online. Common engagement metrics are *time on site* and the *bounce rate*, which is the percentage of visitors who leave the site on the same page they entered it—a low bounce rate is preferable. Knowing where site traffic is coming from is another clue to engagement. Are users typing in the site's URL or clicking a bookmark? Such *direct traffic* indicates a higher level of site loyalty than does *referral traffic*, the users who find the site via a link from another site such as Twitter, or from a website aggregator. Linking to a single story or video from a social media site or from an aggregator is increasingly common.

- Web analytic data offer information for potential advertisers. Information about the users' geographic location, the times of day the site is used, and types of content most often accessed give advertisers a better idea of likely spending patterns.
- Online entrepreneurs should know how to "optimize" a site for search engines—for example, using proper nouns and terms that are highly searched as key terms and in headlines. Google's free service "AdWords" can provide synonyms for search terms, as well as the number of times users have searched these terms in Google. (Kaushik, 2009; R. Simms, Director of Digital Operations of the Alabama Media Group, personal communication, November 4, 2011; Track your traffic, 2010).

A social media strategy is critical. Social media sites like Facebook, Twitter, and Instagram are free, and provide instant feedback and alternative ways to disseminate content and awareness of the product or service. Generating buzz via consumer-generated content works best when started early, when the product serves a useful niche, and when the marketing is a bit edgy (Niederhoffer, Mooth, Wiesenfeld, & Gordon, 2007). Even more important, social media are valuable tools for building audience identification and "community" around the product or service. This is a popular refrain in online journalism and PR, but we see it in other media fields too. For example, indie video game designers are pursuing games with "social values," encouraging connection with friends via social media (Irwin, 2008). It's important to avoid the appearance of shilling a product via social media; frequent social media users are good at sniffing out commercial purposes behind the pose of community interaction. Instead, provide the community helpful and interesting content of real value, and update it frequently; this will more likely attract traffic and build loyalty (Track your traffic, 2010). Also, avoid the pursuit of Twitter followers and Facebook friends for the sake of having followers and friends. If people aren't going to be loyal followers, buy your site's products, or add value to your site, then why seek them? (Briggs, 2012). For more information on startups and social media, see the list of readings at the end of the chapter.

*Revenue streams.* Advertising is the most often pursued revenue stream, as shown in the databases of journalism startups, above. Below are tips for gaining ad revenue, with a particular emphasis on online ventures, the most common type of media startup today:

- Consider hiring sales help, either paid by commission or with sweat equity. Some kind of salary or stipend base can aid reliability, though this luxury may be out of reach.
- It's important to price advertising rates for what the market will bear. Pricing too high creates barriers to purchase, but pricing too low can undercut long-term success because customers become averse to price increases, and because price signals quality level (Ali & Seiders, 2004). Also, in the beginning, keep pricing simple. Develop tiers and options for pricing later, once the market is better known. Rate cards and media kits should be accessible on the site, and easy to read (Briggs, 2012).
- Though charging by number of ad impressions (number of times an ad loads in a browser) is common for online media, it may be better for a new entrepreneur without a reliable audience base to charge for advertising over a designated period of time (Briggs, 2012).
- Much of the current, online advertising is sold via advertising networks, where multiple online publishers are bundled and sold as a package to advertisers. Ad networks link small sites to larger sites, allowing advertisers to reach sizable audiences for lower cost (Hof, 2009). Ad networks can be either self-serve, where the entrepreneur signs up online and ads automatically load on the site (Google AdSense is an example, not to be confused with Google AdWords), or an agency can manage the advertising. Agency networks are more time-consuming and costly up front, but pay more in the long run, while self-serve is easy and cheap to join, but less profitable in the long run (Briggs, 2012).

Though advertising brings media ventures the most money, it's best not to be tied to one revenue stream. Diversification lowers risk in the event of the collapse of any one revenue strategy; however, prioritize the most likely sources of revenue. Just tossing out all possible revenue streams can make an entrepreneur appear unfocused to potential investors (Ellis, 2009). For more information, see the readings at the chapter's end.

- *Affiliate marketing* refers to a mutual, long-term relationship between the entrepreneur and the payer, and may take a number of forms. An affiliate company may sponsor part of a startup site over a long period, or may purchase access to an e-mail list of the site's users. There is also "affiliate advertising," from which neither partner receives revenue unless the ad is clicked and/or a purchase is made from the advertiser's site.

- *Foundation support* as philanthropic giving is a possible source of revenue, but such a strategy should fit with the venture's mission. These ventures often start as a tax exempt 501(c)3 nonprofit (for more information, see the Digital Media Law Project, 2014). For example, a news enterprise with religious, scientific, artistic, public safety, civic, or educational purposes could qualify.
- *Segmented marketing.* Charging for "premium content" or pricing by tiers is becoming popular. A site might develop a list of local services and charge for an enhanced listing, for example. However, as mentioned, this strategy works best for a venture that has gained a clear sense of its niche and market.
- An entrepreneur may sell *professional services* on the side. Media entrepreneurs gain valuable experiences in areas that many are only considering pursuing, and these may be marketable—Web design and social media consulting are examples.
- Entrepreneurs may hold *events* such as webinars on niche knowledge areas and charge for access to those who sign up, or for access to experts in the site's online community.

## SUMMARY

Media companies' financial woes, subsequent layoffs, workers' commitment to their craft, and low barriers to entry online have produced an environment that seems especially ripe for entrepreneurialism. However, making a go of a new media enterprise is challenging work. Venture capital is tough to come by, failure rates are high, and rewards are limited. Yet many do attain success, through either financial reward or increased autonomy and creative freedom.

Research indicates that the entrepreneur's own characteristics—e.g., self-confidence and risk taking—are minor factors in bringing success. It is more important to have a familiar product and a conducive, supportive environment. In fact, locating one's venture in a strong network position, with access to resources, information, and connections, is usually more beneficial than having "that one great idea." Observing pioneers in an area is a good idea, as it's helpful to learn from others' mistakes and successes. Many successful new enterprises were incubated within existing firms, and an entrepreneurial, innovative environment can also help existing firms innovate. Partnerships between firms and new ventures can provide firms with fresh ideas and provide entrepreneurs with stability.

Effective response to opportunities is also critical, as is timing. It's best not to wait until a media outlet or product is perfect before launching, as doing so leads to diminished resources and can deprive the entrepreneur of valuable feedback.

Media entrepreneurs should craft a business plan whether they expect to pursue startup capital or not. A business plan can help clarify a new venture's purpose and target audience, define competitors and collaborators, and generate financial strategy. It is important to become familiar with legal requirements, declaring the form of the business being started and naming the business. Finding volunteer collaborators, keeping costs low, tracking the audience, and pursuing multiple revenue streams are all important to launching a new venture and keeping it afloat as it negotiates increasingly rough waters in pursuit of success.

### ADDITIONAL INFORMATION

Interested in starting your own new media venture? The information below can help.

### Media Entrepreneurialism

Briggs, M. (2012). *Entrepreneurial journalism: How to build what's next for news*. Thousand Oaks, CA: Sage.

Briggs, M. [normalguyguide] (2011, March 13). Entrepreneurial journalism (1/2) [Video file]. Retrieved from www.youtube.com/watch?v=-gY3P3CXFjM

Briggs, M. [normalguyguide] (2011, March 13). Entrepreneurial journalism (2/2) [Video file]. Retrieved from www.youtube.com/watch?v=Q04Qt4cOP6Y

DVorkin, L (2012). *The Forbes model for journalism in the digital age: Training a new generation of entrepreneurial journalists*. San Francisco, CA: Hyperink.

Jarvis, J., Ali, R., Balboni, P., Harris, J., Overholser, G., & Thornton, J. (2010, February 12). Education of the entrepreneurial journalist [Video file]. Retrieved from www.paleycenter. org/carnegie-entepreneurial-journalism/

### General Entrepreneurialism

Entrepreneur.com [Publication with tips on entrepreneurial ventures]

Kawasaki, G. (2004). *The art of the start*. New York, NY: Portfolio.

Stanfordbusiness. (2009, September 25). Do you have what it takes to be an entrepreneur? [Video file]. Retrieved from www.youtube.com/watch?v=z68eB6bnjNk

Stanfordbusiness. (2010, March 24). What they don't teach in business school about entrepreneurship [Video file]. Retrieved from www.youtube.com/watch?v=mHVJF9VaWfo

### Business Plans

Briggs, M. (2012). *Entrepreneurial journalism*. Thousand Oaks, CA: Sage. (See sample business plans at the end of the book.)

Ellis, J. [stanfordbusiness]. (2009, July 28). The business plan [Video file]. Retrieved from www. youtube.com/watch?v=yG6_6UbprFw

Magazine Journalist Business Plan. (2012). BPlans. Retrieved from www.bplans.com/ magazine_journalist_business_plan/executive_summary_fc.cfm

Zacharakis, A. (2004). Writing a business plan. In W.D. Bygrave & A. Zacharakis (Eds.), *The portable MBA in entrepreneurship* (pp. 107–139). Hoboken, NJ: John Wiley & Sons, Inc.

## Using Analytics and Social Media

Barden, B. (2013). A beginner's guide to Google Analytics. Retrieved from www.quickblogtips. com/bonus-content/free-ebook-a-beginners-guide-to-google-analytics/

Googleanalytics. (2011, May 18). Analytics for agencies #1—Introducing the new version of Google Analytics [Video file]. Retrieved from www.youtube.com/watch?v=ulr9eK4er-Y

Kaushik, A. (2009). *Web analytics 2.0: The art of online accountability and science of customer centricity*. New York, NY: John Wiley & Sons.

Kerpen, D. (2011). *Likeable social media: How to delight your customers, create an irresistible brand, and be generally amazing on Facebook (and other social networks)*. New York, NY: McGraw-Hill.

Lurie, I. [ian lurie] (2012, January 12). Google analytics tutorial: Install [Video file]. Retrieved from http://vimeo.com/35388270

Stanfordbusiness. (2010, March 23). Using social media as a marketing tool [Video file]. Retrieved from www.youtube.com/watch?v=8T-zcKNV1wg

## Legal Matters

Caplan, J. (2012, March 4). Practical tips, resources for entrepreneurial journalists with legal questions [Web log post]. Retrieved from www.poynter.org/how-tos/ leadership-management/entrepreneurial/164826/practical-tips-resources-for-entrepreneu rial-journalists-with-legal-questions/

Giammittorio, G., & Tomasetti, L. [DardenMBA]. (2009, June 15). Legal matters: Starting and growing your business [Video file]. Retrieved from www.youtube.com/ watch?v=9VELnWhz8pw

# Case Studies

### CASE 4.1: STARTING A NEW VENTURE

Keisha quit her job as an online editor at the *Urbanton Journal*, a large, struggling, understaffed daily newspaper, to pursue her dream of starting a serious news site that covered East Suburbia, her area of town. After 10 years working for the *Journal* as a reporter, a city editor, and now an online editor, it was hard for Keisha to watch the quality and quantity of local coverage decline. Keisha was well connected to East Suburbia. She had reported on the area before buying a small home there. She had been active in her neighborhood association, leading an effort to clean up a blighted area and create a butterfly garden (the city has a reputation for these gardens, partly due to the work of a prominent entomology department at a local University). Keisha felt her employer had laid off too many employees, watering down the reporting resources needed to cover local government and public issues in her area. She saw a need for a hyperlocal outlet that offered serious journalism on local, public issues. She would include everyday people's voices and avoid mainstream media content. The niche seemed obvious. East Suburbians would not only be eager to read the stories, they could also serve as volunteer "citizen" journalism contributors.

Keisha had a modest amount of startup money from a supportive relative and from her own savings. She had no business experience, but the need for this information seemed obvious, and she felt confident that ad dollars would follow the eyes. A few of her former newspaper colleagues, some laid off and some still employed, were interested in her project—especially a friend in IT, who offered her some pointers. During the 4 months it took her to build the site, Keisha contacted friends in the area about writing for the site, and she herself worked to create content, much of which was timeless, so she would have material for the lean times.

The site debuted in September. About 15 sleepless months later, the site was shuttered. Keisha had run out of money and energy, having acquired neither advertising nor reliable citizen contributors. They were, as it turned out, not very interested in reporting and writing on public issues, which they found time consuming and complex and a little boring.

Revisit the pointers from this chapter. What do you think Keisha did wrong? What opportunities did she miss?

## CASE 4.2: THE BUSINESS PLAN

Let's give Keisha a "do over." Keisha decides to start from scratch and create a business plan for the site. To do so, she conducts informal research and gathers the information, below. Using (a) the information from Case 1, (b) the chapter's discussion on business plans and supplemental readings listed in the chapter, and (c) the additional information below, write an abbreviated business plan (about 6 to 8 pages) for Keisha's site.

- *About East Suburbia.* East Suburbia is a midtown area with several neighborhoods. The area was one of Urbanton's first suburban areas but now finds itself between the city center and newer suburbs and exurbs. Housing generally ranges from mid- to high-end older homes, though some areas still need renovation. The 1990s and early 2000s saw an influx of young families who bought older homes and fixed them up. There is a small arts community, with a handful of galleries and studios, nearby coffee shops and small restaurants, and a small theater that shows art films. The area also has a mix of chain stores and restaurants, and sits next to a large city park with mixed uses.
- *The local media environment.* Urbanton's media include a daily newspaper, two citywide magazines, a business journal, an alternative weekly paper covering city government, arts and entertainment, three local TV stations, two commercial radio stations, and a public radio station. Two years earlier, another resident had started an online neighborhood website, "Look East," but the site was active for only 8 months.
- *What the customers think.* Keisha informally canvasses 20 residents of East Suburbia to find out what they want from a local news source. Below are typical responses.

  o   What kinds of news and information interest you? 10 had most interest in national news; 6 in local entertainment and arts events; 2 in school issues; and 2 in local government.

  o   How are you currently most likely to get your news? 10 said national outlets such as cable news and national public radio; 4 said they took the city paper; 3 said they watched local TV; 3 said they read the city's alternative weekly.

  o   What kinds of advertising do you pay attention to? 9 said they paid no attention to ads; 7 said they paid attention to ads from local shops or restaurants; 4 said they paid attention to ads from shops and restaurants in the general city.

## CASE 4.3: USING ANALYTICS

Keisha launches EastBurb News, a local news site, in September 2011. Her content plan involved coverage of news and events in three eastern suburbs of her city, in real time, on both the blog and social media associated with it. The blog comments, a message board, and Facebook and Twitter accounts provide feedback to Keisha as well as an online community for the residents of the suburbs. She currently posts one or two stories a day to the site's social media accounts. Around the middle and end of each month, Keisha also sends an e-mail newsletter to users who sign up with the site. EastBurb News is essentially a blog, and most of the posts and the traffic end up on the home page. Keisha serves as editor of the site and frequently posts herself, but she also pays freelancers who write news and features and occasionally create video. Video is the most costly aspect of her site, since she pays a premium for video content and posts the videos as downloadable podcasts, costing her bandwidth. She also invites visitors to submit information about local events, and posts them for free.

In early 2012, after spending a few months building an audience through word of mouth and promoting her new site to other sites, Keisha signed up for a Google Analytics account. The Dashboard (Figure 4.1) is what Keisha sees at the end of the first month of analysis. She plans to use the results to make decisions about how to allocate resources and produce content.

About the dashboard: The fever line across the top of the dashboard tracks number of visits to the site during January. The numbers below this line, under "Site Usage" (Visits, Pageviews, etc.) are different ways to measure the way people use the site: number of visits and pageviews, average time spent on the site, etc. The pie chart under "Traffic Sources Overview" shows a breakdown of ways users access the site—i.e., from *Referring Sites*, or links from other websites or social media; from *Direct Traffic*, or those typing in a URL or using a bookmark; from *Search Engines*; or from *Other*. To the right of this pie chart under "Content Overview" is a list of site pages showing the percentage of overall site pageviews each page is getting. The top line in this list with the forward slash (/) is the site's homepage.

Using information in the chapter, suggested readings at the end of the chapter, the Dashboard for East Burb News provided

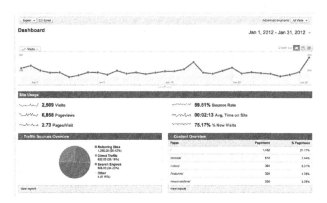

**Figure 4.1**   Google Analytics dashboard for Keisha's EastBurb News
website

(Figure 4.1), and your own research on Google Analytics (see www
.google.com/analytics), answer the following questions.

- What's the difference between pageviews and visits? To
  make more money from ads, Keisha would like to see
  readers visit more than the two to three pages they now
  visit on average. How do you think she could increase the
  number of pages a reader visits on her site?
- What's a "bounce rate"? How might Keisha change the site
  to improve the bounce rate?
- If Keisha is going to use these results to invest in new
  content for her site, what might the "Content Overview"
  list on the Dashboard tell her?
- From what "source" does most of the traffic come? Why do
  you think that's the case?
- Based on the Dashboard results shown here and what you
  know about Keisha's business plan for EastBurb News,
  suggest two possible tactics she might employ to boost
  traffic.
- Besides what is shown on the Dashboard here, what are
  some other metrics Keisha might consult before making
  investment decisions, and why?

# CHAPTER 5

# Planning and Project Management

In the language of management, "planning" is shorthand for "strategic planning," while the term "strategic planning" is synonymous with "strategic management."

Strategic management is the most important responsibility leaders and managers have. All other tasks—leadership, motivation, research, market analysis, finance—are simply necessary steps in realizing the organization's strategic plan. The strategic plan—or vision—defines what the organization's ultimate goal is and outlines a plan for how to achieve it. So important is this process that the majority of all research on media management has focused on strategic management (Mierzejewska & Hollifield, 2006).

In the world of commercial media, an organization's strategic vision must include maximizing profits for owners and shareholders, although it may also include goals of serving society, producing high-quality content products, or being recognized as an industry leader or influential source of information. In the expanding world of nonprofit media, the strategic vision would include achievement of the goals for which the organization was created, while surviving financially. In the increasingly important markets for media entrepreneurs and independent and freelance media professionals, where individuals are, effectively, one-person media organizations, the strategic vision includes out-competing others who provide similar services and thereby earning a steady, worthwhile living.

Regardless of the elements included in a strategic vision, an organization must have a concrete plan, if there is any hope of achieving the vision. This chapter will examine strategic organizational planning processes, including project planning and management. The chapter also will take a detailed look at the management challenges involved in one of the most common—and complex—projects media professionals take on in the digital age—globalization. The next chapter, Chapter 6, will examine another equally common and challenging media project—managing innovation.

## ELEMENTS OF THE ORGANIZATIONAL PLAN

There are three types of organizational plans: long-term, mid-term, and short-term. The key to successful planning for all three time frames is to begin by developing a focused and unified organizational vision that is shared by all units in the organization. That vision is then used to structure all planning, strategies, and activities across the organization, so all departments are working for a common goal, rather than their own unit goals (Reading, 2002).

Most experts agree that "vision" is the defining characteristic of a leader—that it separates leaders from mere managers. The Merriam-Webster dictionary defines "vision" as "the act or power of imagination . . . unusual discernment or foresight" (2012). Applying that idea to business, Wilson refined the definition to "a coherent, powerful statement of what the business can, and should be, X years hence" (2003, p. 56). Wilson argues that a well-crafted vision (a) provides organizations with both a direction and a destination, (b) should be powerful enough to inspire managers and employees, and (c) should be specific enough to be considered a preview of the company's activities for a given time period.

In addition to vision, most organizations also have a mission statement. In some cases, the vision and mission statement are the same thing, but in others, the organizational mission statement is a more narrow statement of the wider vision. Usually, mission statements include a statement of (a) what the company does, that is, what its functions are; (b) who its stakeholders are, meaning for whose benefit it carries out those functions; and (c) how the organization goes about fulfilling its mission (Pfeiffer, 1991). Research shows that most organizational mission statements also include references to survival, growth and profitability, the company's philosophy, the company's self-concept, and its goal for its public image (Pearce & David, 1987).

### Long-Range Planning

Once an organization has identified its vision and crafted its mission statement, the next step is long-range planning. Long-range planning focuses on operationalizing the organization's vision and mission statements by specifying the geographic and market scope the company wants to control over time and the goals it wants to achieve (Tregoe & Tobia, 1991). Long-range planning includes consideration of the environment in which the organization will operate, such as market conditions and technologies, and the tangible and intangible resources the organization or individual controls and can use to realize the vision.

Among organizational experts, the focus on organizational resources as part of the planning process is known as the Resource-Based View (RBV). The Resource-Based View of organizations sees each organization as a collection of unique resources that it can use to develop and carry out strategies. Resources fall into one of two types, property resources and knowledge resources (Chan-Olmsted, 2003). Property resources include tangible things such as facilities, technology, and capital, while knowledge resources are intangible resources including knowledge, talent, and reputation.

The RBV approach to long-term planning emphasizes a firm's ability to successfully utilize its unique resources to compete, particularly emphasizing those resources that are rare, nonsubstitutable, valuable, and difficult for other organizations to imitate. Of the two types of resources, knowledge resources are considered more valuable to long-term planning because they are not easily copied or developed by competitors. A company or individual who focuses on RBV strategies is using knowledge barriers to protect themselves from competition (Barney & Hesterly, 2001).

Regardless of the approach a company or individual takes to long-range planning, long-range thinking has to be fairly general and based on assumptions about the future environment (Tregoe & Tobia, 1991). Therefore, long-range plans aren't effective as tools for daily action. Long-range planning precedes strategic planning, but strategic planning itself is actually mid-range planning. Mid-range planning is much more concrete and action-focused than long-range planning.

## Mid-Range Planning

Mid-range planning, also known as strategic planning, consists of both content and process (Rajagopalan, Rasheed, & Datta, 1994). "Content" refers to the issues or factors that will be considered during the strategic planning process, the nature of the decisions that will come out of the planning process, and how much those decisions will improve the organization's performance.

"Process" concerns *how* an organization goes about developing its strategic plan. Researchers categorize organizational strategic planning processes in many different ways, so there is no one agreed-upon way to do it. But it's helpful to look at some of the different processes that companies use.

One study identified four general approaches to strategic planning processes (Rajagopalan et al., 1994): (a) a rational/analytical process, which tends to be centralized, focused on organizational goals, and based on an assumption of a predictable organizational environment; (b) a political/power/behavioral process, which typically occurs in complex and unpredictable organizations where power is dispersed, making it necessary to negotiate between groups with different priorities; (c) an organizational/bureaucratic process, which is used in fairly predictable organizational environments where priorities are well established, but tend to be set at the departmental level so that there are few shared organization-wide goals; and (d) an organizational adaption process, which is used by companies in complex, unpredictable environments where power is decentralized and rapidly changing business conditions make it necessary to constantly change the organization's goals.

The important question, of course, is how strategic planning processes affect the company or individual's success and outcomes. In the 21st century, this has become a surprisingly controversial question. That controversy is particularly relevant to people who expect to work in the media industry.

Strategic planning has been accepted as the core of good management for decades. That strategic planning might actually be bad for success would be considered heresy in most management circles. But since the Great Recession of 2008/2009, that idea has become less revolutionary. More than a few management experts have argued that because of the tremendous uncertainty and economic turmoil in the global business environment since the turn of the 21st century, strategic planning is less useful than in the past and may even be dysfunctional for some businesses (Lublin & Mattioli, 2010; Wolfe, 2010). No one has argued against the need for strategizing, but the question is whether locking a company into a long-range, or even mid-range, plan will reduce the organization's flexibility and creativity and slow response times when new opportunities and threats appear.

In the media industry, that argument has power. Many companies consider 10 years the long-range planning time frame and 5 years the frame for mid-range plans. But in the current media environment, 5 years is an eternity. New technologies with the potential to disrupt traditional media business models have erupted into the marketplace every 1-to-2 years since the new millennium began. Just since 2010, such widely used social applications as Pinterest and Instagram, and new technologies such as 4G mobile network service—which makes it easier to stream video to mobile devices—have been launched into the market. In the first 3 years after Apple opened its App store in July 2008, the number of available apps rose from 500 to around 425,000. In the following 3 years, by June 2014, that number had climbed to more than 1.2 million with 40 billion downloads. Any one of those apps could turn out to be the next big thing and the next media market disrupter. What value is a 5-year plan to media companies when the next year is likely to bring two or three potentially disruptive technologies into the market?

These arguments notwithstanding, many management experts still believe strategic planning is a critically important process. They counter that every business needs to know where it's going and have a road map for getting there, but that managers also must recognize there may be curves in the road along the way. Flexibility and quick reflexes are necessary to stay on top of a changing business environment, but not having a destination and a route will make it hard to get anywhere.

Regardless of the current debates about the value of long-range and strategic planning, there is little, if any, debate about the central role short-term planning and project management play in 21st century management.

### Short-Term Planning and Project Planning

Putting an organization's strategic plan into action or responding to a sudden shift in business conditions requires specific steps that occur in relatively short time frames. Just what those steps should be varies, of course, according to the specific organization and its situation. Regardless, one of the great challenges for any manager is to successfully execute a plan.

While there is no single prescription for successful short-term planning, one critical step is setting goals. A goal is a clear statement about what is going to be accomplished. While that sounds easy, it isn't, and business leaders often fail to do it effectively. For example, the majority of newspaper publishers in one survey said they had invested in developing online websites with the goal of making their digital editions "successful" (Saksena & Hollifield, 2002). But when pressed, few of the publishers could say what they meant by "successful." Such fuzzy goals are rarely achieved because there is no way of knowing when the goal has been accomplished—or not.

One approach to setting goals uses the acronym SMART: Specific, Measurable, Attainable, Related to the organization's larger goal or strategy, and Time-bound (Nelson & Economy, 1996). That is, when you set a goal, you should make sure that goal contains all of the SMART characteristics. A media manager who sets SMART goals will be able to measure progress toward his or her larger goal and change course quickly when necessary.

## PROJECT MANAGEMENT

Although executing any strategic plan requires many different actions and activities, one of the most important activities is the project. Projects are so critical to organizational development that there is a management career specialty called "Project Management" that requires training and certification. Project planning falls into the category of short-term planning, although some projects may require years to complete.

In media industries, a great deal of production work is organized through projects. Examples of production projects include new technologies, films and TV series, games, apps, and music albums. But major organizational undertakings such as reorganization, adoption, or development of innovations (see Chapter 6), movement into a new market, or the startup or acquisition of new ventures typically are organized as "projects." Since the 1980s, companies that operate in strict time-to-market environments, such as media companies, have become particularly reliant on projects as a means of moving themselves toward strategic goals (Gray & Larson, 2000).

### What Is a Project?

Among experts, projects are defined as "unique undertakings . . . composed of interdependent activities . . . [that] create a quality deliverable . . . involve multiple resources . . . are driven by competing constraints . . . [but] are *not* synonymous with the products of the project" (Webster & Knutson, 2011, pp. 4–5). In other words, a project is the process of creation rather than the creation itself. Further, it is defined by a clear starting point and an equally clear ending point. A project is not an ongoing process.

One of the biggest challenges in project management is to ensure from the start that a project is clearly linked to the organization's long-term goals and strategic plan and that its level of priority within the organization is clear to everyone. Research shows that in medium and large organizations, project selection and prioritization are rarely linked to the company's strategic plan (Gray & Larson, 2000). Organizations that lurch from project to project as every new idea appears wind up squandering resources on actions unrelated to their long-term goals. The same is true for individuals in the freelance market who never become expert in any single production skill because they take any job that comes along.

Projects are a good approach when tasks are so large, or require such a variety of resources, that no one unit in the organization can handle the assignment. They also are appropriate when outside pressures require the organization to focus on different critical activities simultaneously, or when the environment is so uncertain, unfamiliar, or complex that a single team is unlikely to meet the challenge alone (Cleland & Ireland, 2002).

Projects tend to develop a common set of problems that must be managed. These include scope, quality, schedule, budget, resources, and risks (Webster & Knutson, 2011). The *scope* of the project is the question of how large the project will be and what elements it will include and exclude. *Quality* concerns requirements for the quality of the final outcome. *Schedule* refers to the amount of time the project manager has to completion and the complexity of time-order factors in the project. *Time-order factors* refers to the parts of the project that must be completed before another stage or part of the project can begin. It also requires an understanding of the implications for the overall project if a timetable is *not* met somewhere in those time-order linkages.

*Budget*, of course, refers to the total amount of money available for the project and for those parts of the project that will have their own separate budgets. *Resources* includes everything needed for the project: time, money, equipment, talent, etc. If you need to develop a video game as an ancillary product for a soon-to-be-released film, one of the resources you need is skilled game designers and developers. Even if you have the money to hire them, if you can't find enough qualified designers to hire, you have a major resource issue.

Finally, in project management, *risk* is defined as any uncertainty that might "have an impact on at least one project objective" (Project Management Institute, 2008, p. 275). Such uncertainties can be caused by a number of factors including the uniqueness and complexity of the project, the assumptions and constraints surrounding it, the people involved, changes that are required as the project develops, or the dependencies that exist between different parts of the project (Hillson, 2011). It's important to see that the definition of risk focuses not just on negative events that would affect project outcomes. *Risk* also includes possible missed opportunities that might have made the outcomes of the project even better had they been seized.

There are a number of different approaches to project management. The *traditional* or *waterfall* approach to project management is to design the project as a series of specific phases (Webster & Knutson, 2011). Each phase is planned, launched, completed, and evaluated before the project moves on to the next phase. The production and testing of a pilot episode for a proposed television series would be an example of the traditional approach to project management. In contrast, the *iterative* approach sees the project as more of a spiral of phases than a waterfall, with some phases of the project being revisited and adjusted based on the outcomes of later phases. Transmedia productions of programs, such as *The Walking Dead*, are an example of the iterative approach. The production of webisodes and other ancillary materials depend on developments in the production of the main series—but also may shape the main series if something in the ancillary materials gains a viral following.

A third approach to project design is called the *evolving* approach and focuses on prototyping and beta-testing products—or otherwise engaging in *fail fast* strategies. This is a common strategy in development of new technologies and applications. The evolving approach is more tolerant of risks and mistakes than previous project management models and is more likely to invite a project's clients to participate in co-creation as part of the project. Some video game developers use the co-creation or *prosumer* model in game design, and even news organizations are turning to the evolving or prosumer project model as way of organizing coverage of breaking news events and major disasters.

## PLANNING FOR INTERNATIONAL PROJECTS

One of the most significant projects that any media enterprise can undertake is expanding its operations into the global marketplace. Today, in the digital age, when content, technologies, and business ideas move around the globe at the speed of light, fewer and fewer media businesses operate without a global component. While legacy media companies such as local newspapers, broadcast stations, and city magazines may still be almost entirely local, emerging media ideas often must go global almost immediately if they hope to hang on to their markets.

Popular new digital business concepts such as Pandora, Spotify, and Instagram, to name just a few, went from being startups to global companies in virtually a single bound. Instagram, for example, went live to the public in October 2010. By November 2011, the fledgling company was already in Japan and moving fast to get into other Asian markets, even while fending off the global explosion of copycat companies setting up in countries where Instagram was not yet operating (Tsotsis, 2011).

There are other reasons why media producers seek international markets. Information products—both news and entertainment—have specific, economic characteristics that make it necessary for media companies to expand their markets as much as possible (Priest, 1994). Among those characteristics:

- *There is a lot of risk and uncertainty in media production.* Media producers have to decide how much they will invest to produce content without being able to predict audience and advertiser demand for that content. During the summer of 2014, for example, film box office sales were the worst they had been in 17 years, adjusted for inflation. Experts cited a number of causes including the emergence of competing technologies and special sporting events that summer. But producers of the films released during the summer 2014 season had greenlighted those projects and absorbed all the costs of producing them long before it was possible to estimate likely ticket sales. It also is almost impossible to test-market media products. You cannot produce only a few minutes of a film or one chapter of a book and ask people how they like it before you decide whether to pay the full cost of production. Even apps must be nearly fully developed before testing can start, even if additional functionality is to be added later. The inability to test market media content greatly increases the risks and uncertainties of media production.
- *Media have high "first-copy" costs.* In other words, almost all of the costs of producing media products come from producing the very first copy. In the digital age, reproducing that copy costs almost nothing. Because of high first-copy costs, the more people the media company can reach with the product, the more likely it becomes that the producer eventually will break even on his or her production costs. That makes it desirable to distribute to audiences around the globe.
- *Media products vary in their relevance to audience members.* Demand for media products is hard to predict because what appeals to one person may not appeal to another. That makes it hard to forecast the demand for a media product before it is produced. Wide distribution increases the chances that enough people will buy it to allow the producer to make a profit.

As a result of the naturally global nature of digital media, many media professionals and entrepreneurs will find themselves working for global media companies in their first jobs after graduation. More will find themselves working globally as they advance through their careers. Even companies that don't own subsidiaries overseas often have employees working overseas, or have employees who specialize in managing the international marketing and distribution of content that was first produced for the domestic market. Media sectors such as the film, music, and video gaming industries have distributed their products globally from the beginning. Those industries build calculations about the global appeal of each product into the production budget for that project.

Finally, anyone who uses the Internet for content distribution is making their content available internationally, whether or not that's part of the plan. If entrepreneurs never consciously evaluate the potential of international markets, they may permanently lose those markets to more nimble competitors quick to copy a good idea.

### Management Considerations in Global Markets

Managing global media projects offers unique opportunities and special challenges. Companies operating across national borders must serve audiences, users, and advertisers with widely different needs and tastes. When media companies expand overseas, organizational structures become more complicated and workforces become more diverse in language and culture. Media managers must understand global media markets and be able to work in multicultural environments. They must understand the risks and advantages of international expansion and become sensitive to the complexities of international politics, economics, laws, and business practices. Finally, in today's environment, a move into international markets means that media managers must develop a heightened sensitivity to international events and engage in an entirely new level of security planning.

A media corporation expanding into international markets immediately faces the question of how to structure its foreign investments. Decisions about structure affect the level of risk the company takes in its new venture, the human and financial resources it needs to support them, and the financial returns it can expect. A media company usually must consider at least three key structural elements: (a) the ownership structures used for foreign investments, (b) the effect of overseas investments on a media company's overall corporate structure, and

(c) the management issues that structure day-to-day operations in a new business environment.

### Ownership Structures

The simplest approach to globalization is to set up an overseas operation as a wholly owned subsidiary—a company that the parent company owns and operates itself. This makes some operations easier, simplifying decision making and leaving little room for misunderstandings among partners. However, running a wholly owned subsidiary also means that the parent company cannot learn about the new market from a partner with expertise in that market. A company also shoulders all the financial risks of the foreign investment when it doesn't have a partner.

Therefore, many companies use *joint ventures* as a way to expand overseas. A joint venture is when two or more companies share ownership in a venture. Joint ventures spread the risks of market entry or product development among partners. They also allow companies to draw on the technical or local expertise of their partners. Having a partner who understands the local culture particularly helps media companies make sure their content is relevant to the local audience. For this reason, newspaper companies investing overseas often use joint ventures, leaving day-to-day editorial control to the domestic partner. International joint ventures also have become common in film and television production as a way to avoid national and regional import quotas on foreign films and programs.

Such joint ventures have downsides, however. Risks are shared, but so are profits. Management costs are high because key strategic decisions must be negotiated with the partner. International joint ventures often suffer from friction between the partners over differences in national and professional cultures, expectations, and business methods. As a result, research on joint ventures across all industries shows that most have a relatively short lifespan (Kogut, 1989).

A third strategy for foreign-market entry is *licensing*, in which a company develops a product and then sells to another company the rights to produce a version of the product in a specific market. Generally, licensing agreements restrict what the licensee can do, requiring that the licensed product be faithful to the original in terms of design and quality.

Licensing has become common in many media industry sectors. Magazines that are produced in multiple languages often are licensed to local publishers. Generally, the original owner who sells the license provides the majority of the content, with the licensee hiring local writers to translate that copy into the appropriate language and produce enough local copy to give the magazine a local flavor.

In television, licensing or *format programming*, as it's called in the industry, has become increasingly important as cable and broadcast networks seek proven program concepts. There are local versions of *American Idol* broadcast in at least a dozen countries under different names, while programs such as *Sesame Street, Wheel of Fortune, Survivor, Ugly Betty, Who Wants to Be a Millionaire*, and even various soap operas have had various localized versions playing in other countries. In format programming, usually the structure, characters, and story lines are similar to the original, although hosts or actors are local and some adjustments may be made to the original concept to increase cultural relevance. In the South African–licensed version of *Sesame Street*, for example, an HIV-positive character was introduced in 2003 to increase AIDS awareness and education among children in that country, while versions of the program that air in Israel, Palestine, and Northern Ireland feature Muppets that teach tolerance of religious and cultural differences.

Licensing is a low-risk market-entry strategy, allowing owners of a media concept to get revenues from overseas markets with minimal investment. The local licensee makes most of the investment and takes most of the risk. On the other hand, the licensee gains the benefit of buying an already successful concept, thereby reducing the risks of original media production. Additionally, with some licensed products such as magazines, the original owner produces most of the content, reducing first-copy production costs.

The downside of licensing, however, is that neither the original owner nor the licensee makes as much money as they would if they owned the product outright. The original owner has the additional risk that licensees may do something that harms the brand. For example, if the licensee does a bad job with a product, local audiences may reject it, costing the original owner future revenues from that country. Similarly, because audiences rarely know a product is licensed, irresponsible or unethical behavior by the licensee may harm the reputation of the original product and the company that owns it.

### Managerial Structures for Foreign Investments

Once a company decides what type of foreign investment to make, it can choose from four basic management models to oversee the operation: (a) international, (b) multinational, (c) global, and (d) transnational. In the *international* model, a media company focuses on its domestic market and creates content with those audiences in mind. It later exports the product to overseas markets to generate additional sales, perhaps making a few minor changes in order to appeal to foreign audiences. Television series such as *Law and Order* and *Dallas*, created for the U.S. market and then sold in syndication overseas, illustrate this model.

In the *multinational* model, the parent media corporation sets up subsidiaries in foreign countries, but allows those subsidiaries to develop local products. The subsidiaries are supposed to serve their local markets, despite being owned by a global company. For example, in 2013, Viacom's MTV operated 66 MTV-branded channels in more than 160 countries worldwide. Most featured local hosts and focused primarily on local music artists.

In the *global* model, a company develops products that it believes will have global appeal, knowing in advance that they will be distributed globally. Disney Corporation uses this model for many of its products, developing products, stories, and characters that will appeal to audiences worldwide.

In the past two decades, the U.S. film industry also has moved to the global model. In its early years, Hollywood greenlighted films based on their appeal to U.S. audiences, because the U.S. market provided the bulk of box office sales. Films were released first in the United States, premiering in foreign markets about 6 weeks later. Today, the potential appeal of a film to foreign audiences is an important consideration in studios' decisions to approve projects. Films, such as comedies, that may be less relevant to foreign audiences generally get much smaller production budgets. Major films are now released simultaneously in theaters worldwide since the global market is on the verge of becoming more important to Hollywood than the domestic market.

The *transnational* model is a network approach to global expansion. Companies charge their overseas subsidiaries with developing products that serve their surrounding markets, while sending their best ideas back to the parent company for global development and distribution. Conversely, the subsidiaries are expected to take ideas from the company's headquarters or other subsidiaries and adapt them for sale in the country or region the subsidiary serves. The transnational model is based on a fluid exchange of ideas, knowledge, and products across the company's subsidiaries and markets.

The German media company Bertelsmann may be the best example in the media industry of the transnational model. Bertelsmann, which has operations in 50 countries and generates more than 65% of its revenue outside of its home market of Germany, is a major producer of television content, magazines, and books; owns a major global music rights management subsidiary; and provides a variety of digital business services. Strategically, the company is focused on expansion in high-growth regions of the world, while seeking to develop products with global potential. The global-for-local and local-for-global emphasis in product development is the hallmark of a transnational model.

### Structural Issues in Managing International Operations

When a media firm launches a global project or company, all of the management functions and challenges discussed throughout this book take on additional complexity because market conditions, regulations, and cultures change as you cross borders.

Since about 1980, major media corporations have been focusing their overseas investments in less-developed countries undergoing major political and economic changes. The reason is simple: Media markets in developed countries are saturated, and market share among existing players is shrinking. Thus, media companies seeking growth have to go where the media market is in flux, population demographics are changing, and the economy appears likely to grow. In the 1990s and early part of the 21st century, Central Europe was a major focus of global media investment following the fall of the Eastern Bloc in 1989. More recently, attention has shifted to India, China, and other Asian markets, as well as some parts of Latin America, such as Brazil.

Moving into countries that are undergoing major economic and political changes offers the best investment potential, but also carries the greatest risks. Economic change, including economic growth, often creates some degree of social and political turmoil, causing business conditions to change in a variety of different ways. Business regulations, for example, including media laws, may be rewritten multiple times in a short period. In recent years, after loosening its control over the media in the early 1990s, the Russian government has moved to reign in the independent media once again. Similarly, nations that don't have strong knowledge-based economies often choose not to enforce intellectual property and patent laws (Hollifield, Vlad, & Becker, 2003). Media and technology companies that do business in such countries are at higher risk of having their content pirated or their technologies stolen. Given the high first-copy costs of media production and the fact that consumers generally buy a media product only once, losses to piracy can quickly offset the potential advantages of international investment.

While emerging markets are attractive to media investors for their growth potential, that potential also attracts stiff competition. Even a casual reading of major media corporate annual reports shows many of them targeting the same "growth markets" (Bertlesmann, 2013; Time Warner, 2013; Viacom, 2013; Walt Disney Company, 2013). Consequently, competition among media companies may initially be higher than the buying power the local population can support. If that happens, overseas projects may lose money, and managers must be prepared to invest in the market for years with little, if any, profit.

Demographic characteristics in emerging markets also require careful consideration. Literacy rates, language differences, and the distribution of wealth across populations affect the size of the available audience for any given media product. In many countries, there are large economic disparities between different ethnic and cultural groups. The actual market for a media product in a country where the population speaks more than one language is limited to the speakers of the language in which a media product is produced. If one language group controls the economic power in a country, audience members who speak other languages may be less desirable to advertisers, even if they outnumber the more powerful group.

Even where language is not an issue, in countries where a small percentage of the population controls the wealth, the actual audience of interest to advertisers is much smaller than the size of the population. For print and Web-based media products, the potential market is limited to the literate audience and to those with enough income to afford high-speed broadband connections in the home. Such factors must be carefully considered when analyzing the market for overseas investments.

As countries change economically and politically, social values often change as well. That, in turn, affects demand for media. For example, during the 1970s and 1980s when women in the United States began moving out of the home and into the workforce in large numbers, the U.S. daytime television audience shrank sharply, while markets for new types of content for women were created. Expansion of education and economic power in society usually results in more demand for media, while restricted opportunities for targeted groups reduce demand.

In short, media managers must be sensitive to shifts in the political and economic landscape in all markets, but particularly in countries going through political and economic change. Change, even positive change, often creates political and social instability as the result of rising expectations and shifts in the balance of power among groups in society. Instability creates significant security risks for overseas operations and personnel, as shown in the Middle East following the Arab Spring of 2010, and several nations in Southeast Asia, including India, that have been enjoying rapid economic growth.

In the 21st century, an increasingly important element of international management is security and disaster planning. Although security is critical in domestic management, international operations may face a wider range of threats, depending on their location. Those threats include political unrest, terrorism, widespread organized crime in some countries that may involve police and other local authorities, cyberattacks, local cultures of bribery and corruption, and the increased risk of natural disasters associated with climate change. Because of such threats, risk management for international projects may include the need to contract for around-the-clock security for employees, establish off-site secure backup for data and other critical systems, and develop disaster management plans that include plans for the rapid evacuation of all personnel.

### Product Development for Foreign Markets

Once a media company or producer decides to launch an international project, one of the key questions is what types of content are likely to succeed in foreign markets. As noted earlier, a key characteristic of media products is that their relevance to individual audience members varies widely; this is especially apparent in international markets. Research shows that when things such as production values are equal, audiences will favor the media products closest to reflecting their own cultures and values (Straubhaar, 1991).

Some types of content, such as comedy, are particularly difficult to export even between countries sharing languages and cultural traditions such as the United States and Great Britain. Such content sells at deeply discounted prices in international markets.

Often the differences between cultures are so subtle they may be difficult for a nonnative manager to recognize—but they still can spell the difference between success and failure. For example, magazines featuring recipes may have problems as they expand globally because of differences in tastes, cultural acceptance of foods, or availability of ingredients. Lifestyles, such as apartment living as opposed to suburban living, will affect readers' interests and needs. Even accepted medical and scientific beliefs vary across countries.

Similarly, advertisements and layouts must be screened to avoid offending local readers and viewers. In Western Europe, for example, newspapers and magazines often illustrate advertisements and editorial copy with pictures of topless women in order to appeal to male readers. U.S. audiences would consider such publications risqué, which would make obtaining distribution in grocery and mass merchandise retail stores difficult. Even the colors used in publications and productions can signal different things in different countries, as can such commonplace things as hand gestures and items of clothing.

The promotion process may also change as companies move across borders. Promotional slogans and even the name of a publication or program may not translate well into other languages. Common U.S. promotional strategies such as event sponsorship, live broadcasts, and other techniques for increasing audiences may be impossible or unacceptable. Similarly, in many less-developed and transitional countries, it is difficult, if not impossible to collect ratings and readership data, which makes it hard to sell advertising or do audience analysis and target marketing.

### Human Resource Management

One of the greatest challenges in global media management is managing people. Media products are *talent products*, meaning that the quality of individual media products almost wholly depends on the knowledge, experience, and talent of its creators (Reca, 2006). Consequently, successfully hiring, retaining, and managing people is critical in media companies, no matter the company's locale.

Among the key differences media managers can expect to encounter are differences in communication style and work practices. International management and cross-cultural communication theorists have identified a number of ways in which cultures differ and which affect communication styles. Among these is *power distance*, the degree of interpersonal power between supervisors and employees. Power distance affects the level of formality expected in communication (Hofstede, 1980). Another dimension is *individualism*, which focuses on the degree to which society values the individual good over the collective good. Cultures that value individualism, such as the United States, will be more likely to accept confrontational communication styles than will those in collectivist cultures such as found in many Asian countries (Triandis & Albert, 1987).

There also can be differences in nonverbal communication and behavioral norms. Nonverbal behaviors such as personal-space norms, touching behaviors, eye contact, table manners, and dress can differ greatly and create misunderstandings between colleagues. In many countries, comments and behaviors that would constitute sexual harassment in the United States are common in the office environment. In countries with strong divisions between genders, ethnic groups, political parties, or religions, intolerance can be an issue in the workplace affecting working relationships, job assignments, and the ability of management to hire and promote strictly on the basis of merit.

Such challenges are not limited to interpersonal behaviors. Professional cultures, which include professional ethics, routines, and expectations, also differ greatly across countries. For example, journalists in many countries view their role in media and society differently than do journalists in the United States. Consequently, their professional ethics, standards, and expectations differ. Such differences can make it difficult to create a company-wide set of ethics and standards. However, in the era of global communication, news of scandals in one overseas subsidiary can be expected to spread rapidly and tarnish the reputation of the entire organization. Witness the stain on the reputation of the global media corporation News Corp. after journalists in one of its London newspapers were caught hacking the phones of celebrities, politicians, and even private citizens in Britain—leading to the arrests of multiple News Corp. employees.

Finally, expectations and regulations about such things as employee productivity, salary and benefits, and work hours can vary widely across countries. France's official work week is 35 hours, for example, while the average employee in Scandinavia, Belgium, and Germany puts in just over 37 hours per week (European Industrial Relations Observatory, 2011). Media companies in less-developed countries often are significantly over-staffed when compared to commercial media operations in developed countries, and expectations for the productivity of individual employees can be considerably lower. In many nations, regulations restrict the ability of managers to layoff, fire, reassign, or even reschedule staff.

Leadership of global media companies is thus complex and challenging, and selecting the senior leadership for overseas subsidiaries is a crucial decision. At least two possibilities exist: (a) hiring or promoting someone from within the overseas market, or (b) sending an expatriate manager from the parent company to run the overseas operation.

Companies that send out a manager often find tensions arising between the "foreign" manager and the local staff. Because the manager is familiar with the parent company, its expectations, and its operational procedures, relationships between corporate headquarters and the subsidiary tend to be smoother. Conversely, when senior management is hired locally in an overseas market, relationships with the local staff may be better, but, frequently, operational and strategic problems arise between the parent company and the subsidiary. Some global media corporations split the difference, sending expatriate managers overseas to run the business side of their media operations, while hiring the senior editorial staff from within the country to direct the content side.

The difficulties of multicultural leadership also affect domestic media operations. As the producers of talent products, global media companies seek to hire the best and most gifted people wherever they may be found, transferring them between subsidiaries and countries as needed. Consequently, people from all over the world can be found working side by side in the offices of such global media giants as CNN, News Corp., *The Wall Street Journal*, and *The New York Times*. Foreign language fluency and knowledge of—and sensitivity to—differences between nations and cultures will be increasingly important job requirements for future media managers, whatever their location.

### Financial Management

Prior to making overseas investments, corporations undertake detailed cost-benefit analyses and develop projections for earning financial returns. The financial plan must include higher operational costs associated with international travel to, and communication with, the overseas subsidiary. Experienced media managers know that international investments may take years to turn a profit, particularly in less-developed countries or countries going through transitions where the media markets tend to be oversaturated, advertising markets may be underdeveloped, and consumers have limited discretionary income with which to buy media and advertised products.

Detailing how to capitalize an international investment until it becomes profitable is key to the success of any international project, as is setting goals that include periodic progress reviews. If an overseas market does not develop, it may be wiser to sell or close the operation, rather than to keep funding it. Media managers should establish guides to determine that stop-loss point *before* they invest.

Even after operations are established, financial management remains complex. Media managers in transitional countries report having problems finding experienced financial managers capable of helping their companies survive (Hollifield, Becker, & Vlad, 2006; Hollifield, Vlad, & Becker, 2004). Accounting rules and tax laws often differ greatly between countries, sometimes making it difficult to reconcile the subsidiary's approach to financial reporting with the one the parent company must use. In countries where foreign media companies are required to set up a joint venture with local partners, the local partner may be undercapitalized, meaning the foreign investor must invest a disproportionate amount of the capital to keep the operation afloat relative to its ownership share in the joint venture.

Risks associated with different nations' monetary policies and fluctuating foreign exchange rates further complicate things. If a country suddenly experiences rapid inflation, or if its currency's value falls on foreign exchange markets, then any media projects or investments in that country immediately lose value for accounting purposes. That can affect the parent company's finances and the resources available for other projects.

Of course, specialists do the technical work of international financial management. But in the 21st century, more and more media projects and companies will seek international distribution; will need some level of international talent, supplies, or production; or will find themselves facing competition from international media sources. Thus, media professionals in all sectors of the industry need to understand and monitor international markets and trends.

## SUMMARY

Planning and project management are critical skills for media managers. The rapid pace of change in the industry has made long-term planning increasingly difficult, which, in turn, has made mid-term strategic planning, short-term planning, and project management even more important.

The key to all successful planning is to have a clear vision of what the organization or, in the case of entrepreneurs, what the individual wants to achieve. That vision should be clearly stated through a concrete mission statement and should then structure all plans and projects. It is the leader's task to constantly check to ensure that all long-term, mid-term, and short-term plans are in line with the vision and mission, and that all projects are steps toward achieving those plans.

Long-term planning typically focuses on identifying an organization's or individual's unique abilities or resources and figuring out how to best exploit them for success. Mid-term planning, often called strategic planning, focuses on a 5- or 6-year timeframe and involves setting a series of goals to be achieved during that time that contribute to the organization's mission. Although strategic planning has long been considered the cornerstone of organizational planning, today, the value of 5-year plans is being questioned by some who fear such plans may make managers dangerously slow to respond to opportunities and threats (Lublin & Mattioli, 2010; Wolfe, 2010).

Few, however, question the need for short-term planning, which generally takes the form of the tactics or projects that managers use to make progress toward larger strategic goals and the organizational mission. Project management, a form of short-term planning, is now so important to management that it is considered a specialized career in itself. In the media industries, production of many types of content such as TV series, documentaries, films, video games, and albums are done as projects.

There are different ways to design projects. In some projects, one phase leads to the next; while in others, each stage affects the others so that the project is constantly being adjusted until fully completed. A third approach is to see the project as continuously evolving and never finished until the company abandons it for something else. Regardless of the type of project, project management means addressing the challenges of project scope, quality, schedule, budget, resources, and risks.

In the digital age, one type of project that many media organizations and professionals will undertake is globalization. Thanks to global digital networks, content, technologies, and good business ideas spread rapidly. Media innovators need to expand into global markets almost immediately if they don't want to lose their ideas to copycats. Popular content that is not distributed globally as soon as it's released domestically is likely to be quickly pirated. Finally, with high first-copy costs and growing competition for audiences, the economics of information make it increasingly important for media producers to expand their markets as widely as possible.

But as they cross borders, media professionals and organizations face increasingly complex management challenges: Organizational structures change. Cultural differences and different audience tastes complicate product development and promotion. Differences in customs, cultures, communication styles, and professional standards mean that media managers must be sensitive personnel managers and keep in mind the importance of keeping talented employees.

Moving into international markets carries many risks. Media markets in countries that are growing economically provide excellent opportunities but they also bring challenges. Typically, media competition is higher than the local population can support. Business laws and regulations may change as the economy grows, and intellectual property protection often is weak. Most importantly, rapid economic growth may set off political unrest and encourage various forms of corruption. Keeping an overseas project alive may require substantial capital resources and patience.

Even so, the most successful media companies and entrepreneurs are willing to take on those challenges because they recognize the importance of international markets. Consequently, it will be increasingly important for media professionals at all levels to develop their understanding of the global media market and their abilities to work with colleagues from diverse national, ethnic, political, religious, and cultural backgrounds.

The next chapter will explore the management of another type of project that is now so common among media companies as to be almost impossible for media managers to avoid: the management of innovations and new-technology projects.

---

### CASE 5.1: THE CASE OF THE DYING NEWSPAPER

Shannon Jolly has just been appointed Executive Editor of the *University Daily Tribune* (*UDT*). Her 12-month term in the position starts July 1, and she knows she is in for a challenging year.

The *UDT* is the 125-year-old independent, nonprofit, free-circulation student daily newspaper serving Northwest University's (NWU) student body of 45,000. The newspaper is owned by a nonprofit educational foundation that is overseen by a volunteer board of directors. Most of the directors were newspaper owners or publishers when they joined the board, but all but a few are now long-retired from the industry. The average length of membership among board members on the *UDT* board is 28 years, and the average age of board members is 77—although several board members are in their late 80s and two are in their early 90s. Only three of the 35 board members are still active in the industry. When the *UDT* board was interviewing applicants for Executive Editor, one board member had asked Shannon whether she agreed with him that "the Internet was just a fad" and that the public would eventually "abandon online news and return to traditional printed newspapers."

*UDT* is managed on a daily basis by a full-time professional publisher, assisted by a staff of several other full-time professionals. The publisher has been at the paper for 30 years, and gets along extremely well with the board members, to whom he reports. He sees eye-to-eye with the board on most matters, and they appreciate his conservative, traditionalist approach to the management of the paper. *UDT*'s professionals oversee the newspaper's sales, production, circulation, and operations, and one is assigned to serve as an advisor in the newsroom. All of *UDT*'s full-time staff members started their careers in small town, weekly newspapers in the region, and most moved to *UDT* after only a few years of professional newspaper experience. *UDT*'s editorial staff, however, is made up entirely of students, and final editorial control is supposed to rest in their hands—or more specifically, in Shannon's hands, now that she's been given the top job. Circulation is free. The newspaper is placed in newspaper boxes all over campus and in selected locations in town. At its peak, *UDT* printed 25,000 copies per day, 5 days a week.

Until 10 years ago, *UDT* was a financially strong operation. NWU is located in a vibrant university town, population 120,000, three hours from the nearest city. The University is by far the largest employer in town with nearly 10,000 employees, and area businesses are heavily dependent on NWU students, faculty, and staff for customers. As a result, local businesses historically advertised heavily in the *UDT*, giving the student newspaper a "profit" margin that would have made many commercial newspaper corporations blush. As a nonprofit, the newspaper has reinvested its "profits" back into the paper's operations.

Unfortunately, however, the rosy financial picture has changed. Advertising revenues started sliding in 2003 as the Internet began gaining traction, and plunged sharply after the start of the Great Recession in 2008. Circulation trends for *UDT* have been even worse. A readership survey undertaken by the newspaper in 2005 showed that about a third of NWU's students read the paper at least several times a week, usually reading it while waiting for class to start. Shannon's older brother Bill, who was Executive Editor of *UDT* in 2004, talked of finding almost every classroom littered with discarded copies of the *Tribune*, left behind by students earlier in the day. These days, Shannon sees few such signs of the newspaper's popularity. She feels lucky if she finds a single discarded copy of *UDT* in one of her classes late in the day. Instead of reading the student daily while they wait for class, Shannon's fellow students busy themselves with their laptops, tablets, smartphones, and MP3 players. *UDT* has cut its print run down to 5,000 per day, but most of those remain unread in the newspaper boxes, waiting to be collected for recycling. The paper has had a website for the past 5 years, but traffic is low—only about 200 unique visitors per day. Previous editors have focused on producing copy for the print run, shoveling the print stories onto the website only as an afterthought once the print edition was at the printer.

Given the paper's declining readership and the growing number of alternative advertising options available, it's not surprising that local advertisers aren't returning to *UDT* in great numbers, even though the economy has improved. For the time being, *UDT* is still "profitable," that is, it still brings in more revenue than it has expenses on a yearly basis. The publisher has told the board, however, that he doesn't expect that to last much longer. In fact, at the last board meeting, he told the directors he expects *UDT* to be losing money in another 2 years.

As Shannon sees it, the job of saving the venerable student daily has fallen to her. If the publisher is right and *UDT* will start losing money the year after next, it is imperative that Shannon take drastic steps *this* year to start turning the newspaper around. Shannon knows that audiences and advertisers don't change behaviors in a day. Even if Shannon makes the right changes, it will be several more years before *UDT*'s revenues and circulation improve. If Shannon does nothing during her year at the helm, it may be too late for the editors who follow her to make a difference. Shannon is determined that 125 years of NWU journalistic tradition is not going to be lost on *her* watch.

### Assignment

1. You are members of Shannon's student editorial team in the *UDT* newsroom. She has told you the paper's situation and expressed her concern about its long-term survival. You share her sense of urgency about the need to do something to save this NWU institution. Work together to develop long-term and mid-term plans for the future of *UDT*.

2. How do you think your editorial advisor, the publisher, and the board will react to your plans—and to the fact that you, as the student editorial staff—are essentially meddling in the business management of the paper? Develop a plan for when and how Shannon should inform each of these individuals or groups about the work your team is doing. Your goal should be to maximize the likelihood that they will support your plans. Consider whether you should involve them in the planning or develop the plan

independently and present it to them after it's completed. Develop plans for dealing with opposition, obstructionism, or outright rejection of your ideas by any one or all of these groups.

3. Develop a short-term plan for putting your long- and mid-term plans into action. Be sure that your short-term plans include SMART goals and tactics to achieve them.

4. What part of your plan will need to be implemented through discrete projects? Will you need new technologies, new apps, new approaches, or new content? Will you need new expertise on staff? Develop a thorough project management plan using the principles and guidelines outlined in the chapter. Be sure that you understand what will be required to carry out your proposed projects. For example, what goes into building a new app? How long does it take and how much does it cost? Even if you don't have the expertise to complete the project yourself, as project manager, you need to fully research and understand what the projects you will be managing will need in terms of time, expertise, resources, and risks.

### CASE 5.2: PLANNING AN INTERNATIONAL INVESTMENT PROJECT

Karl Markinson has just been promoted to Vice President of International Operations for Doxton Media Corp. Doxton is a 10-year-old U.S. media corporation created by Sarah Dorner-Braxton. A decade ago, when it became clear that the Internet was going to severely disrupt legacy media companies, Dorner-Braxton had seen an opportunity. She started selectively buying up legacy media units that were being sold by struggling media companies, as well as investing in new-technology startups with good ideas but no cash.

Today, Doxton Media's portfolio includes three nonfiction entertainment cable/satellite networks. One programs fashion news and features such content as designer profiles and video of fashion shows in the United States and Europe. The company's second network programs small business news and tips. The third network programs educational documentaries about science targeted to young people aged 8 to 18. Doxton Media also has a small magazine division that publishes titles with content similar to that of the video networks: a women's fashion magazine; a science magazine that covers everything from archaeology to physics (written in a highly engaging way for adults who are interested in science and innovation but are not scientists); and a business magazine targeted to small business owners and entrepreneurs. All of the magazines have digital editions, and the company has been trying to encourage its U.S. subscribers to move from print to online subscriptions in order to cut costs.

Doxton also owns a group of radio stations located in rural areas throughout the United States. Although most commercial radio has been struggling in the United States, Doxton's radio division has been booming. The secret has been a decision to abandon the slick, prerecorded radio content now programmed by so many U.S. stations in favor of intensely local content. Doxton's stations use local volunteers and contributors to program hyperlocal music, talk shows, cultural programming, and community news. Rural audiences have loved it and come flocking back to the dial, bringing local advertisers with them. Finally, Doxton also has a new technology division that focuses on creating video and text-based content for distribution on smartphones and tablets through Doxton's proprietary content apps.

Karl has been with Doxton since its start-up and, as Vice President of Strategic Operations, played a key role in the company's success. Last year, he had told Sarah he thought Doxton's opportunities for future growth were limited, however, given the fragmentation, turbulence, and saturation of U.S. media markets. He suggested Doxton begin to think about expanding overseas. Sarah agreed. Recognizing that overseas expansion is inherently risky, she told him she wanted a media industry expert that she could trust implicitly to oversee the project, in other words: him. Thus, Karl became Doxton's first Vice President of International Operations.

After significant research, Karl schedules a meeting with Sarah. "There are many different ways we could do this," he tells her when they sit down. "The first questions we need to answer are first, are we going to take our existing products overseas? Or are we going to expand by buying companies over there. The second question is into what regions or markets do we want to expand?"

"What are your thoughts?" Sarah responded.

"Let's take the second question first," Karl said. "Central and Western European media markets are as saturated as North American markets—or nearly so. So are Australia and New Zealand, and Latin America is not far behind. Eastern Europe, China, and many of the countries in the Middle East are largely closed to foreign media. That leaves south Asia and Africa. Most of the major media conglomerates are fighting over south Asian markets, but very few are looking to Africa yet. I say that's where we focus."

"Hmmm," Sarah mused. "There's a lot of diversity in Africa. Where exactly were you thinking of looking?"

"I don't know yet," said Karl. "But I thought I'd start with some of the largest countries: Ethiopia, Kenya, Nigeria, Namibia, and Madagascar, but those are just my initial thoughts."

Sarah nodded. "Good. Look into it and let me know what you learn."

### Sources

CIA. The World Factbook. www.cia.gov/library/publications/the-world-factbook/
CIA. The World Factbook Guide to Country Comparisons. www.cia.gov/library/
    publications/the-world-factbook/rankorder/rankorderguide.html
NationMaster. Comparative Media Statistics at http://www.nationmaster.com
The African Media Initiative. www.africanmediainitiative.org/

LexisNexis Academic (a subscription service that is usually available at university libraries and law firms).
Google up-to-date information about existing media and media ownership in each country.

### Assignment

*Note to Instructors: You may want to consider dividing the assignment of each country to a single group or individual with instructions to cover all options for that country. Alternatively, you could assign a specific media product to a group or individual, asking them to explore the opportunities for that media product in each country.*

You're Karl's assistant. Help him research the listed countries, or other countries your professor selects, and answer the following questions for Sarah.

1. Consider the media titles and networks Doxton already owns in the United States. Which of these, if any, would you recommend to Sarah that she try to place into Africa? Carefully consider each country and, in your report to Sarah, tell her which titles or products you would and would not recommend distributing in each country—and why. Be sure to consider geographic, demographic, technological, socioeconomic, linguistic, ethnic, religious, competitive, and cultural issues in your recommendations, as well as recent political, ethnic, and religious developments.

2. Look at your recommendations for Question 1. Write a detailed analysis of how Doxton would need to strategically place its product into the chosen market(s). What content elements would need to be adjusted to make the product attractive to local consumers in the markets you are recommending? What other things will Doxton need to consider if it's to succeed in distributing its media in these countries?

3. Given Doxton's current media portfolio and expertise, what opportunities are there for expanding into these countries by buying an existing media company, setting up a joint venture with an existing company, or licensing one of Doxton's properties to an existing media company? Consider carefully the expertise and compatibility of the companies you look at to make sure they would make a good partner for Doxton. A good partnership requires both sociocultural compatibility and shared expertise in the type of media products the partnership will produce. Be sure to consider the nature of the media market in which that African company operates, including geographic, demographic, technological, socioeconomic, linguistic, ethnic, religious, competitive, and cultural issues in your recommendations, as well as any recent political, ethnic, and religious developments.

4. Consider your recommendations for Question 3. What structural, economic, and human resource issues is Doxton likely to face, if it follows your recommendations and tries to move into one or more of these markets with the partner you recommend? How do you recommend that Doxton handle those issues?

5. Think about what you've learned about these
selected countries and their media markets. Based on
that, tell Sarah what you think would be the best approach
to expanding into one or more of these countries.
Specifically, which country(ies) would you recommend for
Doxton's investment? What types of media products do
you think would be most successful in the countries you've
identified—regardless of whether or not Doxton
produces them? What would be the best type of ownership
structure to use for Doxton's expansion, given the
countries and products you are recommending? What
would be the best corporate structure for Doxton to
use in running its expansion and why? What types of
social, cultural, political, economic, technological,
and competitive risks will Doxton have to manage
during this project if Sarah and Karl follow your
recommendations?

---

### CASE 5.3. PLANNING FOR THE UNTHINKABLE AND THE INEVITABLE

Sandy Larkin sat with the phone pressed to his ear, shaking his head in slow disbelief. The news director of a southern California television station, Sandy was hearing a story that was the stuff of every news director's nightmares.

Lauren Holtz, a long-time friend from journalism school days and now news director of a TV station in the South, was on the other end of the line. A week ago, Lauren's city had taken a direct hit from a major tornado. The city had been absolutely devastated.

"This place looks like it's been hit by a bomb," Lauren told him. "It's the worst experience I've ever been through. But the worst part of it, Sandy, was that *we*, the newsroom, were completely unprepared!"

"What do you mean," Sandy asked. "You have tornados around there all the time. How could you have been completely unprepared?"

"Oh, we had a severe weather coverage plan, of course," Lauren replied. "And we had all meteorologists and reporters in place, but we blew it. We hadn't planned for the things that really mattered."

"What do you mean?" Sandy asked.

Lauren sighed. "When the storm hit, the tornado took out the northwest side of the city, which is the area where most of my news staff lives. At the time, we already had several teams over in that area, in place to cover the storm. The storm took out all the cell towers in the area, so for hours we didn't know where some of our teams were—whether they were OK, hurt, or dead. On top of that, as damage reports started rolling in and we realized how bad it was—that several schools and entire neighborhoods in that area had been leveled—my people started just taking off and heading home. You can't blame them. They were terrified for their families and distraught about their homes. But at the time when our community needed us most, we found ourselves without most of our reporters.

"On top of that," Lauren continued, "the storm brought flooding rains, and we'd already been having heavy rain for the last month. After about four hours, the river near the station flooded and the station was inundated. We have backup generators, of course, but they were on ground level so they also flooded. We were completely knocked off the air and the station was surrounded by water and effectively cutoff for two days."

"Whew," Sandy said. "I bet you're glad that's all behind you."

"It's not," Lauren replied. "The flood waters did enormous damage to our equipment, and we're still not fully operational. Most of my people are now homeless and living in emergency shelters since all the surviving hotels and motels are jammed. Some have family members in the hospital. Almost all have children and pets they don't know what to do with since all the schools are closed, and the shelters won't take animals. The only consolation is that all the other stations in town are in the same situation. One of them took a direct hit and isn't back on the air yet. The other isn't much more operational than we are. We're all feeling like failures. Never has our community needed us more, and our station and all the news media here are in chaos!"

Sandy felt a chill run down his back as he hung up the phone. Southern California is earthquake country, and geologists have repeatedly warned that the clock to the next major earthquake is rapidly running down. He knew that at any time, he could find himself in Lauren's situation—or worse.

**Assignment**

1. Your project is to write a disaster plan for Sandy's newsroom. Research the type of damage cities normally experience in earthquakes. What happens to the power grid, the water and sewer systems? What happens to transportation and communication systems? How should news media companies—television, radio, newspapers, online news sites—prepare themselves so that they will be able to continue operations following a major earthquake or other natural or man-made disaster? Your report should contain specific plans for maintaining critical operations while still assisting employees who may be personally affected by the disaster. It also should contain plans for supporting employees in the weeks following a disaster that creates long-term disruption to normal life. Your plan should contain ideas about how your news organization will maintain operations when access to food, water, shelter, and communications is difficult and many basic community infrastructures (highways, bridges) have been destroyed. Your plan also should consider the cost of disaster recovery to the station, including the extra costs of long-term disaster coverage by the newsroom, at the same time that many local businesses have been destroyed and the station's local advertising revenue falls.

2. Think about the types of disasters that are most common or most likely in the region where you live. Develop a disaster plan for a local news media company that will help ensure it will be able to continue providing critical news and information to the public both during and after a disaster.

# CHAPTER 6

# Innovation

Innovation generally is an idea with a purpose—a means to an end. It is the job of managers to determine how well that innovation serves its purpose and its effect on the people who use it.

This is especially true in a media company. Knowing the innovation's capacities and limitations facilitates managing. Understanding the limitations of a cellphone camera helps a photo editor decide what news situations require more sophisticated cameras. Similarly, innovation determines internal structure. A TV station manager knows that producing the 6 o'clock news requires dividing work into journalistic, promotional, engineering, and advertising components, each with its own department and procedures. So that internal structure, in turn, determines employee behavior and efficiency.

As innovations change, media managers must understand the strategic ramifications. Media firms—with their time-sensitive products—must grasp the market significance of rapidly developing and converging technologies, such as the Internet and broadband, and adapt. Doing so could mean the difference between new, growing revenue streams and a stagnant, noncompetitive future. Remember when the only way to watch TV was on a TV set? Advertisers then had to adjust to VCRs, which allowed audiences to time-shift, i.e., watch whenever they wanted. Now, with advanced telephony and digitization, users also can space-shift—watch their favorite programs *wherever* they want. To keep pace with the audience and fund their programming, TV managers had to rethink how and where they placed the ads.

Ongoing innovation has usually characterized media, but digitization and the Internet accelerated the pace of change (Küng, 2008), making it all the more important that media managers learn to navigate their organizations so as to take competitive advantage of that change. To do so, the manager must understand innovation's organizational role and impact. This chapter puts you in the managerial mindset as it pertains to innovation.

## APPROACH

A manager needs to think about what he or she wants to do before he or she does it. A news director sets the tone for how well his or her staff uses mobile trucks; his or her constant complaints about the truck's equipment breakdowns undermine staff trust in the trucks. If he or she consistently praises the editing system and helps staffers master the system's potential, he or she enhances the producers' ability to edit and cue video effectively, thus enhancing productivity.

Of course, any innovation to some extent dictates the news director's approach. But constant, evolving technological advances—often called "disruptive" for their ability to create new industry or transform an existing one (Day & Schoemaker, 2000)—and continuing economic woes have threatened the way media conduct business. For example, customers have more latitude and choice regarding when and where they consume news, thus threatening business models (the predictable way a media firm generates revenue). Changes such as increasing digitization and competition, declining advertising revenue, and shifting audience preferences have placed journalism in an age of uncertainty (Singer, 2011). Such changes require new, more sophisticated strategies to protect the long-term health of a media organization. No longer does the only strategy issue involve how much to increase everyone's budget. Such an uncertain, "emergent" business climate poses a new challenge to media managers, who will need to determine the best direction for their companies and, simultaneously, a direction that—if innovation continues at its current, unpredictable pace—will not pose a danger to the company's financial health. So in this environment, strategy takes on even more importance than normal.

### Strategy

Strategy or the planning and action that managers take to achieve goals can be planned in three different ways (Küng, 2008): rationally, adaptively, or interpretively. In rational mode, a manager starts with a focus on external environments—e.g., competition, political landscape, regulatory structure, economy, technological development, and whatever affects customer behavior. He or she then methodically and linearly plans a response that will take advantage of that environment, by either maximizing resources or setting up some way to comfortably exist in it.

But the truth is that environments are never static and, in rapidly changing environments, some rationalist approaches may not work as well as an adaptive strategy that expects change and provides for times when the organization needs to readjust. If you think of the rationalist approach as creating a plan and then executing it, then an adaptive strategy appears only when needed. In contrast, interpretive approaches try to see things as those on the inside of the organization would, thus taking advantage of organizational intangibles—e.g., employee culture, motivation, and values—and depending on employees to help make sense of, and respond to, the environment (Weick, 1995).

Because conventional strategy alone is not enough, managers must beware of market *and* internal organizational influences (such as the adoption process to be discussed later in this chapter) accompanying technology. A manager needs to adopt a broad approach, relying on as much information as possible, when considering innovation. He or she may want to consider an open system theory (Katz & Kahn, 1978) because it recognizes and charts the recurring organizational sequences of input/effort, change, output/production, and renewed input/effort. In other words, organizations bring in energy or materials from the environment, transform that energy/matter into some product, export that product into the environment, and then reenergize the organization from environmental sources. This allows the manager to see his or her organization (and thus its resulting product) as a collection of interrelated parts working in unison toward a common goal. The manager then realizes that the system (organization) constantly interacts with its environment. That interaction yields a vast reservoir of relevant information with which to successfully manage.

For example, unaccustomed to thinking like marketers, many managers have previously concentrated on internal operations and concerns, with poor results. Interviews with 14 newspaper online executives (Chyi & Sylvie, 2000) showed they had difficulty defining their markets, not to mention their primary competitors, leading them to believe that their audiences wanted repackaged, repurposed local content from the print product. In reality, much of the audience came from outside the local market and instead wanted content that the newspaper already was providing, but which no other media outside the market could generate. In contrast, knowing that audiences increasingly were wanting to watch TV entertainment programming online whenever it was convenient for them led officials at NBC Universal and News Corp. to plan, develop, and launch Hulu.com (Liu & Chan-Olmsted, 2003).

Anyone can develop a strategy, but it takes a really able manager to effectively implement it. Regardless of the type of strategy, the media manager must create procedures and policies to support implementation (Gershon, 2001). This managerial skill is especially vital in the current convergent atmosphere transforming the media industry. Industry experts thought the structural and technological boundaries that historically separated markets and industries could be erased (Albarran, 2010), requiring managers to develop multiplatform media enterprises.

For example, where once local broadcast stations and newspapers fiercely competed for certain news, some cooperation and mutual promotion now often exists through convergence. Starting around 2000, some newspaper reporters appeared on TV. The newspapers promoted the TV's newscast, or both were promoted via a joint online venture. This means editors and producers must be flexible in helping staff manage their time; train reporters unfamiliar with print, broadcast, or online styles; and coax journalists leery of the convergence effort. Much energy is needed to maintain and nurture such partnerships (e.g., Strupp, 2000).

Apparently, some organizations could not meet that need, as print journalists and broadcast journalists in convergent arrangements displayed intergroup prejudice; each group—while high on their own career choice—was less positive about working in the other medium (Filak, 2004). Even the task of learning the terminology of each area was, at times, a one-way proposition, as a study of the convergence attempt by the Phoenix newspaper and a local TV station showed (Silcock & Keith, 2006). Time pressures, especially on the broadcast side, prompted part of this failure to develop a common professional culture and also created conflict. Although most convergent newsroom journalists thought at one time that these ventures created more solid news with multiple features (Singer, 2006), most such partnerships practiced relatively little real convergence and were mostly focused on cross-promotion. In one study of such efforts, three-fifths of the respondents said they did not share stories, with ingrained competition and distrust cited as possible stumbling blocks (Dailey, Demo, & Spillman, 2009). Obviously, when adopting a strategy, managers must have a willingness to honestly and openly examine core values and beliefs, and study the forces restraining change as well (Thornton & Keith, 2009).

In fact, cross-media strategies, while providing media companies a chance to add value to their product at a fraction of the cost, can also get complicated (Küng, Leandros, Picard, Schroeder, & van der Wurff, 2008): Where is the convergence attempt going to be—our company or theirs? Who'll be in charge of it—us or them? How much money should we put forth—what's our "share?" Which of our departments will benefit the most—and what do we say to the ones who won't? How do we coordinate our interests with theirs? If we develop a new application for the iPhone, who will control our content or have the upper hand in the arrangement—us or Apple? Such risks, in the case of convergent partnerships, have instead resulted in some media increasing their "Webvergence," in which former partners each focus on autonomously produced multimedia content on their own websites (Thornton & Keith, 2009).

Too, there's the danger of adopting the wrong strategy. For example, the *Los Angeles Times*—with a strong investigative reputation—responded to a change in leadership in 1989 by bringing in a new editor who extended the paper's use of color, graphics, shorter articles, and other market research-motivated features to create more reader-friendly sections. Many talented and veteran reporters, dismayed by what they saw as a lack of professionally driven changes, started leaving the paper, creating speculation as to whether *the Times* could maintain its journalistic standing. A new publisher in 1995 adopted an even more aggressive consumer-oriented strategy, aggravating journalists to the point of open resistance (Sylvie & Moon, 2007)—definitely not an interpretive strategy, much less a successful one.

The result makes even more remarkable the success of a similar strategy at another newspaper. When introduced, *USA TODAY* emphasized reader wants, color graphics and maps, shorter-than-normal stories, and detailed sports coverage—all of which, again, represented a departure from central, traditional journalistic values and assumptions such as these: Journalists know news/content better than readers; news is largely conveyed via text and an occasional photo; the best news is detailed; and other types of content (entertainment and sports) are lesser versions of news. Assembling such a newspaper was an adventure because it required a large group of journalists to change their thinking, work habits, and the end result. In essence, it required an uncommon type of journalist—one willing to risk change and view innovation as an opportunity, not a threat. Such vision, with the aid of other factors, helps change-agents/managers complete their task. Sylvie and Witherspoon (2002) suggested journalists and other newspaper employees must evaluate resistance to create a longer-term, more meaningful, or strategic change (see Figure 6.1) and to avoid change that is reactive, control-oriented, or based on inappropriate models. The issue then becomes, Sylvie and Witherspoon argue, how to create, properly communicate, and strategically implement the vision that enables successful change.

The British Broadcasting Co. (BBC) repeated this feat when—beginning in the late 1990s and extending into the current millennium—it overcame lack of funding and Internet skills; a centralized and intricate hierarchy; and a traditional, local-media focus to successfully launch BBC

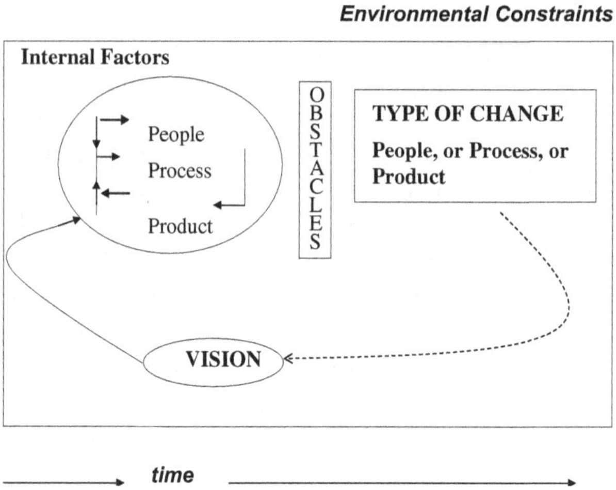

Environmental Constraints

**Figure 6.1** How Newspaper Change Occurs

News Online. The operation, independent from its parent firm, avoided the BBC's traditional conservative nature by exploiting the staff's belief that the BBC should maintain its dominance in the UK market, their inherent motivation to find ways to improve their work, and the ability of its leadership to work in tandem and collaboratively (Küng, 2007). Because the network's successful online transition also benefitted from its leadership's foresight that the Internet would, indeed, become a large, viable broadcast vehicle, we explore this capability next.

**Peripheral Vision**
Technologically driven products cannot be managed without forethought. Media visionaries continually maintain and update their understanding of business/product objectives and "define their business' identity within whatever future comes" (Brown & Eisenhardt, 1998, p. 148). This is not the same as strategy or the visionary's tool or plan for executing the vision. Nor is it the same as seeing the future; even the media operations that used videotext in the 1980s were probably unaware they were working on the forerunner of the Internet. In a sense, then, vision is being able to articulate an organization's role and identity *prior* to developing a strategy (Hitt, Keats, & DeMarie, 1998).

Managers create visions through methodically thinking about the future and evaluating the wants and needs of the organization's client groups (Nanus, 1992). Managers must acquire or develop structures and processes to initiate and foster vision; managers who are leaders help their subordinates understand the innovation by how they (the managers) convey that idea (Vaill, 1993). As Figure 6.1 attempts to show, the leader—by having the vision—can determine how that vision affects his or her employees, their work processes, and what they produce. Foreseeing the consequences of the vision allows the leader to then frame or portray the innovation in such a way as to make his or her subordinates eagerly or willingly implement the innovation. In the case of BBC News Online, one manager outlined the vision and provided the financial support while another conveyed it to BBC staffers and executed it by removing obstacles, running interference against the organization's bureaucracy, and encouraging staffers to experiment in creating the Internet interface. As the organization became successful, it grew, but began to feel constraining. A third, different manager took over, establishing a more cooperative link to the parent organization, upgrading processes and support, and thus clarifying roles and alleviating staff stress that had accrued (Küng, 2007). These three managers thus allowed the original vision to became a natural, integral part of managing, enabling managers to "win tomorrow today" (Brown & Eisenhardt, 1998, pp. 127–129).

Vision and strategy, then, have a symbiotic relationship: They're reciprocal. That is, whereas a strategy is the operational process that enables a media firm to match or achieve a vision, the vision is the leadership trait that also informs and shapes the strategy. The connection for media, however, is muddied by the pace of innovation and its resulting continual string of new technologies. And as our discussion at the beginning of this chapter suggests, the current ongoing nature of media-product changes is such that the audiences are gaining an increasingly larger hand in saying what constitutes the value of those products (Picard, 2006). Media managers then probably should pay more attention to consumers' opinions—rather than solely those of creative or journalistic employees, despite what the interpretive approach might seem to suggest.

So if you think by now that there's more to vision—such as the necessity for infrastructure, coordination, and motivation, to name a few—you're not alone. One framework (Chan-Olmsted, 2006) suggests additional, more complex reasons for adoption, including characteristics of the firm, traits of the innovation, the perceived overall strategic value of adoption, available alternatives to the innovation, available strategic networks, the intensity and timing of the innovation's adoption, and market conditions. Once the manager understands these factors, i.e., develops something akin to a "peripheral" vision that accounts for most factors, he or she should have a better idea of how to implement it.

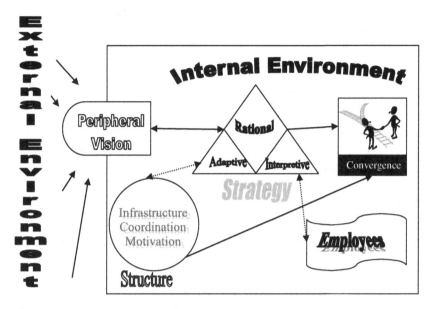

**Figure 6.2**    Interplay of Convergence Influences

### Vehicle

Strategy pertains to the actual implementation of the innovation, while vision—as a strategic influence and guide—finds itself expressed in that strategy. Meanwhile, the innovation begins to take organizational shape in the form of the vehicle, or management's chosen instrument or conduit to carry and execute the change. The instrument varies, depending on management's strategy and intent.

For example, a structural approach employs formal devices such as rules and organizational hierarchy to instigate an innovation, such as when *The Dallas Morning News*—after the competing *Dallas Times-Herald* closed down—tried to serve the *Times-Herald* subscribers by buying its presses, editing system, and equipment. Such an approach changed the organization's structure. But in this case, the change didn't work: Flawless integration of the two systems proved impossible; constant production delays arose, deadlines were missed, and newspapers didn't get delivered in time (Sylvie & Witherspoon, 2002).

So, just because managers recognize that technology fulfills a need doesn't necessarily make it easy for them to exactly calculate the impact. Management often must heavily rely on employees' skills, talents, and judgment at all phases of production. It may be impractical to view the innovation without including the employee/user in the picture to a limited degree—another reason many managers try the technological-task approach—which complements the structural approach by emphasizing a particular innovation's obvious, direct impact on procedures and tasks. In *The Morning News* case, the broadcast senior managers then tried to improve the production process by buying a new pagination system, which allowed editors for the first time to electronically assemble news page elements, as opposed to nonjournalists ("composers") assembling pages by hand. The system was supposed to facilitate strategic and operating objectives—to deliver more newspapers faster and more efficiently. But in putting it in place, upper management gave the newspaper's information technology (IT) department free reign in implementation, which included little training and few attempts to get advice from other employees. This approach resulted in numerous newsroom complaints and little journalistic buy-in; therefore, management aborted the experiment (Sylvie & Witherspoon, 2002).

In such instances where managers use the technological-task approach, they usually see the technology as controllable, with a measurable response in organizational performance: They choose a technology, hoping it will increase productivity by enhancing the processes and routine tasks. This approach—essentially the substitution of one innovation for another—often occurs in technology-dependent news media. Yet using it carries potential problems or trade-offs. An alternative approach is the sociotechnical adoption of innovations—stressing the needs and actions of the innovation's users as well as examining the innovation's attributes and characteristics. Sociotechnical managers see person and machine interacting to the organization's benefit, or detriment. They view innovation's purpose as dynamic and changing and to be used according to its perceived utility (Argyris, 1962), as did the editors at *The Dallas Morning News* when they formed the newsroom technology group with the sole concern of finding, developing, and implementing an efficient pagination system that newsroom users would adopt. Management spent 6 months planning and soliciting employee opinions about what would work, allotted additional funds to develop in-house trainers, and followed an extensive, thorough training process. Managers hired part-timers to replace the trainees while they trained, organized groups as sounding boards, developed a 21-chapter user's manual, and conducted pilot tests. Final adoption went smoothly (Sylvie & Witherspoon, 2002).

Acceptance of the sociotechnical approach may grow as more managers become sensitive to employee needs and growth. Often recognizing that formal organizational values may infringe on an employee's personal values or skills, these managers realize that psychological and social planning play an important part in new technology introduction. They evaluate innovation not just according to objectives, but also according to the process of change that the innovation introduces and its impact on employees' motivations, skills, and organizational competence (Blackler & Brown, 1985). For example, as more newsrooms begin to converge, they will require revisiting the occupational cultures of the employee groups they want to mix and match.

These three approaches illustrate that management has to have a basic orientation in dealing with innovation. The approaches stress the element of control, although some research shows that managers also view innovation in terms of cost and market (Noon, 1994). Still, as mentioned at the start, managers need a basic objective when adopting innovation. The objective in no small part determines how well the adoption (or rejection) process occurs and how well a manager can predict the innovation's impact on management and employee and market behavior. The adoption process must be examined and placed in context.

Still, one final piece to the approach question—involving those who determine the approach—probably trumps all the others.

### Leadership

The importance of bottom-up participation in managing innovation illustrates the difficulty of implementing such innovation: There's much work involved in persuading employees to change how they go about their routine tasks. Some would argue that most change efforts fail for reasons related to such efforts—call it conservativeness, inertia, reluctance, routines, tradition, or what you will, managers must prime, spin, and frame change (Lund, 2008).

Change management requires priming because an innovation nearly always challenges some traditional way of operating. The change agent (i.e., the manager as leader) has to prepare employees—usually by showing that the traditional way will be enhanced, rather than supplanted or hurt. An editor strongly needs to use priming, for example, when his or her subordinate journalists believe that the current continual movement toward digitization, multiplatform-delivery, market-driven change, and convergence threatens to de-professionalize journalism by granting citizens equal access (on par with journalists) to some information; encouraging (via new technologies) journalists to do more technical, production-oriented tasks; and de-emphasizing the public service nature of journalism in favor of producing greater profits (Witschge & Nygren, 2009).

In framing, the media manager would emphasize certain advantages or desirable outcomes of an innovation while ignoring its more negative attributes. For example, a news director who wants his or her top investigative journalist to start a blog probably would suggest that the blog would enhance the reporter's visibility among viewers, thus creating a new stream of viewer-suggested investigative topics or story sources. The news director probably also would point to the increased feedback (and likely fans) that the blog's automatic reader-response function would generate, as well as the additional branding and investigatory credibility the blog would provide. Those items, the news director would argue, surely outweigh—or return 10-fold in benefits—the extra 30 to 60 minutes of daily time that the blog would require of the journalist.

But media managers—since they work in communication organizations—must recognize that other individuals (usually informal leaders or other assertive persons within the organization) can frame as well, so it's not as simple as just a one-on-one conversation or publishing an interdepartmental memo or sending an e-mail. Although management is in charge of most change efforts, it must not ignore employee culture. The frame doesn't exist in a vacuum, meaning few media organizations can imitate *The Chicago Tribune's* dominating management team of the 1980s and 1990s, when senior managers instigated many technological synergies among its related media holdings with little pushback from its newsroom culture (Sylvie & Moon, 2007). The other extreme can be seen in certain convergence attempts, where management teams from each participating organization were powerless to control how the other organization's journalists perceived and critiqued the effort, resulting—for a newspaper and a TV station in Phoenix, for example—in the lack of trust in each other's work routines (Silcock & Keith, 2006).

Spinning, on the other hand, deters opponents of an innovation by deliberately focusing on the positives or fruits of the change—a kind of extreme framing in which favorable attributes may be exaggerated, in a sense. Returning to BBC News Online's successful implementation, managers often stressed that the online unit—though working in relative obscurity apart from other units in the organization—represented a chance for its employees to gain a sense of adventure and be autonomously creative. Although some viewed the News Online subculture as "outlaws" of a kind, management used such terminology to motivate online staffers to continue to experiment and see themselves as a special "team" (Küng, 2007).

Managers always have the upper hand when it comes to change. As one survey of four converged newsrooms discovered, journalists all saw the beginning drive for convergence coming from management, as something their superiors sought, but which was not implemented authoritatively, top-down (Singer, 2004b). And management's ability to act as a change-agent—to, in effect, lead the change—is the one element that it can fully control in attempting to avoid or resolve "a confrontation between leaders and the led" (Sánchez-Tabernero, 2004, p. 29).

Managing this internal tension, "the challenge of conflicting dual demands in the organization that cannot be resolved by simple organizational structures or choices" (Achtenhagen & Raviola, 2007, p. 129), is a reality for all businesses. Belgian multimedia conglomerate Concentra Media realized as much when it reorganized warring internal units and implemented a new content management system to promote editing and sharing of content across different media units (e.g., for newspapers, TV, magazines, and radio). Company managers believed the move would lessen conflict between (and competition among) each unit's advertising divisions and encourage use across different media. So did Dutch publishing giant PCM, when it restructured its newspaper and book properties along brand lines in order to converge operations and lessen conflict between each property's editorial and business departments. Harmony—and additional conflict—ensued at Concentra and PCM, largely because managers still didn't fully understand the core tensions among the opposing groups (Achtenhagen & Raviola, 2007).

For that reason, leadership style (See Chapter 1) recently has come under greater scrutiny by media management scholars. The prevailing thought is that managers' thought and decision-making processes may need to change if media companies are to meet the challenge of innovation. For example, at convergence-practicing news media, most reporters said their managers used a relationship-oriented or person-centered managing style. In fact, as relationship behavior of news managers increased, so did the level of convergence (Powers, 2006). A study of frontline U.S. newspaper managers showed that personal values drove decision making and that managers with certain demographic traits—e.g., gender, race, and experience—used different value sets on which to base their decisions than did other managers. As to managing innovation, the data hinted that developing innovation involves a complex matching of an innovation's traits with the existing set of managers' values (Sylvie & Huang, 2008a).

A secondary analysis of the same data showed that audience-related values had no predictive power in the editors' decision-making approaches. While the editors' social, journalistic, and organizational value systems *did* have some role in decision making, values that corresponded to audience-oriented values did not. These results suggest that the editors were not as sensitive to audience-oriented values as to value systems involving journalistic practices, organizational, and social concerns. Hence, in 2005 (when the survey was taken), editors were not as market-driven as perhaps they needed to be (Sylvie & Huang, 2008b). Such a mistaken emphasis—and the resulting economic damage it may foster—should provide all the more motivation to learn how to recognize innovations' impacts.

## IMPACT

Innovation may have several types of effects: desirable/undesirable, direct/indirect, and anticipated/unanticipated (Rogers, 1983). Another effect might be termed disruptive/undisruptive (Day & Schoemaker, 2000). These consequences are approached from various internal and external perspectives.

Internally, managers focus on the adoption process and its effects. When an organization decides to adopt a technology or innovation, several steps (Rogers, 1983) precede and follow the decision.

### Agenda Setting

Akin to strategy, agenda setting is a kind of introductory process—prior to the actual implementation of an innovation—that occurs when management identifies a need for a technology. This may also include the research and development phase of the innovation (Andriessen, 1994). In any case, management assesses the industry as much as possible, reading related publications (print and online), and consulting technological experts for potential solutions. In mass media, technologies often seem to set their own agenda. For example, interest in the Internet burgeoned to the point where many media companies created websites simply to keep pace with the market for Web-based information. But just as often, media managers respond to particular needs that employees identify in the work process.

### Matching

Here, the manager aligns the agenda (or some detail or issue on that agenda) with a technology that fits with it. For example, the BBC chose to create BBC News Online to address its lack of Web-based presence

(Küng, 2007)—a fairly typical occurrence at most news media organizations in the early days of the Internet (Lawson-Borders, 2003). Another example might be a Web 'zine that has marketing problems, particularly in attracting older readers, could hire a variety of consultants over several months to increase readership. Similarly, an independent filmmaker/producer who can't afford quality film may decide to use a video or digital camera. Once the magazine hires the consultants or the filmmaker makes a choice, they must implement the decision, which brings us to the next step.

### Redefining/Restructuring

Redefining occurs when a manager changes the technology or idea to fit her particular agenda, objective, or situation. She asks herself, for example, whether the reorganization of her news team's work process is suitable for convergence purposes. In short, in what ways, if any, has the initial concept of the tool or idea changed as it was implemented? Then she introduces the idea to pertinent staffers, who interact with it in various ways. Their interaction results in the effects types mentioned earlier: (a) direct (changes that occur in immediate response) or indirect (changes resulting from immediate responses); (b) desirable (helps the user or system function more effectively) or undesirable (dysfunctional); (c) anticipated (changes recognized and intended by management) or unanticipated (changes neither recognized nor intended); or (d) undisruptive (procedures continue with minimum difficulty) or disruptive (tasks persist with much trouble).

For example, say that a digital camera sounds just right for an independent film producer but, after a week's worth of shooting, she recognizes she really can't get the depth and shading on her video that she would like. She has to decide whether to continue as is (and risk criticism of the film's visual quality when it's finally shown) or to figure out a way to pay for quality film and use the standard camera. But she realizes that it's never that simple: She starts questioning her initial objectives for making the film and how visual quality impacts (if at all) the film's message. What does she want to say? Does the "how" of set lighting really matter? Would video seem a more "authentic" medium to the intended audience?

These individual-hardware/idea/process interactions can be mental or physical, pleasant or unpleasant, work or play, positive or negative. For instance, in convergence efforts, it can be from as trivial as whether newspaper journalists need to worry about wearing ironed shirts in case they appear on camera, (Singer, 2004b, p. 10) to as important as whether they should break stories first on TV (Thornton & Keith, 2009, p. 262).

Media firms often experience interactions fairly quickly because of the product's changing nature and the work's sequential and routinized nature. So a typical TV journalist asked for the first time to write for both print, online, and broadcast likely will quickly report to his or her news director the differences in writing for all three along with any suggestions for changes. And the news director likely will mull the viability of the idea for this particular employee and what changes, if any, need implementation. Yet the process still is incomplete.

**Clarifying**

Let's say 3 months pass, and our TV reporter's productivity is up 60%—good but not great considering he's been asked to write for TV, Web, and print. Theoretically his productivity should triple (i.e., go up 200%). The news director confirms that the reporter followed the plan correctly, but hasn't kept pace and often misses online deadlines. The manager talks separately with the online editor, the producer, and the reporter, emphasizing perhaps the producer's role in editing the story, and urging the reporter to view the task as reaching different readers. Not only are the different audience segments new, but they also look for different kinds of information and emphases in a story. The news director must ensure that the reporter, the online managing editor, and the producer properly align in function and timing so that the reporter's stories make it to the Web.

In clarifying stages, the manager must review how adopters—such as the reporter or the news director—perceive an idea or new technology and more plainly describe the innovation in such a way that employees understand it and recognize it as useful. Managers usually report such perceptions in terms of (a) *relative advantage* (the degree to which employees perceive a technology as better than the idea it replaces); (b) *compatibility* (the degree to which employees perceive a technology as consistent with existing values, past experiences, and needs of potential adopters); (c) *complexity* (the degree to which employees perceive a technology as relatively difficult to understand and use); (d) *trialability* (the degree to which employees perceive a technology may be experimented with before adoption is confirmed); and (e) *observability* (the degree to which nonadopters can see a technology's impact). So it's important that the news director in our current example delve into and concede that print and broadcast practices may lead to certain group cultural problems, such as unfairly labeling partners from the newspaper as elitist, egotistical, dull, or not trendy (Silcock & Keith, 2006, p. 620). Each perception or attribute can lead to good or bad consequences (Rogers, 1983). For example, if our TV reporter—after all the adjustments—begins to see substantially increased audience feedback and better, more exclusive story ideas follow, then this advantage may prompt the reporter to generate more stories, to blog more, and to encourage others in the newsroom to follow suit. This may plant the seeds for a better, revised work structure that may evolve, as described in the next section.

### Routinizing

In this final step, the innovation firmly becomes part of work. At the TV station, our reporter learns how to write so that he either automatically downloads the online version of his story to the website, or "tweaks" it slightly so it is online appropriate. That mere fact proves that our news director selected a technology or idea that controls work routines and dictates somewhat predictable outcomes

The resulting employee–technology interaction influences management's perceptions of the technology's (or idea's) usefulness, the employees gain experience leading them to new and updated uses of the technology—in turn leading the organization to modify the use of the innovation. Such a learning mechanism slowly self-adjusts, so that the innovation eventually loses its newness and becomes embedded in company operations. In our example, multimedia writing becomes part of the furniture, instead of some new experiment, and an accepted or preferred way of doing business. The same thing has happened in Armenia, where traditional American journalistic values have, in large part, taken root (Torosyan & Starck, 2006), as it did in Tampa, Florida, where a TV station and the local daily newspaper have a convergent operation (Silcock & Keith, 2006), and as it's happening across the United States in terms of social media use at community news sites (Remez, 2012).

Rules, new job descriptions, or rewards of some kind help bring about these changes. For example, one newspaper newsroom switched its structure to topic-team reporting because analyses showed that topics such as science, health, and medicine received inadequate coverage. Teams helped solve the problem, increasing such coverage; but the policy changes in coverage and news display led to adoption of a new set of news values (Russial, 1997). Staff sizes at the major news networks dropped because of budget cuts, and ABC News abandoned traditional multistaffer crews in favor of backpack journalists—one person simultaneously performing multiple technical, production, and reporting functions (Guskin & Rosenstiel, 2012). Such adjustments typify newsrooms today because managing is, by nature, adjustment. Classic managerial functions include planning, staffing, organizing, controlling, and motivating. Introducing innovation requires using one or all these functions at some time in the adoption process; good managers know when to perform which function and when—in the adoption process—to adjust. Nowhere is timing more important than in convergence.

## CONVERGENCE AND INNOVATION AS PRODUCTS

Up to now, this chapter has provided brief glimpses of convergence in the strategic and adoption developments. But there's more: Convergence—generally accepted as the merger of one or more media into one, new medium—has become more routine for managers who work in a constantly and rapidly evolving swirl of computer-driven innovations. Fierce competition in the media (Compaine & Gomery, 2000) leaves managers no choice but to adopt technological products out of necessity, the consequences of which create uncertainty, making many media managers cautious and conservative.

For example, TV (probably because the Internet changes so quickly and because of lingering audience acceptance of mobile delivery) has lagged behind other media in digitization. Viewers continue to prefer on-demand content, which creates problems for stations in negotiating content rights, particularly for attractive sports events. It also didn't help when a national content provider failed because of lack of subscribers (Wong, 2010). All that could change in the next few years, of course, because of the introduction of tablets, if more people decide that the tablet TV-watching experience far exceeds that on a cellphone. Still, savvy managers must know the difference between the mechanically possible and the profitable.

For example, many newspapers created online products in a fairly hit-or-miss fashion, spending unsubstantial amounts of money, including few personnel, and doing little research (Saksena & Hollifield, 2002). A later study showed less than a third of weekly newspapers formed a business plan for creating their website or set quantifiable aims, and that nearly three-fourths did no audience research. But for those that did set goals, slightly more than half achieved the goals (Adams, 2008).

So as the interplay of innovation-as-product (primarily via the growing media trend toward technological convergence or digitization) and managerial impact gains importance, our knowledge about convergence grows. For example, technological convergence (in which a technology is created to replace or combine two or more other technologies) is one of four types of media convergence—the others include functional (in which various functions become unified); competitive/complementary (in which two products are suddenly seen as competitors or complementary); and strategic/industry (in which previously separate industries converge, as in buyout or mergers) (Wirth, 2006). This section deals with how convergence affects both media structure (functional convergence) and strategic management, which influence and support each other (Wirtz, 2001). But first, we'll examine the basic mechanism driving that competition and, thus, managerial behavior and uncertainty.

### Value

In today's technology and media convergence era, media managers are searching for new digital media products—most often the online extension of the "legacy" product (the one that historically has driven the company's profits)—that will generate meaningful revenues. The search took on serious momentum when it became apparent that online products were "inferior goods" that—while having value—didn't have enough inherent value to attract audiences large, long, or often enough to yield profits rivaling those from legacy media (Chyi & Yang, 2009).

The marketplace influences value, i.e., how good, significant, useful, substantive, practical, important, worthy, helpful, attractive, or meritorious a product is in the eyes of its consumer. Managers traditionally use the value chain—a conceptual tool that breaks down a firm's core activities—to form distinct bases for creating competitive advantage, or value. These activities include primary activities (inbound logistics, operations, outbound logistics, marketing and sales, and service) and support (procurement, technology development, human resource management, and firm infrastructure) activities—that "design, produce, market, deliver and support" the firm's product (Porter, 1985; 33–43, 36). Figure 6.3 illustrates a traditional media value chain.

With the advent of convergence, managers have realized that the value chain doesn't have to remain static; it can be unbundled and

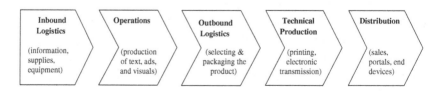

**Figure 6.3** Media Value Chain

reconfigured to help media transform themselves to take advantage of technology—in a sense, add value to their products. The new, rearranged value chain has parts that will strategically help managers target new audiences because these parts enable the company to add value to existing products, repackage those products into something new (and possibly restructure the company) that uses or takes advantage of an innovation (Wirtz, 2001; see Figure 6.4).

This means that media are changing what they do—including how they manage their organizations—because audiences are changing what *they* do. The rest of this section examines what areas are changing and how.

### Brand Awareness and Strategy

Enhanced, technologically driven products require media managers to understand they have a niche and an identity—a brand—to maintain and expand. This works several ways.

For example, local broadcasters have limited resources with which to cover and generate news. Whereas a typical, small-city newspaper has one journalist per every 1,000 subscribers, a corresponding local TV station might have one-fifth that number. As a result, TV news directors constantly search for ways to supplement local reporting; a local station can expand its newscast and, thus, its brand by appearing to have its own regional, national, and international correspondents in using its affiliated network, which daily provides several hundred stories to local affiliates via satellite technology (Barkin, 2001). Broadcasters also have begun promoting themselves in other media (Eastman, Ferguson, & Klein, 2006), such as their websites (Gregson, 2008) and social media accounts (Petner, 2009)—the latter most often to promote singular news items (Greer & Ferguson, 2011).

Future media managers (or at least those driven by technology-sensitive products) must learn and gain advantage from the previous experience and current branding of the traditional product. For instance, video rental stores started replacing VHS-format videotaped films with films on

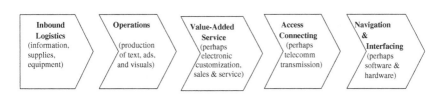

**Figure 6.4**   Reconfigured Media Value Chain

digital video discs (DVDs) in an effort to not only try to catch up to increasing sales of DVD players, but also to learn from their video customers as to what constituted a comfortable viewing experience (Emling, 2002). So a brand-conscious media manager makes the future happen through a new technologically driven product, thus energizing the existing business (Brown & Eisenhardt, 1998). When it comes to convergence, the Internet allowed all traditional mass media to implement this brand extension.

Brands enhance a product's value beyond the product function (Keller, 2008), but, more importantly, they also give the manager a crucial, strategic tool. Convergence gives managers additional media/markets to consider, but also provides an important task—brand management—to which managers must tend, particularly as media brands proliferate and they begin to expand the channels and methods they use to promote themselves. Brands essentially provide consumers a "lifestyle statement" (McDowell, 2011, p. 42) and a competitive advantage to the company represented by the brand. In an era when journalistic and business concerns are beginning to clash somewhat (managers want journalists to begin to view audiences as consumers, rather than as citizens), branding's no small feat. Creating and maintaining a news brand, for example, makes it all the more imperative for news media to cover news with a quality orientation (Siegert, Gerth, & Rademacher, 2011).

But some media have a long way to go in learning how to brand. For example, a recent study of newspaper slogans found them lacking in traditional branding elements: While showcasing important advantages, local relevance, and consumer needs, most slogans didn't include memory aids, note the brand, or suggest consumers do something (Ghanem & Selber, 2009). As mentioned earlier in the brand section—online products' "inferior" value fails to attract audiences in numbers that would produce profits rivaling those from legacy media (Chyi & Yang, 2009). Consequently, for traditional media to successfully brand in the convergent era, their managers have to construct a brand image that will lead consumers to the new (probably online) product, as well as to return to the traditional product and explain why both provide different yet crucial benefits. But there's no evidence of that happening. While newspaper branding efforts by major, traditional, U.S. news organizations generated more online site traffic from 2002 to 2006, their local news operations' sites traffic declined as the primary choice for political information (Shaver & Shaver, 2008).

Probably the best example of media branding comes from ESPN's branding activities, which have even been the subject of academic articles (e.g., Sharma, 2009). The sports entertainment giant has learned to traverse its many outlets by emphasizing sports, authority, and personality (Hyman, 2011). Research shows that if a strong cable channel has high brand equity—the degree of response by consumers to marketing efforts unique to a brand—then brand extensions have a high degree of potential success. For example, ESPN has created many brand extensions: ESPN Classic, *ESPN The Magazine*, ESPN2, ESPN Radio, ESPN Deportes, etc. Too, managers must consistently maintain the quality of the varying subbrands and perhaps try not to create too many of such extensions (Chang & Chan-Olmsted, 2010). For example, ESPN tried to launch a mobile cellphone, but retreated after it was clear that no one wanted to pay an extra $200 for Mobile ESPN and switch signal carriers as well—not even avid sports fans.

### Superior Supervision

Convergence forces changes in the ways that managers handle employees, especially in an era of uncertainty. Cooperation is required when media converge to produce a collaborative, cross-promotional product. Chapter 2—in discussing organizational groups and cultures, retention, and motivational challenges—also notes that convergence typically translates into more work for the worker and probably additional stress. The chapter recommends that managers expect such issues, and vary their supervisory approach by working with other departments to facilitate interdepartmental cooperation (Gade, 2008), rethink how they frame convergence (Sylvie & Moon, 2007), and assure journalists that convergence aligns with their professional expectations (Kunelius & Ruusunoksa, 2008). So management techniques sensitive to motivation appear likely to pay dividends in facilitating the adoption of convergence.

But in media organizations, managing will seem somewhat circular, in that every issue connects to every other issue—particularly in convergent circumstances. Whereas an editor may be very much aware of motivational issues such as those above, much morale hinges on how he or she structures the work processes. For instance, an editor asking journalists to report in additional media and become familiar with how those media work soon will have an unhappy staff if he or she provides no accompanying training sessions to alleviate concerns about the perceived complexities of new media formats (Singer, 2004b). These sessions should not only train, but also help managers spot those subordinates willing to be trained, because convergent climates also need to spark creativity among employees in order to meet changing audience demands (Killebrew, 2003;

Sylvie & Gade, 2009). This creativity, in turn, will lead to enhancing employee autonomy (Krumsvik, 2008), another motivation-connected matter. In general, giving employees high autonomy in structuring work promotes creativity and satisfaction with the new media format (Bailyn, 1985).

To avoid getting lost in such "circles," the media manager will need a comprehensive strategy, as noted earlier in this chapter. For internal consequences of adoption and convergence, that strategy obviously will have to be complex, requiring a manager who can allot information and authority, value subordinates, foster creativity, and have influential interpersonal skills, among other things. Using communication, commitment, cooperation, compensation, cultural change, competition, and customers as reference points (Lawson-Borders, 2003), this strategy will address the fears of convergent journalists who aren't really concerned with convergence itself but, rather, with the way managers implement it (Singer, 2004b). Most of this can be viewed within Sylvie and Witherspoon's (2002) suggestions for newspaper leaders in facilitating change (see Table 6.1).

**Table 6.1**  Media Leadership Skills to Enhance Change

| SKILL | SKILL ATTRIBUTES |
| --- | --- |
| Share Control | Follow subordinates' lead; establish feedback mechanisms; allow employees to devise new methods of work; overcome fear of lack of control; gain more confidence. |
| Continuously Communicate | Communicate vision of change clearly and often and through as many means and channels as possible. |
| Institutionalize Commitment to Change | Pay employees enough to make them want to stay; train employees for now and for the future. |
| Teach Continuous Improvement | Tear down or breach departmental walls; foster synergy; frame cooperation as a positive; challenge employees to create new markets; add emotional component to the newspaper. |
| Cultivate Decision-Making Resources | Approach decision making with the "big picture" in mind; define problems carefully and within a larger framework; actively set aside time for thinking; make decisions proactively. |

**External Concerns**

Many of the suggestions in Table 6.1 go a long way, as well, in managing external impact—another way of saying that managing change or innovation directly implies dealing with elements of market structure and how they intertwine. The discussion below highlights some of the more basic market elements. We start with a description of U.S. media audience trends as this text headed toward publication (Mitchell & Rosenstiel, 2012):

- Development of technology (and the audiences that use it) is not controlled by media management. Media companies that generate content traditionally have not devoted resources to research and development, from which technological ideas spring. Companies such as ATT, Apple, Facebook, and Microsoft lead in this area.
- Relatedly, the technology companies, through continuous testing and research, have generated multiple mobile technologies that create the numerous platforms—tablets, cell telephones, social websites—to which media companies must conform their content in order to distribute their products. This attracts additional, new media companies that then compete for audiences and, thus, advertising revenue. Combined with the 2008–2010 recession era, this has meant declining revenue for traditional media companies.
- The new technologies have given audiences easier access to news, annually increasing the number of unique visitors to news sites and, especially with social media, spreading news. Many of traditional media's audiences have reached prerecession levels, thanks to the influx of digitally driven users.
- Still—and despite the financial success of their digital initiatives—many of those traditional media continue to experience declining profit levels or revenue shortfalls, meaning their business models haven't yet enabled them to replace declining traditional revenue with digital dollars. Particularly hard hit are newspapers, network news, magazines, and radio.

**Competition**

These trends suggest that a brand-conscious manager must beware of competition. Not only, for example, have newspapers essentially lost most classified advertising to digital competitors the likes of Craigslist or Monster.com, or radio stations lost listeners to such audio services as Pandora or Spotify, but television websites compete with their newspaper peers in terms of news video. Many newspapers themselves must compete with the Patch sites, which offer "hyperlocal," community-oriented news at a microlevel. And, as more newspaper websites begin to charge audiences for certain content, the local TV website becomes a more viable competitor. Meanwhile, magazines featuring long-form journalism must monitor mobile platforms and other new technologies that may change reading habits and begin to erode their audience bases.

Again, strategy is a manager's best friend. Because consumers rely on brands for regular delivery of goods or services, the manager simultaneously wants to encourage that reliance (so that it becomes a habit) and discourage the likelihood of ending that reliance. Your product must meet or exceed whatever product or service your competitor offers or introduces. As a result, the value chain mentioned earlier becomes all the more important in the manager's toolbox. The manager must decide whether organization restructuring will provide some new or added competitive advantage; i.e., can the manager leverage either the company's assets or abilities to the point that his or her product differentiates itself from competitors' products?

Of course, other types of competition face the media manager beyond just the competition for audiences. Wirtz (2011) developed an effective conceptualization of these competition types:

1. Mission—whether economic or journalistic, monetary or information oriented
2. Submarket—competition in markets in which other media compete for customers (e.g., advertising and news)
3. Conduit—intramediary (competition between the product and all similar products within the relevant medium) vs. intermediary (competition between the product and all similar products across different media)
4. Consumer—competition for the audience's time, money, attention, etc.

But unique products and services also challenge a manager. With newer and more companies entering markets with greater ease because of convergent technology, their products provide adequate substitutes for each other. This encourages market blurring. No longer does a local newspaper have the safe, relative monopoly of its print edition when it starts an online version. The advent of the Internet and online editions means other newspapers compete with the local paper in advertising and information markets (Chyi & Sylvie, 1998). Only by differentiating their products can these media create more distinct markets, but the question then becomes "What is the market *now*?" or, "How *local* is local?"

This one-product, two-market conundrum has presented interesting challenges for newspaper managers: Local advertising still accounts for the overwhelming majority of advertising revenue (upward to 90%); yet more than half of the newspaper's online traffic is from *outside* the local market. So the decision becomes whether to try to build on that nonlocal traffic (and create content geared toward it) or stick to the audience you know best (Sylvie & Chyi, 2007). Options can vary, depending on the company's core abilities. For example, *The Dallas Morning News*'s main website caters to Dallas-proper readers. But—because high school football is so popular in Texas and the newspaper has an extensive suburban/rural network of "stringers" (freelance journalists who cover the games)—the newspaper decided to create SportsDayHS, a cellphone application and site that constantly updates scores and player statistics to followers around the large Dallas–Ft. Worth metropolitan area in North Central Texas (Batsell, 2012).

### Consumer Behavior

As we've seen, media companies try to shelter themselves by identifying their strengths and creatively using those strengths to enhance their existing products and enter new markets. If your TV news network is losing audience share and advertising revenues, you must begin to seek different revenue sources. But to do so, you must have a good understanding of consumer behavior. For example, you should know that although at varying times 288 million American viewers in 2011 watched traditional TV, another 284 million used the Internet, DVRs, and cellphones to do so (Nielsen, 2012). You also need to know that your competitors' revenues went up to prerecession levels, thanks to their other holdings (Mitchell & Rosenstiel, 2012). That says audiences like your competitors, but not you—meaning you must plumb through the data, examine what you do, determine the driving influences, and identify or create strengths to use to compete effectively

Consumers use media to survey the environment, to help make decisions, to provide entertainment, to help them socially, or to help them learn about themselves (Lacy & Simon, 1993). Not only do innovation and technology help improve the measurement of those audiences, as mentioned earlier, it encourages media consumption habits and behaviors. More recently, it has transformed the consumer from a passive listener/

viewer/reader of information to an active participant in the production process. Now consumers do not have to wait until the evening newscast for the current weather or short-term forecast. They need only use a cellphone weather application, find the local weather map on the Web, or watch cable TV's Weather Channel.

As a consequence, audiences have become searchers, seeking media content for informational or entertainment purposes when they want it. Books have been written about the impending decline in citizen behavior that will follow from this kind of media consumption (e.g., Papacharissi, 2009), but managers have little time to worry about anything except increasing audience share. The more popular cellphone applications in 2011 (Nielsen, 2012; see Table 6.2) illustrate audiences searching, which especially concerns managers because half of consumers don't mind receiving advertising on those "apps" if it comes with free content. Using audience behavioral data, as discussed in Chapter 8, represents traditional management discretion in the broadcast and advertising industries and the marketing departments of other media, particularly in the case of audience targeting (e.g., see Smith, Boyle, & Cannon, 2010). But online newsrooms also are becoming somewhat familiar with the practice. Journalists realize that building a news site begins with having audience tracking data—that is, information that shows what people read, when, and for how long, all of which is easily available from website servers (Deuze, 2001). But news managers walk a fine line. They must take care not to replace audience values—i.e., what the audience wants in the way of content—with their own journalistic values that essentially equate to the organizational brand, because the audience can now find quality substitutes for the organization's journalism content if it fails to meet audience needs (MacGregor, 2007; Strömback & Karlsson, 2011).

Certainly, managers should beware letting audience behavior dominate decision making. Steve Jobs, the late cofounder and driving creative force behind Apple's market dominance, preferred his intuition to market research "because customers don't know what they want until

**Table 6.2** Most Popular Cellphone Applications in 2012

| | |
|---|---|
| Games 68% | Sports 31% |
| Maps 45% | Banking 30% |
| Music 45% | Books 23% |
| Social Networking 45% | Restaurants 23% |
| News 33% | Coupons 22% |
| Entertainment 31% | Recommendations 16% |

we've shown them" (Isaacson, 2012, p. 143). Of course, managers should exercise leadership whenever appropriate, but not everyone has Jobs's level of empathy for consumer behavior, or the luxury of the monopolies and the reputation that Apple has. That's especially true for entrepreneurial ventures that are trying to establish a market niche. For example, in 2006, the organizers behind the online upstart *Long Beach Post* tried to create a quality, independent, community-oriented, professional-journalist- *and* citizen-journalist-driven alternative to the established daily newspaper in that California city. But they had to continually watch site traffic to determine if their product was building trust and credibility—and also to assure advertisers that an online ad was an equally safe investment as a print ad during an ongoing recession. Knowing the audience numbers also helped the managers decide whether to restructure and pare down the alternative organization, add new content, extend promotional activities, revamp the ad pricing format, enlarge ad opportunities, and partner with other media (Klein & Vázquez, 2011).

One of the more strategic actions that managers may use in regard to audience behavior comes in the bundling phenomenon, in which the organization sells two or more separate products together at a discounted price. Management assumes the audience will buy a new product—and lessen its uncertainty about that product—if it is sold with a more established, known product. This strategy also allows the company to enter a new market and out-compete another company that doesn't bundle. Television, cable, telephone, Internet, Voice-over-Internet phoning, and cellphone services often get bundled, with the discounted price encouraging audiences to stay loyal to the bundling provider. Cable operators particularly like to provide trial offers and vary the level of discounts, depending on the consumer's choice, while telephone providers such as ATT parlay their brand reputation in offering new cellphone services (Chan-Olmsted & Guo, 2011). No doubt, print and other nonbroadcast media—particularly those with declining audience shares—will begin to offer bundling options as a way to rejuvenate their image and revenue, and as a response to either convergence-driven development of new product offerings or in response to alliance offers from a content-less technology firm.

Regardless, managers must take the possibly perilous action—which Jobs continuously mastered—of understanding how, and in what context, the consumer experiences the product. Coincidentally, that experience constitutes the brand. But many media managers only view the brand as their product's content, which essentially is only one way a consumer can experience media. Other ways include advertising and marketing efforts

(Calder & Malthouse, 2008). Truly visionary media managers will seek to understand, recognize, and take advantage of the new consumer experiences that will continually arise in the future. Their vision will provide insight to new technologies, but also to what consumers want from those technologies. This, in turn, will facilitate media management.

## SUMMARY

This chapter examines managerial approaches to technology, the process of how a company uses or adopts technology, and how technology may affect media organizations and their markets. To summarize, technology has internal and external impacts. Managers have to understand that technology demands adjustment. They must be sensitive as to how and when to manage. A media manager's job is to turn the technology to the company's advantage by using the correct approach.

Before the approach is taken, however, the media manager must have a strategy, peripheral vision, a vehicle for the strategy, and must exercise some leadership. Strategy helps avoid overreacting or unintended results. But strategizing is incomplete without the ability to skillfully lead the strategy, using the right assets, people, and tools (the three components of a vehicle). Vision precedes these three elements, however, because strategy is but a plan for obtaining the vision, which is a succinct characterization of the role and identity of where and what the organization wants to be.

The next step involves choosing from among the structural, technological-task, and sociotechnical approaches, all rooted in a slightly different managerial orientation and each with advantages and disadvantages. Most modern-day managers use some form of the sociotechnical approach. A media company adopts a technology for its own particular reasons. Then it introduces the technology to employees, who interact in various ways with the technology depending on the employee and nature of the task involved. Then management perceptions and employee reactions prompt a period of adjustment, ultimately leading to adoption or rejection of the technology. This adoption process includes the stages of agenda setting, matching, redefining/restructuring, clarifying, and either routinizing or rejecting the technology or idea.

Because most media have begun convergent activities, media management of technology has transformed into a constant managerial function. Ongoing adjustment to technological development and changing audience tastes requires the media manager to manage in an atmosphere of constant change and adjustment—and requires attention to such issues as economic value, branding strategy, communication framing, competitive advantage, and how consumer behavior influences and reacts to those factors. How and when a manager takes action with regard to technology and innovation greatly impacts the company's future.

---

**CASE 6.1 PLANNING CONVERGENCE, PART I**

Your boss asks you to design a converged newsroom operation, capable of producing content for print, broadcast, and online media for your medium-sized market. It must introduce print reporters to an online newsroom. Before you start, however, the boss has given you some questions to answer for her. The questions are:

**Assignment**

1. How will the space basically be organized within the newsroom? How would you place the news, sports, features, etc., editors? How would subject matter fit into space allocation? How would you place reporters and why? Where would print, broadcast, and online staffs go? Would you segregate them?
2. What, in your opinion, is the most important strategic management competency that middle managers should know and which upper management should encourage?
3. What kind of newsroom culture would you want to encourage and how? How would you frame the issue of citizen journalism to current staffers?
4. How can we do this and save operational costs (not including software and equipment)?

---

**CASE 6.2 PLANNING CONVERGENCE, PART II**

With visions of dollar signs dancing in his head, the station's general manager has taken to the idea of "convergence" as another way of cutting costs and increasing profits. As the news director, you've been asked to call a meeting with the local newspaper editor to discuss the feasibility of the idea. But first the GM wants you to sell the idea to your staff—"I want immediate buy-in, and I want to see more team efforts and reporting groups from the reporters," he huffed after your last meeting with him. You narrowly escaped having to implement another idea of his to merge the videography and reporting staffs as a cost-saving move.

The newspaper newsroom already has been issued a directive to reorganize: "The changes should reinforce our long-standing belief in great reporting and writing as the vital center of the paper's journalism. We want to empower journalists and encourage them to work across departments and platforms. In addition, we want to simplify the handling of words, pages, images, and new media, building on the prior move to 'two-touch' editing. Decisions about space and play must happen faster, both in print and online, and in a way that pulls together our now-separate newsrooms. A single editor ultimately ought to be able to oversee all versions of a story, whether it appears in print, online, or on a BlackBerry or iPhone. Space in the newspaper, and editing firepower in general, should be allocated based on a day's news priorities, not a predetermined formula." The paper created a "universal desk" to combine departmental copy-reading processes and bring together many people in varying lower editing positions, as well as many website producers. The desk will do all editing, and decide space allocation and story placement. Stories edited previously for online will provide the start for a print version, and vice versa.

You rose through the ranks, dreaming of producing stories for television. You majored in broadcast at State U. and grew up hating newspapers for the trashy way the print types looked down on broadcast types in college. Of course, you know the newspaper folks probably feel the same way about your staff (you've heard plenty of "Ron Burgundy" jokes).

Your assignments editor says that your typical TV newsroom already has started talking. Here's a list of comments he's overheard just today: "We don't have time to do what we have to do now, much less do anything new," said the crime reporter. "It's just another screwy management move," opined the education reporter. Your veteran anchor has chimed in with: "Sounds good. You first." And then, the weekend producer expressed what most of his colleagues were thinking: "This is about cutting jobs, isn't it?" Finally, the station meteorologist, a native Texan, on seeing a newspaper reporter at the station, said: "I don't know what y'all would do to him in the newsroom, but we—we would treat him pretty ugly down in Texas."

**Assignment**
1. What sort of cultural maneuvering will you need to do to get the staff to buy into the idea? How would you overcome the competitive animosity? What would be the first thing you would do?
2. How would you go about developing some sort of team structure? Would you do so according to ability? Experience? Age? Gender? What trait or characteristic would you use first in making team assignments? Why? Which would you avoid using? Why? Would you mimic the newspaper's organizational intentions?
3. What message would you bring to an organizational meeting with the editor of the cooperating newspaper newsroom? What framing strategy would you use to immediately defuse any stereotypical comments or concerns on either side?
4. Let's say you disagree with your GM's plan. Write a memo telling him as much. Have a three-classmate panel read the memo, take it to the rest of the class (which constitutes the GM's advisory board), and have them vote as to whether you should be fired, directed to implement the partnership regardless, given a chance to implement a modified version of the partnership, or patted on the back and taken to lunch.

**CASE 6.3 DECIPHERING THE MARKET**

You are Carol Ann Conant, the publisher of a small community newspaper, *Kain Courant Frenchman*. The paper has 1,000 subscribers in the small rural community of Kain Courant—and is nearing war with a competing publication, *The Sassafron Timeless*.

The *Frenchman* has teamed with the local college's engineering school to create a cellphone application specifically targeted to the African American community in Kain Courant. The app, KainDo, will start selling for $1.99 as soon as next month, and you expect to eventually have about 3,000 sold in the Sassafron area and another 3,000 nationally to former Kain Courant residents and their descendants. The area is known for its unique southern French culture, architecture, and legacy; many natives moved out of the area in the 1960s and 1970s in search of better jobs and opportunities, but are still connected to the town and its culture.

The app is very much neighborhood- and community-oriented and will allow neighbors to interact with one another, report loose livestock and auto accidents directly to the county, announce festivals, garage and bake sales, and school-related events, warn neighbors about crime, post musings about the neighborhood, ask the newspaper and fellow subscribers questions, and post pictures of weddings, new babies, and anniversaries. The app ideally creates a neighborhood within a real community and will serve the news needs of subscribers anywhere, especially those in Sassafron, where *the Frenchman* has the lowest concentration of readers. Despite the impending launch, you feel further research is needed on models of good weekly apps.

*Timeless* publisher and editor in chief Charles "Boo" Dan has warned you he'll come out with a better, cheaper app if you go ahead with your plans. "We really have *Frenchman* news," he said, referring to Kain Courant natives, although historically folks from "The Courant" have eschewed living in Sassafron because they feel that the town establishments discriminate against country folk. The *Timeless* is owned by a large, regional newspaper chain and is edited in the chain's largest paper in the state, the *Jefferson Standard*.

You know focus groups suggested that no app could serve the area like *the Frenchman*'s innovation, so Dan has been imploring his superiors to bring out an app that would facilitate price searching and coupon marketing to small communities such as Sassafron.

Information gathered from the latest U.S. Census Bureau report estimated that of Sassafron's 19,540 residents, 2,365 residents, or more than 12%, had Kain Courant roots. Almost 5% of the state's four million residents are of French origin.

Dan's remarks illustrate views of other Sassafronians, who say that the city needs to extend a much-needed hand to Kain Courant because it's historically been undercovered and underserved. The 7,000-circulation *Timeless* covers a city dominated by Etatcoin U., they say, and it is easy to overlook the less-affluent, rural residents down the highway in Kain Courant.

You've been hesitant, however, to admit *The Timeless* is a competitor, insisting it all depends on how a community newspaper is defined. Does it start out with some point of view or advocacy? You think so. You wanted to have a very good newspaper covering the community of Kain Courant.

But experts on community media say it takes more than stories on people to make a community newspaper and that if *The Timeless* owners could leverage relationships with major advertisers to create a campaign courting Kain Courant—accessing advertising dollars traditionally earmarked for smaller media—it wouldn't matter if the new app lived up to the classic mission of a community newspaper. Your publisher friends in similarly sized papers insist that for years they've gone to major advertisers and been denied advertising. They've told you that if *The Timeless* comes into Kain Courant and brings all its advertiser buddies, it will send a signal to all the chains out there, and then you (and they) won't be able to compete. So they're looking at how you handle this test.

All this attention surprises you. The criticism intensified when you fired your editor, Kain Courant-native Jannee Rachal, for reasons known only to you. It heightened the suspicions that the paper's management might not be comfortable with Kain Courant ways, which have a history of diehard advocacy for all things French. "Having a *Frenchman* without the advocacy won't work," you were told by your friend, Etatcoin media management professor Woods Farmer.

You admit that *the Frenchman* is a hybrid of sorts between a traditional community paper and an alternative. If this seems phony to Kain folk, they won't buy it, you believe.

**Assignment**
1. At the moment, what is your most pressing problem as publisher of *the Frenchman*?
2. Of the external impacts listed in this chapter, which is your greatest weakness in this situation and how would you resolve it?
3. Should *the Frenchman* be classified as a "French newspaper"? Why or why not? Should you rehire Rachal?
4. Where is the town of Sassafron in the adoption process regarding your app? What is your brand and what strategy would help extend it? Should it be extended?

5. Should *The Timeless* help Kain Courant with local advertisers? Should you be concerned at all—and if so, to what degree—with *The Timeless*?
6. How does the model of starting a community or rural paper differ from the one of starting a small-town paper? Did Conant err in any way?

---

### CASE 6.4 THE CASE OF SOCIAL MEDIA

You are the research director for *The Blitz*, a magazine that covers the music scene in Waterloo, the capital of the state of Mind and a top 20 market. Last week, the publisher insisted on meeting with you to discuss the magazine's strategy regarding social media and tablet readers. He thinks the magazine should be developing a strategy so that it can create a new, viable revenue stream in 2 years. You're skeptical, so you've put your staff to work on several questions:

1. What are the user issues surrounding social media? What added value could you produce for something like Facebook? Are publications making any money in that medium? How much use could Facebook users have for a music publication within a Facebook setting?
2. What kind of 140-character messages (like those in Twitter) would emanate from *The Blitz*? What use would followers have for such short messages? How would you market such messages in *The Blitz* itself? Could actual journalism occur in such messages or would they be more of a headline service? To what degree would *Blitz* staff writers use this tool? What's the added value that you could provide readers?
3. What would you do to separate yourself from competing national magazines in using Facebook and Twitter? How would you position the local music scene? What type of storytelling would this tend to foster and does it fit with what subscribers would want in the actual print magazine? How would you get buy-in from the reporting staff?
4. What would social media add to the magazine's brand? Currently, this is what you have on your website: "Mind is known for its rareness—not just Minders but the Mind

way of life. Most folks can't explain Minders, but they certainly notice them and their singular Mind conceit. It is in the rich Mind history. There is something different about Mind. Minders, when it comes to music, are especially pleased. Although some non-Minders associate us with rock icons only, Minders know that Mind inculcates a wide variety of music; our music echoes the culture. Today, the Mind music tableau is bigger, more lively and rising swifter than ever. We feature Minders' incredible role in and for music. Our hue-full, lustrous journal is a Minder's start for all things music in Mind. We inform and amuse our readers. We inform them about great Mind bands, as well as dish up a heaping helping of music history. We amuse them with funny anecdotes about many of the state's flamboyant characters, as well as cover music events from around Mind, like mud in the water."

5. How would you sell advertisers on the social media products?

**Assignment**

1. Pick one of the questions above, research it, and report back to the class.
2. Which is the greater concern or unknown with this product now—technology, audience, branding, strategy, competition, or consumer behavior—and why?
3. What would it cost to finance testing and development of this technology?
4. Is this technology more likely to be developed by a journalistic-oriented organization (e.g., *The Blitz*), or by a technology-based group? Which would have the most trouble managing the product once it's developed?

# CHAPTER 7

# Market Analysis

At no other time in the past century has it been as critically important as it is now for emerging media professionals to understand market analysis. As noted throughout this book, rapid changes in media markets and technologies have transformed the nature of audience demand for content and dramatically increased competition for audiences and advertisers. Additionally, new technologies are making entirely new media businesses possible, while the restructuring of traditional media industries means more and more media professionals now work either freelance or on contract for specific projects.

For the media entrepreneur, knowing how to analyze the market for their content or professional skills is a matter of basic survival: It can mean the difference between profit or bankruptcy for a new business, or getting a freelance or contract assignment—or not. Even legacy media companies now seek evidence that job applicants understand the media market environment—and their own role in it as a branded media product—when considering new hires. Many media executives say they look for evidence that job applicants are actively—and professionally—branding themselves and their professional abilities via their blogs, Web pages, and social media accounts—and thereby attracting a personal following that can translate into larger and more loyal audiences for their employers (various media executives, personal communication, 2012). No longer is market analysis the job of midlevel media managers. Today, it's part of the responsibilities of nearly everyone in the industry.

This chapter explores the fundamentals of media market analysis and examines how those principles should be applied by media managers, media entrepreneurs, and emerging media professionals.

### THE FUNDAMENTALS OF MARKET ANALYSIS

Simply defined, market analysis is the process of identifying the opportunities and risks for a particular company in a particular market or for a particular product. Two primary approaches to market analysis have evolved. One focuses on the firm or individual's resources and capabilities, while the other focuses on the customer's needs and uses for the product (Day, 1981). Both approaches play critical roles in media management and go hand in hand with planning (see Chapter 5) and marketing research (see Chapter 8).

You can think about market analysis in three ways. First, it is part of the daily routine for media managers and, increasingly, media personnel at all levels. In today's rapidly changing media environment, everyone at every level needs to constantly scan the competitive environment, looking for new competitors, new technologies or applications that could be a new business opportunity or threat, and new product ideas and production techniques. The goal of market analysis is to spot unseized opportunities and emerging competitive threats (Paley, 2004).

Second, market analysis also can be a formal project conducted before a company or entrepreneur makes a major new investment, develops a new product, or changes an overall business strategy. More to the point for emerging media professionals, it is a critical and necessary first step when launching your own media company or before investing your time and money in developing your own media product.

The third and increasingly important application of market analysis is to one's own career. Analyzing the market for a news story, film, app, game, etc. before pitching it to a supervisor or investor makes it more likely that you'll get the support you need. Editors, news directors, and agents will be more interested if you can tell them what your project's market niche will be, what it will cost to produce in terms of both time and money, how it compares to existing content in the market, and what it is likely to return in terms of profit, circulation or ratings, and prestige. But perhaps even more important to career management is the need for media professionals to understand *themselves* as a product in the highly competitive media labor market and to critically analyze—and market—the differences in what they can offer potential employers or investors compared to their competition.

### DEFINING THE "MARKET" IN A MARKET ANALYSIS

The first step in a market analysis is to define the market that needs to be analyzed. A market usually is defined by two elements: (a) geography and

(b) product (Albarran, 1996). Geography refers to where the product is sold or bought. For example, a newspaper's geographic market includes the area in which it distributes its papers, either through home delivery, newsstand sales, or significant digital distribution. A television or radio station's geographic market is the area reached by its broadcast signal, while a local cable system's market is the area in which it serves subscribers. While local media companies may have carefully defined geographic markets, some media sectors—film, television, music, online producers, and video game developers—see the entire world as their geographic market.

Product refers to the type of product a company sells. A market analysis for a product would include demand for that product and the number of competitors selling that product, or substitutes for it, in the geographic market. For example, how many local televisions stations broadcast in the community? How many other types of video competitors are there also competing for audiences and advertisers, such as cable and satellite networks, online video streaming services, etc.?

For media companies that depend on advertising as a major source of revenue, analyzing the product aspect of their markets is more complicated than for most industries because advertising-supported media products are *joint commodities*, also called *dual products*. A *joint commodity* is a product that is sold simultaneously into two different markets (Albarran, 2010). Media companies such as newspapers and broadcasters "sell" content to the audience, while selling advertisers the time or space around that content. Consequently, managing advertising-supported media means separately analyzing the demand and competition for audience attention and advertiser revenue.

Media economists have identified a third market that media managers and entrepreneurs must analyze and manage: the investment market for the media company itself (Albarran, 1996). Publicly traded media corporations compete with other media companies and other industries to attract investors. Success in the investment market increases the value of the company and makes it easier for the company to get cash or loans to use for growth and to buy or start new enterprises. Consequently, many management decisions—content choices, the acquisition or sale of subsidiaries, and even hiring and layoffs—are influenced by how the decision will affect the company's stock price or overall value in the investment market.

For many media entrepreneurs, the investment market is different, but no less important. Few individuals have the cash they need to launch a business and keep it alive until it becomes profitable. Entrepreneurs must, after all, buy all the equipment needed to produce their media products, hire and pay people either for their expertise or assistance; market their product so that potential customers know it exists; pay for the business's space and other overhead, such as insurance and utilities; and support their personal living expenses for as long as it takes for the company to become profitable—which usually takes several years.

Potential entrepreneurs, therefore, also need to analyze their business's position in the investment market. For entrepreneurs, that usually means analyzing how well they can compete with other entrepreneurs and inventors for *venture capital* investments. *Venture capitalists* are wealthy individuals—and sometimes large corporations—who make direct investments in high-risk startup companies. Venture capitalists carefully evaluate all the proposals they receive from entrepreneurs, and invest when they think an idea has true profit potential—and a company founder who has the management ability to turn that idea into a successful business. Venture capitalists' goal, of course, is to be an early investor in the next Facebook or Apple Inc.

### CONDUCTING A MARKET ANALYSIS

The market analysis process carefully examines three types of factors: (a) external conditions, (b) internal conditions, and (c) financial conditions (Stevens, Sherwood, & Dunn, 1993) (Table 7.1).

Most discussions of market analysis focus on external conditions because more external than internal factors exist, and managers have less control over them. The specific external conditions that a manager examines vary by situation.

In practice, these factors overlap and mutually influence one another. However, the categories provide a useful framework for trying to make sense out of a complex process.

### External Conditions

*Forecasting long-term industry trends.* The first questions to ask in a market analysis are fairly general: (a) What are the overall trends in the market? (b) Are there new technologies or other factors on the horizon that may change the market?

Unfortunately, long-term forecasts are increasingly difficult to make. They require examining a number of factors, including trends in new technologies, trends in audience demand for media products, demographic and lifestyle trends in society, and trends in advertiser demand in the various media sectors.

**Table 7.1**  The Market Analysis Process

---

The Market Analysis Process
*External Conditions*
Forecasting long-term trends
Trends in market growth and development
Trends in product demand
Price
Price of substitutes and complements
Consumer income
Consumer tastes
Trends in political/regulatory conditions
Technology forecasting
Specific market factors
Market structure
Seller concentration
Buyer concentration
Barriers to entry
Product differentiation
Cost structures
Vertical integration
Access to distribution channels
Target market
Economic and sociological conditions
*Internal Conditions*
Company mission and objectives
Organizational structure and culture
Expertise and product mix
Resources
Strengths
Weaknesses
Opportunities
Threats
*Financial Conditions*
Revenues
Costs
Return on investment
Availability of capital
Intangible returns

---

*Trends in new technologies.* Since the turn of the 21st century, the flurry of new digital-media technologies emerging on the market has made life difficult for media forecasters. For example, the video game industry and social media have emerged as new competitors to existing media for audiences and advertisers. Smartphone apps and tablets have made accessing mobile media content easier, so the audience for digitally distributed content continues to rise, affecting audience and advertiser demand in traditional media markets such as newspapers, magazines, and film. Simultaneously, the development of low-cost digital-media production technologies such as cameras and video editing software, combined with the development of sites such as YouTube, has flooded the Internet with new competitors. People around the world are producing video and blogs and uploading them to the Web without seeking any financial return for their contributions. This free content has been stunningly successful at competing with professionally produced content for audiences, further reducing audience demand—and therefore advertiser demand—for paid content. As new media innovations constantly beget other new media innovations, predicting the "Next Big Thing" and its effect on the market will be increasingly difficult.

*Trends in audience demand for media products.* Demand is a measure of the quantity of a product that people will buy at a particular price (Hoskins, McFadyen, & Finn, 2004). It is a function of the cost of the product, the cost of substitutes and complements for the product, the ability of consumers to pay the costs of consumption, and consumers' tastes and utilities (Stigler, 1952).

Research shows that consumer demand for media products, in general, has risen steadily in recent decades (Wakslag, 2008). Unfortunately, increased competition has fragmented the audience into smaller and smaller pieces, and changing consumer tastes have slowed demand for specific types of media products. For example, between 2000 and 2011, total daily newspaper circulation in America dropped more than 20%, even as the U.S. population rose more than 10.5% during the same period (Newspaper Association of America, 2014; U.S. Census Bureau, 2014). Broadcast television networks also suffered. While total primetime viewing continued to rise, primetime viewing of traditional television sources, such as the major broadcast networks, public television, and local independent stations, all declined (Stelter, 2013). Similarly, the introduction of wireless electronic readers and tablets in recent years have greatly affected consumer preferences for how they receive books, magazines, and newspapers, reducing demand for printed versions of those media products.

*Product price.* The cost of most types of products consumers buy is measured strictly by price. With media products, however, the cost to the consumer includes time, as well as money, because consuming media products takes time (Priest, 1994). You have to invest hours in watching a movie, reading a book, or playing a video game—time that then can't be used for other purposes. Indeed, for many consumers, the time-cost of media consumption is a bigger factor in their product choices than the financial cost.

In predicting demand for media products, most media managers calculate that demand will fall as the time required for consumption rises—although obvious exceptions exist and technologies may be changing some traditional viewing patterns. Editors have shortened news stories because research shows audiences are more likely to change channels or turn the page if a story runs long. Television miniseries, which require viewers to watch every episode in order to keep track of the story, are now relegated mostly to premium cable channels. Too small a percentage of viewers have been willing to commit to appointment viewing in recent years to make such content attractive to advertisers.

Now, however, more consumers are using time-shifted viewing, so the consumption of miniseries and other long-form or multiprogram episodes may increase. Consumers also view on smartphones or tablets, either saving the content on devices for future reading and viewing, or using on-demand apps such as HBO GO, where episodes of shows or miniseries can be viewed anytime, anywhere. Only through market analysis can such new trends or technologies, or new interpretations of time for consumers, be assessed for their potential influence on future products and profitability.

In the competition for audiences' and advertisers' money, price negatively relates to demand for most products and services: As prices go up, demand goes down and vice versa (Hoskins et al., 2004). The relationship between the change in price and the change in demand is called elasticity of demand, and the sensitivity of demand-to-price varies by product. When the price of a product increases 1%, if demand decreases more than 1%, demand for the product is said to be elastic. If demand decreases less than 1% when the price rises 1%, demand for the product is inelastic. If price and demand change at the same rate, the product is said to have unit elasticity.

Media managers engaged in market analysis need to understand the demand for their products because it affects their ability to set prices. If demand for a product is inelastic, increasing the price likely will result in higher revenues because demand will fall more slowly than the price rises. However, if demand for a product is elastic, then an increase in the price can actually cost the company money as demand falls faster than revenue rises.

For example, look at the case of a city magazine we'll call *Downtown*, which has a circulation of 100,000 per month (Table 7.2). If the subscription price is $1 per copy, *Downtown* will generate $100,000 per month in revenue from circulation. If demand for the magazine is inelastic, when management increases the cover price 25% to $1.25, the company will increase its monthly circulation revenue to $112,500, even if the number of subscribers falls 10% to 90,000. The gain in revenue from the price increase will exceed the loss in revenue from the drop in circulation. However, if demand were elastic so that a 25% increase in cover price produced a 26% decrease in circulation, circulation revenue would fall.

The fact that most media are joint commodities further complicates the process of pricing because the market analyst also has to consider the potential impact on advertising revenue. Advertisers buy ads on the basis of circulation size or ratings. Usually prices are set on the basis of cost-per-thousand (CPM) readers or viewers reached. Thus, in the case *Downtown*, advertising rates and, thus, revenue also may fall when circulation drops.

If demand had unit elasticity and a 10% decline in circulation for *Downtown* caused a 10% drop in advertising revenue, the magazine would still enjoy an increase in total revenues. However, the increase would be small because the loss in advertising revenue would almost offset the growth in circulation revenue. If reader demand for the magazine were elastic, however, following a cover-price increase, the publication would wind up with much lower revenues, even if ad rates and the volume of advertising sold stayed the same. The potential effects of price increases on sales to readers and advertisers must be considered when a media company thinks about raising its prices.

Elasticity of demand also refers to the effects that changes in the health of the overall economy may have on consumer demand for a

**Table 7.2**  The Effects of Elasticity of Demand and Price Increases on Revenue

|  | CURRENT | INELASTIC | ELASTIC |
| --- | --- | --- | --- |
| Price | $1.00 | $1.25 (125%) | $1.25 (125%) |
| Circulation | 100,000 | 90,000 (210%) | 74,000 (226%) |
| Circ. Revenue | $100,000 | $112,500 | $92,500 |
| Ad Rate (CPM) | $10 | $10 | $10 |
| Number of ads per issue | 100 | 100 | 100 |
| Ad Revenue | $100,000 | $90,000 | $74,000 |
| Total Revenue | $200,000 | $202,500 | $166,500 |

particular product—known as "income elasticity." The money an advertiser spends on advertising is somewhat flexible, and companies often cut those funds first in economic downturns. As a result, demand for advertising can be elastic, and as the Great Recession that began in 2008 clearly demonstrated, the media industry is highly vulnerable to changes in the national or local economy.

On the consumer side, demand for media products tends to be relatively inelastic, although it varies from product to product. Audience demand for broadcast radio and television content is immune to changes in price and the economy because consumers pay nothing to receive it. Sales of expensive premium cable channels and tickets to movies are much more sensitive to price and economic swings.

*Substitutes and complements.* Price elasticity also relates to the number and prices of substitute and complement products available to consumers. A substitute is a product that can be used in place of another product. A complement is a product purchased to use with another product. Video games complement video game consoles, which are nearly useless without the game software.

If the price of a substitute product is significantly lower than your product, and the substitute's utility or usefulness is comparable, then the elasticity of demand for both products increases. This was demonstrated over the past decade as newspapers launched websites that allowed audiences to access online content without paying for it. Paid subscriptions dropped at least in part because of the availability of the free Web access. In response, news organizations began setting up paywalls on their websites, forcing readers to pay for content whether they received it digitally or in print.

Similarly, if the prices of complementary products are too high or the quality is inferior, then demand for the product will fall. Demand for video game consoles is driven largely by the price, quality, and variety of the games that are created for a given console.

Media managers and entrepreneurs must carefully evaluate the value their product offers that audiences and advertisers cannot get from substitute products. Part of that evaluation focuses on price. Audiences may accept lower quality if they can pay less for it. Thus, it's necessary to look at the total value returned to the target audience or advertiser for the price paid, as compared to competing products or services.

*Consumer income.* A person's demand for products is related to his or her income. As individual income rises, audiences have more discretionary money to spend on optional goods and services such as information and entertainment—in other words, media.

Because most media products are joint commodities, consumer income also has an impact on advertising demand. Advertisers generally prefer to reach more affluent audience segments, because those individuals have more money to spend on both necessities and luxuries. Advertisers often are willing to pay a higher CPM to reach more affluent audiences.

*Consumer tastes and utilities.* Consumer taste refers to the question of why audiences choose one product over another. Few theories predict changes in consumer taste but, from an economic view, consumers must find *utility* in a product in order to be willing to buy it. *Utility* is the usefulness or satisfaction a product provides.

While consumer tastes change and often defy prediction, research has identified some of the reasons people choose some types of media content over others. These practices, which are known as "uses and gratifications," of media use include keeping up with what's going on in the world, decision making, entertainment and diversion, using media as part of social-cultural interactions, improving self-understanding, and fulfilling psychological needs (such as watching a funny video to make yourself laugh after a bad day) (Lacy & Simon, 1993; Severin & Tankard, 1992).

Predicting consumer demand for media is always difficult. But however hard it may be, it is a critical element in successful market analysis. Fortunately, there are some indicators, such as socioeconomic and demographic trends, that help.

### Trends in Advertiser Demand for Media Products

As media audiences fragment and new technologies create new vehicles for advertising, many advertisers are rethinking their traditional approaches to advertising and marketing. Throughout the last half of the 20th century, national advertisers built their campaigns around television, newspapers, and magazines. Today, advertisers are broadening their approaches, spreading their ad budgets across some combination of online placements, social media, search engine optimization, webisodes and similar creative messaging such as branded entertainment, event sponsorship, direct mail and e-mail, theaters, video games, and product placements in films and at sporting and entertainment events.

This fragmentation of the advertising market since 2000 has made it increasingly difficult for media businesses to survive on advertising-only business models. Today, the biggest challenge facing media managers worldwide is the need to develop new business models that generate enough revenue to keep their media companies alive.

## POLITICAL AND REGULATORY CONDITIONS

Changes in laws, policies, and regulations affect all media companies. Laws regulating wages, benefits, labor relations, working conditions, taxes, employee health and safety, and the environment apply to all businesses. Because regulatory policies change over time, market analyses must consider the current state of regulation in product and geographic markets and any changes that might happen. For a full discussion of legal, policy, and ethical issues affecting media, see Chapter 9.

Within the media industry, some industry sectors such as broadcasting and cable tend to be more subject to government regulation than are the print media. For example, in most countries, broadcasters must get a license from the government in order to go on the air, and in the United States, broadcasters operate under federal rules governing decency and obscenity in content. These regulations are imposed on broadcasters because the scarcity of broadcast spectrum limits the number of broadcast licenses that can be issued. Thus, broadcasters are generally required to serve the general public and its wide range of tastes, rather than to focus on niche audiences. In contrast, the content of cable and satellite networks tends to be less strictly regulated because people pay to receive it and can cancel their subscriptions if the content offends them.

Digitally distributed content is subject to very little regulation since users must seek it out. Criminal statutes, such as laws against fraud and child pornography, apply to digital content just as they do content distributed across traditional platforms. Some nations also limit their citizens' access to certain content on the Internet for political reasons. But in most cases, media managers and entrepreneurs developing online-based media products and services face fewer regulations.

## SPECIFIC MARKET FACTORS

In addition to long-term forecasting, market analysis includes examination of the specific conditions that will affect success in a given product or geographic market. Among those conditions are market structure, the target market, and the market's economic and sociological environments.

### Market Structure

The structure of a market is one of the most important considerations in a market analysis. When conducting a market analysis, you need to examine the structure of both the product and geographic markets of interest to you. The elements of market structure that should concern managers and entrepreneurs are seller concentration, buyer concentration, vertical integration, product differentiation, cost structures, and barriers to entry.

### Seller Concentration

*Seller concentration* refers to the number of companies competing in the market. Too much or too little seller concentration in a market makes it hard for a startup company to survive. In the digital online market, for example, there are so many websites competing for the audience's attention, it's hard to attract an audience large enough to generate the revenue needed to survive. On the other hand, if there are only a few competitors in a market, the established players usually have enough market share to capture economies of scale. That reduces their production costs, and they can pass those savings on to customers, offering lower prices than smaller companies can afford to match. The ideal level of seller concentration in a market depends on the size of the market and the demand for the product.

Analyzing seller concentration in media markets is hard because different types of media products substitute for one another for both consumers and advertisers. Someone who once subscribed to the local daily newspaper can now get local news online from sources such as *Yahoo* or local bloggers without having to pay for it. More to the point, all forms of media—news media, theaters, video games, social media, etc.—compete for the local audience's time and attention and, increasingly, for advertising revenue.

### Buyer Concentration

*Buyer concentration* is the opposite of seller concentration; it measures the number of buyers in the market for a particular product. Again, media managers and entrepreneurs have to examine this from the perspective of both audiences and potential advertisers, if advertising is part of the business model.

Buyer concentration asks whether there are enough potential buyers in a market to make it worthwhile to produce and distribute a product. For example, if there were only one video production company in a small, outlying university town a couple hour's drive from the nearest major urban area, there would be too much buyer concentration in the video labor market to support 20 new video production graduates who all want to stay in town and make a living freelancing. Similarly, a video-production house that depends on one or two major clients for most of its business could be in serious trouble if it loses a client.

It is particularly important to analyze buyer concentration among advertisers when advertising is part of the media business model. Again, having too little or too much buyer concentration is a problem. Too little buyer concentration means there may be many advertisers, but they buy only small amounts of time or space. In such cases, it may cost the media company more to locate, negotiate with, and produce and distribute ads for small customers than those customers actually pay for the advertising. The fragmenting of advertising markets in recent years has made this a familiar problem to media managers and entrepreneurs.

The opposite problem is having too much buyer concentration. Not all businesses are potential advertisers. Most companies that advertise through the mass media sell products or services directly to consumers, such as automobile dealers, fast-food restaurants, banks, and insurers. When a media company is forced to depend on one or two large advertisers or subscribers for most of its revenue—which can easily happen in small towns—it becomes vulnerable to control by those customers. Large advertisers can negotiate lower prices and other benefits, such as positive news coverage, because the media company can't afford to risk losing the client.

## Vertical Integration

Another element of market structure is *vertical integration*, where a company also owns its suppliers or distributors. Vertical integration gives a company competitive advantage because it has better control over costs, supply, or distribution.

For example, if you develop a terrific idea for a new niche cable network, the challenge would be getting distribution by cable and satellite systems. Given that the channel capacity of cable and satellite systems is limited, getting carriage for a new, unproven, independently owned network is extremely difficult. In contrast, if a cable or satellite distribution company develops a new cable network, the new network can be distributed first on its own systems. Once the new network has had a chance to prove it can attract audiences, it becomes much easier to convince other systems to carry it.

## Product Differentiation

*Product differentiation* is the degree to which products in the market are different enough to offer consumers real choices. Media companies often fail to provide audiences much product variety, filling their schedules with sequels, spin-offs, and thinly disguised copies of already-popular programs. In the United States, when *Law and Order* became a hit in the 1990s, NBC spun off multiple versions of the same concept for the next decade. CBS did the same thing with *CSI*. In the reality TV genre, *American Idol* and *America's Got Talent* clearly target the same audience, as do shows such as *Survivor* and *Amazing Race*.

The media manager and entrepreneur have to ask whether an idea differs too much or too little from what's already available. If it differs too little, audiences won't have much reason to choose it over the original version. If it differs too much, the investment risk goes up because it may not ever find an audience.

The fact that demand for media content varies a great deal from person to person increases the risks for media project managers (Priest, 1994). You might love a book or movie, but your best friend hates it. Worse, the product usually has to be fully produced before it can be test marketed. A film has to be finished or nearly finished before it can show sneak previews. With the possible exception of such forms as Wiki books and Zines, most authors don't produce and sell a chapter of their book before sitting down to write the whole story. By the time the audience sees a media product, the producer has paid most of the cost of production and stands to lose big if the audience doesn't like it.

The usual response to this production risk among media managers is to produce sequels and spin-offs. If the first film or television series was successful, the sequel probably will have a built-in fan base. An entirely new idea, or a production that uses unknown talent, may have no audience at all. Therefore, media managers and entrepreneurs must try to maximize product differentiation while, at the same time, minimizing risk.

### Cost Structures

Media producers and entrepreneurs also have to consider their cost structures. *Cost structures* refers to production costs and includes fixed and variable costs. Fixed costs are costs over which managers have little control because you can't eliminate them. High fixed costs require the manager or entrepreneur to generate higher revenues in order to be able to stay in business. A prime example of this problem can be seen right now in the newspaper industry. The cost of replacing the high-speed, four-color Web presses needed to print most daily newspapers is extremely high. Web presses can cost $40 million or more (Wilson, 2012). With newspaper circulation and revenues falling in the United States, many experts say the printed newspaper will largely disappear in the next generation as existing presses wear out, and newspapers find it impossible to pay to replace them.

Variable costs are costs over which a manager has some control, such as travel and entertainment budgets and, to a more limited degree, personnel, advertising, and marketing expenses. Media products are "talent products" (Reca, 2006), which means media products are created through the knowledge and talents of the specific individuals who produce them. Because of that, personnel generally is one of the biggest costs in a media company's budget.

### Barriers to Entry

A *barrier to entry* is anything that makes it difficult for a new competitor to enter the market. If a media company already is in a market, having barriers to entry against new competitors is desirable. If you're trying to start a new company or move into a new market, barriers to entry are a problem.

All the elements of market structure discussed so far are barriers to entry of one kind or another, but there are others as well. For example, a shortage of people with the right skills in the local labor force can be a barrier to entry. For digital media entrepreneurs, a lack of knowledge about technology or computer programming can be a barrier to entry. For graduating broadcasting and film students, the entertainment industry's tendency to depend on proven talent is a barrier to entry in the job market. Media managers constantly scan their current and proposed markets for barriers to entry, both the obvious ones and those that are more subtle.

### The Target Market

A market analysis necessarily includes an analysis of the target market. From the standpoint of media companies, not all audiences are created equal. Some audiences are more desirable to advertisers than others, which makes those audiences more valuable as target markets, if advertising is part of the business model. For media businesses that depend on sales or subscriptions, the targeted audience not only has to want the product, they also have to have the money to buy it.

As a general rule, women 18 to 49 years old are the most desirable target market for advertisers because they tend to make most of the household buying decisions. Advertisers also believe that people 18 to 49 still have flexible brand preferences and are more likely than older viewers to be influenced by advertising. For content or products sold directly to audiences, the growth in women's earning power over recent decades also makes them a desirable target market.

Despite the general preference for women, advertisers often are willing to pay a premium to place ads around content that successfully attracts narrow or hard-to-reach audience segments (Napoli, 2003). For example, young men spend less time using traditional media than young women, so content that attracts young men often is sold to advertisers at a higher CPM. The same thing can be true for any content that succeeds in reaching particularly desirable niche audiences, such as business executives and some ethnic groups. When a media outlet targets a mass audience, as a daily newspaper or the broadcast networks do, advertisers may reach more people, but only a small percentage of the people they're paying to reach are potential customers. Buying time or space in media targeted to a narrow audience allows advertisers to know exactly who they are reaching and increases the chances that their audience will become their customers.

Unfortunately, as more media abandon mass audiences for niche audiences, large segments of the population—those groups that are less attractive to advertisers—find themselves underserved by content that meets their information and entertainment needs. People older than 49 find few television programs with storylines built around their interests, issues, or lives. Similarly, in the past decade, radio stations that program music from the 1950s and 1960s for Baby Boomers have had problems keeping advertisers. As more stations changed their music formats in the early part of the last decade to appeal to younger listeners, the over-49 age group became earlier adopters of subscriber-supported satellite radio, because it offered channels of the music they liked.

Historically, media companies also have ignored ethnic minorities because relatively few advertisers specifically targeted minorities as potential customers. Fortunately, that has started to change. The number of cable networks targeted to specific ethnic and language audiences in the United States has grown faster since 2000 than the populations of the targeted groups (Coffey, 2007). Indeed, Spanish-language television and radio is one of the fastest-growing formats in the United States, and many other countries are seeing similar expansions of multicultural programming.

But if targeting audience sectors may leave some audiences underserved, that may spell opportunity for the media entrepreneur. Serving an underserved market is what entrepreneurship is all about. To do that successfully, however, media managers and entrepreneurs must understand the nature and limitations of their targeted audiences. They must be sure their targeted market can generate enough revenue through sales or advertising to return the investment on production.

### Demographic, Economic, and Sociological Conditions

The final element in an analysis of the external conditions in a market is demographic, economic, and sociological conditions in the targeted market. In targeted geographic markets, that might include such things as the unemployment rate, long-term growth trends in the area, and the diversity of business and industry in the area economy. For demographically targeted audiences, external conditions might include median income, education, religion, political and social values, language preferences, and cultural history, preferences, or sensitivities.

The reasons why managers and entrepreneurs would want to understand local economic conditions probably are obvious—people living in more affluent communities will have more money to buy both media products and advertised consumer goods. Thus, revenue from both direct sales and advertising is likely to be higher for media companies serving wealthier communities. Additionally, the business mix and economic environment in a community also predicts advertising sales for advertising-supported media.

For media managers, however, it also is important to understand a community's sociological profile or *psychographics*. Psychographics refers to people's attitudes, values, goals, and preferences. These characteristics shape people's lifestyles and the type of media content they will consume.

In recent decades, there have enormous changes in the demographics and psychographics of the United States and, indeed, many countries around the world. The world's population has been growing rapidly, and that growth has been accompanied by global migrations. Millions of people around the world have been on the move, searching for greater economic opportunities and fleeing war, political oppression, natural disasters, and environmental changes. Consequently, more and more countries are becoming heterogeneous in terms of race, religion, cultures, values, and politics. In other words, the "mass" audience of the past has become far less of a "mass" in most media markets.

By way of example, in the United States, the 2010 census showed that only about 70% of the U.S. population still identified itself as "White only, non-Hispanic," down from 75% in 2000 (U.S. Census Bureau, 2011). The census also showed that the Asian population was the fastest growing group in the United States during the decade. Just as importantly, the economic power of U.S. minority communities grew significantly during the decade. The combined buying power of the U.S.'s African American, Native American, and Asian communities grew an estimated 65% between 2000 and 2009 (Humphreys, 2009). That growth, combined with immigration, greatly increased both audience and advertiser demand for non-English language media channels and ethnically targeted media products.

Other demographic and lifestyle changes affect media markets. For example, in many developed countries, including the United States, Europe, and many Asian countries, birth rates have fallen since the 1960s, and the population is aging. That changes the type of media content demanded by audiences, and it also creates problems with advertiser demand because most advertisers target more advertising-susceptible young adults.

One reason birth rates have dropped is because women have entered the global workforce in large numbers. That's also changed demand for media content. Ratings for daytime television programming have declined in countries where large percentages of women work. In the United States, the impact of that was seen in 2009 and 2011 when CBS and ABC cancelled several long-running soap operas such as *As the World Turns* and *All My Children*. The networks cited falling ratings as the reason for shutting down production on the programs, some of which had been on the air daily for more than 50 years.

Other types of psychographic changes in society also influence audience tastes and demand. Changes in the religious profile of the audience in a media market, a community's shift one way or the other on the political spectrum, the emergence of an important social movement, or a significant change in social values all impact demand for content. In the United States, for example, the increasingly widespread acceptance of same-sex relationships has made it possible for broadcast and cable networks to develop shows featuring gay, lesbian, bisexual, and transgender (LGBT) characters. There also has been a surge among media entrepreneurs developing mainstream media products targeted specifically to LBGT audiences.

Variations between cultures, religions, and ethnic groups can be large. Images and topics that would be expected, and even demanded, by one culture will offend another. Some cultures, for example, find it offensive to publicly discuss disease and illness. Similarly, there are well-known differences between cultures on such things as the acceptable use of religious symbols or discussion of religion, and the visibility of women or the roles in which women appear. More than a few media managers have found themselves under siege for violating the norms of one subset of their community or another.

## INTERNAL CONDITIONS

Analyzing internal conditions in the course of a market analysis is a process of self-examination. At issue is whether the company or entrepreneur has the internal resources needed to succeed with a new product or business.

### SWOT Analysis

One technique for analyzing internal conditions is the SWOT analysis (Pearce & Robinson, 1997). SWOT stands for Strengths, Weaknesses, Opportunities, and Threats. A SWOT analysis includes an examination of the company's mission statements, goals, organizational structure, market position, leadership, personnel, financial resources, organizational and professional cultures, and existing product mix and markets. With each factor, the manager asks herself what the company's strengths and weaknesses are in that area, and what opportunities and threats exists.

*Company mission and objectives.* Whether you conduct a formal SWOT analysis or not, you should always ask whether a proposed investment or project is consistent with the company's mission statement and goals (see Chapter 5). If not, then it probably should not be undertaken.

*Organizational structure and culture.* Another immediate question is how the new project or investment will relate to the company's structure and culture. For example, does the company have the physical infrastructure it needs to undertake the project, or will it need new office space, new equipment, or new personnel to launch the project? Is the proposal highly innovative, risky, or disruptive in a conservative, risk-averse, or change-averse company?

Questions about the company's culture are particularly important because culture clashes within organizations are common sources of problems. Each organization and profession has its own culture. When two organizations try to merge or collaborate, differences between cultures often lead to project failure. For example, experts cited the clash of cultures between the AOL and Time Warner corporations as a major reason for the problems and huge financial losses that followed their merger in 2000 (Munk, 2002).

Successful entrepreneurial organizations often fail when it becomes necessary for the company—and its leadership—to transform the company culture from its small, free-wheeling entrepreneurial beginnings into the more settled, organized approach to business required by larger organizations. Despite their creative genius, few entrepreneurs are capable of transforming *themselves* from entrepreneurial leaders into corporate leaders and leading their organizations through the necessary change in culture. Even such business legends as the late Steve Jobs of Apple Inc. have stumbled during that transition. In most cases, either the entrepreneurial founder is forced out in favor of new leadership as the company grows, or the company stalls or fails.

*Project fit.* Another question that should be asked during a SWOT analysis is how does the new project fit into the existing product mix? Knowing how to run a newspaper does not mean that a manager will know how to run online and mobile news distribution operations. Many media executives have tried to diversify their business operations, hoping to gain financial stability in this disrupted business environment. Research suggests, however, that in most cases, diversification has reduced media companies' financial performance as management found itself in less familiar business lines (Kolo & Vogt, 2003).

*Company resources.* When examining internal conditions, the company's position in its existing markets also should be considered. Is it in a strong position? Is it a market leader? Or does it face serious, competitive threats or an eroding market? Many companies make the strategic decision to exit markets in which they are not one of the top two or three players, rather than tying up resources that could be used more efficiently in other ventures. If the internal analysis shows the company in a strong position, it probably will be a good time to make new investments. New projects may be harder to launch if the company faces serious competitive threats in its existing markets. Even so, if the company's business is eroding, it may be difficult, but advantageous, to begin moving into new lines of business with a better, long-term future.

An obvious question is whether the company has the financial resources to make the investment. Can it afford to support the new project for as long as it takes to become profitable or absorb the losses if profitability never happens? Does it have the credit rating and financial stability necessary to take out loans or attract investors?

This creates a difficult problem for media managers. There are two schools of thought on the issue of sustainability. One approach is to launch only projects that you can support long enough to give the idea a chance to prove itself. The other approach is to "fail fast," i.e., try things and move on if ideas aren't quickly successful.

Knowing the balance to strike between the two approaches is difficult. Historically, most media products—including some of the most famous and successful—required *years* of investment before they became profitable. Had their founders used the "fail fast" approach, those companies wouldn't exist today. The magazine *Sports Illustrated* took 11 years to turn a profit (Fabrikant, 1985), for example; while more recently, ESPN lost $100 million over 5 years before first turning a profit in 1985 (Eskenazi, 1989). On the other hand, financial success has never been guaranteed to any media entrepreneur, but achieving it in today's disrupted market is an even more doubtful prospect. Continuing to pour time and money into failure is as unwise as pulling the plug too quickly.

One thing to keep in mind in a market analysis is that an organization's weakness in one set of circumstances may become a strength, if conditions change—and vice versa. An internal analysis should ask how the company or project would perform under different conditions. For example, being an entrepreneurial startup means an organization has far fewer financial and personnel resources than larger competitors. But it also has far less bureaucracy and hierarchy, which may make it more nimble and quicker to respond to opportunities. Most new business ideas create both opportunities and threats, and they need to be carefully—and honestly—examined.

*Financial conditions.* Finally, a market analysis should estimate the financial costs and returns that will result from the project. This involves forecasting the revenues that the new investment or project will generate; the costs involved (including the costs of other opportunities the company or individual might have been able to pursue instead of this project, which are known as *opportunity costs*); what long-term returns on investment (ROI) to expect; the availability of capital to finance the project or investment; and the possibility of intangible benefits that the company might gain.

Return on investment (ROI) measures how much profit the owner will make relative to the investment required. Companies seek the highest ROI possible. Therefore, when an investor compares competing investment options, he or she usually will invest in the one with the highest ROI potential. A good investment decision requires an estimate of the likely ROI.

If the project will require a substantial investment, it's also necessary to examine the availability and cost of financing. Companies usually finance investments in one of three ways: (a) revenue, (b) borrowing, or (c) expanding ownership. All three methods have risks.

When a company uses revenue, it pays for the project out of the money it generates from its existing business, reducing profits at least temporarily, which can hurt the stock price in publicly held companies. Alternatively, borrowing involves taking on debt, which must be repaid with interest—the cost of financing. Taking out a loan requires careful attention to interest rates because revenues must be used to pay those costs. If the combination of operating costs and debt service exceed the company's revenues over a long time, the company will fail. Several U.S. newspaper companies that aggressively bought newspapers in the late 1990s found themselves in that situation a decade later as plunging circulation and advertising revenues left them unable to meet the interest payments on their debt.

Inviting more people to share ownership also can help finance a company, but multiple investors can increase the costs and complexity of corporate decisions by requiring negotiation with more people. In some instances, it can lead to battles for corporate control. Expanding ownership by selling stock publicly means the company faces additional state and federal securities regulations, and compliance with those regulations increases operating costs. With expanded ownership, management also will face new pressures to continuously maximize shareholder value, which affects the company's range of options.

Even more difficult to evaluate are the intangible elements of a financial analysis. One of those is opportunity cost. If you weren't investing in this project, what could you invest in instead and how much would that return? If you were working for someone else, rather than starting your own business, what would you be making in salary and benefits and how does that compare with the value of your startup? There are other important intangibles to consider as well. In addition to revenues and profits, new projects can return value in the form of public relations, reputation, and prestige. Over the long term, that may generate additional business and thereby return revenues and profits. However, there is no guarantee that actual financial benefit will result and such returns are difficult, if not impossible, to measure. Nevertheless, they often are used to justify major investments and should be considered.

If a company purchases an existing business, information will be available to help evaluate the project's likely financial performance. However, when launching entirely new ideas or creating new products and markets—for example, social media and location-based apps in recent years—relevant revenue and cost data won't be available. Nevertheless, it's still necessary to try to forecast how long it will take to become profitable and what the eventual return to investors is likely to be. As noted at the beginning of the chapter, market decisions must all be made with an eye to their impact on the company's investment market, whether that's the stock market or the private-capital market.

## MARKET ANALYSIS: THE MEDIA JOB MARKET

Up until now in this chapter, we've focused on how media managers and media entrepreneurs use market analysis to analyze the potential for new products, services, and acquisitions. But there is another market that probably is of more interest to most emerging media professionals: the job market. Almost all of the elements we've discussed as being part of a sophisticated market analysis also should be applied to your analysis of the job market you'll face upon graduation. And it is very important to be honest in your personal market analysis about whether you present a desirable brand to employers in your chosen field.

### Defining the Market

The first questions are, of course, what are your product and geographic markets? Are you placing yourself in the market for lighting directors? Videographers? News reporters? News producers? Social media coordinators? Scriptwriters? Game developers?

The first step is to have an idea about the media specialty in which you want to start your career. Your skills in that area are your product. Geography also is important. The more willing you are to go wherever opportunity takes you, the more likely you are to have a career in media. In most cases, the person who limits his or her job search to one town or city is much less likely to have a media career.

### Long-Term Forecasting

Before your settle on a career area, take the time to do some long-term trend forecasting, including demand forecasting and technology forecasting. What are the long-term trends in the field you're targeting? Is the job you want likely to be replaced by technology in the near future, the way robotic cameras have replaced human studio-camera operators in television? Are consumer tastes changing toward or away from the media sector that interests you the most, such as newspapers? What knowledge and technical skills will you need to rise above an entry-level position in your chosen career? What abilities do employers expect people in this career to have after 3 to 5 years in the job?

### Buyer Concentration/Seller Concentration

Buyer concentration is the number of potential employers who could buy your services. The more buyer concentration there is in your target career, the harder it will be to get a job. If you are interested in animation, there are increasing opportunities to create animation for video production, advertising, video gaming, and even websites. However, if you define your career as *film animation*, there are very few companies that do that work.

Seller concentration is the number of competitors for the job you want or in your chosen media specialty. Your competition in the job market is defined as everyone who also is applying for that job. If there is only one position available, that means you have to be the best person in the applicant pool. "Best" is defined not only by knowledge, skills, and experience, it also includes maturity, reliability, attitude, collegiality, work ethic, passion for the job, and willingness to learn, among other things.

Once you have a job, your competition is defined as everyone against whom your performance will be compared. That may be all other reporters, everyone in the newsroom regardless of job, in your department, or everyone in your company. If, as is increasingly common, you find yourself working freelance or on contract, your competition is everyone in your geographic market who potentially could supply the same services.

There is a hard reality in the professional world: There is no such thing as grade inflation. In universities, grade inflation has led to the majority of students being awarded As and Bs in most classes, which stand for "Exceptional" and "Above Average" performance, respectively. It is, of course, mathematically impossible for even a majority of people in any group to be above average for that group. Not surprisingly, then, in the professional world, a person has to be more competent than almost all of his or her coworkers in both job skills and interpersonal skills to be considered "above average" and, therefore, worthy of promotion.

For those who work in media specialties, such as lighting, videography, audio engineering, screenwriting, etc., where most jobs are freelance or contract, being dedicated enough to your profession to make it into the top tier among your competitors is critical. The top handful of lighting directors, audio engineers, and editors in any market will be on speed dial for every major film and video production company in the region. They'll have as much work as they want. Their competitors, who are only average in ability, will work on the jobs that are leftover.

## Cost Structures and Price

In the job market, your cost structures are your basic living expenses. Before heading out into the job market, realistically analyze how much it will cost you to live for a year in the city where you'll be working. That will tell you your minimum target salary before you enter negotiations. Your cost calculations should include rent; utilities; phone and Internet; transportation costs such as car payments, car insurance, gas, and repair costs, or public transportation costs for a year of commuting; health care insurance plus whatever amount you have for your insurance deductible; food; clothing, including enough professional clothing to get you through a work week in two different seasons; student loan payments; etc.

You'll find basic expenses quickly add up, even before you add in such optional expenses as dining out, entertainment, and vacation. If you have a pet, add an additional $1,200—the estimated cost of the first year of owning a dog or cat. Additionally, you should plan to save some minimum amount every month as a buffer against emergencies. Finally, the uncertainty about the future of Social Security and pension plans means that every person must begin seriously saving for retirement as soon as they start working.

When you've finished your cost-of-living calculations, the total is what you must receive in salary *after* you've paid taxes and Social Security.

"Price," in the job market, is your salary demand. As in every market, the law of supply and demand is at work. The more competition you face in your chosen profession, the lower your salary will be. The "glamour" of media jobs and the potential of celebrity draw many people to media, which is one reason salaries are so low compared with many other professions. The law of supply and demand also applies to your salary requirements. The higher the starting salary you request, the less likely you are to be hired.

## Product Differentiation and Branding

Product differentiation is what you have to offer that other good competitors for the job you want either don't have or can't do as well. Analyze your professional and personal strengths and be prepared to sell them. Work hard to differentiate your skills from those that most others are able to offer. Have you learned the latest editing or photo software update before anyone else? Do you "see" things when shooting photos or video that others don't? Are you able to create lighting effects, investigate news stories, or write compelling scripts in ways that others around you can't or don't? Have you learned how to program and code, as well as create?

Focus on your professional skills, but don't overlook the personal characteristics that employers find as valuable and, sometimes, more valuable than skills alone: Maturity; flexibility; willingness to learn, to take direction, to adapt, and to change; passion for the job or the cause; willingness to take responsibility; being a problem-solver rather than a problem-creator; self-confidence; interpersonal skills; initiative; and being driven to be excellent without being an obsessive-compulsive perfectionist. The list of desirable personal qualities is long.

Don't overlook things that you've done that signal to potential employers that you have these characteristics or can bring special skills to the workplace. Having studied abroad or traveled extensively overseas is a sign of confidence, flexibility, and a broad perspective. Having organized a charity event shows management experience and initiative. Speaking a second or third language fluently is a valuable skill in a multicultural market.

Once you've identified the skills and experiences that differentiate you from others, it is necessary to market them—and to brand yourself. As noted earlier, media are talent products and personnel are the biggest budget line for many media companies. Media companies are increasingly looking not only for talented employees, but employees who can market themselves and make themselves a recognizable and valuable part of their employer's media brand.

This idea of employees as part of the media brand is a role television news anchors and newspaper columnists traditionally have played. Today, however, media managers want almost every employee to become his or her own brand. They expect reporters, screenwriters, producers, and employees at all levels to use blogs, columns, comment sections, and social media to develop a personal following among the audience. That following then translates to larger audiences and stronger brand loyalty for the media company.

Increasingly, employers expect potential employees to demonstrate during the application process that they understand the importance of personal branding and marketing. Many media employers look to see whether you list a URL for a personal website on your resume—and then look at the site to see how well you present yourself. They also check to see if you're using social media accounts to build your professional reputation. As you develop your product differentiation strategy for the job market, you should ask yourself how you can effectively brand yourself around your unique abilities and communicate your value to an audience of potential employers. You also should ask yourself whether you should remove any pictures or content that may present the wrong impression of your brand to potential employers.

## Internal Conditions

Finally, you need to ask yourself about your internal conditions. Do you have the talent, drive, commitment, and abilities to be a serious competitor in the media job market of your choice? What is your personal tolerance for risk and uncertainty? How self-disciplined and determined are you, and do you persevere in the face of adversity? Is the lifestyle that goes along with your media career goal a good fit with the other things you want in life, such as family, free time, job security, etc.?

The reality is that most people's needs and desires change over their lives, and at least partly as a result, most people change careers several times. Starting out in the media field doesn't mean you can't move on when your internal conditions change. However, many emerging media professionals are unrealistic about the professions they are choosing. Working in a newsroom, for example, means being a first responder. In other words, you work nights, weekends, holidays, and whenever news is breaking. Being a national sports reporter or videographer means working almost exclusively nights and weekends, which is hard on your social life, and spending nearly every holiday—Thanksgiving, Christmas, New Year's—away from home. Working in the film industry usually means working freelance and, therefore, living without job security. Your job market analysis should include serious thought about whether the media profession of your choice is a good fit with your personality, risk tolerance, and life goals.

## SUMMARY

A market analysis carefully and critically considers the factors that may affect a company's, entrepreneur's, or individual's success in a geographic or product market. Undertaken as a formal project, it generally is done to evaluate the potential for a new investment or a new product. Effective media professionals constantly scan the competitive environment in which they work, searching for unrealized opportunities and emerging threats.

Understanding the market analysis process also can help authors, producers, reporters, and other content creators. It can make it more likely they will get support for their projects because they'll be able to explain the potential market and estimate the likely returns when they approach supervisors or investors.

Finally, conducting an ongoing analysis of the labor market in the media industry is absolutely crucial for ambitious professionals. Successful professionals are constantly estimating demand in their industry for their skills and experience, evaluating their abilities against those of colleagues and competitors, and forecasting future trends in the industry so they can stay one step ahead in gaining required skills.

Although the specific issues in a market analysis will vary from project to project, generally, the process includes an examination of external conditions, internal conditions, and financial conditions. This entails careful evaluation of long-term trends and developments in the market, the actual conditions in the product or geographic market being considered, the compatibility of the idea with the company's or individual's mission, objectives, and capabilities, and the likelihood of long-term success.

A market analysis serves several critical functions. It helps managers and professionals effectively monitor the competitive environment in which they are operating so they can take advantage of new opportunities or deal with emerging threats, and it helps them make better short- and long-term decisions. In the media industry, the ability to effectively evaluate the market is a critical skill for managers at all levels of a media business, for entrepreneurs, and, increasingly, for emerging media professionals.

---

**CASE 7.1 MAKING A CHOICE**

You and your colleagues are senior analysts with RCR Media Consulting Co. Sarah McLaren, owner of a small television station group called McLaren Communications, has contacted RCR. Ms. McLaren is aware of two TV stations in two different, but comparably sized markets going up for sale. She only has the capital to buy one of the two. She has hired RCR to conduct a market analysis of the two stations and make a recommendation as to which of the two—if either—she should buy (see Tables 7.3, 7.4, 7.5, 7.6, and 7.7).

McLaren Communications currently owns three TV stations in three small markets, all sized 150+. All three of the company's current holdings are in the Midwest plains states. Two of the stations are Fox affiliate stations. The other one is a CBS affiliate.

**Table 7.3** Profiles of Midtown and Areaville

| | COMMUNITY PROFILES | |
| --- | --- | --- |
| | **MIDTOWN** | **AREAVILLE** |
| **Market Size** | | |
| Radio market size | 193 | 175 |
| Television size | 91 | 87 |
| **Population** | | |
| Total population | 174,400 | 396,487 |
| Total households | 72,500 | 94,700 |
| **Households by income** | % | % |
| Under $19,999 | 8.2 | 15.4 |
| $20,000–39,999 | 11.1 | 20.9 |
| $40,000–74,999 | 22.6 | 28.6 |
| $75,000–99,999 | 14.8 | 13.9 |
| $100,000+ | 43.3 | 21.2 |
| Median income | $87,059 | $55,253 |
| Unemployment rate | 7.2% | 4.2% |
| **Ethnic population** | % | % |
| Caucasian | 92.5 | 75.4 |
| African American | 2.4 | 8.3 |
| Hispanic | 4.5 | 11.1 |
| Asian | 0.6 | 5.2 |
| **Education** | % | % |
| Grades 0–11 | 15.1 | 11.9 |
| High School graduate | 26.7 | 28.7 |
| College 1–3 years | 23.3 | 31.8 |
| College 4+ years | 34.9 | 27.6 |
| **Occupation** | % | % |
| Managerial | 35.5 | 20.5 |
| Technical | 33.5 | 25.7 |
| Service worker | 9.4 | 15.5 |
| Farm worker | 1.2 | 9.0 |
| Precision production | 10.6 | 11.3 |
| Operator | 9.8 | 18.0 |
| **Transportation to work** | % | % |
| Public | 12.4 | 0.8 |
| Driving | 75.9 | 70.3 |
| Carpool | 6.4 | 12.6 |
| Other | 5.3 | 16.3 |
| Average travel time (min.) | 60 | 15 |

|  | COMMUNITY PROFILES | |
| --- | --- | --- |
|  | **MIDTOWN** | **AREAVILLE** |
| **Retail sales Data** | $ | S |
| Total retail sales | 3,373,986 | 3,446,047 |
| Retail expenditure per household | 57,687 | 33,789 |
| Grocery, food & beverage | 878,118 | 881,351 |
| Restaurants & bars | 320,581 | 324,586 |
| General retail & clothing | 800,037 | 810,222 |
| Motor vehicles and parts | 783,146 | 798,543 |
| Building supplies | 319,548 | 323,456 |
| Health & personal care | 153,247 | 150,672 |
| Furniture, appliances, & electronics | 119,309 | 123,428 |
| **Radio: time spent listening (TSL) (Mon.–Sun. 6 a.m.–Mid.)** | **(Min.)** | **(Min.)** |
| Persons 12 + (Min.) | 17:30 | 18:30 |
| Men 18–34 | 16:30 | 19:30 |
| Men 25–54 | 18:45 | 21:30 |
| Men 35–64 | 20:15 | 21:15 |
| Women 18–34 | 18:30 | 17:15 |
| Women 25–54 | 19:00 | 18:00 |
| Women 35–64 | 17:45 | 17:00 |

McLaren Communications's company mission statement says: "McLaren Communications is a strong, positive commercial enterprise that succeeds through serving its communities with high-quality information and entertainment programming that reflects strong community values."

McLaren Communications has done its own analysis of internal and financial conditions and determined that it has the financial resources to buy either one of the two stations. It has the management expertise to run an additional station, if acquired. Specific financial data for the two stations will not be available until McLaren Communications opens negotiations with the owners, but some general estimates are available.

The preliminary market analysis that Ms. McLaren is hiring RCR to conduct should provide some insight into what types of

**Table 7.4** Midtown Radio Stations

| RANK 12+ 6 AM-MID. | CALL LETTERS | DIAL POSITION | FORMAT | AQH SHARE | OWNER | INSIDE /OUTSIDE METRO AREA | WATTS | ANT. HGHT |
|---|---|---|---|---|---|---|---|---|
| 1 | WVAD-FM | 98.3 | Hot adult contemporary | 14.3 | Jayson Media | In | 1,300 | 140 |
| 2 | WGGR-FM | 99.9 | Adult contemporary | 8.0 | Big Group* | Out | 27,500 | 204 |
| 3 | WSSS-FM | 95.1 | Album-oriented rock | 7.9 | Toms Radio | In | 29,500 | 194 |
| 4 | WDGF-FM | 101.1 | Oldies | 4.2 | Smith Radio* | Out | 6,800 | 404 |
| 5 | WRUF-AM | 660 | All sports | 3.9 | CPU Radio | In | 50,000 | |
| 6 | WBAT-FM | 100.5 | Oldies | 3.5 | Big Group* | In | 900 | 186 |
| 7 | WWAR-FM | 92.5 | Country | 3.4 | Smith Radio* | Out | 17,000 | 268 |
| 8 | WNBB-AM | 770 | News Talk Information | 2.5 | CPU Radio | In | 50,000 | |
| 9 | WATH-FM | 104.7 | Pop Contemporary Hit | 1.9 | State Commun. | Out | 7,400 | 381 |
| 9 | WCOL-FM | 102.9 | Oldies | 1.9 | Smith Radio* | In | 19,500 | 247 |
| 11 | WMLC-AM | 940 | Nostalgia | 1.8 | Jayson Media | In | 680 | |
| 12 | WSAC-FM | 105.5 | Pop Contemporary Hit | 1.7 | Seascape Media | In | 16,500 | 173 |
| 13 | WSEA-FM | 101.3 | Country | 1.2 | Seascape Media | Out | 10,000 | 326 |
| 14 | WQYQ-FM | 93.7 | Rhythmic Oldies | 1.0 | CRC Radio | Out | 21,000 | 238 |
| 14 | WZRT-FM | 97.3 | Pop Contemporary Hit | 1.0 | State Commun. | In | 6,000 | 473 |
| 16 | WSTS-FM | 100.7 | Urban | 0.8 | CPU Radio | Out | 50,000 | 152 |

* Denotes a major media group: more than 150 radio stations nationwide, 15% or more of the total TV viewing audience nationwide, 10% or more of the local cable systems nationwide, 15+ daily newspapers nationwide.

**Table 7.5**   Midtown Television Stations

| RANK (EVENING NEWS) | CALL LETTERS | CHANNEL | NETWORK | OWNER |
|---|---|---|---|---|
| 1 | WCTV-TV | 2 | NBC | Ligon Communications* |
| 2 | WRDV-TV | 11 | CBS | Parker Television* |
| 3 | WQQT-TV | 6 | Fox | Byers Media |
| 4 | WNBB-TV | 4 | ABC | Claude Communications* |
| 7* | WPBS-TV | 7 | PBS | Midtown Unified School District |

* Denotes a major media group: more than 150 radio stations nationwide; 15% or more of the total TV viewing audience nationwide; 10% or more of the local cable systems nationwide; 15+ daily newspapers nationwide.

**Midtown Cable**
Owner: National MSO Cable.*
Channel Capacity: 80 Channels
Available channels: 5
1 Channel of local programming
Technology: Digital
Homes passed: 69,897
Subscribers: 35,400
* Denotes a major media group: more than 150 radio stations nationwide, 15% or more of the total TV viewing audience nationwide, 10% or more of the local cable systems nationwide, 15+ daily newspapers nationwide.

**Midtown Print Media**
Local Daily: *Midtown Daily Register*. Distributed mornings, Monday–Sunday. Circulation 59,658. Owner: Major Group Newspapers.*
*Midtown City Life*. Monthly city and lifestyle magazine. Circulation 5,000. Owner: Major Group Newspapers.*
Two city dailies for the nearby metropolitan areas also are distributed in Midtown
* Denotes a major media group: more than 150 radio stations nationwide, 15% or more of the total TV viewing audience nationwide, 10% or more of the local cable systems nationwide, 15+ daily newspapers nationwide.

short- and long-term revenue and profitability she might expect from the properties based upon the markets they are in, the competition they face, and the prospects for growth. She has told RCR that she does not expect specific financial figures, but rather a general description of which one of the two properties is likely to generate the best ROI in the short and long term based upon the information that is publicly available.

The two stations up for sale are WCRZ-TV in Midtown and KRVW-TV in Areaville. The president of RCR assigns you to conduct the market analysis of the proposed acquisitions for McLaren Communication. Your job is to write a thorough, detailed market analysis that concludes with a firm recommendation to McLaren Communications as to which of the TV stations

**Table 7.6** Areaville Radio Stations

| RANK 12+ 6 AM–MID. | CALL LETTERS | DIAL POSITION | FORMAT | AQH SHARE | OWNER | INSIDE /OUTSIDE METRO AREA | WATTS | ANT. HGHT (MTRS) |
|---|---|---|---|---|---|---|---|---|
| 1 | KKID-AM | 1240 | News Talk Information | 10.0 | Big Group* | In | 1,000 | 177 |
| 2 | KHRH-FM | 96.9 | Country | 8.3 | Smith Radio* | In | 100,000 | 177 |
| 3 | KSPK-FM | 102.7 | Pop Contemporary Hit | 7.6 | Big Group* | In | 100,000 | 131 |
| 4 | KBRZ-FM | 106.3 | Album Oriented Rock | 6.7 | R Squared* | In | 3,000 | 65 |
| 5 | KSWT-AM | 1400 | News Talk Information | 5.6 | Big Group* | In | 670 | |
| 6 | KCOW-FM | 105.3 | Oldies | 5.0 | Big Group* | In | 3,000 | 100 |
| 7 | KKRN-FM | 107.3 | Hot Adult Contemporary | 4.9 | Smith Radio* | In | 100,000 | 168 |
| 8 | KJNK-FM | 98.1 | Country | 4.3 | R Squared* | In | 100,000 | 299 |
| 9 | KCRP-FM | 104.1 | Pop Contemporary Hit | 4.2 | Areaville Radio Inc. | In | 31,000 | 187 |
| 10 | KQTE-FM | 97.7 | Rhythmic Contemporary Hit | 3.6 | Big Group* | Out | 100,000 | 297 |
| 11 | KNEE-FM | 95.1 | Classic Rock | 3.3 | Johnson Radio | In | 50,000 | 87 |
| 12 | KRNN-FM | 96.1 | Adult Contemporary | 1.8 | Areaville Radio | In | 100,000 | 430 |
| 12 | KMRY-AM | 1480 | All Sports | 1.8 | Smith Radio* | In | 1,000 | |
| 13 | KWRM-AM | 590 | Album Oriented Rock | 1.6 | Wyatt Radio | Out | 5,000 | |
| 14 | KSNT-FM | 98.5 | Urban | 1.0 | Areaville Radio | In | 100,000 | 358 |

* Denotes a major media group: more than 150 radio stations nationwide, 15% or more of the total TV viewing audience nationwide, 10% or more of the local cable systems nationwide, 15+ daily newspapers nationwide.

she should buy and why, provided you decide to recommend that she buy one at all. Your report should include a step-by-step discussion of the critical factors that a market analysis includes; a comparison of those factors between the two markets under consideration; an analysis of what you think those factors will mean in terms of the stations' short- and long-term performances and why; a final recommendation as to which station McLaren Communications should buy, if either one; and why you are making that recommendation based upon the factors you identified in your market analysis.

*Midtown.* Midtown is a small community in a rural, Midwest state east of the Mississippi River. It lies in hills and forests one hour from two different major metropolitan areas. Signals from some of the media based in those cities reach Midtown.

Historically, the community has had a strong manufacturing and agricultural base of family farms that have provided a solidly middle-class lifestyle to its population. However, most of the most affluent members of the community are in the health and financial services industries, which provide only a comparatively small percentage of the jobs in the community.

In recent years, two major manufacturing plants in town have closed as their owners have moved their manufacturing operations overseas, leaving only three still in operation: a chemical manufacturing plant, a textile mill, and a paper mill. Additionally, the consolidation of the agricultural industry has forced a number of local farmers out of business. As a result, the unemployment and poverty rates in the community have risen, and the population has fallen as people have left to look for employment elsewhere. However, the community also is home to a branch campus of the state's flagship university, and it is in a popular recreation area, with numerous state parks, hiking trails, lakes, and rivers.

From a geographic standpoint, Midtown is in a small valley bordered on one side by a river and on the other by steep, hilly terrain, limiting its ability to grow. The community is connected to each of the two nearby cities by a two-lane highway.

Lifestyle scales have identified the population of Midtown as being dominated by a combination of "Working Towns"—that is "older families, lower-income blue collars" and "Ex-Urban Blues," somewhat younger, middle-class, blue-collar families in midsized towns. Politically, the community is moderately conservative, but not particularly religious.

In terms of media, WCRZ-TV is the only television station in town, although signals reach Midtown from the stations in both of the nearby cities. The community has 16 radio stations, about half of which are owned by major, international media corporations. It has one local cable system operator, also the subsidiary of a national company. The cable system has 80 channels and sells local advertising. Finally, the town has one locally owned daily newspaper, which has been losing circulation and has a household penetration rate below the national average.

*Areaville.* Areaville is a mid-sized community in the Pacific Northwest that is rapidly transforming itself from a farming town into a small city. It is located 3 hours from the nearest major urban area, and a range of hills between the two communities blocks most of the city's radio and television signals from reaching Areaville. However, some of the TV signals are carried on the Areaville cable system. The community is 3 hours from the sea in a valley dotted with orchards, farms, and small lakes.

Historically, the community has been solidly middle class. It is a university town and has the state's only medical school. Consequently, a large percentage of the town's population works in health care and other professional services. Additionally, in recent years, Areaville has benefited from an exurban migration by young professionals, who are moving their families out of the city because they are able to use the community's excellent broadband infrastructure to connect to their clients. Additionally, the pastoral lifestyle and excellent medical care in the area have started attracting media and entertainment professionals from Southern California. The result has been an increase in both the size and affluence of the local population.

The picture is not entirely rosy, however. Despite the recent growth, there are major income disparities in Areaville and its surrounding areas. The rural counties around Areaville have suffered for decades from persistent poverty related to the decline in the farming, mining, and forestry industries, once the economic core of the region. None of those industries is expected to recover. Consequently, while median household income is comparatively high, so is the percentage of households living in poverty.

Sociologically, the community is ethnically diverse. Of particular note is its large and growing Hispanic population. Its psychographic profile has been identified as a mix of "Landed Gentry": elite exurban, small-town executives, and young, middle-class town families; "Affluentials": upwardly mobile, white-collar professional suburban families; and "Heartlanders": farmers, rangers, and tenants. The community is politically liberal with strong support for such issues as immigration rights and the environment. Outdoor activities are popular.

In terms of media, the community has 10 radio stations, all but two owned by national media corporations. The local cable system operator is also the subsidiary of a national cable provider. The system is now fully digital, offers almost 200 channels and broadband services, and sells local advertising. The local daily newspaper is

**Table 7.7** Areaville Television Stations

| RANK (EVENING NEWS) | CALL LETTERS | CHANNEL | NETWORK | OWNER |
|---|---|---|---|---|
| 1 | KSTC-TV | 2 | CBS | Big Group Television* |
| 2 | KDCR-TV | 11 | ABC | Terrell Family Media |
| 3 | KRVW-TV | 6 | NBC | RMR Television* |
| 4 | KRSS-TV | 4 | Fox | Pictures Communications* |
| 5 | KUCT-TV | 9 | WB | Jones Communications* |
| 6 | KRCRTV | 13 | UPN | Jones Communications* |
| 7 | KPBS-TV | 8 | PBS | University of Areaville |

* Denotes a major media group: more than 150 radio stations nationwide, 15% or more of the total TV viewing audience nationwide, 10% or more of the local cable systems nationwide, 15+ daily newspapers nationwide.

**Cable in Areaville**
Owner: National MSO Cable*
Channel Capacity: 100 Channels
Available channels: 2
3 Channels of local programming
Technology: Digital
Homes passed: 83,450
Subscribers: 58,415

**Newspapers in Areaville**
*Areaville News Herald*. Distributed mornings, Monday–Sunday. Circulation 73,589. Owner: Terrell Family Media.

owned by a national newspaper chain and has a household penetration rate above the national average.

**Additional Sources**

In addition to the data provided, you may wish to do your own research, particularly in order to forecast trends. You may wish to consult the following sources, among others:

Statistical Abstracts of the United States [available in print and online]
Veronis & Suhler Communications Industry Forecast
Investing in Television
National Association of Broadcasters website
Current books, trade publications, and journal articles on the television industry

---

**CASE 7.2 DOING YOUR OWN ANALYSIS**

Select a newspaper, magazine, radio station, local cable-system operator, television station, or Web company in your community or a nearby community. Conduct your own market analysis of its position in the market. Write your report as if you were writing it for a potential investor.

Make sure that your report includes a detailed analysis of the media company you've selected and its market. Address the issues outlined in the chapter. Make a buy/don't buy recommendation to the investor based upon your market analysis and explain the reasons behind your recommendation.

---

**CASE 7.3 ENTREPRENEURSHIP IN ACTION**

Today there are more opportunities than ever for people with good ideas to start their own media businesses. Develop an idea for a for-profit media outlet in the product and geographic markets of your choice. Take this opportunity to develop the market analysis for your idea as a business plan for that media opportunity. Discuss each of the important factors in a market analysis in detail.

Your business idea does not have to be proposed as a bricks and mortar company. Think creatively. Today, many people are making a living producing and distributing niche content on the Web or mobile phones, or offering Web-based or digital services of some kind. Don't overlook niche opportunities in society, travel, sports, religion, food, hobbies, business content, or any underserved area that comes to mind. The one requirement is that you must determine through your market analysis whether it's realistic to think your idea can become a profitable business and, if so, how that will happen and how long it will take.

---

### CASE 7.4 PITCHING AN IDEA

Identify a major project you would like to pursue: an important long-term investigative news story, a film idea, a television series, a new digital or game offering, etc. Do a detailed market analysis for your project addressing the important factors that need to be considered. Then take one of the two following actions:

1. Use the market analysis process to identify an existing media company that might be interested in supporting your project. Describe in detail the factors in the company's market that are relevant to your project idea. Explain why you think your project might be appropriate for that company to support based upon the analyses you've done for your project idea and for your target investor.
2. Visualize yourself as an employee in an existing media company, such as a local newspaper, or television station, that might be interested in your project. Use the market analysis process to identify that company's market. Develop an effective approach that you can use with your supervisor to get his or her support for your idea. Your "pitch" should be based upon the market analysis you have done for your project and for the company. You should explain to your supervisor how the company's market position will be improved, if you are allowed to pursue your idea.

#### Additional Sources

Sources you may want to consult as you do your research include, Bacon's Media Directories

Blair's Television and Cable Factbook
Broadcasting and Cable Yearbook
Editor and Publisher Yearbook
National Association of Broadcasters Television Financial Report
Standard Rate & Data
Statistical Abstracts of the United States
Veronis & Suhler Communications Industry Forecast
Community Web websites and local Chambers of Commerce
Current books, trade publications, and journal articles
National Association of Broadcasters website

There are many other resources, directories, fact books, and sources of information that could provide you with valuable information for a market analysis. Ask your librarian for help in locating them.

**CASE 7.5 YOUR CAREER**
Conduct an analysis of the short- and long-term labor market for the career you plan to pursue. Write a report that includes all sections of a market analysis to identify the long-term prospects for a career in that field. Also decide whether you are qualified to enter your desired job market and what additional skills or expertise you may need to acquire.

**Additional Sources**
The following sources may be helpful for this assignment:

Annual Surveys of Journalism and Mass Communication Graduates. Provides data about the education, skills, qualifications, job-seeking and employment experiences, and starting salaries and benefits for journalism and mass-communication graduates throughout the United States since the mid-1980s. Specific information is available by mass communication major, race, and gender. Available online at www.grady.uga.edu/annualsurveys/.

Analyze the help-wanted ads in the trade publications and association websites that serve the industry in which you want to make your career. Systematically identify where most of the jobs of interest to you are located geographically; what types of companies are hiring; what education, skills, and experience employers are demanding at different levels along your desired career track; and what salary levels are.

Use the phone book, websites, and your state's Film Commission's directory of creative service professionals to identify video production houses and freelance media professionals in the markets around you. Contact some of those professionals in the professional specialization that interests you most, and ask if you can set up an appointment to interview them about their business and the knowledge and skills needed. Talk with several individuals to get different perspectives.

Use community websites, U.S. census data, and other sources to estimate the cost of living in cities where you are likely to apply for jobs.

Interview a senior executive in the type of company for which you would like to work.

# CHAPTER 8

# Marketing and Research

The market analysis chapter (Chapter 7) discussed how media managers must understand the interaction of supply and demand in the advertising, information, and intellectual markets. Market analysis is central to managerial decision making because it yields information and analysis to use when making decisions. Managers need to understand research to identify whether the information or data obtained from a research study for use in market analysis or other decision-making tasks is of the proper nature and quality. Managers need to understand the basic steps of the research process and the factors to consider when deciding whether a research study was conducted properly and yields the appropriate data to fit the decision being made.

Managers often hire research firms or expect a research director at their media organization to conduct research to solve problems or help in conducting a market analysis. A manager who does not understand the research process or the important factors to consider in evaluating research is at a disadvantage. If a manager cannot properly evaluate the quality of information, that manager cannot tell whether the appropriate information is being used to solve a problem or make a decision.

Once a manager decides upon the appropriate content changes for a media organization, the potential audiences to consume that content and the potential advertisers who seek to reach those audiences are identified and targeted. Understanding marketing and advertising enables a manager to promote that content effectively to the right audiences and advertisers. It enables the manager to provide the appropriate information to advertisers so they will purchase time or space on the media outlet to reach the audience.

The goal of this chapter is to encourage you to develop a broad perspective on marketing and research and to develop the habit of following research trends in the media trade press. Many marketing decisions, research questions, methods, and information gathering techniques are common across media organizations. Therefore, the basic types of research questions and methods used by media organizations are discussed.

With the increasing competitiveness and constantly changing technologies of the media industry, marketing and research activities are central to the job of media management. Marketing activities revolve around decisions about the marketing mix or four Ps—*product, pricing, placement* (distribution), and *promotion*. To make these decisions, managers need answers to questions about their customers. For media managers, the two types of customers are (a) consumers or audiences (readers, viewers, or listeners), and (b) advertisers. One way media managers use research is to develop profiles of their audiences to market their space or time to advertisers.

## MARKETING AND ADVERTISING IN TODAY'S MEDIA ENVIRONMENT

Marketing is the "process of planning and executing the conception, pricing, promotion, and distribution of ideas, goods, and services to create exchanges that satisfy individual and organizational objectives" (AMA Board, 1985, p. 1). Marketers consider the correct blend and emphasis of the marketing mix elements needed to attract and satisfy their primary customers or target segments. These marketing mix decisions are crucial to determining the message content and media placement of advertising.

Advertising's role in the marketing mix is to communicate the value that a brand, product, service, or media outlet has to offer to the desired target segment. An advertising campaign is "a series of coordinated advertisements that communicate a reasonably cohesive and integrated theme" and "can be . . . a single advertisement placed in multiple media, or . . . made up of several different advertisements with a similar look, feel and message" (O'Guinn, Allen & Semenik, 2009, p. 12). But most advertising campaigns would make little sense without the audience's knowledge about the advertised brand or product from previous campaigns. A brand is "a name, term, sign, symbol or any other features that identifies one seller's good or service as distinct from those of other sellers" (O'Guinn et al., 2009, p. 22). Some famous brands include Coca-Cola, Microsoft, Nike, McDonald's, and Disney. While an ad campaign has a coordinated theme and message for the short term, advertisers recognize audiences learn about brands and products from multiple ad campaigns and other sources over the long term.

Advertisers use integrated brand promotion (IBP) for promotional planning. IBP is defined as "the process of using a wide range of promotional tools working together to create widespread brand exposure" (O'Guinn et al., 2009, p. 11). These promotional tools include: (a) advertising in mass media; (b) sales promotions including coupons, sweepstakes, sampling, and frequent-user programs; (c) point-of-purchase or in-store advertising; (d) Internet and mobile advertising; (e) blogs; (f) podcasting; (g) event sponsorships; (h) branded entertainment such as product placement in television programming, Webcasts, and films; (i) outdoor signage and billboard, transit, and aerial advertising; (j) public relations; (k) social media; and (l) influencer marketing or word-of-mouth advertising, known as peer-to-peer persuasion (O'Guinn et al., 2009, p. 11).

The need for coordinated brand building grew because mass media audiences became more fragmented and advertisers began using new methods to reach and engage specific audiences or target markets. For example, Doritos and Pepsi Max encouraged consumers to enter a contest to create brand advertisements to air during the Super Bowl. Finalists' ads were posted online and other consumers voted for the winner, encouraging consumers to interact and develop an affinity for each brand (Parpis, 2011).

Regularly conducted research is needed to ensure coordinated brand building reaches the intended audience. For example, video and online games were once used to reach the elusive young male demographic. By 2011, however, computer and video games were played in 72% of American households and the average age of game players was 37 years. Of all gamers, 18% were under 18 years of age, 53% were 18 to 49 years old, and 29% were age 50 or older. Now women age 18 or older represent a significantly larger group of game players (37%) than males age 17 or younger (13%). The average age of the most frequent game purchaser is 41 years (ESA, 2011). That is why Farmers Insurance placed an in-game campaign to reach Zynga's 250 million users. About 6 million Farmville players elected to get the Farmers virtual airship to protect their farms as part of the campaign. Farmers Insurance had 30,000 fans prior to the campaign and 135,000 after. Many players kept the airship on their farms after the campaign, resulting in one billion impressions after 6 months (Geron, 2011).

Engagement is important because audiences often multitask when consuming media. For example, about 40% of U.S. tablet and smartphone owners use them while watching television; they check e-mail during programs and commercials, surf for unrelated information, visit social networking sites, and check sports scores (Nielsen Wire: 40%, 2011).

Advertisers want to know what primary media audiences consume while multitasking and why. Media managers use research to determine which advertising venues highly engage various target segments.

The growth of cable, satellite, video-on-demand, mobile devices, and the Internet increasingly fragments mass media audiences. IBP increased in importance because advertisers must define and attract smaller, more precise segments of consumers who share similar characteristics. Fragmentation results in advertisers considering a wider range of options for advertising placement besides those mentioned already, including TV screens in airport waiting areas, posters at public events, grocery-store cart or floor advertising, subway posters or car cards on buses, video screens in stores and sports arenas, trade shows, convention exhibits, and video-on-demand online. Traditional mass media may offer larger audiences during popular primetime programming and major sporting events such as the Super Bowl. But media managers must respond and plan based on the reality that advertisers now consider many communication options when deciding where to place advertisements (Kelley, Jugenheimer, & Sheehan, 2012).

Positioning involves designing and representing one's product, service, or brand so it occupies a distinctive and valued place in the target consumer's mind relative to other brands (O'Guinn et al., 2009, p. 200). Positioning develops a perceptual space, shaping how a brand (or media outlet) is perceived on a variety of dimensions, such as quality or social display value. For example, *The New York Times* positions itself as a high-quality, in-depth, informative paper for educated, sophisticated, and affluent readers. Advertisers communicate the position of the brand or product—media or otherwise—using advertising and IBP to create the desired image in the minds of targeted consumers.

Media develop content to attract a specific target audience, just as manufacturers create products designed to attract a target segment of consumers. Often, media products are designed for audiences that advertisers desire to reach (e.g., the TV program *American Idol* targets young adult viewers). In this case, the advertiser and media manager target the same audience, and the media manager also targets the advertiser by targeting the advertiser's audience. Alternatively, the media manager may accept the audience attracted by the editorial content of the media vehicle and then find advertisers interested in communicating with that audience.

Since the 1960s, the development of marketing, IBP, and positioning created the need for a new organizational function—marketing research, which enables media managers to discover their audience's needs and wants and determine how best to meet them. Once a manager decides on a change of content, perhaps as the result of a market analysis, that new content must be marketed to audiences and advertisers. Marketing research is conducted to help managers identify their audiences, identify the content those audiences might prefer, or provide other information to help in the advertising and marketing process. This chapter discusses the marketing research process, how to develop and design research, and some of the major media research companies.

## THE MARKETING RESEARCH PROCESS

It is important to conduct research systematically and objectively to ensure the quality of the information obtained. No manager wants to spend thousands of dollars gathering information unless it accurately reflects reality. *Systematic* research is well planned and organized. All details are outlined in advance of data collection. *Objective* research is void of bias. Bias appears in many forms, but often results from a researcher's preconceived desires or expectations for the outcome of the research study. The Advertising Research Foundation (ARF, 2003) developed its Guidelines for Market Research to demonstrate how to conduct systematic and objective studies. The American Association for Public Opinion Research (AAPOR) publicizes ethical standards and practices on its website to ensure survey research is objective and also publicizes practices it deems unethical (AAPOR Standards and Ethics, 2011).

### Stages of Marketing Research

The marketing research process resembles the research process in other areas of study. It has eight stages.

*Research question.* Also referred to as setting research objectives, this stage may concern a particular problem, such as these: Why do consumers buy one product rather than another? Which newspaper design do readers prefer? Some researchers prefer to set objectives rather than state questions. For example, the second question phrased as an objective is this: Determine the newspaper design readers prefer.

*Secondary research review.* A researcher reviews the available information on a topic of interest before conducting research. Often enough data are available to save the time and money necessary for a new research study. Media managers often use secondary research, a fact discussed later in the chapter.

*Primary research design.* The researcher develops a plan or *design* for the study. Will the study be qualitative and use intuitive data collection, or quantitative and use specific measurement techniques such as surveys? What type of quantitative or qualitative research would be best? Why? The design for the study is driven by the research questions.

*Data-collection procedure.* The researcher identifies the specific data needed to answer the research question and creates a plan to appropriately collect the data.

*Sampling design.* Due to financial and time constraints, researchers study a subset of the population of interest. This smaller group, a "sample," must be representative of the population of concern. A design for obtaining a representative sample must be outlined.

*Data collection.* The data are collected, often the most time-consuming and costly part of a research study.

*Data processing and analysis.* Researchers typically edit or verify data before analyzing it. Verification means reviewing the data for completeness and bias. Then the researcher enters the data into a computer program and interprets or analyzes them.

*Report writing.* Finally, the researcher writes a report that clearly details the study, the results obtained, and how the results answer the research question(s).


## TYPES OF RESEARCH AND RESEARCH QUESTIONS

Media managers must understand certain basic research concepts to develop objective and systematic research or assess whether they need a research firm. Media research examines variables or factors, defined as phenomena or events measured or manipulated, such as the characteristics of a newspaper's readers or TV program's viewers. A researcher systematically varies independent variables to see how they affect dependent variables, which are what the researcher wishes to explain. For example, do full- or half-page ads (independent variable: ad size) attract more readership (dependent variable: number of readers who recall information from each different ad size)? The values of the dependent variable are not manipulated, but rather measured or observed. *Reliability*, or a reliable measure, is dependable, stable, and consistently gives the same answer over time. *Validity*, or a valid measure, actually measures what it is designed to measure (Wimmer & Dominick, 2011). A manager considers all these factors when evaluating the quality of research.

The type of research problem suggests the method to use. Having knowledge of research methods enables managers to select between competing research proposals submitted by outside suppliers (including evaluating the research design, methods, questionnaires, and sampling techniques used) or to design and implement research in-house. Managers also must understand and interpret research findings to use the results effectively.

Consider three issues before designing a research study: First, how much is already known about the problem at hand? Second, how much information is needed about each audience member? Third, how important is it that the study results generalize, that is, are interpreted as applying to other people and situations beyond the specific group studied? The answers direct the researcher to some types of research and not others. The following is a discussion of the different categories of research available and some considerations for choosing any of them.

### Primary vs. Secondary Research

The researcher conducts primary research for a specific purpose and designs it to answer a specific question posed. Secondary research is conducted for purposes other than the researcher's specific purpose, is often cheaper and easier to collect than primary research, more quickly accessible, and provides sufficient, if not perfect, information. For example, many TV stations and advertisers use Nielsen ratings to evaluate TV program audiences.

Media managers often use secondary research, especially syndicated research, which is used to answer research questions about the audience (e.g., a publication's readership or the surfers of a website), the effectiveness of an advertising message (message or evaluative research), and the placement of advertising by advertisers (advertising activity or media planning research). Syndicated research is conducted on an ongoing basis by a specialized firm to serve a group of companies in the industry rather than contracted to meet the needs of one company. Major providers of syndicated research include Nielsen (www.nielsen. com/us/en), MRI or Mediamark Research Inc. (www.gfkmri.com), and Simmons (www.experian.com/simmons-research/simmons-consumer-research.html).

### Exploratory, Descriptive, and Causal Research

*Exploratory research* is conducted when a researcher approaches a relatively new topic and little information is available. Research questions may not be well defined, and there may be many issues of interest that cannot be narrowed for study. As such, exploratory research identifies key variables, issues, or ideas that help the researcher better understand the general problem and define more specific research questions.

A TV network might want to create a new podcasting hub based on its own programming to attract the young male audience. For example, ESPN has its PodCenter (http://espn.go.com/espnradio/podcast/) with sports-themed podcasts online. Researchers might test options by speaking to small numbers of young men in a focus group. This allows for free thinking and reveals important ideas that network executives failed to envision. The exploratory research identifies directions for developing podcasting, as well as identifying other possible options for products and giving the researchers a more focused set of research questions to study. In the advertising world, exploratory research used to generate advertising messages before the ads are made is called *developmental advertising research* (O'Guinn et al., 2009).

*Descriptive research* describes a group or a situation in detail across a set of variables defined in the research questions. A local newspaper interested in making its website relevant to potential young readers might analyze which online content would attract readers ages 18 to 34 and which content to safely drop without losing its core readers ages 45 to 64. The newspaper polls these demographic groups to identify what content they prefer and what content it could eliminate or edit on the website. Descriptive research helps identify audience-segmenting characteristics and estimate the size of those segments.

Managers usually ask questions that are inherently causal. When a manager considers strategic options, he or she really asks: Which strategies will result in the outcome I want? Only causal research can answer questions that pose a tailored question about a strategy causing an observable effect on an outcome—typically audience behavior. A broadcast programming executive expects the decision of when to air a program to affect the size and characteristics of that program's audience and the programs appearing before and after it.

*Causal research* is difficult and expensive. It requires data accumulated over time, allowing for multiple causes to be examined and for competing theories as to why behavior occurs to be controlled. No single research project can establish causality. Because business decisions often do not allow time for causal research, media managers usually accept the ability to reliably predict behavior as a replacement for understanding causal relationships.

### Designs for Data Collection

Once the researcher defines the problem, reviews secondary data, and decides that primary data collection is necessary, he or she develops a study design. Exploratory research typically uses *qualitative research* designs that are not reliant on the measurement of variables, but which use subjective or intuitive data collection or analysis. Qualitative research provides a relatively quick insight on a problem so as to plan further action. It often uses small, convenience samples, rather than large, representative samples, so you should not base risky decisions on its use. Qualitative research techniques include *focus group* and *depth interview* techniques (Wimmer & Dominick, 2011).

A focus group usually consists of 6 to 12 people representing the population of concern who are interviewed simultaneously, with a trained moderator leading a discussion on the topic under study (Wimmer & Dominick, 2011). Focus groups provide an open-ended response situation where synergy among the participants enhances the generation of ideas. Discussions typically last between one and a half and two hours. Information collected during a focus group is valuable, but it cannot be generalized to the greater population with confidence because of the small sample size and the unique nature of interaction.

Depth interviews are often unstructured personal interviews where a trained interviewer probes the subject's behaviors and feelings for up to two hours. They generate a great deal of information, often unexpected, for any one individual. However, their problems include small sample size, limited generalizability, and higher cost than focus groups and other data-collection methods.

Descriptive research is often conducted using *quantitative* methods or a description of a phenomenon involving the specific measurement of variables via such methods as surveys or observational methods (Wimmer & Dominick, 2011). Quantitative methods use larger, randomly collected samples, allowing researchers to generalize the results to other people and situations.

The survey or self-report method asks people to report their behaviors, attitudes, opinions, and characteristics relevant to the managerial problem. A survey consists of administering a questionnaire specially designed to answer the research questions. The questionnaire is administered face to face through a phone interview or website, or it is mailed or e-mailed to subjects. Results are then compiled to describe the research problem and potential outcomes.

Surveys are often cross-sectional or performed at one moment in time. A longitudinal study is used when data need to be collected at more than one point in time to evaluate the research question. For example, Toluna (www.toluna-group.com) collects information from its online panel of four million members in 42 countries. Research companies such as

NPD (www.npd.com), TNS (www.tnsglobal.com), Kantar Media (www.kantarmedia.com), and WPP (www.wpp.com) provide cross-sectional or panel studies of American and global consumers.

Observation does not rely on self-reports, but observes consumer behavior using obtrusive (known to the observed individual) or unobtrusive (unknown to the observed individual) methods. Some widely used observational data-collection methods include scanner data and tracking of Internet users' surfing behavior. Scanner data are used at point-of-purchase sites such as grocery stores to collect information on purchase behavior.

Many grocery chains provide preferred customer cards that are scanned each time a purchase is made. The customer receives a coupon, discount, or other reward when the card is used. Because the customer provided demographic information to the grocer to receive the card, the list of purchases is associated with that individual's demographic profile. This same approach is used online, having browsers register at a website, providing demographic and lifestyle preferences in order to receive coupons, free downloads, or conduct searches.

Content analysis provides an objective and systematic means to investigate media content. It is used to describe message composition and content. For example, content analysis is often used to examine typography, layout, and makeup in newspapers and magazines. It is used to study how the media portray minority groups, differences in news coverage, and the level of violence in TV programming.

The ability of descriptive research to accurately describe a large population relies on two elements of research. First, the sample studied must be randomly selected from the larger population the sample represents to prevent biases related to income, gender, ethnic background, and so on. Every subject should have an equal chance of being selected so no group or age is overrepresented. Random sampling allows researchers to reduce and estimate the probability that the biases exist. Second, a large sample size is needed because the larger a random sample, the less likely it is to be biased. Generally speaking, the larger the sample the better; samples should be larger than 400, and a sample of more than 1,000 works well for multivariate studies (Wimmer & Dominick, 2011).

Causal research is performed using laboratory experiments when control over extraneous conditions is important and feasible. For example, the same newspaper lifestyle section is tested by having one group of individuals read one version and a second group read a second version in a controlled setting without disruptions. This makes it more likely that different reactions to the two sections are because of the lifestyle content and not some external factor. Yet exposure to the lifestyle section in a laboratory setting is contrived and may differ from reading it at home, resulting in a different or less-than-natural reaction to the section.

Field experiments are conducted in natural settings to minimize the disadvantages of experiments. For example, two versions of a newspaper's lifestyle section are tested by delivering one version to residents in one geographic region of a city and a second version in another region. Readers' reactions are monitored in both regions to discover which section was preferred more by which readers. Real-life conditions are present, yet a field experiment lacks researcher control, allowing many factors to influence the outcome. The researcher may never be sure that the readers' reactions varied only because of differences in the two lifestyle sections.

An experimental design isolates the cause-effect relationship between the managerial factor of concern (the independent variable) and the desired audience behavioral outcome (the dependent variable) to achieve internal validity. When an experiment has internal validity, the probability is high that only the independent variable caused the dependent variable to change. An experiment has external validity if its results can be generalized to other situations and people. To increase the likelihood of external validity, researchers should randomly select the sample used in the experiment from the larger population.

You cannot have perfect internal and external validity in the same experiment. Internal validity requires control over all factors extraneous to the independent and dependent variables of concern. Controlled lab situations enhance internal validity, but decrease external validity by removing outside factors. External validity requires that extraneous variables not be controlled as in field experiments. However, once extraneous variables are allowed to fluctuate, internal validity suffers. There is always a trade-off between internal and external validity, so the research objectives should guide the balance between the two.

## TYPES OF APPLIED MEDIA RESEARCH

Basic research identifies the general principles of practice and answers general questions for media managers. Applied research is conducted to obtain information for a specific decision in a unique situation. For example, *The New York Times* might conduct a study to identify its readers' reactions to the publishing of a commemorative edition of the New York Yankees baseball team in print, for the iPad, or online. Media companies ask similar applied research questions regardless of the nature of the company. The following discusses five basic types of applied media research, including how the information gained is used by advertisers and how it is used to market the media company.

### Audience Research: Secondary Data

Audience research examines the characteristics of present and potential target audiences. A company can perform primary audience research or use the many secondary, syndicated sources of audience data. Audience research often identifies the demographic, geographic, and psychographic characteristics of potential audiences. Demographic characteristics include age, education, gender, race, marital status, occupation, and income. Audiences are segmented by geographics including region of the country, state, city, or neighborhood. Geodemographic segmentation uses data from the U.S. Census Bureau and zip codes to identify neighborhoods around the country that share demographic characteristics. For example, the American Dream segment comprises upwardly mobile ethnic minorities found in metropolitan neighborhoods, while the Rural Industrial segment is young families with one or both parents working at low-wage jobs in small towns (O'Guinn et al., 2009, p. 205–206).

Psychographics describe the individual's lifestyle, activities, interests, and opinions in order to provide insights into consumers' motivations (O'Guinn et al., 2009). The VALS (values and lifestyles) typology divides audience members into 8 categories based on demographic and psychographic profiles (www.strategicbusinessinsights.com/vals/). The SRDS (Standard Rate and Data Service) Local Market Audience Analyst provides demographic and psychographic data for cities and counties nationwide and lifestyle profiles of various consumer interest and demographic groups.

Managers of media outlets should learn how advertisers use secondary data to develop effective ways to sell time or space to advertisers. Advertisers and media planners analyze secondary data to decide how to spend an advertising budget, how much their competitors spend in major media, how many in the target audience should see the ad, and where and when to place the ads to effectively reach the targeted audience. The media planner analyzes secondary data to select vehicles in which to place the ads (e.g., *The New York Times* is a vehicle in the newspaper medium). The media buyer purchases time and space in the vehicles that efficiently reach the target audience. Media firms use these same secondary data to identify their audiences and those of competing media outlets.

*Using audience research.* Simmons and MRI/Mediamark Research Inc. report usage rates of national media and brands to identify users of a product or service, including heavy, medium, and light users. The information allows advertisers and media managers to define a target segment by demographics, geographics, and media-usage habits. A Public Broadcasting Service or PBS TV station manager could use MRI data to identify and describe the target segment of major contributors (or U.S. adults who contributed to PBS or Public Broadcasting Service; see Table 8.1).

The "Total" column and row show an estimated 230,416,000 adults in the United States. The next "Donors '000" column and "Total" row show the projected estimate of 9,243,000 adults who contributed to PBS. (Any column having 000 in the title signifies that you add three zeros to data or numbers provided in that column.) The "Donors" column and the "Educ: graduated college plus" row show an estimated 4,514,000 of contributors to PBS earned a college degree. The "Percent (Pct) Down" column shows that 48.8% of contributors have a college degree (or 4,514,000/9,243,000 PBS contributors = 48.8%). The "Percent Across" column shows that 7.2% of all college graduates contribute to PBS (or 4,514,000 contributors with college degrees/62,874,000 total U.S. collegraduates = 7.2%). (An asterisk next to a column indicates fewer than 50 subjects responded, as shown for the category "Age 18–24" so consider these results cautiously.)

The "Index" column shows an index of 179 for PBS contributors who graduated from college. Many secondary research reports use indices; an index shows a relationship between two percentages, as shown in the following formula for calculating index numbers. MRI defines an index as the "probability of finding a user in a specific group relative to the probability of finding a user in the general population. Indices of user demographics and media preferences are used to indicate the direction and amount of difference from the average. The index of the average is 100. Thus, an index of 112 reflects a 12% above-average incidence. An index of 89 indicates an 11% below average incidence" (MRI User, 2011):

$$\text{Index number} = \frac{\text{Percentage of users in a demographic segment}}{\text{Percentage of population in the same demographic segment}} \times 100$$

The 179 index represents the 48.8% of major contributors who have a college degree divided by the 27.3% of all U.S. adults who are college graduates (or 62,874,000 total U.S. adults with a college degree divided

**Table 8.1** MRI PBS Contributors Fall 2011

**MRI—MEDIAMARK**

Fall 2011 Product Financial Contributions

Public Broadcasting Service (PBS) **Adults**

| | | Total '000 | Donors '000 | Percent Across | Pct Down | Index |
|---|---|---|---|---|---|---|
| * Denotes sample size is less than 50. | | | | | | |
| Total | | 230,416 | 9,243 | 4 | 100 | 100 |
| Men | | 111,472 | 3,742 | 3.4 | 40.5 | 84 |
| Women | | 118,944 | 5,500 | 4.6 | 59.5 | 115 |
| Educ: graduated college plus | | 62,874 | 4,514 | 7.2 | 48.8 | 179 |
| Educ: attended college | | 44620 | 1,245 | 2.8 | 13.5 | 70 |
| Educ: graduated high school | | 71,520 | 2,259 | 3.2 | 24.4 | 79 |
| Educ: did not graduate HS | * | 28,911 | 412 | 1.4 | 4.5 | 35 |
| Educ: post graduate | | 25,462 | 2,561 | 10.1 | 27.7 | 251 |
| Educ: no college | | 100,996 | 2,516 | 2.5 | 27.2 | 62 |
| Age 18–24 | * | 9,973 | 90 | 0.9 | 1 | 23 |
| Age 25–34 | | 34,912 | 477 | 1.4 | 5.2 | 34 |
| Age 35–44 | | 43,741 | 893 | 2 | 9.7 | 51 |
| Age 45–54 | | 56,928 | 2,041 | 3.6 | 22.1 | 89 |
| Age 55–64 | | 41,914 | 2,289 | 5.5 | 24.8 | 136 |
| Age 65+ | | 42,948 | 3,453 | 8 | 37.4 | 200 |
| Adults 18–34 | | 44,885 | 567 | 1.3 | 6.1 | 31 |
| Adults 18–49 | | 116,097 | 2,544 | 2.2 | 27.5 | 55 |
| Adults 25–54 | | 135,580 | 3,410 | 2.5 | 36.9 | 63 |
| Men 18–34 | * | 22,124 | 221 | 1 | 2.4 | 25 |
| Men 18–49 | | 57,743 | 1,023 | 1.8 | 11.1 | 44 |
| Men 25–54 | | 67,991 | 1,392 | 2 | 15.1 | 51 |
| Women 18–34 | * | 22,762 | 346 | 1.5 | 3.7 | 38 |
| Women 18–49 | | 58,354 | 1,520 | 2.6 | 16.4 | 65 |
| Women 25–54 | | 67,590 | 2,018 | 3 | 21.8 | 74 |
| Occupation: Professional and Related Occupations | | 32,784 | 1,776 | 5.4 | 19.2 | 135 |
| Occupation: Management, Business and Financial Operations | | 29,406 | 1,306 | 4.4 | 14.1 | 111 |
| Occupation: Sales and Office Occupations | | 28,436 | 832 | 2.9 | 9 | 73 |
| Occupation: Natural Resources, Construction and Maintenance Occupations | * | 18,872 | 299 | 1.6 | 3.2 | 39 |
| Occupation: Other Employed | | 45,887 | 891 | 1.9 | 9.6 | 48 |
| HHI $150,000+ | | 23,190 | 1,497 | 6.5 | 16.2 | 161 |
| HHI $75,000-$149,999 | | 65,125 | 3,354 | 5.1 | 36.3 | 128 |
| HHI $60,000-$74,999 | | 25,140 | 1,045 | 4.2 | 11.3 | 104 |
| HHI $50,000-$59,999 | | 19,101 | 879 | 4.6 | 9.5 | 115 |
| HHI $40,000-$49,999 | | 20,210 | 596 | 2.9 | 6.4 | 73 |

| | | | | | |
|---|---|---|---|---|---|
| HHI $30,000–$39,999 | | 22,680 | 787 | 3.5 | 8.5 | 87 |
| HHI $20,000–$29,999 | | 23,130 | 589 | 2.5 | 6.4 | 64 |
| HHI <$20,000 | | 31,841 | 496 | 1.6 | 5.4 | 39 |
| Census Region: North East | | 42,073 | 2,143 | 5.1 | 23.2 | 127 |
| Census Region: South | | 85,319 | 2,571 | 3 | 27.8 | 75 |
| Census Region: Midwest | | 50,234 | 2,057 | 4.1 | 22.3 | 102 |
| Census Region: West | | 52,791 | 2,472 | 4.7 | 26.7 | 117 |
| MediaMarkets | | | | | | |
| MediaMarkets: Top 5 | | 48,318 | 2,005 | 4.2 | 21.7 | 103 |
| MediaMarkets: Next 5 | | 23,432 | 1,349 | 5.8 | 14.6 | 143 |
| County Size: A | | 95,063 | 4,295 | 4.5 | 46.5 | 113 |
| County Size: B | | 70,099 | 2,737 | 3.9 | 29.6 | 97 |
| County Size: C | | 33,501 | 1,313 | 3.9 | 14.2 | 98 |
| County Size: D | | 31,752 | 898 | 2.8 | 9.7 | 70 |
| Marital Status: Never Married | | 61,869 | 1,371 | 2.2 | 14.8 | 55 |
| Marital Status: Now Married | | 124,761 | 5,926 | 4.7 | 64.1 | 118 |
| Marital Status: Engaged | * | 11,084 | 217 | 2 | 2.3 | 49 |
| Marital Status: Widowed*/Divorced*/Separated (legally)* | | 43,787 | 1,946 | 4.4 | 21.1 | 111 |
| Child age: <12 months | * | 9,500 | 165 | 1.7 | 1.8 | 43 |
| Child age: 12–23 month | * | 8,495 | 100 | 1.2 | 1.1 | 29 |
| Child age: 12–23 month | * | 8,495 | 100 | 1.2 | 1.1 | 29 |
| Child age: <2 years | * | 17,482 | 265 | 1.5 | 2.9 | 38 |
| Child age: <6 years | | 42,809 | 693 | 1.6 | 7.5 | 40 |
| Child age: 2–5 years | | 32,943 | 505 | 1.5 | 5.5 | 38 |
| Child age: 6–11 years | | 41,976 | 849 | 2 | 9.2 | 50 |
| Child age: 12–17 years | | 46,071 | 1117 | 2.4 | 12.1 | 60 |
| Years At Present Address: <1 year | | 37,652 | 1,000 | 2.7 | 10.8 | 66 |
| Years At Present Address: 1–4 Years | | 63,159 | 1,527 | 2.4 | 16.5 | 60 |
| Years At Present Address: 5+ Years | | 129,605 | 6,715 | 5.2 | 72.7 | 129 |
| Home: Owned | | 158,235 | 7,589 | 4.8 | 82.1 | 120 |
| Home value: <$50,000 | * | 9,675 | 119 | 1.2 | 1.3 | 31 |
| Home value: $50,000–$99,999 | * | 21,700 | 511 | 2.4 | 5.5 | 59 |
| Home value: $100,000–$199,999 | | 52,150 | 2,075 | 4 | 22.5 | 99 |
| Home value: $200,000–$499,999 | | 60,093 | 3,616 | 6 | 39.1 | 150 |
| Home value: $500,000+ | | 14,619 | 1,268 | 8.7 | 13.7 | 216 |
| Race: White | | 175,384 | 8,319 | 4.7 | 90 | 118 |
| Race: Black/African American | | 26,750 | 517 | 1.9 | 5.6 | 48 |
| Race: American Indian or Alaska Native | * | 2,522 | 85 | 3.4 | 0.9 | 84 |
| Race: Asian | * | 7,363 | 131 | 1.8 | 1.4 | 44 |

(Continued)

**Table 8.1** (Continued)

**MRI—MEDIAMARK**

| | **Adults** | | | | |
|---|---|---|---|---|---|
| | Total '000 | Donors '000 | Percent Across | Pct Down | Index |
| Race: Other | * 21,850 | 303 | 1.4 | 3.3 | 35 |
| Race: White only | 172,794 | 8,247 | 4.8 | 89.2 | 119 |
| Race: Black/African American only | 25,976 | 483 | 1.9 | 5.2 | 46 |
| Race: Other Race/Multiple Classifications | 31,646 | 513 | 1.6 | 5.5 | 40 |
| Spanish spoken in home (most often or other) | 35,158 | 870 | 2.5 | 9.4 | 62 |
| Magazines I (Heavy) | 46,055 | 1,999 | 4.3 | 21.6 | 108 |
| Magazines II | 46,099 | 2,325 | 5 | 25.2 | 126 |
| Magazines III | 46,095 | 2,016 | 4.4 | 21.8 | 109 |
| Magazines IV | 46,074 | 1,739 | 3.8 | 18.8 | 94 |
| Magazines V (Light) | 46,092 | 1,164 | 2.5 | 12.6 | 63 |
| Newspaper I (Heavy) | 46,101 | 3,469 | 7.5 | 37.5 | 188 |
| Newspaper II | 46,092 | 2,046 | 4.4 | 22.1 | 111 |
| Newspaper III | 46,075 | 1,520 | 3.3 | 16.4 | 82 |
| Newspaper IV | 46,083 | 1,053 | 2.3 | 11.4 | 57 |
| Newspaper V (Light) | 46,064 | 1,154 | 2.5 | 12.5 | 62 |
| Radio I (Heavy) | 46,099 | 1,735 | 3.8 | 18.8 | 94 |
| Radio II | 46,078 | 1,909 | 4.1 | 20.7 | 103 |
| Radio III | 46,087 | 1,841 | 4 | 19.9 | 100 |
| Radio IV | 46,073 | 1,892 | 4.1 | 20.5 | 102 |
| Radio V (Light) | 46,080 | 1,867 | 4.1 | 20.2 | 101 |
| TV (total) I (Heavy) | 46,047 | 1,668 | 3.6 | 18 | 90 |
| TV (total) II | 46,085 | 1,899 | 4.1 | 20.5 | 103 |
| TV (total) III | 46,087 | 1,774 | 3.8 | 19.2 | 96 |
| TV (total) IV | 46,109 | 2,141 | 4.6 | 23.2 | 116 |
| TV (total) V (Light) | 46,088 | 1,761 | 3.8 | 19 | 95 |
| Internet I (Heavy) | 46,104 | 1,613 | 3.5 | 17.5 | 87 |
| Internet II | 46,086 | 1,974 | 4.3 | 21.4 | 107 |
| Internet III | 46,070 | 2,158 | 4.7 | 23.3 | 117 |
| Internet IV | 46,089 | 1,871 | 4.1 | 20.2 | 101 |
| Internet V (Light) | 46,068 | 1,627 | 3.5 | 17.6 | 88 |
| Outdoor I (Heavy) | 46,118 | 2,003 | 4.3 | 21.7 | 108 |
| Outdoor II | 46,089 | 1,831 | 4 | 19.8 | 99 |
| Outdoor III | 46,081 | 2,010 | 4.4 | 21.7 | 109 |
| Outdoor IV | 46,062 | 1,803 | 3.9 | 19.5 | 98 |
| Outdoor V (Light) | 46,067 | 1,595 | 3.5 | 17.3 | 86 |
| TV (Prime time) I (Heavy) | 46,069 | 2,111 | 4.6 | 22.8 | 114 |
| TV (Prime time) II | 46,089 | 1,739 | 3.8 | 18.8 | 94 |
| TV (Prime time) III | 46,093 | 1,909 | 4.1 | 20.7 | 103 |
| TV (Prime time) IV | 46,097 | 1,919 | 4.2 | 20.8 | 104 |
| TV (Prime time) V (Light) | 46,069 | 1,566 | 3.4 | 16.9 | 85 |

| | | | | | |
|---|---|---|---|---|---|
| TV (Day time) I (Heavy) | | 24,119 | 8,10 | 3.4 | 8.8 | 84 |
| TV (Day time) II | | 24,109 | 8,54 | 3.5 | 9.2 | 88 |
| TV (Day time) III (Light) | | 24,100 | 899 | 3.7 | 9.7 | 93 |
| HH subscribe to Cable | | 12,7989 | 5,571 | 4.4 | 60.3 | 109 |
| HH subscribe to digital cable | | 97,850 | 4,463 | 4.6 | 48.3 | 114 |
| HH have a satellite dish | | 64,393 | 2,137 | 3.3 | 23.1 | 83 |
| Watched any pay-per-view/ last 12 months | | 32,528 | 1,156 | 3.6 | 12.5 | 89 |
| Watched any Video-on-Demand/last 12 months | | 49,519 | 1,982 | 4 | 21.4 | 100 |
| Any cable viewing/last week | | 18,9241 | 7,641 | 4 | 82.7 | 101 |
| Cable Services: ABC Family Channel | | 49,103 | 1,411 | 2.9 | 15.3 | 72 |
| Cable Services: Adult Swim | * | 18,777 | 164 | 0.9 | 1.8 | 22 |
| Cable Services: A&E Television Network | | 52,138 | 1,722 | 3.3 | 18.6 | 82 |
| Cable Services: AMC (American Movie Classics) | | 42,560 | 1,470 | 3.5 | 15.9 | 86 |
| Cable Services: Animal Planet | | 52,454 | 1,733 | 3.3 | 18.7 | 82 |
| Cable Services: BBC America | | 15,585 | 1,165 | 7.5 | 12.6 | 186 |
| Cable Services: BET (Black Entertainment TV) | | 22,625 | 460 | 2 | 5 | 51 |
| Cable Services: Biography Channel | | 9,965 | 453 | 4.5 | 4.9 | 113 |
| Cable Services: Bloomberg Television | * | 4,281 | 253 | 5.9 | 2.7 | 147 |
| Cable Services: Bravo | | 30,889 | 1033 | 3.3 | 11.2 | 83 |
| Cable Services: Cartoon Network | * | 28,119 | 336 | 1.2 | 3.6 | 30 |
| Cable Services: CBS Sports Network | | 15,112 | 507 | 3.4 | 5.5 | 84 |
| Cable Services: Centric | * | 4,768 | 55 | 1.1 | 0.6 | 29 |
| Cable Services: Chiller | * | 6,592 | 128 | 1.9 | 1.4 | 49 |
| Cable Services: CLOO | * | 5,101 | 193 | 3.8 | 2.1 | 94 |
| Cable Services: CMT (Country Music Television) | | 22,603 | 391 | 1.7 | 4.2 | 43 |
| Cable Services: CNBC | | 30,381 | 1,537 | 5.1 | 16.6 | 126 |
| Cable Services: CNN (Cable News Network) | | 66,415 | 3,347 | 5 | 36.2 | 126 |
| Cable Services: Comedy Central | | 48,333 | 1,091 | 2.3 | 11.8 | 56 |
| Cable Services: Cooking Channel | | 29,269 | 1,140 | 3.9 | 12.3 | 97 |
| Cable Services: Current TV | * | 1,938 | 77 | 4 | 0.8 | 100 |
| Cable Services: The Discovery Channel | | 72,488 | 2,657 | 3.7 | 28.7 | 91 |
| Cable Services: The Disney Channel | | 36,650 | 848 | 2.3 | 9.2 | 58 |
| Cable Services: Disney XD | * | 10,780 | 168 | 1.6 | 1.8 | 39 |

*(Continued)*

**Table 8.1**  (Continued)

**MRI—MEDIAMARK**

| | | Total '000 | Donors '000 | Percent Across | Pct Down | Index |
|---|---|---|---|---|---|---|
| Cable Services: DIY (Do It Yourself Network) | | 14,302 | 553 | 3.9 | 6 | 96 |
| Cable Services: E! (Entertainment Television) | | 36,465 | 1,021 | 2.8 | 11 | 70 |
| Cable Services: ESPN | | 67,639 | 2,462 | 3.6 | 26.6 | 91 |
| Cable Services: ESPN2 | | 40,767 | 1,502 | 3.7 | 16.3 | 92 |
| Cable Services: #ESPNU | * | 5,062 | 180 | 3.5 | 1.9 | 88 |
| Cable Services: ESPN Classic | * | 10,866 | 269 | 2.5 | 2.9 | 62 |
| Cable Services: ESPNews | | 27,821 | 924 | 3.3 | 10 | 83 |
| Cable Services: FamilyNet | * | 2,795 | 59 | 2.1 | 0.6 | 52 |
| Cable Services: Flix | * | 3,231 | 60 | 1.8 | 0.6 | 46 |
| Cable Services: Food Network | | 56,075 | 2,019 | 3.6 | 21.8 | 90 |
| Cable Services: #Fox Business Network | | 6,455 | 524 | 8.1 | 5.7 | 202 |
| Cable Services: Fox News Channel | | 68,853 | 2,802 | 4.1 | 30.3 | 101 |
| Cable Services: FSC (Fox Soccer Channel) | * | 3,951 | 121 | 3.1 | 1.3 | 76 |
| Cable Services: FSN | | 11,085 | 421 | 3.8 | 4.6 | 95 |
| Cable Services: FUEL TV | * | 2,504 | 22 | 0.9 | 0.2 | 22 |
| Cable Services: Fuse | * | 5,910 | 104 | 1.8 | 1.1 | 44 |
| Cable Services: FX | | 39,761 | 934 | 2.3 | 10.1 | 59 |
| Cable Services: G4 | * | 12,650 | 184 | 1.5 | 2 | 36 |
| Cable Services: Galavision | * | 8,158 | 84 | 1 | 0.9 | 26 |
| Cable Services: GSN (Game Show Network) | * | 6,759 | 139 | 2.1 | 1.5 | 51 |
| Cable Services: Golf Channel | | 10,743 | 688 | 6.4 | 7.4 | 160 |
| Cable Services: GMC | * | 2,942 | 69 | 2.3 | 0.7 | 59 |
| Cable Services: (GAC) Great American Country | * | 7,283 | 157 | 2.2 | 1.7 | 54 |
| Cable Services: H2 | | 14,335 | 574 | 4 | 6.2 | 100 |
| Cable Services: Hallmark Channel | | 29,694 | 1,149 | 3.9 | 12.4 | 96 |
| Cable Services: Hallmark Movie Channel | | 22,151 | 877 | 4 | 9.5 | 99 |
| Cable Services: History Channel | | 81,006 | 3,110 | 3.8 | 33.6 | 96 |
| Cable Services: HLN | | 8,700 | 368 | 4.2 | 4 | 105 |
| Cable Services: HGTV (Home & Garden Television) | | 42,257 | 1,950 | 4.6 | 21.1 | 115 |
| Cable Services: HSN (Home Shopping Network) | * | 6,780 | 243 | 3.6 | 2.6 | 89 |
| Cable Services: IFC (Independent Film Channel) | | 6,612 | 331 | 5 | 3.6 | 125 |

| | | | | | | |
|---|---|---|---|---|---|---|
| Cable Services: INSP (Inspiration Network) | * | 3,033 | 126 | 4.1 | 1.4 | 103 |
| Cable Services: Investigation Discovery | | 16,553 | 439 | 2.7 | 4.7 | 66 |
| Cable Services: Lifetime | | 50,586 | 1,658 | 3.3 | 17.9 | 82 |
| Cable Services: Lifetime Movie Network (LMN) | | 25,296 | 944 | 3.7 | 10.2 | 93 |
| Cable Services: Logo | * | 2,579 | 109 | 4.2 | 1.2 | 106 |
| Cable Services: Military Channel | | 15,870 | 652 | 4.1 | 7.1 | 102 |
| Cable Services: MLB Network | | 9,929 | 391 | 3.9 | 4.2 | 98 |
| Cable Services: MSNBC News | | 36,720 | 2,158 | 5.9 | 23.3 | 147 |
| Cable Services: MTV | | 38,972 | 530 | 1.4 | 5.7 | 34 |
| Cable Services: MTV Tr3s | * | 4,724 | 100 | 2.1 | 1.1 | 53 |
| Cable Services: MTV2 | * | 14,347 | 225 | 1.6 | 2.4 | 39 |
| Cable Services: Music Choice | * | 9,679 | 264 | 2.7 | 2.9 | 68 |
| Cable Services: Nat Geo Wild | | 13,666 | 510 | 3.7 | 5.5 | 93 |
| Cable Services: National Geographic Channel | | 43,659 | 1,894 | 4.3 | 20.5 | 108 |
| Cable Services: #NBA TV | * | 5,073 | 154 | 3 | 1.7 | 76 |
| Cable Services: NFL Network | | 21,992 | 520 | 2.4 | 5.6 | 59 |
| Cable Services: Nick at Nite | * | 16,061 | 272 | 1.7 | 2.9 | 42 |
| Cable Services: Nickelodeon | | 29,784 | 641 | 2.2 | 6.9 | 54 |
| Cable Services: Outdoor Channel | * | 9,563 | 243 | 2.5 | 2.6 | 63 |
| Cable Services: Ovation | * | 1,017 | 100 | 9.9 | 1.1 | 246 |
| Cable Services: OWN | | 18,069 | 644 | 3.6 | 7 | 89 |
| Cable Services: Oxygen | | 20,354 | 527 | 2.6 | 5.7 | 65 |
| Cable Services: Palladia HD | * | 2,665 | 130 | 4.9 | 1.4 | 121 |
| Cable Services: PBS Kids Sprout | * | 7,017 | 177 | 2.5 | 1.9 | 63 |
| Cable Services: Planet Green | * | 5,986 | 215 | 3.6 | 2.3 | 90 |
| Cable Services: QVC | | 9,437 | 390 | 4.1 | 4.2 | 103 |
| Cable Services: Reelz Channel | * | 2,925 | 142 | 4.9 | 1.5 | 121 |
| Cable Services: SCI | | 12,922 | 575 | 4.4 | 6.2 | 111 |
| Cable Services: SOAPnet | * | 9,349 | 262 | 2.8 | 2.8 | 70 |
| Cable Services: Speed Channel | | 17,357 | 467 | 2.7 | 5.1 | 67 |
| Cable Services: Spike TV | | 39,011 | 682 | 1.7 | 7.4 | 44 |
| Cable Services: Style | * | 10,130 | 246 | 2.4 | 2.7 | 60 |
| Cable Services: Sundance Channel | | 5,524 | 356 | 6.4 | 3.9 | 161 |
| Cable Services: Syfy | | 35,117 | 849 | 2.4 | 9.2 | 60 |
| Cable Services: TBN | * | 7180 | 319 | 4.4 | 3.5 | 111 |
| Cable Services: TBS | | 66,976 | 1987 | 3 | 21.5 | 74 |
| Cable Services: TeenNick | * | 6,081 | 31 | 0.5 | 0.3 | 13 |

(*Continued*)

**Table 8.1** (Continued)

## MRI—MEDIAMARK

| | Adults | | | | |
|---|---|---|---|---|---|
| | | Total '000 | Donors '000 | Percent Across | Pct Down | Index |
| Cable Services: The Tennis Channel | * | 2,208 | 173 | 7.8 | 1.9 | 195 |
| Cable Services: TLC (The Learning Channel) | | 45,016 | 1665 | 3.7 | 18 | 92 |
| Cable Services: Travel Channel | | 20,860 | 812 | 3.9 | 8.8 | 97 |
| Cable Services: truTV | | 28,341 | 715 | 2.5 | 7.7 | 63 |
| Cable Services: TNT (Turner Network Television) | | 66,292 | 2351 | 3.5 | 25.4 | 88 |
| Cable Services: TCM (Turner Classic Movies) | | 26,413 | 1544 | 5.8 | 16.7 | 146 |
| Cable Services: TV Guide Network | | 13,149 | 516 | 3.9 | 5.6 | 98 |
| Cable Services: TV Land | | 26,435 | 664 | 2.5 | 7.2 | 63 |
| Cable Services: TV One | * | 6,993 | 152 | 2.2 | 1.6 | 54 |
| Cable Services: USA Network | | 59,766 | 1,907 | 3.2 | 20.6 | 80 |
| Cable Services: VERSUS | | 15,307 | 630 | 4.1 | 6.8 | 103 |
| Cable Services: Vh1 | * | 26,331 | 312 | 1.2 | 3.4 | 30 |
| Cable Services: Vh1 Classic | * | 6,997 | 180 | 2.6 | 1.9 | 64 |
| Cable Services: The Weather Channel | | 75,806 | 3291 | 4.3 | 35.6 | 108 |
| Cable Services: WE tv | * | 10,649 | 245 | 2.3 | 2.7 | 57 |
| Cable Services: WGN America | | 15,588 | 558 | 3.6 | 6 | 89 |
| Magazines: AARP The Magazine | | 34,035 | 2873 | 8.4 | 31.1 | 210 |
| Magazines: All You | * | 3,524 | 90 | 2.6 | 1 | 64 |
| Magazines: Allure | * | 6,591 | 170 | 2.6 | 1.8 | 64 |
| Magazines: American Baby | * | 6,163 | 142 | 2.3 | 1.5 | 58 |
| Magazines: American Hunter | * | 4,924 | 109 | 2.2 | 1.2 | 55 |
| Magazines: American Legion | * | 3,195 | 297 | 9.3 | 3.2 | 232 |
| Magazines: American Rifleman | * | 5,290 | 160 | 3 | 1.7 | 75 |
| Magazines: American Way | * | 1,300 | 53 | 4.1 | 0.6 | 101 |
| Magazines: American Woodworker | * | 3,347 | 188 | 5.6 | 2 | 140 |
| Magazines: Architectural Digest | | 4,380 | 508 | 11.6 | 5.5 | 289 |
| Magazines: Arthritis Today | * | 4,287 | 374 | 8.7 | 4 | 218 |
| Magazines: Arthur Frommer's Budget Travel | * | 2,311 | 108 | 4.7 | 1.2 | 116 |
| Magazines: The Atlantic | * | 1,040 | 159 | 15.3 | 1.7 | 382 |
| Magazines: Audubon | * | 1,492 | 189 | 12.7 | 2 | 317 |
| Magazines: Automobile | * | 3,622 | 142 | 3.9 | 1.5 | 98 |
| Magazines: Baby Talk | * | 4,424 | 41 | 0.9 | 0.4 | 23 |

| Magazine | | | | | | |
|---|---|---|---|---|---|---|
| Magazines: Barron's | * | 911 | 141 | 15.4 | 1.5 | 385 |
| Magazines: Bassmaster | * | 3,537 | 72 | 2 | 0.8 | 51 |
| Magazines: Better Homes & Gardens | | 38,331 | 1,951 | 5.1 | 21.1 | 127 |
| Magazines: Bicycling | * | 2,080 | 111 | 5.3 | 1.2 | 133 |
| Magazines: Birds & Blooms | | 6,315 | 453 | 7.2 | 4.9 | 179 |
| Magazines: Black Enterprise | * | 3,427 | 80 | 2.3 | 0.9 | 58 |
| Magazines: Boating | * | 2,190 | 89 | 4.1 | 1 | 101 |
| Magazines: Bon Appetit | | 5,803 | 471 | 8.1 | 5.1 | 202 |
| Magazines: Bridal Guide | * | 4,376 | 57 | 1.3 | 0.6 | 32 |
| Magazines: Brides | * | 5,517 | 75 | 1.4 | 0.8 | 34 |
| Magazines: Car And Driver | | 9,748 | 329 | 3.4 | 3.6 | 84 |
| Magazines: Car Craft | * | 2,247 | 38 | 1.7 | 0.4 | 42 |
| Magazines: Catholic Digest | * | 2,092 | 73 | 3.5 | 0.8 | 87 |
| Magazines: Chicago Tribune (Sunday) | * | 2,170 | 172 | 7.9 | 1.9 | 198 |
| Magazines: Cigar Aficionado | * | 1,979 | 123 | 6.2 | 1.3 | 154 |
| Magazines: Coastal Living | * | 3,662 | 229 | 6.3 | 2.5 | 156 |
| Magazines: Conde Nast Traveler | | 3,574 | 338 | 9.5 | 3.7 | 236 |
| Magazines: Consumer Reports | | 16,371 | 1,335 | 8.2 | 14.4 | 203 |
| Magazines: Cooking Light | | 11,172 | 649 | 5.8 | 7 | 145 |
| Magazines: Cooking with Paula Deen | * | 6,307 | 199 | 3.2 | 2.2 | 79 |
| Magazines: Cosmopolitan | | 18,175 | 487 | 2.7 | 5.3 | 67 |
| Magazines: The Costco Connection | | 20,395 | 1,458 | 7.2 | 15.8 | 178 |
| Magazines: Country Living | | 11,109 | 570 | 5.1 | 6.2 | 128 |
| Magazines: Country Sampler | * | 2,002 | 53 | 2.6 | 0.6 | 65 |
| Magazines: Cycle World | * | 2,777 | 54 | 1.9 | 0.6 | 48 |
| Magazines: Delta Sky Magazine | | 4,956 | 442 | 8.9 | 4.8 | 222 |
| Magazines: Diabetes Forecast | * | 3,525 | 158 | 4.5 | 1.7 | 112 |
| Magazines: Diabetes Self-Management | * | 4,850 | 182 | 3.8 | 2 | 94 |
| Magazines: Diabetic Cooking | * | 6,380 | 131 | 2 | 1.4 | 51 |
| Magazines: Discover | | 6,621 | 350 | 5.3 | 3.8 | 132 |
| Magazines: Ducks Unlimited | * | 2,567 | 91 | 3.6 | 1 | 89 |
| Magazines: Ebony | * | 9,477 | 204 | 2.2 | 2.2 | 54 |
| Magazines: The Economist | * | 2,644 | 239 | 9 | 2.6 | 225 |
| Magazines: Elle | * | 6,302 | 220 | 3.5 | 2.4 | 87 |
| Magazines: Elle Decor | * | 1,942 | 115 | 5.9 | 1.2 | 147 |
| Magazines: Entertainment Weekly | | 9,470 | 371 | 3.9 | 4 | 98 |
| Magazines: Entrepreneur | * | 3,037 | 213 | 7 | 2.3 | 175 |
| Magazines: ESPN The Magazine | * | 15,948 | 346 | 2.2 | 3.7 | 54 |

(Continued)

**Table 8.1**  (Continued)

**MRI—MEDIAMARK**

| | | Adults Total '000 | Donors '000 | Percent Across | Pct Down | Index |
|---|---|---|---|---|---|---|
| Magazines: Esquire | * | 2,790 | 157 | 5.6 | 1.7 | 141 |
| Magazines: Essence | * | 7,493 | 193 | 2.6 | 2.1 | 64 |
| Magazines: Every Day with Rachael Ray | * | 7,208 | 338 | 4.7 | 3.7 | 117 |
| Magazines: Everyday Food | * | 4,477 | 193 | 4.3 | 2.1 | 108 |
| Magazines: Family Circle | | 17,558 | 924 | 5.3 | 10 | 131 |
| Magazines: Family Handyman | * | 4,552 | 294 | 6.5 | 3.2 | 161 |
| Magazines: FamilyFun | * | 5,711 | 144 | 2.5 | 1.6 | 63 |
| Magazines: Field & Stream | * | 8,437 | 226 | 2.7 | 2.4 | 67 |
| Magazines: First For Women | * | 3,866 | 108 | 2.8 | 1.2 | 70 |
| Magazines: Fit Pregnancy | * | 1,931 | 103 | 5.3 | 1.1 | 133 |
| Magazines: Fitness | * | 7,653 | 228 | 3 | 2.5 | 74 |
| Magazines: Food & Wine | | 7,366 | 457 | 6.2 | 4.9 | 155 |
| Magazines: Food Network Magazine | * | 9,072 | 396 | 4.4 | 4.3 | 109 |
| Magazines: Forbes | | 5,111 | 330 | 6.5 | 3.6 | 161 |
| Magazines: Fortune | * | 3,898 | 237 | 6.1 | 2.6 | 152 |
| Magazines: 4 Wheel & Off Road | * | 2,844 | 100 | 3.5 | 1.1 | 87 |
| Magazines: Four Wheeler | * | 2,800 | 159 | 5.7 | 1.7 | 141 |
| Magazines: Game & Fish/ Sportsman | * | 4,170 | 86 | 2.1 | 0.9 | 51 |
| Magazines: Game Informer | * | 8,938 | 95 | 1.1 | 1 | 27 |
| Magazines: Garden Design | * | 4,254 | 247 | 5.8 | 2.7 | 145 |
| Magazines: Gardening How-To | * | 4,520 | 236 | 5.2 | 2.6 | 130 |
| Magazines: Glamour | * | 11,939 | 334 | 2.8 | 3.6 | 70 |
| Magazines: Golf Digest | | 6,253 | 337 | 5.4 | 3.6 | 134 |
| Magazines: Golf Magazine | * | 5,442 | 248 | 4.6 | 2.7 | 113 |
| Magazines: Good Housekeeping | | 22,299 | 1317 | 5.9 | 14.2 | 147 |
| Magazines: GQ (Gentlemen's Quarterly) | * | 6,518 | 263 | 4 | 2.8 | 101 |
| Magazines: Guideposts | * | 6,361 | 375 | 5.9 | 4.1 | 147 |
| Magazines: Guns & Ammo | * | 7,872 | 209 | 2.6 | 2.3 | 66 |
| Magazines: Handy | * | 1,930 | 111 | 5.8 | 1.2 | 144 |
| Magazines: Harper's Bazaar | * | 3,290 | 121 | 3.7 | 1.3 | 92 |
| Magazines: Health | | 7,819 | 465 | 5.9 | 5 | 148 |
| Magazines: Hot Rod | * | 6,249 | 142 | 2.3 | 1.5 | 57 |
| Magazines: House Beautiful | | 5,619 | 373 | 6.6 | 4 | 165 |
| Magazines: Hunting | * | 2,979 | 99 | 3.3 | 1.1 | 83 |
| Magazines: In-Fisherman | * | 2,805 | 47 | 1.7 | 0.5 | 42 |
| Magazines: In Style | | 10,481 | 447 | 4.3 | 4.8 | 106 |
| Magazines: In Touch | * | 7,042 | 128 | 1.8 | 1.4 | 45 |

| Magazine | | | | | | |
|---|---|---|---|---|---|---|
| Magazines: Inc. | * | 1,374 | 110 | 8 | 1.2 | 200 |
| Magazines: Jet | * | 6,307 | 118 | 1.9 | 1.3 | 47 |
| Magazines: Kiplinger's Personal Finance | * | 2,141 | 290 | 13.5 | 3.1 | 338 |
| Magazines: Ladies' Home Journal | | 11,638 | 881 | 7.6 | 9.5 | 189 |
| Magazines: Latina | * | 2,590 | 68 | 2.6 | 0.7 | 65 |
| Magazines: Life & Style Weekly | * | 4,334 | 82 | 1.9 | 0.9 | 47 |
| Magazines: Los Angeles Times (Sunday) | * | 2,190 | 139 | 6.3 | 1.5 | 158 |
| Magazines: Lucky | * | 2,772 | 100 | 3.6 | 1.1 | 90 |
| Magazines: Macworld | * | 1,699 | 92 | 5.4 | 1 | 136 |
| Magazines: Marie Claire | * | 3,700 | 122 | 3.3 | 1.3 | 82 |
| Magazines: Martha Stewart Living | | 10,619 | 675 | 6.4 | 7.3 | 159 |
| Magazines: Maxim | * | 10,621 | 206 | 1.9 | 2.2 | 48 |
| Magazines: Men's Fitness | * | 7,725 | 206 | 2.7 | 2.2 | 66 |
| Magazines: Men's Health | | 12,473 | 388 | 3.1 | 4.2 | 78 |
| Magazines: Men's Journal | * | 3,615 | 117 | 3.2 | 1.3 | 80 |
| Magazines: Metro-Puck Carrier Newspapers | | 53,338 | 3,138 | 5.9 | 34 | 147 |
| Magazines: Midwest Living | * | 3,553 | 256 | 7.2 | 2.8 | 179 |
| Magazines: Money | | 7,503 | 544 | 7.3 | 5.9 | 181 |
| Magazines: More | * | 1,793 | 175 | 9.8 | 1.9 | 244 |
| Magazines: Mother Earth News | * | 2,294 | 150 | 6.5 | 1.6 | 163 |
| Magazines: Motor Trend | * | 6,764 | 150 | 2.2 | 1.6 | 55 |
| Magazines: Motorcyclist | * | 2,191 | 75 | 3.4 | 0.8 | 85 |
| Magazines: Muscle & Fitness | * | 5,555 | 117 | 2.1 | 1.3 | 53 |
| Magazines: National Enquirer | * | 8,246 | 222 | 2.7 | 2.4 | 67 |
| Magazines: National Geographic | | 32,742 | 1,828 | 5.6 | 19.8 | 139 |
| Magazines: National Geographic Kids | * | 5,576 | 293 | 5.3 | 3.2 | 131 |
| Magazines: National Geographic Traveler | | 8,784 | 459 | 5.2 | 5 | 130 |
| Magazines: National Wildlife | * | 5,007 | 403 | 8.1 | 4.4 | 201 |
| Magazines: New York Magazine | * | 1,533 | 164 | 10.7 | 1.8 | 267 |
| Magazines: New York Times (Daily) | | 2,296 | 267 | 11.6 | 2.9 | 289 |
| Magazines: New York Times (Sunday) | | 3,496 | 437 | 12.5 | 4.7 | 311 |
| Magazines: The New Yorker | | 3,607 | 406 | 11.3 | 4.4 | 281 |
| Magazines: Newsweek | | 12,468 | 978 | 7.8 | 10.6 | 196 |
| Magazines: NNN Top 10 (Daily) | | 23,006 | 1,679 | 7.3 | 18.2 | 182 |
| Magazines: NNN Top 100 (Daily) | | 62,542 | 4,136 | 6.6 | 44.8 | 165 |

(Continued)

**Table 8.1**   (Continued)

**MRI—MEDIAMARK**

|  |  | Total '000 | Donors '000 | Percent Across | Pct Down | Index |
|---|---|---|---|---|---|---|
| **Adults** |  |  |  |  |  |  |
| Magazines: NNN Top 100 (Sunday) |  | 81,552 | 4,909 | 6 | 53.1 | 150 |
| Magazines: NNN Top 25 (Daily) |  | 37,570 | 2,933 | 7.8 | 31.7 | 195 |
| Magazines: NNN Top 25 (Sunday) |  | 47,758 | 3,399 | 7.1 | 36.8 | 177 |
| Magazines: North American Fisherman | * | 2,951 | 85 | 2.9 | 0.9 | 72 |
| Magazines: North American Hunter | * | 5,223 | 63 | 1.2 | 0.7 | 30 |
| Magazines: O, The Oprah Magazine |  | 14,331 | 984 | 6.9 | 10.6 | 171 |
| Magazines: Official Xbox Magazine | * | 5,558 | 67 | 1.2 | 0.7 | 30 |
| Magazines: OK! | * | 5,898 | 73 | 1.2 | 0.8 | 31 |
| Magazines: Outdoor Life | * | 5,112 | 202 | 3.9 | 2.2 | 98 |
| Magazines: Outside | * | 2,221 | 83 | 3.7 | 0.9 | 93 |
| Magazines: Parade Carrier Newspapers |  | 64,590 | 3,849 | 6 | 41.6 | 149 |
| Magazines: Parenting | * | 9,838 | 244 | 2.5 | 2.6 | 62 |
| Magazines: Parents | * | 14,824 | 363 | 2.5 | 3.9 | 61 |
| Magazines: PC Gamer | * | 2,312 | 49 | 2.1 | 0.5 | 52 |
| Magazines: PC World | * | 3,647 | 174 | 4.8 | 1.9 | 119 |
| Magazines: Penthouse | * | 1,919 | 20 | 1.1 | 0.2 | 26 |
| Magazines: People |  | 42,938 | 1,923 | 4.5 | 20.8 | 112 |
| Magazines: People en Espanol | * | 7,248 | 172 | 2.4 | 1.9 | 59 |
| Magazines: Playboy | * | 6,113 | 114 | 1.9 | 1.2 | 47 |
| Magazines: Popular Mechanics | * | 8,109 | 281 | 3.5 | 3 | 86 |
| Magazines: Popular Science |  | 6,556 | 338 | 5.2 | 3.7 | 129 |
| Magazines: Prevention |  | 9,318 | 602 | 6.5 | 6.5 | 161 |
| Magazines: Psychology Today | * | 3,114 | 168 | 5.4 | 1.8 | 135 |
| Magazines: Reader's Digest |  | 25,397 | 1,385 | 5.5 | 15 | 136 |
| Magazines: Real Simple |  | 7,130 | 462 | 6.5 | 5 | 162 |
| Magazines: Redbook | * | 8,336 | 365 | 4.4 | 4 | 109 |
| Magazines: Road & Track | * | 4,750 | 174 | 3.7 | 1.9 | 91 |
| Magazines: Rolling Stone |  | 11,899 | 510 | 4.3 | 5.5 | 107 |
| Magazines: Runner's World | * | 2,827 | 113 | 4 | 1.2 | 100 |
| Magazines: Saltwater Sportsman | * | 1,339 | 25 | 1.9 | 0.3 | 47 |
| Magazines: Saturday Evening Post | * | 2,251 | 210 | 9.3 | 2.3 | 232 |

| | | | | | | |
|---|---|---|---|---|---|---|
| Magazines: Scholastic Parent & Child | * | 7,244 | 139 | 1.9 | 1.5 | 48 |
| Magazines: Scientific American | * | 2,838 | 327 | 11.5 | 3.5 | 287 |
| Magazines: Self | * | 5,969 | 169 | 2.8 | 1.8 | 71 |
| Magazines: Seventeen | * | 8,870 | 97 | 1.1 | 1.1 | 27 |
| Magazines: Shape | * | 6,377 | 199 | 3.1 | 2.1 | 78 |
| Magazines: Ski | * | 1,368 | 92 | 6.7 | 1 | 167 |
| Magazines: Smart Money | * | 3,731 | 311 | 8.3 | 3.4 | 208 |
| Magazines: Smithsonian | | 6,591 | 1,004 | 15.2 | 10.9 | 380 |
| Magazines: Soap Opera Digest | * | 4,019 | 80 | 2 | 0.9 | 49 |
| Magazines: Soap Opera Weekly | * | 2,900 | 85 | 2.9 | 0.9 | 73 |
| Magazines: Southern Living | | 15,110 | 777 | 5.1 | 8.4 | 128 |
| Magazines: Southwest Spirit | * | 2,996 | 221 | 7.4 | 2.4 | 184 |
| Magazines: Spin | * | 1,315 | 46 | 3.5 | 0.5 | 87 |
| Magazines: Sporting News | * | 3,240 | 55 | 1.7 | 0.6 | 42 |
| Magazines: Sports Illustrated | | 20,142 | 618 | 3.1 | 6.7 | 76 |
| Magazines: Star | * | 9,804 | 290 | 3 | 3.1 | 74 |
| Magazines: Street Rodder | * | 1,952 | 56 | 2.9 | 0.6 | 72 |
| Magazines: Sunday Mag/Net Carrier Newspapers | | 14,459 | 1,255 | 8.7 | 13.6 | 216 |
| Magazines: Sunset | | 4,700 | 501 | 10.7 | 5.4 | 266 |
| Magazines: Super Chevy | * | 2,758 | 53 | 1.9 | 0.6 | 48 |
| Magazines: Teen Vogue | * | 3,584 | 122 | 3.4 | 1.3 | 85 |
| Magazines: Tennis | * | 1,631 | 108 | 6.6 | 1.2 | 165 |
| Magazines: Texas Monthly | * | 2,520 | 116 | 4.6 | 1.2 | 114 |
| Magazines: This Old House | | 5,383 | 505 | 9.4 | 5.5 | 234 |
| Magazines: Time | | 18,422 | 1324 | 7.2 | 14.3 | 179 |
| Magazines: Town & Country | * | 3,144 | 109 | 3.5 | 1.2 | 86 |
| Magazines: Traditional Home | * | 4,652 | 395 | 8.5 | 4.3 | 212 |
| Magazines: Travel + Leisure | | 5,330 | 406 | 7.6 | 4.4 | 190 |
| Magazines: Tribune (8) Daily | | 4,947 | 527 | 10.6 | 5.7 | 265 |
| Magazines: Tribune (8) Sunday | | 7,539 | 572 | 7.6 | 6.2 | 189 |
| Magazines: TV Guide | | 12,405 | 420 | 3.4 | 4.5 | 84 |
| Magazines: US Airways Magazine | * | 2,941 | 133 | 4.5 | 1.4 | 113 |
| Magazines: US Weekly | * | 13,566 | 350 | 2.6 | 3.8 | 64 |
| Magazines: USA Today | * | 3,110 | 132 | 4.2 | 1.4 | 106 |
| Magazines: USA Weekend Carrier Newspapers | | 39,747 | 2,435 | 6.1 | 26.3 | 153 |
| Magazines: Vanity Fair | | 6,566 | 532 | 8.1 | 5.8 | 202 |
| Magazines: Veranda | * | 1,246 | 131 | 10.5 | 1.4 | 262 |
| Magazines: VFW Magazine | * | 2,757 | 189 | 6.8 | 2 | 171 |
| Magazines: Vogue | | 11,493 | 370 | 3.2 | 4 | 80 |
| Magazines: W | * | 1,324 | 109 | 8.2 | 1.2 | 205 |

(Continued)

**Table 8.1** (Continued)

**MRI—MEDIAMARK**

|  | | Total '000 | Donors '000 | Percent Across | Pct Down | Index |
|---|---|---|---|---|---|---|
| Magazines: Wall Street Journal | | 3,661 | 355 | 9.7 | 3.8 | 242 |
| Magazines: Washington Post (Sunday) | | 1,924 | 229 | 11.9 | 2.5 | 296 |
| Magazines: WebMD the Magazine | | 9,167 | 407 | 4.4 | 4.4 | 111 |
| Magazines: Weight Watchers | * | 10,900 | 410 | 3.8 | 4.4 | 94 |
| Magazines: Wine Spectator | * | 3,043 | 223 | 7.3 | 2.4 | 183 |
| Magazines: Wired | * | 2,549 | 113 | 4.5 | 1.2 | 111 |
| Magazines: Woman's Day | | 19,710 | 990 | 5 | 10.7 | 125 |
| Magazines: Woman's World | * | 6,994 | 303 | 4.3 | 3.3 | 108 |
| Magazines: Women's Health | * | 10,476 | 324 | 3.1 | 3.5 | 77 |
| Magazines: Working Mother | * | 2,219 | 78 | 3.5 | 0.8 | 87 |
| Magazines: WWE Magazine | * | 3,441 | 80 | 2.3 | 0.9 | 58 |
| Magazines: Yankee | * | 1,502 | 275 | 18.3 | 3 | 456 |
| Magazines: Yoga Journal | * | 1,996 | 61 | 3.1 | 0.7 | 77 |
| Magazine Types: Airline | | 11,403 | 811 | 7.1 | 8.8 | 177 |
| Magazine Types: Automotive | | 23,844 | 712 | 3 | 7.7 | 74 |
| Magazine Types: Babies | * | 9,074 | 191 | 2.1 | 2.1 | 53 |
| Magazine Types: Boating | * | 3,946 | 158 | 4 | 1.7 | 100 |
| Magazine Types: Bridal | * | 7,564 | 114 | 1.5 | 1.2 | 38 |
| Magazine Types: Business/ Finance | | 37,797 | 2,608 | 6.9 | 28.2 | 172 |
| Magazine Types: Computers | * | 5,385 | 239 | 4.4 | 2.6 | 111 |
| Magazine Types: Epicurean | | 40,412 | 1,999 | 4.9 | 21.6 | 123 |
| Magazine Types: Fishing/ Hunting | | 27,445 | 738 | 2.7 | 8 | 67 |
| Magazine Types: Fraternal | | 5,181 | 398 | 7.7 | 4.3 | 191 |
| Magazine Types: General Editorial | | 94,490 | 5,150 | 5.5 | 55.7 | 136 |
| Magazine Types: Health | | 39,464 | 1,999 | 5.1 | 21.6 | 126 |
| Magazine Types: Home Service | | 67,958 | 3,966 | 5.8 | 42.9 | 145 |
| Magazine Types: Men | | 39,556 | 1,281 | 3.2 | 13.9 | 81 |
| Magazine Types: Motorcycle | * | 6,399 | 113 | 1.8 | 1.2 | 44 |
| Magazine Types: Music | | 12,592 | 529 | 4.2 | 5.7 | 105 |
| Magazine Types: News and Entertainment Weeklies | | 82,400 | 3,792 | 4.6 | 41 | 115 |
| Magazine Types: Newspaper Distributed | | 10,6740 | 5,996 | 5.6 | 64.9 | 140 |
| Magazine Types: Outdoor Recreation | * | 2,220 | 208 | 9.4 | 2.2 | 233 |
| Magazine Types: Parenthood | | 26,323 | 622 | 2.4 | 6.7 | 59 |

| | | | | | |
|---|---|---|---|---|---|
| Magazine Types: Photography | * | 2,514 | 105 | 4.2 | 1.1 | 104 |
| Magazine Types: Science/Technology | | 13,631 | 823 | 6 | 8.9 | 151 |
| Magazine Types: Sports | | 35,606 | 1,428 | 4 | 15.5 | 100 |
| Magazine Types: Travel | | 15,703 | 996 | 6.3 | 10.8 | 158 |
| Magazine Types: Video Games/PC & Console | * | 16,019 | 180 | 1.1 | 1.9 | 28 |
| Magazine Types: Women | | 92,298 | 4,156 | 4.5 | 45 | 112 |
| Magazine Types: Women Fashion | | 22,053 | 709 | 3.2 | 7.7 | 80 |
| Radio: Weekday 6:00 am–10:00 am | | 112,812 | 4,671 | 4.1 | 50.5 | 103 |
| Radio: Weekday 10:00 am–3:00 pm | | 83,563 | 3,341 | 4 | 36.1 | 100 |
| Radio: Weekday 3:00 pm–7:00 pm | | 99,263 | 3,804 | 3.8 | 41.2 | 96 |
| Radio: Weekday 7:00 pm–Midnight | | 36,113 | 1,238 | 3.4 | 13.4 | 85 |
| Radio: Weekday Midnight–6:00 am | | 11,132 | 283 | 2.5 | 3.1 | 63 |
| Radio: Weekend 6:00 am–10:00 am | | 69,693 | 3,067 | 4.4 | 33.2 | 110 |
| Radio: Weekend 10:00 am–3:00 pm | | 96,317 | 3,852 | 4 | 41.7 | 100 |
| Radio: Weekend 3:00 pm–7:00 pm | | 72,153 | 2,802 | 3.9 | 30.3 | 97 |
| Radio: Weekend 7:00 pm–Midnight | | 36,417 | 1,188 | 3.3 | 12.9 | 81 |
| Radio: Weekend Midnight–6:00 am | * | 9,130 | 294 | 3.2 | 3.2 | 80 |
| TV Dayparts: Weekdays: 9:00 am–4:00 pm | * | 31,356 | 1,065 | 3.4 | 11.5 | 85 |
| TV Dayparts: Weekdays: 4:00 pm–7:30 pm | | 61,928 | 2,541 | 4.1 | 27.5 | 102 |
| TV Dayparts: Weekdays: 11:30 pm–1:00 am | | 28,532 | 990 | 3.5 | 10.7 | 87 |
| TV Dayparts: Weekend children's shows: Saturday-Sunday morning | * | 28,942 | 930 | 3.2 | 10.1 | 80 |
| TV Dayparts: Weekend Sports: Saturday-Sunday afternoon | * | 51,942 | 1,751 | 3.4 | 18.9 | 84 |
| TV Show Types: Auto Racing—Specials | * | 12,760 | 465 | 3.6 | 5 | 91 |
| TV Show Types: Awards-Specials | * | 17,135 | 962 | 5.6 | 10.4 | 140 |
| TV Show Types: Baseball Specials | | 38,127 | 1,776 | 4.7 | 19.2 | 116 |
| TV Show Types: Basketball Specials—College | * | 16,262 | 812 | 5 | 8.8 | 124 |

(Continued)

**Table 8.1** (Continued)

**MRI—MEDIAMARK**

| | **Adults** | | | | |
|---|---|---|---|---|---|
| | | Total '000 | Donors '000 | Percent Across | Pct Down | Index |
| TV Show Types: Basketball Specials—Professional | | 22,551 | 770 | 3.4 | 8.3 | 85 |
| TV Show Types: Comedy/ Variety | * | 12,835 | 400 | 3.1 | 4.3 | 78 |
| TV Show Types: Daytime Dramas | * | 6054 | 170 | 2.8 | 1.8 | 70 |
| TV Show Types: Daytime Game Shows | * | 9,285 | 231 | 2.5 | 2.5 | 62 |
| TV Show Types: Daytime Talk/ Variety | * | 5,547 | 357 | 6.4 | 3.9 | 160 |
| TV Show Types: Documentary Informational—Primetime | | 12,848 | 792 | 6.2 | 8.6 | 154 |
| TV Show Types: Early Evening Network News—Mon–Fri | | 15,568 | 1,173 | 7.5 | 12.7 | 188 |
| TV Show Types: Early Evening Network News—Weekend | | 14,437 | 947 | 6.6 | 10.2 | 163 |
| TV Show Types: Early Evening Weekday News Programs (Local)—Mon–Fri | | 20,151 | 976 | 4.8 | 10.6 | 121 |
| TV Show Types: Early Morning News | | 16,198 | 903 | 5.6 | 9.8 | 139 |
| TV Show Types: Early Morning Talk/Informational/News | | 13,625 | 826 | 6.1 | 8.9 | 151 |
| TV Show Types: Entertainment Specials | * | 20,567 | 1,031 | 5 | 11.2 | 125 |
| TV Show Types: Feature Film—Primetime | * | 3,711 | 213 | 5.7 | 2.3 | 143 |
| TV Show Types: Football— College Weekend | | 33,490 | 1,329 | 4 | 14.4 | 99 |
| TV Show Types: Football— Pro Weekend | | 57,312 | 2,255 | 3.9 | 24.4 | 98 |
| TV Show Types: Football Bowl Games—Specials | | 23,366 | 966 | 4.1 | 10.5 | 103 |
| TV Show Types: Football Pro Pregame Shows | | 34,906 | 1,213 | 3.5 | 13.1 | 87 |
| TV Show Types: Football Specials—Professional | | 71,788 | 2,877 | 4 | 31.1 | 100 |
| TV Show Types: Game Shows—Primetime | * | 9,639 | 280 | 2.9 | 3 | 72 |
| TV Show Types: General Drama—Primetime | * | 9,794 | 492 | 5 | 5.3 | 125 |
| TV Show Types: Golf | * | 6,450 | 499 | 7.7 | 5.4 | 193 |
| TV Show Types: Gymnastics | * | 5,459 | 386 | 7.1 | 4.2 | 176 |
| TV Show Types: Hockey | | 25,659 | 1,353 | 5.3 | 14.6 | 131 |

| TV Show Types / Websites | | | | | | |
|---|:---:|---|---|---|---|---|
| TV Show Types: Horse Racing | | 13,230 | 1,050 | 7.9 | 11.4 | 198 |
| TV Show Types: Late Evening Weekday News Programs (Local)—Mon–Fri | | 20,597 | 983 | 4.8 | 10.6 | 119 |
| TV Show Types: Late Night Network News/Info—Mon–Fri | * | 3,037 | 174 | 5.7 | 1.9 | 143 |
| TV Show Types: Late Night Talk/Variety | * | 4,295 | 256 | 5.9 | 2.8 | 148 |
| TV Show Types: News—Specials | | 21,899 | 1,546 | 7.1 | 16.7 | 176 |
| TV Show Types: Pageants—Specials | * | 13,214 | 557 | 4.2 | 6 | 105 |
| TV Show Types: Reality-based | * | 7,370 | 292 | 4 | 3.2 | 99 |
| TV Show Types: Situation Comedies—Primetime | * | 7,522 | 317 | 4.2 | 3.4 | 105 |
| TV Show Types: Skating—Specials | | 11,978 | 1,073 | 9 | 11.6 | 223 |
| TV Show Types: Soccer | | 14,369 | 779 | 5.4 | 8.4 | 135 |
| TV Show Types: Sports Anthologies—Weekend | * | 12,893 | 466 | 3.6 | 5 | 90 |
| TV Show Types: Sunday News/Interview | | 8,535 | 563 | 6.6 | 6.1 | 165 |
| TV Show Types: Syndicated Adult General | * | 6,720 | 243 | 3.6 | 2.6 | 90 |
| TV Show Types: Tennis | * | 10,025 | 792 | 7.9 | 8.6 | 197 |
| TV Show Types: Track & Field Games | * | 6,061 | 405 | 6.7 | 4.4 | 166 |
| Websites: AOL Mail | | 18,626 | 1,097 | 5.9 | 11.9 | 147 |
| Websites: Gmail.com | | 45,114 | 1,909 | 4.2 | 20.7 | 105 |
| Websites: Windows Live Hotmail | | 25,062 | 842 | 3.4 | 9.1 | 84 |
| Websites: Yahoo! Mail | | 67692 | 2,101 | 3.1 | 22.7 | 77 |
| Websites: abc.com | | 8,901 | 542 | 6.1 | 5.9 | 152 |
| Websites: cbs.com | | 6,872 | 367 | 5.3 | 4 | 133 |
| Websites: disney.com | * | 5,634 | 107 | 1.9 | 1.2 | 47 |
| Websites: FarmVille | * | 1,855 | 96 | 5.2 | 1 | 129 |
| Websites: fox.com | * | 9,093 | 427 | 4.7 | 4.6 | 117 |
| Websites: Hulu.com | | 13,415 | 476 | 3.5 | 5.1 | 88 |
| Websites: IMDb.com | | 9,831 | 357 | 3.6 | 3.9 | 90 |
| Websites: iTunes.com | | 30,407 | 1,168 | 3.8 | 12.6 | 96 |
| Websites: iVillage.com | * | 571 | 6 | 1 | 0.1 | 25 |
| Websites: Moviefone.com | * | 3,428 | 96 | 2.8 | 1 | 70 |
| Websites: MSN Movies | * | 1,414 | 47 | 3.3 | 0.5 | 83 |
| Websites: MTV.com | * | 4,153 | 87 | 2.1 | 0.9 | 52 |
| Websites: nbc.com | | 6,716 | 475 | 7.1 | 5.1 | 176 |
| Websites: Pandora.com | | 23,312 | 757 | 3.2 | 8.2 | 81 |
| Websites: pbs.org | | 5,437 | 762 | 14 | 8.2 | 349 |
| Websites: Ticketmaster.com | | 11,084 | 529 | 4.8 | 5.7 | 119 |

*(Continued)*

**Table 8.1** (Continued)

**MRI—MEDIAMARK**

| | | Total '000 | Donors '000 | Percent Across | Pct Down | Index |
|---|:---:|---:|---:|---:|---:|---:|
| | **Adults** | | | | | |
| Websites: Yahoo! Movies | * | 6,715 | 134 | 2 | 1.4 | 50 |
| Websites: About.com | * | 5,545 | 264 | 4.8 | 2.9 | 119 |
| Websites: Answers.com/ WikiAnswers | * | 5,641 | 323 | 5.7 | 3.5 | 143 |
| Websites: bankrate.com | * | 2,596 | 119 | 4.6 | 1.3 | 114 |
| Websites: eHow.com | * | 5,355 | 303 | 5.7 | 3.3 | 141 |
| Websites: Superpages.com | * | 1,282 | 69 | 5.4 | 0.7 | 134 |
| Websites: WebMD.com | | 23,686 | 1,231 | 5.2 | 13.3 | 130 |
| Websites: WhitePages.com | | 12,665 | 790 | 6.2 | 8.5 | 155 |
| Websites: Wikipedia.org | | 40,942 | 2,318 | 5.7 | 25.1 | 141 |
| Websites: #Yahoo! Answers | * | 6,878 | 249 | 3.6 | 2.7 | 90 |
| Websites: Yellowpages.com (YP.com) | | 20,185 | 908 | 4.5 | 9.8 | 112 |
| Websites: CareerBuilder.com | | 13,523 | 385 | 2.8 | 4.2 | 71 |
| Websites: monster.com | * | 11,897 | 347 | 2.9 | 3.7 | 73 |
| Websites: ABCNews.com | | 7,614 | 547 | 7.2 | 5.9 | 179 |
| Websites: AOL News | | 8,508 | 471 | 5.5 | 5.1 | 138 |
| Websites: CBSNews.com | | 5,081 | 334 | 6.6 | 3.6 | 164 |
| Websites: CNN.com | | 22,065 | 1,191 | 5.4 | 12.9 | 135 |
| Websites: foxnews.com | | 17,643 | 721 | 4.1 | 7.8 | 102 |
| Websites: #HuffingtonPost. com | * | 4,357 | 319 | 7.3 | 3.5 | 183 |
| Websites: msnbc.com | | 14,665 | 1,017 | 6.9 | 11 | 173 |
| Websites: nytimes.com | | 12,293 | 1,087 | 8.8 | 11.8 | 220 |
| Websites: USA Today.com | | 9,361 | 410 | 4.4 | 4.4 | 109 |
| Websites: wsj.com | | 7,242 | 455 | 6.3 | 4.9 | 157 |
| Websites: Yahoo! News | | 31,026 | 1,098 | 3.5 | 11.9 | 88 |
| Websites: Amazon.com | | 47,311 | 2,395 | 5.1 | 25.9 | 126 |
| Websites: Coupons.com | | 8,497 | 463 | 5.4 | 5 | 136 |
| Websites: Ebay.com | | 37,420 | 1,356 | 3.6 | 14.7 | 90 |
| Websites: Groupon.com | | 13,252 | 691 | 5.2 | 7.5 | 130 |
| Websites: Overstock.com | | 13,400 | 696 | 5.2 | 7.5 | 130 |
| Websites: Univision.com | * | 3,861 | 61 | 1.6 | 0.7 | 39 |
| Websites: Yahoo! en Espanol | * | 1,844 | 35 | 1.9 | 0.4 | 47 |
| Websites: Any Spanish Language Website | * | 5,743 | 104 | 1.8 | 1.1 | 45 |
| Websites: AOL.SportingNews. com | * | 721 | 12 | 1.6 | 0.1 | 41 |
| Websites: CBSSports.com | * | 4,905 | 184 | 3.8 | 2 | 94 |
| Websites: ESPN.com | | 29,082 | 1,106 | 3.8 | 12 | 95 |
| Websites: foxsports.com | | 9,699 | 386 | 4 | 4.2 | 99 |
| Websites: MLB.com | * | 7,410 | 316 | 4.3 | 3.4 | 106 |

| Websites: NASCAR.com | * | 5,496 | 135 | 2.5 | 1.5 | 61 |
|---|---|---|---|---|---|---|
| Websites: NBA.com · | * | 6,380 | 230 | 3.6 | 2.5 | 90 |
| Websites: NBC Sports | * | 3,413 | 164 | 4.8 | 1.8 | 120 |
| Websites: NFL.com | | 14,626 | 491 | 3.4 | 5.3 | 84 |
| Websites: #WWE.com | * | 1,369 | 43 | 3.1 | 0.5 | 78 |
| Websites: Yahoo! Sports | | 14,911 | 318 | 2.1 | 3.4 | 53 |
| Websites: CNET.com | | 7,027 | 351 | 5 | 3.8 | 124 |
| Websites: Bing Maps | * | 5,678 | 240 | 4.2 | 2.6 | 105 |
| Websites: CheapTickets.com | | 9,820 | 434 | 4.4 | 4.7 | 110 |
| Websites: Expedia.com | | 17,624 | 946 | 5.4 | 10.2 | 134 |
| Websites: Hotels.com | | 8,999 | 435 | 4.8 | 4.7 | 121 |
| Websites: Hotwire.com | * | 7,055 | 347 | 4.9 | 3.8 | 123 |
| Websites: MapQuest.com | | 42,684 | 2,337 | 5.5 | 25.3 | 136 |
| Websites: Maps.google.com (Google Maps) | | 43,273 | 2,107 | 4.9 | 22.8 | 121 |
| Websites: Orbitz.com | | 10,649 | 548 | 5.1 | 5.9 | 128 |
| Websites: Priceline.com | | 9,637 | 476 | 4.9 | 5.2 | 123 |
| Websites: Travelocity.com | | 14,032 | 861 | 6.1 | 9.3 | 153 |
| Websites: Tripadvisor.com | | 5,583 | 421 | 7.5 | 4.6 | 188 |
| Websites: Yahoo! Maps | | 18,675 | 691 | 3.7 | 7.5 | 92 |
| Websites: AccuWeather.com | | 12,763 | 839 | 6.6 | 9.1 | 164 |
| Websites: Weather.com | | 58,720 | 2,764 | 4.7 | 29.9 | 117 |
| Websites: weatherbug.com | | 10,256 | 418 | 4.1 | 4.5 | 102 |

* Denotes sample size is less than 50.

by the total of 230,416,000 adults in the United States), rounded and multiplied by 100 or:

$$179 = \frac{48.8\% \text{ of PBS Contributors who earned a college degree or more education}}{27.3\% \text{ of U.S. Adults who earned a college degree or more education}} \times 100$$

Again, an index of 100 is equal to the average, so the 179 index tells us that PBS contributors are 79% more likely than the average U.S. adult to have a college degree or more education. Index numbers are viewed as central tendencies such as averages or means. An index, like an average, describes the group as a whole rather than one person. Index numbers between 90 and 110 are generally considered to be insignificant. Therefore, the MRI data suggest that adults who are college graduates (with an index of 179) or who earned post graduate degrees (with an index of 251) are more likely to contribute to PBS.

Demographic or other characteristics having indices over 100 are not necessarily the best to select. Consider segment size, level of use or consumption, and other primary or secondary research when selecting a target segment. Sometimes several categories of the same demographic or characteristic are included in the target segment. For example, the age 65 or older group has the highest index of 200 and comprises 37.4% of PBS contributors. Yet if the manager only targeted person 65 years and older, many major contributors would be omitted. By adding contributors ages 55 to 64 (24.8% with an index of 136), the total percentage of contributors targeted would be 62.2% (37.4% + 24.8%). Note that researchers should combine only mutually exclusive categories within the same characteristic such as Age. For example, mutually exclusive categories such as Age 18–24, Age 25–34, Age 35–44, Age 45–54, and Age 65+ could be added as shown above. The Age categories Adults 18–34 through Adults 25–54, and so forth, comprise Age categories with some duplication between the ages in each category. Therefore, combining such overlapping categories would be erroneous due to double counting some respondents. The PBS station manager might also consider a research project to determine why younger listeners are less likely to donate.

Which characteristics best exemplify the national target segment of contributors to PBS? The MRI data in Table 8.1 suggest major contributors are adults ages 55 or older who earned college or postgraduate college degrees and have annual household incomes of $75,000 or more. Contributors appear likely to be employed in professional occupations and may be empty-nesters who own homes valued at $200,000 or more. They tend to read major newspapers such as *The New York Times* during the week and/or on Sundays. Their TV and cable TV preferences include BBC America, early evening network news, horse racing, and ice skating specials. They enjoy reading magazines such as *Architectural Digest*, *Bon Appetit*, *The Economist*, *The New Yorker*, *Scientific American*, and *Smithsonian*. Their online preferences include msnbc.com, nytimes.com, pbs.org, and Tripadvisor.com. Although these are national data, a local public station manager could conduct research to assess whether these characteristics hold true locally. For example, the station's printed or online contribution forms could include a brief demographic and media usage questionnaire for obtaining local data.

Managers of media outlets should understand reach and frequency because advertisers and media planners use these concepts when developing media schedules or plans. Reach refers to the percentage of the target segment exposed to a vehicle, ad, or program at least once in a given period. Reach is a measure of dispersion or how widely the message is received. Frequency is a measure of repetition and refers to how often the audience segment is reached on average (Kelley et al., 2012). An advertiser may select a particular medium or combination of media based on whether the product is sold to the public at large or a specialized segment (such as major contributors to public TV).

As discussed in Chapter 7, advertisers and media planners also consider cost per thousand (CPM) when making advertising placement decisions. CPM is the cost to deliver 1,000 people or households to an advertiser. It is an estimate of media efficiency for reaching the desired segment. CPMs are used for comparing one media vehicle to another, as well as comparing one medium to another. CPMs are used for inter-media (or comparing different media) and intramedia comparisons (i.e. comparisons among vehicles in the same class like newspapers or magazines). Although intermedia comparisons are made to select among different media classes, remember these media are not directly comparable in terms of how the audience is measured and commercial impact. Intramedia CPMs compare ads of the same sizes and types (e.g., compare full-page, four-color ads among magazines or compare 30-second ads among primetime TV shows). The basic CPM formula is as follows (Kelley et al., 2012).

$$CPM = \frac{\text{Cost of ad or unit} \times 1000}{\substack{\text{Circulation or Number of Prospects or Target Segment or} \\ \text{Number of households or persons viewing a particular} \\ \text{program or in a particular daypart or time period} \left(\text{e.g., prime time}\right)}}$$

Advertisers and media planners evaluate factors including CPMs, reach, frequency, indices, and audience size (such as the number and percentage of target readers and target subsegments) to select the most effective mix of vehicles to reach as many different members of the target segment as possible. A media planner considering where to place ads for a firm that wants to inform contributors of its sponsorship of PBS programs could use the MRI data to select appropriate vehicles. Which combination of magazines appears to best reach major contributors to public TV with varying interests? A planner might select *Bon Appetit*, with an estimated 5.1%, or 471,000 PBS contributors (with an index of 202), to reach the PBS contributor subsegment with epicurean interests. By adding *Scientific American* (3.5%, 327,000, index of 287), the contributor subsegment with scientific interests is added. By adding *National Geographic* (19.8%, 1,828,000, index of 139) contributors with interests including nature, the environment, and travel are added. Finally, by adding *Fortune* (2.6%, 237,000, index of 152) and/or *Forbes* (3.6%, 330,000, index of 161), contributors in the business subsegment are included in the media plan. Obviously, some major contributors may subscribe to more than one of these vehicles, increasing the frequency of exposure to the ad or campaign.

CPMs help ensure that the media plan or schedule is as cost-efficient as possible in reaching the desired target segment. Assume that the advertiser gave the media planner a limited budget, so choices must be made on maximizing reach among various target subsegments. The media planner decides only one business-oriented magazine can be used. *Forbes* with an index of 161 reaches 330,000 or 3.6% of major contributors (see www.forbesmedia.com/forbes-magazine-rates and register free for rate information). *Forbes* charges $135,730 for one full-page, four-color ad. *Fortune* with an index of 152 reaches 237,000 or 2.6% of major contributors (see www.fortunemediakit.com/). *Fortune* charges $140,000 for one full-page, four-color ad. Yet how do these vehicles stack up in terms of cost efficiency? The intramedia CPMs for a full-page, four-color ad in each business magazine vehicle are the following.

### Forbes Target CPM
*Full-page, four-color ad*

$$\text{Ad CPM} \frac{\$135,730}{330,000} \times 1000 = \$411.30$$

### Fortune Target CPM
*Full-page, four-color ad*

$$\text{Ad CPM} \frac{\$140,000}{237,000} \times 1000 = \$590.72$$

Typically differences of $10 or more are meaningful in comparing CPMs. The CPM analysis suggests *Forbes* has a significantly lower cost per thousand among the target market than *Fortune*. In addition, the data for *Fortune* must be considered carefully because of the small number of respondents upon which the readership estimate is based (as there is an asterisk next to the magazine title). Therefore, given a similar index, a higher number of target market readers, and cost efficiency, the MRI data suggest using *Forbes* rather than *Fortune* in the media plan. The media planner would check other data sources and each magazine's media kits to determine whether there is a compelling reason to use *Fortune* instead of *Forbes*. In contrast, if the CPMs were similar and all data were reliable and valid, the media planner would evaluate audience and other data to discern if one vehicle is better than the other for reaching contributors or for garnering reader involvement or engagement. Media planners also consider whether either magazine has a longer issue life, or tends to be saved and read again by the subscriber or other people, thus having a larger secondary audience through pass-along readership (Kelley et al., 2012).

Advertisers and media planners analyze the viewing and listening levels of various programs on different stations and channels to decide which broadcast vehicles best reach the target segment. In many markets, the level of program viewing and listening, as well as demographic and other data, are measured by Nielsen (www.nielsen.com/us/en), during the *sweeps* periods. The most important periods for measuring ratings, called sweeps, occur in February, May, July, and November.

Nielsen assigns stations to only one viewing or listening market area where they receive the largest audience share. Nielsen calls these nonoverlapping, mutually exclusive market areas comprised of counties grouped around cities or towns "Designated Market Areas" (DMAs). Each county or parish in the continental United States is assigned to only one DMA. "Households Using TV" (HUT) or "Persons Using TV" (PUT) is the total percentage of homes (or persons) in a DMA watching TV during any daypart, such as primetime (8:00 p.m. to 11:00 p.m. Eastern time) (Kelley et al., 2012).

Broadcast managers worry about sweeps results because the price of advertising time is based on ratings and shares. A TV *rating* is the number of households (or persons) who watch a TV show divided by all TVHH or TV households (or persons) in that market area having a TV set. Ratings measure overall reach. A *share* is the estimated percentage of HUTs or PUTs during a specified time watching a program (i.e. the number of households [or persons] watching a particular program, divided by the total number of households [or persons] with TV sets actually turned on when the program airs). Shares are always larger than ratings because there is never a time when every single household has a TV on (Kelley et al., 2012).

Shares help evaluate how one program fares against its competition and whether it gained or lost audience members over different times of the year. A program's rating depends on its popularity and the daypart when it airs. The rating of a show that airs during the day is normally much smaller than a primetime show. Yet that daytime show may have a higher share of viewers using TV in its time period or daypart. HUTs and PUTs are lower in the summer when fewer people watch TV and higher in the winter when more time is spent indoors watching. If you looked only at ratings, you would miss the differences in viewing levels at various times of year (see also Nielsen's Television Measurement page at www.nielsen.com/ to learn how ratings data are collected.)

Ratings and shares are used in a local DMA to analyze the performance of local programs. The general manager at the ABC-affiliated station in the Port City DMA is analyzing the performance of her 6 p.m. newscast. She may conduct primary research, if the analysis suggests her investment in a new anchor and equipment may affect the ratings. From Table 8.2, it appears that her newscast's audience size increased over the past year, especially in November. Had she considered only ratings, she would miss that her audience share increased in May, although the rating did not increase due to a smaller HUT level. (Shares for each sweeps period do not add up to the HUT levels because some local

**Table 8.2**  Using Ratings and Shares Sweeps Period

|                          | FEBRUARY 2012 | MAY 2012 | JULY 2012 | NOVEMBER 2012 |
|--------------------------|---------------|----------|-----------|---------------|
| ABC Action 2 News        |               |          |           |               |
| Rating                   | 15            | 15       | 16        | 20            |
| Share                    | 25            | 28.8     | 33.3      | 35.7          |
| NBC Ch. 7                |               |          |           |               |
| NBC *Hometown News*      |               |          |           |               |
| Rating                   | 25            | 23       | 21        | 21            |
| Share                    | 41.6          | 44.2     | 43.8      | 37.5          |
| CBS Ch. 12 News          |               |          |           |               |
| You Can Use              |               |          |           |               |
| Rating                   | 8             | 7        | 7         | 7             |
| Share                    | 13.3          | 13.5     | 14.6      | 12.5          |
| Port City                |               |          |           |               |
| HUT Levels 6–6:30 p.m.   | 60            | 52       | 48        | 56            |

viewers were watching other local stations and cable channels from 6:00–6:30 p.m.)

Advertisers, media planners, and broadcast managers use the cost per point (CPP), which "compares broadcast vehicles on the basis of how much it costs to reach 1% of the audience" (Kelley et al., 2012, p. 110). A CPP is an estimate of the dollars required to deliver one rating point (or 1% of the audience) of any DMA. Media planners use it to compare broadcast vehicles because it is an easy way to assess costs across various dayparts or markets. The formula is:

$$\text{CPP} \frac{\text{Cost of a commercial}}{\text{Rating}}$$

SQAD (www.sqad.com) is a media cost forecasting company that provides CPPs and CPMs for TV and radio market areas nationwide. A media planner having a SQAD report and ratings books can estimate the cost of ads and media plans, as well as evaluate the cost efficiency of placing broadcast ads in programs in different markets.

Although measurement methods change continually as new technologies develop, broadcast media usage generally has been measured using diaries (surveys) and electronic meters (observation). Diaries are booklets in which viewers and listeners write down the stations they watch or listen to and when. National TV audiences are measured using people meters that automatically register the channel numbers tuned in, day of week, and time of day. Sample household members push a button to indicate when they view. Set meters that log set-tuning information only and diaries for demographic data measure local TV viewing in large- to mid-size markets. The other local TV and radio markets are measured using diaries (Wimmer & Dominick, 2011).

Arbitron, now Nielsen Audio, implemented its portable people meter (PPM) to measure what radio stations consumers listen to, as well as to conduct cross-platform measurements. A panel of consumers each carry a PPM device, similar to a cell phone, that captures each panel member's exposure to television, radio, online video, cinema, and commercials, wherever that exposure occurs. The PPM was designed to measure the wide variety of media to which consumers are exposed in and out of the home on a typical day.

The Audit Bureau of Circulations provides information on the number of copies of a newspaper or magazine circulated (see www.auditbureau. org). ABC Interactive provides website traffic data, verifies e-mail newsletter delivery during a particular audit period, and independently verifies mobile media audits including mobile audience by device type and daypart, audience access points including apps or mobile browsers, as well as page views and unique visitors to sites. Nielsen provides information on various audiences and how they engage with online media.

CPM is used by media planners for assessing online campaigns. For example, assume *Bloomberg Businessweek* online charges a CPM of $40 to run a banner ad (sized 300 x 250 pixels). Therefore $40 divided by 1,000 equals 0.04 per impression, so 500,000 impressions x 0.04 = $20,000 estimated cost of an ad to reach that number of impressions. Viewed another way, a different site that charges $15,000 per banner and guarantees 600,000 impressions has a CPM of $25 (or $15,000 divided by 600 or 600 thousands). With CPC, or cost-per-click, advertisers pay websites based on the number of clicks a specific banner ad gets, such as $0.04 to $0.20 per click. CPC is calculated by dividing the media cost by the number of clicks obtained within a certain time period. CPA or cost-per-action is the cost of generating a sale, acquiring a customer, or making a transaction (Kelley et al., 2012, pp. 112–113).

The Interactive Advertising Bureau (IAB) regularly updates guidelines and standards for online advertising (www.iab.net/guidelines). The IAB identified the Universal Ad Package, which includes four ad sizes that are accepted by many sites (Search online for: Interactive Advertsing Bureau). The Mobile Marketing Association (MMA) works to develop measurement standards and best practices of mobile advertising, including a universal mobile ad package and rich media mobile advertising guidelines (http://mmaglobal.com/policies/committees/mobile-advertising).

### Audience Research: Primary Data Collection

A media manager may conduct primary audience research to answer questions unanswered by syndicated data. For example, more specific information on the audience's demographic or lifestyle characteristics may be needed. Or a newspaper or website manager may need to discover which sections are preferred, and why, by important audience segments such as young professionals ages 18 to 34 with household incomes of $75,000 or more. The major types of research used by newspaper managers include circulation, readership, and advertising studies.

*Circulation studies.* Geography is important to local newspaper managers because it defines the area where readers are attracted. Circulation studies reveal the newspaper's market share, market share of competing media, existing circulation patterns, and areas of potential circulation growth. A newspaper manager then conducts a situation or market analysis to determine which areas to target for increasing circulation.

*Readership studies.* Readership studies describe the people living in the target areas. They often include questions about demographics, psychographics, and media usage to discover who reads the newspaper, why, the sections they prefer, and the benefits they obtain from reading it. A large, metropolitan newspaper might develop a lifestyle section appealing to upper income city residents moving to a particular zip code. A small town newspaper might increase soccer coverage in the sports section when research shows many local children and parents participate in soccer.

Studies incorporating demographics, psychographics, and media usage are used to measure the audience characteristics of competing media. Information about who exclusively reads each local daily, weekly, and shopper; who reads a combination of these publications and why; and how these and other publications are used may reveal untapped readership segments.

*Advertising studies.* The media manager or media representative sells media time or space to media buyers using a media kit. A media kit positions the media product as an ideal vehicle for the advertiser. Media outlets may conduct research to accurately describe the demographic and psychographic composition of their audiences. Industry groups provide advertising advice and data for media kits. The Chamber of Commerce, other local economic development offices, or state agencies concerned with economic development provide market information. State or regional press associations may compile primary and secondary market information, include CPM data in media kits, or make them available to advertisers.

Many vehicles with online sites include a media kit, rate card, and information on their audiences. Many media outlets list media kits on their websites, including *Forbes* and *Fortune*, noted previously. Various media and marketing trade organizations provide information on various aspects of IBP. These include the Television Bureau of Advertising (www .tvb.org), Video Advertising Bureau (www.thevab.tv), Radio Advertising Bureau (www.rab.com), The Association of Magazine Media (www. magazine.org), Newspaper Association of America (www.naa.org), Interactive Advertising Bureau (www.iab.net), Electronic Retailing Association (www.retailing.org), Outdoor Advertising Association of America (www.oaaa.org), Direct Marketing Association (www.thedma.org), The Global Association for Marketing at Retail (or at point of purchase— www.popai.com), Promotional Products Association International (www .ppai.org), Digital Content Next (www. digitalcontentnext.org), Word of Mouth Marketing Association (womma.org), Brand Activation Association (www.baalink.org) and Entertainment Resources & Marketing Association (www.erma.org).

Positioning research includes studies of audience perceptions to discover a brand or product's unique attribute (or combination of attributes) to better meet consumers' needs. Positioning research diagnoses why audiences are not attracted to a product and includes other factors such as how a product compares to competitors'. It often uses exploratory and descriptive methods such as focus groups or surveys. Identifying consumer habits, lifestyles, behaviors, and desires through primary target segment research provides the information basis for product positioning.

For media organizations, positioning concerns the audience's image of the media outlet or company, or the *product* in this case. A new website's name is critical to its successful positioning because it may be the only information the audience hears about it. At the media content level, studies of audience reactions to and preferences for broadcast and cable programming, news and magazine articles and format, and the structure and content of Web and mobile sites are critical to maintaining audience commitment. A manager conducts a mail or telephone survey, focus group, or personal interviews to determine whether the local community favors the news talent and newscast. Results may be used to determine local news anchor changes.

## MEDIA CONTENT: EVALUATIVE, FORMATIVE, AND SUMMATIVE RESEARCH

Evaluative research determines how well the media content conveys what it is intended to convey. Causal research methods such as experiments are often used to conduct this research. Advertisers and their advertising agencies use evaluative research to test messages before (pretesting) and after (post-testing) ads are conveyed to the general public.

Test marketing evaluates audience tastes for broadcast and cable programming, print editorial content, website structure and content, and advertising. An ad might be aired in one market before it airs nationally to project what its effect on consumer behavior might be. Ads might be shown in two different markets or on a two-way cable system in one city, with subscribers in one part of the city seeing one version of a program or commercial and those living in another area seeing another version. Results of a random telephone survey reveal which program version earned higher ratings or which commercial spurred more sales.

With formative research, production companies and TV networks pretest programming, and advertisers pretest ads, before committing full resources to them. Concept testing assesses a program's potential popularity or the potential effectiveness of an ad's key selling concept before exposure to the general public. A concept is tested by having subjects read a one-page program summary or showing them a mock-up of a commercial. Subjects may be invited to a theater to view a pilot program. After viewing, they report their feelings about the program to help network executives determine how popular various characters and endings might be (Wimmer & Dominick, 2011).

Summative research examines whether the appropriate message is conveyed to the target market. This allows the media or advertising manager to evaluate whether the media or advertising content objectives were actually accomplished. Summative research can be performed in the field during a campaign or purchased as secondary data.

## SUMMARY

All media managers must understand research from a broad perspective to use it effectively. It is important to understand research methods and concepts like variables, reliability, and validity to conduct or effectively assess research.

Before designing a research study, a manager considers three issues: First, how much is already known about the problem at hand? Second, how much information is needed about each audience member? Third, how important is it that the study results generalize to other people and situations? The answers direct the researcher to some types of research and not to others.

Advertising, print, broadcast, cable, and online managers use similar kinds of data, research sources, and research techniques in different ways. Media outlet managers must comprehend how advertisers use audience data and media planning concepts such as indices, reach, frequency, CPMs, and CPPs to select media vehicles for advertising buys. Understanding how advertisers and agencies use these concepts helps a manager sell advertising time or space effectively.

Some of the research categories that are important to effective media management are primary, secondary, syndicated, exploratory, descriptive, and causal research. Applied research methods include audience, positioning, formative, and summative research. Data-collection designs available to the researcher include focus groups, in-depth interviews, surveys, and experiments. By collecting information about the consumer, the media manager makes more informed strategic decisions and thus markets the media vehicle more effectively to advertisers.

### CASE 8.1 THE CASE OF THE RATINGS INCREASE

Sue Al-Matrouk, general manager of WPRT-TV 2 in Port City, was delighted to receive the latest sweeps report, which showed the ratings and shares for Action News at 6 p.m. appeared to increase over the past four sweeps periods (see Table 8.2). She wondered whether the increase was because of her investment in a new anchor and set, additions to the website, or new equipment like the Doppler radar, news helicopter, and remote truck. It was expensive to retain the news helicopter, so she would cut that expense if it were not a factor in the ratings increase. Yet News Director John Small said he had received a great deal of positive feedback about it. Perhaps she could share the cost of the helicopter with another media outlet. She also wondered whether the new promotional campaign by Promotions Director Janice Biaggi had had an effect.

Sue noted the ratings and shares of the long-standing newscast leader in the market, NBC's "*Hometown News,*" appeared to have been declining since May. She wanted to know why. The CBS "News You Can Use" newscast remained solidly in third position and could be losing viewers. She wondered whether these changes were because of improvements in her newscast, factors related to the competing newscasts, other factors in the market, or a combination of all these factors. She planned to call Robert Howard, her station's group owner, to inform him of the ratings increase and ask him to support a research project to learn what contributed to the newscast's success.

Avery Atkin, sales manager at WPRT, came into her office with a big smile on his face. "In all my years in this market, I've never seen a book like this. I've never seen us so close to *Hometown News.* We may have the best sales quarter ever after my team and I go out and sell advertising based on this book."

"I'm excited too," Sue replied. "I'm really proud of our team because all the hard work paid off. And I know you and the sales staff will do a great job selling us based on this book. But I want to be sure we stay on this upward track. We may be able to overtake and pass *Hometown News,* and I don't want to squander this opportunity."

"Yeah," Avery agreed. "This is great, but we really do need to understand why this is happening so we can keep it up."

Just then John and Janice came in looking quite happy.

"Good news sure travels fast," Sue said. "Great job, gang! I know how hard you've worked and I'm so proud of what we've accomplished."

"Thanks! Yeah, this is great. I just want to keep this train on the track, so to speak," Janice said.

"Thanks and me, too," said John. "I've been in the news business too long to sit on my laurels."

Sue thought for a moment and said, "Let's plan to have a meeting tomorrow. I want each of you to tell me why you think this is happening and what we need to do to maintain this success. I also want each of you to propose ideas and objectives for a research study. We need some good research to plan and maintain this success in the future. I think Robert will support a study and might even give us some extra money, if we give him a good research proposal."

### Assignment

1. Evaluate the ratings, shares, and HUTS in Table 8.2 carefully. Write a paragraph or two explaining what these ratings and shares appear to suggest about each station's performance and why. Explain whether it appears viewership for each station is increasing, declining, or staying the same, and why.

2. How much confidence do you have in your answers to Question 1? What do the ratings and share data really reveal? Do the data in Table 8.2 tell us why the ratings and shares of the station have changed? Why or why not?

3. Write a few detailed paragraphs that answer the following questions: How can Sue determine whether the ratings and shares for her 6 p.m. newscast are improving due to the investments she's made in talent, her online edition, and equipment? Can she answer this question? Why or why not? What can Sue realistically do to get ideas about why viewership of her newscast may be increasing?

4. What type of research study should each of the following managers propose to Sue? What type of research study is needed to determine external factors that may be having an effect? Name and describe the research objectives, type of study, or research, methods, and data analysis techniques to use, and so on, to answer Questions 4a through 4d.

a. What type of research study should the news director propose? Why?
b. What type of research study should the sales manager propose? Why?
c. What type of research study should the promotions manager propose? Why?
d. What type of research study should be developed to discover what other factors (e.g., changes in the other stations' newscasts, etc.) may be having an influence?

5. Using your answers to Question 4, design a research plan for Sue to present to the station's owner. For what type of research study or studies should Sue contract? What type of study or studies could Sue contract for to serve the needs and meet the research objectives of news, promotions, and sales and examine external factors? Should she contract for more than one study? If yes, which ones should she contract for and in what order?

---

### CASE 8.2 EVALUATING CONTRIBUTORS TO PUBLIC TV

Assume you are the general manager of the public TV station in your city or the nearest major city. You just completed your latest fundraising campaign and are dissatisfied with the results. You want to discover why your fundraising campaign was not as successful as you had anticipated.

Review the MRI data for Contributors to Public TV (see Table 8.1). Evaluate Simmons or more recent MRI data if available. If the SRDS Local Market Audience Analyst (LMAA) is available online at your library, review data on the relevant demographic segment and lifestyle profiles. Evaluate any other available data about the target segment of contributors to PBS or public TV.

Check Adweek or Mediaweek to see if an analysis of your city has been published recently (for example, see Bachman, 2010). Review the census data for demographic and economic information about your city or the nearest major city. Try to find out who major individual and business contributors might be.

See if the *Demographics USA—County Edition* (2005) is available in your library and obtain the basic demographics, occupation employment data, 5-year projections, effective buying income, population by age and sex, household data, and other relevant information contained there.

Look for other sources of secondary or syndicated media research that provide information about your city or market. Ask your Reference Librarian for other sources of information. In other words, conduct a thorough secondary research review on contributors to public TV and your market or city. (Note: Published sources of secondary or syndicated research tend to have instructions on how to use and interpret their data at the beginning or end of the report or in a separate pamphlet or publication that may accompany the report. Some include instructions, advice, or answers to frequently asked questions [FAQs] on their websites.)

### Assignment

Write a report detailing the primary target segment of contributors to public TV nationwide, including demographics, geographics, psychographics, and any other information you find. Identify and describe the major potential corporate contributors or supporters in your city (including the major companies and industries located there). Then write a proposal for a research project to assess why your most recent fundraising campaign was unsuccessful and whether local contributors have similar characteristics to contributors nationally. Include each of the following sections in your final report and research proposal.

1. Provide a description and analysis of the target segment of contributors to public TV. Include all major characteristics including demographics, geographics, and psychographics. If possible, identify how many persons or households appear to be in the major public TV contributors target segment (e.g., the number of households in your city headed by college graduates and adults with postgraduate degrees, persons 55 or older, and/or households having incomes of $75,000 or more, etc., from the LMAA). Write a detailed and concise report on the target segment of national public TV contributors.
2. Provide a detailed, yet concise description of your market area or major city. Provide information about the city's major economic conditions, industries, characteristics, and

so on. The goal is to describe your city accurately, describe local economic conditions, and identify major local industries, companies, etc.

3. Use the research you developed in Question 2 to provide a detailed, yet concise description of potential corporate contributors. Identify the major companies and industries in your city, and describe how and why each might be persuaded to contribute to or support your local public TV station.

4. Write a research proposal to discover why your most recent fundraising campaign was not as successful as hoped and the characteristics of present and potential local individual contributors (or whether they are similar to the national target segment of individuals who contribute to public TV). Develop a part of your research proposal to discover the major local companies and industries that have/have not contributed to the local public TV station and why.

Your research proposal should discuss the major aspects of the marketing research process, including research questions, a secondary research review, primary research design, data-collection procedures, sampling design, data collection, data processing and analysis, report writing, and potential research firms to contact about conducting the study. Identify local or national research firms you might hire to conduct the research you propose. Explain why the research company or companies are qualified and are appropriate choices for the type of study you propose to conduct. Identify which research company is the best to hire to conduct your research and why. Provide an appendix in your report that includes examples of the types of questions to ask individual and corporate contributors in your study.

---

### CASE 8.3 DEVELOPING A NEW DIGITAL OUTLET OR SITE

Your task is to develop a proposal for a new digital outlet such as a blog, online newspaper, magazine, category portal, etc. The goal is to create a digital outlet that is economically viable. Your outlet or site may have a targeted national audience (e.g., *Huffington*

*Post* online newspaper) or be targeted to a certain region (e.g., such as *Southern Living* magazine), state (e.g., *Texas Monthly*), or city. Your outlet could be targeted to a particular device or sets of devices (e.g., tablets such as iPads, smartphones, etc.). You could target a particular demographic or psychographic segment (e.g., such as *Bon Appetit*, targeting gourmet cooks, etc.). Your primary criteria are that a significant and viable audience segment and group of major advertisers exist to support the digital outlet. You must provide supportive data that are realistic and suggest the venue you propose could survive and prosper.

You might begin by evaluating information including blogs, reports, and industry trends at the Digital Content Next homepage (www.digitalcontentnext.org). including the research reports it offers. Visit the Mobile Marketing Association (mmaglobal.com) and the MPA—Association of Magazine Media's site (www.magazine. org) for information and reports. Visit the Newspaper Association of America (www.naa.org), which includes information on digital publishing. The latest MPA Magazine Handbook includes a variety of information including the market for e-reading (www.magazine. org/insights-resources). You might also visit Conde Nast Digital to see a media kit site for various outlets (www.condenast.com).

Check to see whether your library has these Standard Rate and Data Service reports, either printed or via online access, including the Digital Media, Consumer Magazine Media, Business Publication Media, Local Media by DMA, Newspaper Media, and TV & Cable Media reports. Review the SRDS reports that have information regarding your proposed type of outlet to see which outlets already exist in the categories or locations you are considering, what their editorial descriptions are, their regular features and sections, who they target, how much they charge for advertising, and so on. Conduct a search on ABI Inform/ ProQuest, Lexis-Nexis Academic Universe, or EBSCO for other articles and data.

Once you have narrowed your ideas to a few categories and/ or locations, evaluate the relevant data in MRI, Simmons, and/or the SRDS Local Market Audience Analyst (LMAA), if available in your library. For example, if you are considering a digital outlet targeted to dog owners, review the demographics, geographics, and media usage data for people who buy dog food in MRI. If your library subscribes to the LMAA, look for information regarding the demographics, lifestyles, and geographics for your proposed outlet. Or assume that you plan to develop an outlet targeting adults with a liberal or conservative political viewpoint nationwide (or choose another psychographic characteristic). Have your professor or librarian show you how to find the information on where persons having the chosen psychographic characteristic live using the LMAA. Have your professor or reference librarian show you how to use this important market research tool to find other information on the audience segment you propose to target in your new outlet.

Reports such as MRI or Simmons contain the names of major brands in the category (e.g., major dog food companies such as Purina, Hill's Science Diet, Iams, etc., and their various brands or varieties). Write down those company and brand names and ask your reference librarian whether their advertising spending data are available in your library. Find out whether advertising data for other major companies, outlets, etc., for the category or locations you are considering are available as well. Check to see which major advertisers advertised in media outlets or categories that are similar to the one you are proposing. Try to find out the amount of spending and media outlets used by other major advertisers that might advertise in your proposed outlet as well.

Review the information or data for the appropriate demographic and/or lifestyle segments for the type of outlet you propose. Review the other lifestyle activities and interests enjoyed by your proposed segment. This helps you to identify potential sections or features, as well as other potential advertisers, for your proposed outlet. Review the instructions in the LMAA to see whether there is other information of interest. If you are thinking about proposing a city magazine, check out the LMAA demographic and psychographic data for the DMA and major counties included in your city of interest. This also will provide ideas and data to help justify your choices of sections and features to offer. Then go online and visit a local library, bookstore, or newsstand to review copies of existing digital outlets or publications in your proposed category.

In other words, find and evaluate as much information, research, and data as possible to develop a thorough digital outlet proposal. Be sure you've developed a comprehensive understanding of the category and audience for which you wish to launch your outlet. Ask your professor and reference librarian for suggestions of other available information sources or databases to use. Use your imagination to develop original and useful information to include in your proposal.

### Assignment

After conducting a thorough and detailed information search, write a proposal to start a new digital outlet. You must support your proposal with relevant and credible information and data. Your proposal must include each of the following sections.

1. Provide a title and overall description of the proposed digital outlet, including its editorial mission and descriptions, features and sections, types of articles or content to include, and so on. Explain why you propose the title you selected. Provide as much detail as you can about the proposed outlet and its content.
   Provide data and information to support why you selected the outlet, type, and category, etc., for your proposal. Explain how and why it is different from other existing outlets with which it may compete. Identify the unfilled niche or position it fills. Make a strong case based on actual recent data and information.
2. Identify and describe your target audience segment in as much detail as possible. Provide an estimate of the audience size or number of potential readers, viewers, or subscribers nationwide (e.g., the number of persons or households owning a dog from MRI, the number of persons having the demographic or lifestyle characteristic of interest, etc.) or in your region, state, or city. Provide as much detail as possible about the major characteristics of your potential target audience, including demographics, geographics, psychographics, and so on. Explain how and why your proposed outlet will be of interest to your target audience. Explain how and why it matches them and their interests. Provide information and data to support your recommendations.

3. Identify and describe a minimum of five potential advertising categories and examples of major advertisers in each (e.g., dog food advertisers such as Purina for a dog-oriented outlet, etc.). Ask your librarian if there are reports having information about how much major advertisers spend on advertising, and in which media categories or vehicles they spend. Search for articles on advertising spending on online databases such as ProQuest, Lexis-Nexis, EBSCO, etc., by typing in the company or brand name and advertising.

Once your search is complete, provide whatever data you can on advertising spending in the five advertising categories you select, as well as the major companies and brands in those categories. If possible, provide data for how advertising spending in the category increased over the past 5 years or decade in order to demonstrate that the potential profitability is increasing for your proposed outlet. Provide information about how much each company or brand that advertises in competing media outlets that may be substitutes for your proposed outlet spends on advertising, if you can. If possible, identify the outlets in which these advertisers have placed ads. Explain why your proposed digital outlet will be an attractive advertising vehicle for these advertisers, providing as much detail, data, and support as you can.

---

**CASE 8.4 UPDATING A DIGITAL OR ONLINE SITE AND MEDIA KIT**

Assume you work for a major daily, weekly, ethnic, or community newspaper, magazine, or shopper, or other media outlet, in your town or the nearest city. Your job is to update the website and online media kit for the outlet. Find a media kit for an outlet in your town or city that seems outdated or less well developed than others found locally. Your job is to analyze that "worst" media kit, propose how to update it, and make suggestions for how to improve the online version of the outlet as well.

Once you've selected the "worst" local media kit, begin by reviewing the online sites and media kits for publications such as *The New York Times* (nytmediakit.com), *USA TODAY* (static.usatoday.com/en/home/), *Sports Illustrated* (www.simediakit. com), and *People* (www.people.com/people/static/mediakit/) as well as sites and mobile media kits such as the Weather Channel's (advertising.weather.com). Find these and others by typing in the name of the publication or outlet and "media kit" in a search engine such as Google. Go through these sites and media kits carefully and thoroughly to discover the types and quality of information you should include in a digital media kit, and the types of information or categories included in most sites in your area. Next review the websites of the existing major media outlets in your city or market (e.g., those for TV stations, radio stations, cable outlets, magazines, other newspaper sites, online sites, digital sites, etc.), to get a good idea of what these local outlet sites and online media kits typically include. Your goal is to make yours the best.

Then review pertinent information about interactive marketing and advertising at the Interactive Advertising Bureau's website (www.iab.net). Visit the Digital Content Next site digitalcontentnext.org for reports and data. Also review the Digital Media section of the Topics & Tools link on the Newspaper Association of America's home page (www.naa.org), as well as other relevant information. Review information related to mobile advertising on the Mobile Marketing Association's site, including the reports on its mobile advertising page (mmaglobal.com/). This page includes reports such as the Universal Mobile Ad Package, which you can open and scroll down to find the standard sizes and types of ads used for mobile advertising. Also check to see whether online traffic and demographic data regarding your site are available at Quantcast (www.quantcast.com) by entering the online address of your outlet in the search box (e.g., entering nola.com if you are using the online version of the *New Orleans Times-Picayune*).

Next go back and review the types of information and data the local online media kits include as well as how they describe the benefits of advertising in these outlets. Develop your own list of pros and cons from reviewing these sites and media kits. Obtain ideas for what to include, what not to include, what to do, and what not to do in updating (or developing, if necessary) the outlet's site and media kit. Consider the pros and cons of the outlet's existing media kit and website. Consider what new information is needed, especially regarding mobile, iPad or tablet, and/or other digital advertising, in the updated site and media kit.

**Assignment**

Provide recommendations for updating and improving your outlet's online site and media kit. Provide details, data, and specific information wherever possible. At the end of each question, provide a section on how the outlet's media kit or website should be improved or changed. (See the suggestions after Questions 1 and 2 for examples.)

1. Online version of the outlet: Provide background information about the outlet, its mission, and descriptions of major pages or features on the site. Then discuss what should be added, changed, dropped, etc.
2. Online editorial sections and descriptions: Provide a brief overview of each section of the outlet and the kinds of articles often found in each section. Identify whether each section targets any specific or special reader segments. Then discuss which sections should be added or dropped, any new reader segments that should be targeted, etc.
3. Online editorial calendar: Provide an editorial calendar showing which special online issues should be published, and when, during the year, if available or applicable.
4. Online audience data: Provide an audience profile including demographics, psychographics, and all other information available. Provide any information you have on reader loyalty, how long readers visit the site, and so on. Compare and contrast the online and regular newspaper readers.
5. Comparative data on other local media websites: Provide any information that identifies the advantages of advertising on your outlet's website versus the websites of other local media outlets. Explain why advertisers should advertise on your outlet's site rather than, or in addition to, other local websites.
6. Online rate information: Provide information about Web, mobile, and digital rates, advertising acceptability standards (i.e. what ads the paper will/will not accept for publication), and other information for selling the site not included earlier.

7. Online advertising units: Recommend the types of online, mobile, and digital ads to offer for sale to advertisers. Justify and support your choices.

8. Obtaining reader information: Provide ideas and suggestions for obtaining demographic, psychographic, or other information from readers. For example, should you require readers to register when first visiting your site and obtain demographic and other information then? What other ways could you collect information for your media kit online that respect the privacy of your audience? What information should you try to collect (e.g., age, income, zip code, education, etc.) and why (especially information that is not already being collected by the outlet)?

9. Discuss any other improvements or changes that are needed. Provide any other advice or guidance for developing or updating the site and the online media kit for the outlet. Provide any other data, design advice, methods, resources, and so on that might be helpful in developing or improving the site and media kit so they are useful to advertisers and the audience.

---

### CASE 8.5 DEALING WITH CABLE CUSTOMER DISSATISFACTION

You are the manager of the cable system in your city (or the nearest city). You are concerned about the constant complaints from customers regarding service. You received 20 letters this week alone; you shudder to think how many complaints the receptionist received by phone. You also are concerned because the local city government is beginning to make noise about the poor level of service the cable company provides.

You decide to conduct a survey of subscribers to identify the major service problems and how they might be solved. You have never conducted a survey and cannot afford to hire a research firm. You must design a study that can be conducted by you and your employees.

### Assignment

Prepare a report describing how you could design and conduct such a survey from scratch using only company employees and resources. Include the following in your report:

1. Identify and describe the appropriate method to use to conduct the survey and how it can be handled in-house. In other words, what kind of survey can be handled by local cable employees and why?
2. Discuss the sources of free or low-cost information to consult for developing your consumer survey. Explain how these sources can be used and why they are appropriate for this situation.
3. Explain how questions for the questionnaire will be developed. In other words, how can you discover what the major problems are before you conduct the survey? How can you decide which questions to include in the survey and why? How can you allow for employee input on which questions to include? How can you allow for community input on which questions to include?
4. Provide examples of the types of questions that accurately measure what your major service problems are.
5. Suggest other questions to include, if any, besides questions regarding the problems and their solutions. Describe the other types of questions to include and explain why they are needed.
6. Make a decision regarding the kind of survey to conduct. Explain and support your decision.

### CASE 8.6 PROPOSAL FOR DEVELOPING OR REVISING A TABLET APP

Develop a new or revised tablet app (e.g., for the latest iPad, etc.) for a media outlet. Select an outlet where additional information or features could be developed for a tablet. Be sure your existing outlet, or proposed app for that outlet, reaches tablet users. To get started, look for recent information on who uses tablets and how they are used. Look for more recent reports that are similar to the Digital Content Next, "A Portrait of Today's Tablet User-June 2011" (http://digitalcontentnext.org/blog/press/tablet-study-and-implications-for-the-online-advertising-industry/). This portrait report includes information such as: tablet users prefer using apps on the tablet to other devices; users watch videos on tablets; which activities are done regularly on a tablet, and which content apps are the most popular for tablets; people's views about newspaper and magazine apps; and tablet advertising opportunities. If possible, have a classmate or your professor bring in a tablet to review relevant apps.

Review information on how organizations manage digital and print content editions. For example, see articles similar to Lauren Indvik's article on Mashable.com, "Inside Sports Illustrated: Building a Magazine for the Digital Age" (http://mashable. com/2011/07/31/sports-illustrated-inside-look/) to see how digital and print editions are coordinated. Search iTunes or online to find descriptions of tablet apps for major outlets, such as CNN, Fox News, *New York Times*, etc., to see how major media outlets use apps. Find out whether and how much these major media outlets charge for their tablet apps. Find out whether media outlets offer 3- or 6-month (or annual) subscriptions designed for tablets and how much they charge for subscriptions.

If EBSCO Business is available through your library, find a list of the major media outlets using apps in "Steve Smith's Eye on Digital Media—Quarterly App Review" in the *Media Industry Newsletter* (Smith, 2011). Conduct an online database search for articles or additional information about how media outlets use apps for tablets. Find and read about any other information or research related to developing a successful app for a media outlet for a tablet.

For more information about current standards, guidelines, and practices for mobile advertising and marketing visit the Mobile Marketing Association's (MMA) Education page (http://www. mmaglobal.com/education). Check to see whether the MMA has developed a revised Universal Mobile Advertising Package for tablets (http://www.mmaglobal.com/files/umap.pdf). For other information that may be helpful, the iPad has a page for app developers (http://developer.apple.com/ipad/sdk/). To get ideas on the types of existing apps for various platforms, review the Android list (https:// market.android.com/details?id=apps_tablet_featured).

**Assignment**

Select a media outlet in your town or city, or in a nearby major city or DMA, that needs to develop an app for a tablet, or could improve the app it has (unless your professor assigns a market or outlet). Develop a proposal for a tablet app for that outlet. Explain what the content will be, the target audience for the app, and so forth.

In other words, provide specific recommendations for the new or updated app. At the end of each question, if you're revising an existing tablet app, describe how the app for that outlet should be improved or changed.

1. Name and Mission: Provide a name for the app and, if you can, a picture or drawing of the app icon. Provide background information about your new or existing tablet app; include the outlet's primary mission and how it differs from other editions. In other words, update the mission to reflect the type of content to be posted on the tablet app. Explain how the tablet app content will differ from other digital, printed, or broadcast editions of the outlet. Then discuss what should be added, changed, dropped, etc.

2. Editorial Sections: Provide a brief overview of each section of the outlet and the kinds of articles often found in each section. For example, CNN includes sections on Top Stories, World News, U.S. News, Politics, Justice, Entertainment, Health, Tech, Travel, etc. Explain how the content in these sections will differ from the outlet's other digital, print, and/or broadcast editions. Identify whether each section targets any specific or special reader segments. Then discuss which sections should be added or dropped, any new audience segments that should be targeted, etc.

3. Editorial Calendar: Provide an editorial calendar showing which special tablet app issues or sections should be published, and when, during the year, if available or applicable. Describe the special issues or sections and be sure they match the audience profile in Question 4.

4. Audience Profile: Provide an audience profile including demographics, psychographics, and all other information available about the audience. Also provide relevant information about tablet app users and how they differ from the users of the outlet's other editions. Explain how and why the content and sections you propose will attract the desired audience.

5. Direct Competitors: Answer Questions 1 through 4 for one or two primary competitors (or the other tablet apps the

consumer would buy, if yours wasn't available). Analyze the differences and similarities between the competing tablet app(s) and your new or revised app.

6. App Uniqueness: Based on your analysis of Question 5, explain how your tablet app is unique or different from its major direct competitor(s). Explain how and why it is different or unique.

7. Interactive Content: Provide examples of the types of interactive content that will be useful to readers and advertisers. For example, if a reader swipes her finger over a photo in the "Celebrity" section, the site for the outfit the celebrity is wearing appears and the reader can go there to learn more about it or to purchase the clothing. Or in a "Technology" section, when a reader swipes her finger over an image of the newest version of the iPad, a Verizon or AT&T link appears where she can go to learn the cost and new features. Provide specific interactive ideas for readers and advertisers.

8. App Pricing Model: Explain whether the outlet should charge for the tablet app or how much it should charge to download the app, if applicable, and why. Explain whether your proposed app should use a subscription model for content access and pricing, how much it should charge for the subscription terms it offers, if applicable, and why. Provide all pricing and term information for your proposed app. In other words, if you propose a free download of the app with a subscription model, discuss how much is charged for a 3- or 6-month subscription, or an annual subscription, or for every such subscription term you recommend. If you propose a paid download with no subscription model, explain how and why this model will be profitable for the outlet. Whatever you propose, discuss how and why it should be profitable for the outlet.

9. Other: Discuss any other improvements or changes that are needed. Provide any other advice or guidance for developing or revising the tablet app. Provide any other data, design advice, methods, resources, and so on that might be helpful in developing or improving the tablet app so it is useful to advertisers and the audience.

# CHAPTER 9

# Law, Regulation, and Ethics

Managers make decisions for a variety of legitimate reasons, most falling into three categories: to advance the organization's goals, to meet legal requirements, and occasionally, to do something just because it is the right thing to do. The other chapters in this text deal with the first reason; this chapter addresses the last two.

Learning about law and ethics is crucial for managers because ignoring them can affect an organization's ability to achieve its goals. Laws, regulations, and ethics act as constraints on the managers' decisions. This chapter provides a basic, concise overview of these constraints; more in-depth examinations of media law and ethics are left to other texts.

## DEFINING LAW, REGULATION, AND ETHICS

*Law* refers to rules created by legitimate authority, such as federal, state, county, and city governments. This includes a country's constitution, laws passed by legislative bodies, and common law that comes from the collective body of court interpretations. *Regulation* is administrative law, which includes laws and rules created by agencies set up through statute by legislative bodies. At the federal level, this includes the rules made by agencies such as the Federal Communication Commission and Federal Trade Commission. *Ethics* refers to standards of conduct and moral principles, or to a process of reaching morally acceptable decisions. Such standards are usually called *codes of ethics*, and the process of reaching decisions is called a *moral reasoning process* (Folkerts & Lacy, 2004). This chapter will address a subset of law, regulations, and ethics of specific interest to managers in organizations that produce and distribute content.

Types of media laws and regulations are not equal and have an order of precedence. That order in the United States is federal Constitution, federal statutory law passed by the federal legislative body (Congress), federal regulations (administrative law) created by administrative bodies, state constitutions, state statutory law created by state legislatures, and state administrative law (Folkerts & Lacy, 2004).

Whereas laws and regulations exist through formal actions by governing bodies, ethics develop informally through social interactions and individual reflections. Although social activities affect ethics, they reside in individuals' minds, and these individuals demonstrate their ethics through behavior. A newspaper reporter's observations and discussions with others in the newsroom obviously affect her perception of fairness, but ultimately the reporter must decide how to produce a fair story.

Because individuals contribute to the development of their ethics, great differences exist among managers' and media workers' definition of ethical. Individual news companies and professional groups have codified ethics in the form of lists of dos and don'ts, but media employees may or may not accept those lists. In addition, the lists themselves can vary as to what is and is not acceptable behavior. These variations can contribute to the difficulty of managing media workers. Usually, variations between an organization's ethical codes and an individual employee's ethics are not great enough to create dysfunctional behavior. Employees who do not accept their company's standards tend to move on. But an organization imposing standards of behavior conflicting with the ethics of a large number of employees inhibits its ability to meet its goals effectively and efficiently.

Law, regulation, and ethics all deal with what should and shouldn't occur. Laws and regulations have the force of government authority and ethics do not. A defining question facing managers is whether to do something that is legal but that their customers may consider unethical. For example, some states have outlawed using the names of rape victims, but others do not. Journalists who can publish rape victim names must decide whether they should, given the feelings among many people that this is not appropriate.

Decisions about legal but ethically questionable policies can have business repercussions. If the public perceives a media company as unethical, consumers and advertisers might decide not to use that particular media product. Conversely, customers also might punish a company valuing money more than taking ethical stances. If a television station runs advertising for a dangerous or worthless product, viewers might choose to watch other stations. This loss of goodwill can reduce the effectiveness of the station's advertising time.

## MEDIA LAW

Laws affecting media organizations fall into several categories. We are particularly interested in prior restraint, libel, privacy, information access, political versus commercial speech, indecency, obscenity, and business law, all of which vary in how much First Amendment protection they receive, but no type of speech is absolutely protected.

### Prior Restraint

Prior restraint concerns government's ability to prevent the publication of information. Over the years, courts have created a high standard for prior restraint. To prevent information from being distributed, government must show a "clear and present danger" from that publication, i.e., that the danger is not vague and is immediate. For this reason, prior restraint of commercial media is unusual.

The classic case of prior restraint involved the Pentagon Papers, a secret history of the United States' involvement in the Vietnam War. Secretary of Defense Robert McNamara commissioned the study, which was classified as top secret. Former CIA employee-turned-antiwar-advocate Daniel Ellsberg leaked copies of the Pentagon Papers to the press. The Nixon Administration received a restraining order to stop publication at several newspapers. However, the Supreme Court ruled that publication did not present a clear and present danger and ruled for the press. Even though newspapers such as the *Washington Post* and *The New York Times* eventually won the case, the companies took a significant risk in challenging the administration. Not only did the case have legal costs, but if the administration had won, it would have significantly reduced the ability of the press to get information about the government (Middleton & Lee, 2011). Managers should monitor major cases and the political landscape to see how it can affect their organization.

### Libel

Prior restraint involves preventing publication, but libel law involves punishing organizations and individuals who injure another through published information. Libel occurs when publication results in false defamation of a person that causes damages. Defamation makes others think less of a person's character, but the defamation must cause some actual loss for the plaintiff to win the libel case.

Libel involves information that likely will be perceived as fact. Opinion cannot be libel. For example, someone could safely express the opinion that the food at Mac's Hamburgers tastes terrible. However, if the same person falsely said the hamburgers were made with uninspected camel meat, he or she likely would lose a libel suit. Courts also have exempted satire from libel laws.

Libel laws do not apply to all people equally. Statements about *public officials* (elected or appointed government agents) and *public figures* (people such as actors, who have put themselves in the public eye) must meet a more stringent definition to be libelous. The higher standard for public figures and officials, called "reckless disregard for the truth," occurs when someone publishes a defamatory lie while knowing it was a lie (*actual malice*) or the person publishes a lie because of inadequate fact checking (*gross negligence*). The higher standard was established in 1964 in *New York Times v. Sullivan.* The Supreme Court ruled that some issues were so important to society that errors in truth had to be tolerated in order to promote vigorous public debate (Middleton & Lee, 2011).

The Associated Press (AP) provides guidelines for avoiding libel actions: stories should be accurate and fair, especially those that "involve negative reports about individuals or companies" (AP, 2011, p. 415). When evaluating stories, consider whether the statement(s) is/are (a) capable of defamatory meaning; (b) factual or capable of being proven true or false, or protected as opinion or rhetoric that a reasonable reader would recognize as hyperbole; (c) understood to be about a specific person, whether or not named or identified; (d) provable as true without violating confidential sources; and (e) wrong or incorrect; if so, would a jury think the reporter did something that any reasonable journalist would have done to ensure the facts were accurate? If these five questions could be answered in the plaintiff's favor, is there a privilege or reason that justifies publication? (e.g., If it is a fair and accurate report on an official government proceeding or document [AP, 2011, p. 414–415].) It is likely these actions are recognized as ethical by many journalists, anyway.

Defamation is part of journalism. Sometimes people who violate the public trust or commit crimes need to be exposed. In doing so, news organizations risk that they might make a mistake and wrongly defame someone. The result can be a lost libel suit, which costs a news organization the damages awarded by the court and the loss of goodwill in the community. However, a news organization that does not pursue risky stories fails to serve its community and can be shown up by competitors.

### Privacy

Privacy laws apply to the reporting of information that people would prefer not be known by the public. Privacy is not found specifically in the

U.S. Constitution, but is a derivative of the Fourth Amendment. Courts have ruled that people have the right to keep confidential some facts about themselves. Three areas of privacy law merit closer inspection: *disclosure of embarrassing facts, intrusion upon seclusion or solitude*, and *false light* (Middleton & Lee, 2011).

Disclosure of embarrassing facts covers a range of events. A television station broadcasting photographs of someone's facelift without permission could be considered an invasion of privacy. A website posting nude photographs of a person without permission also could be invasion of privacy. As with libel, there are several defenses for invasion of privacy. One important defense is that the particular person is newsworthy and coverage of the private facts serves the public. As with libel, public officials and public figures have less protection than do private citizens because they are of interest to the public, by definition. Another defense is that a supposed private act occurred in public view. If someone behaves in an embarrassing way in public, the action is not private. Consent also is a strong defense. If an actor signs a consent form to perform in a pornographic film, that actor is not likely to successfully sue if the film is placed online at some future point. Unlike libel, where truth is an absolute defense, truth only makes the damage of privacy invasion worse. If the fact is false, then privacy law does not apply. The fact has to be true before it becomes embarrassing.

Another type of privacy law involves intrusion upon seclusion or solitude. This area concerns the process of reporting rather than the publishing, posting, or broadcasting of information. Media workers have no right to enter private areas such as homes or automobiles and take information. The key issue centers on what is a private or public place. A person's home is private, but garbage placed on the street for pick-up is not. A strong defense would show the area intruded upon was not private.

Some of the same management issues associated with libel relate to invasion of privacy. If someone sues a media organization for invasion of privacy, the managers must decide whether the organization settles or fights the suit. Either would cost money and could have an impact on how people perceive the news organization. As in all management decisions, financial costs and benefits need to be considered before a decision.

Making people think less of someone, defamation, plays an integral part of investigative journalism; invading privacy does not. Investigative reporting often works best when reporters use publicly available information to discover wrongdoing. However, publishing embarrassing facts often falls within the realm of sensationalism. Ethical concerns about stories that could lead to both libel and privacy suits should be evaluated before the stories are run. What are the repercussions of a controversial story? How would the repercussions serve the community and how might it hurt the community? Were ethical standards followed when the information was collected and published or broadcast?

### Information Access

Because the First Amendment protects journalism as a government watchdog, the press often conflicts with politicians and bureaucrats. Government agencies seeking to control what the public knows are more likely to try to control the flow of information. Controlling information helps politicians and bureaucrats hide mistakes and criminal activities. Media companies cannot report about what they do not know.

To promote the flow of information and improve the democratic process, federal and state governments passed freedom of information acts (FOIA) that specify the process by which media organizations can obtain information from certain government agencies. The process and applicable agencies vary by state and much government information remains secret. For example, the federal FOIA applies only to portions of the executive branch, such as cabinet departments and regulatory agencies. The law does not apply to Congress, the Supreme Court, and the president's staff. FOIAs can be useful for journalists investigating government activities, but using FOIA may not be easy. Agencies can charge for providing information, and the laws have loopholes that can be used to circumvent the spirit of the laws.

Equally important to journalists is access to government meetings where laws are discussed and passed. Access to federal and state government meetings tends not to be a serious problem because many news organizations monitor these levels of government. However, at local levels, where news coverage is limited, city councils and county commissions do not always discuss issues and actions in public settings. To help ensure public and journalistic access to local governments, states have passed open meetings laws. These laws define what local government units can do in private and what must be done in public.

Because most news organizations cover local governments, open meetings acts are valuable tools for learning about government activities and conveying that information to news consumers. To that end, editors and journalists need to know about applicable open meetings laws, and must, on occasion, be willing to go to court to make sure the meeting laws are followed. Unlike libel and privacy laws, which apply to individual reputations, pursuing the enforcement of opening meetings is unlikely to hurt a news organization's goodwill. Most people support open meetings so much that suing to force a city council to be open to the public actually can improve community goodwill.

## Political vs. Commercial Speech

Political speech or dissemination of information related to the operation of democratic government is the type of communication addressed by the First Amendment. The protection stems from the need for vigorous, open debate about issues and people of concern to citizens. In 1942, a distinction was made between political and commercial speech in *Valentine v. Chrestensen* when the Supreme Court ruled the First Amendment did not protect "purely commercial advertising." The ruling said governments under some conditions could regulate the distribution of commercial speech. In *Central Hudson Gas & Electric v. Public Service Commission of New York* (1980), the Supreme Court created a four-part test for whether speech can be regulated by governments: (1) the speech must be eligible for First Amendment protection, it cannot concern illegal activity or mislead; (2) the asserted government interest must be substantial; (3) the regulation must directly advance government interest; and (4) the regulation must be sufficiently narrow or not more extensive than necessary (Middleton & Lee, 2011).

Distinguishing between commercial and political speech can be confusing because political candidates and organizations supporting political change often buy advertising. The famous libel case *New York Times v. Sullivan* (1964) involved an advertisement regarding the civil rights struggle that ran in the *Times*. (A copy of the ad is found on page 124 of Middleton & Lee [2011].) Because news organizations participate in political and commercial speech, media managers need to have an understanding of the legal issues related to both. They need to decide when to accept and reject advertising and when the First Amendment protects advertising.

## Indecency and Obscenity Laws

Media content that large portions of society consider offensive falls into two categories: indecency and obscenity. Obscenity involves content that appeals to prurient interest (obsessive interest in sex), but indecency may not. For example, the Federal Communication Commission can restrict the use of certain words, only some of which involve sexual activity. Indecent material is not as offensive as obscene material; a legally obscene work may be censored and its producers may be punished. Because indecent material has First Amendment protection in print media and online media, most issues regarding indecency involve electronic media.

In *Roth v. U.S.* (1957), the Supreme Court confirmed that the First Amendment did not protect obscene material, the portrayal of sex is not necessarily obscene, and that obscenity is without redeeming social importance. In *Miller v. California* (1973), the court set up a three-part test for obscenity. To be obscene, an average person, applying contemporary community standards, would find that the work as a whole appeals to prurient interests; the work depicts patently offensive sexual conduct specifically defined by state law; and the work, as a whole, lacks serious literary, artistic, political, or scientific value. All three parts of the test must be met before a work can be declared legally obscene (Middleton & Lee, 2011). Of course, it is not always clear what content appeals to prurient interests. The terms "serious literary, artistic, political, or scientific value" and "patently offensive" have a variety of interpretations. A further difficulty is that "community standards" vary and change over time. What would be considered obscene in Alabama may not be in California.

Although obscenity laws have become more liberal over the years, changing federal, state, and local political environments can alter what is legal. Media managers who deal with entertainment content must be aware of what constitutes indecent and obscene material because it can affect a variety of business decisions. The issue of indecency will be dealt with in the regulation section.

## BUSINESS LAW
Business laws apply to most businesses and media companies are no exception. This section will briefly address some of the many business laws applicable to media organizations and how media managers can avoid violating these laws.

### Antitrust
In *Associated Press v. U.S.* (1945), the Supreme Court said the First Amendment did not prevent the federal government from applying antitrust laws to newspapers. Antitrust laws prohibit business practices that seek to prevent competition or monopolize a market. The Sherman Act of 1890 outlaws contracts, combinations, and trusts that restrain trade, as well as outlawing monopolies and efforts to monopolize. An anticompetitive monopoly is when one company controls a product or service in a market and maintains that monopoly by unreasonably excluding other companies or impairing their ability to compete against it. For example, a newspaper with a monopoly in a small town could not refuse to run advertisements from businesses that also advertise on a local television station (Bureau of Competition, 2010, p. 4).

Other major antitrust laws include the Federal Trade Commission (FTC) Act and The Clayton Act. The FTC Act prohibits unfair methods of competition as well as unfair or deceptive acts or practices. The Clayton Act prohibits mergers and acquisitions that substantially lessen competition or create a monopoly, as well as interlocking directorates where the same person makes business decisions for competing companies (Bureau of Competition, 2008). Antitrust action can take the form of a criminal case if a government agency brings suit, or a civil case if a company sues a competitor. As media markets become more concentrated, mergers and sales of individual and media properties increasingly must receive antitrust approval to take place.

Antitrust laws are based on the assumption that competition among media outlets serves customers and advertisers, which has some support in research. Moderate levels of competition increase the amount of money spent on reporting in newspaper and television newsrooms, reduce the cost per thousand for advertising, increase the number of viewpoints available about public issues, and result in more stories about more topics (Lacy & Martin, 2005). Research also suggests, however, that very high levels of competition, such as what many media firms are facing in the digital age, can have negative effects on audiences and advertisers (Becker, Hollifield, Jacobsson, Jacobsson, & Vlad, 2009; Hollifield, 2006; Jacobsson & Jacobsson, 2003). As increased competition cuts into revenues, media organizations cut newsroom and production budgets, layoff the most experienced staff who have the highest salaries, lower entry level wages, and may sacrifice ethics for revenue. Some have argued that the news sites and blogs created by citizen journalists that have added to media competition have increased the variety in media voices. However, such sites generally are not substitutes for a daily newspaper site; often, they do not provide daily updates of news content, they cover fewer topics, and they depend mostly on volunteers rather than paid, professional journalists (Lacy, Duffy, Riffe, Thorson, & Fleming, 2010).

Nevertheless, under current law, media managers whose companies consider acquiring or merging with other companies need to consider the antitrust implications of their plans, including the possibility of criminal and civil actions. Clearance by the Justice Department may not prevent competitors from filing a civil antitrust case. If a case goes to court, the plaintiff must show that the merger or acquisition will lessen competition and have a negative impact on the company filing the lawsuit. Media companies should discuss possible lawsuits with lawyers who specialize in antitrust law.

Antitrust concerns create a conflict for managers at news organizations. Reducing competition would improve a media company's financial performance, but having at least some competition better serves a community. The conflict occurs because, as discussed in the ethics section, many journalists assume that the First Amendment carries an implicit responsibility to serve society.

### Copyright Laws

Because media companies produce information as content, managers' decisions are affected by intellectual property law, which includes copyright. Copyright laws dictate who owns and uses content and information with the goal of encouraging creativity and the production of creative works. Copyright law protects the creative endeavors of people and organizations. Without copyright law, anyone could take another's content and resell it, making it difficult for creative people to earn a living (Middleton & Lee, 2011). For example, about $58 billion in economic output is lost to the U.S. economy annually from copyright theft of movies, music, and video games (Motion Picture Association of America, 2011).

Copyright law covers the presentation of ideas and facts, not the ideas and facts themselves, and includes music, literature, photographs, graphics, movies, journalism, recordings, television programs, radio broadcasts, online works, and multimedia works ("Copyright Law," 2011). If a website publishes a story about a governor's illegal activities, the website story is copyrighted, but other news outlets can cover the same story. However, other news outlets cannot simply copy the story and related material from the website. Copyright does not allow one company to control an idea because the free flow of ideas is crucial to the working of a democracy. For example, the inability of the *Washington Post* to copyright the idea that President Nixon committed crimes during his presidency allowed *The New York Times* and other news outlets to compete in developing this story. As a result, the story of the president's crimes came out more quickly than had only one news organization pursued the story.

To balance the need for information to flow freely in a democracy vs. the need for individuals or companies to own the information they produce, limits were established on how long a person or company owns the copyright and the conditions whereby a person can use content. Currently, a work's creator holds the copyright for 70 years after the creator's death. The duration of protection is different for works made for hire, such as a work prepared by an employee within the scope of employment, where the employer is considered to be the work's author. For works for hire, the copyright lasts 95 years from the year it was first published or 120 years from creation, whichever is shorter ("Copyright basics," 2011).

Even though a person or organization owns a copyright, they cannot exclude others entirely from using the copyrighted content without permission. Fair use allows a work to be used without permission due to the need of society to have access to information and includes criticism, comment, news reporting, teaching, and research. There are four factors to consider when determining whether a particular use is fair (U.S. Government Printing Office, 2009, p. 1; Middleton & Lee, 2011, p. 266):

1. the purpose and character of the use, including whether such use is of commercial nature or is for nonprofit educational purposes;
2. the nature of the copyrighted work;
3. the amount and substantiality of the portion used in relation to the copyrighted work as a whole;
4. the effect of the use on the potential market for, or value of, the copyrighted work.

As media organizations increasingly become international in marketing and ownership, copyright in other countries becomes more important. There is no international copyright that automatically protects a work throughout the world. Protection against unauthorized use in a particular country depends on the national laws of that country. International copyright treaties and conventions, such as the Berne Convention, can provide protection in a country that is a party to one of the international copyright conventions. Some countries such as Afghanistan, Iran, and Iraq offer no protection to any foreign works (U.S. Government Printing Office, 2010).

International intellectual property piracy is a serious problem. The United States Trade Representative (USTR) reported that the piracy of music, films, ring tones, apps, games, and scanned books using mobile telephones, tablets, and flash drives is increasing overseas. It created a priority watch list of countries where intellectual property protection, enforcement, or market access problems exist, including China, Russia, Argentina, Canada, Pakistan, and India. Consider that China has an estimated 457 million Internet users, as compared with 223 million users in the United States. The USTR reported that 99% of all music downloads in China are illegal and the unauthorized retransmission of live sports telecasts over the Internet is increasing there (Kirk, 2011).

## Wage and Contract Law

Managers need to understand wage and contract law because a company's payroll makes up a large portion of its total budget. The budget, in turn, affects the company's profit. How managers deal with wage and contract also can affect employees' morale. Employees who feel valued and appreciated are more likely to invest their own efforts and time in the company.

A number of state and federal laws affect how much media employees are paid. At the low end of employee pay, state and federal laws dictate the minimum wage an employee can make, and at the high end, contract law defines the wage relationship in a negotiated wage. Just how much any individual is paid also reflects market dynamics. Highly skilled, creative, and well-known employees can bargain with management for their salaries. These employees include television anchors and newspaper columnists in news media organizations, as well as radio personalities, actors, writers, and directors in entertainment companies. Of course, not all employees in these categories can bargain for higher than minimal pay. The ability to ask for and receive a premium salary reflects supply and demand for particular skills and the individual's "brand" and professional reputation. Highly paid broadcasters and columnists such as Diane Sawyer and Thomas Friedman have a following among viewers and readers that is comparable to a product brand. Being an employee with a brand can apply at a national level as with Sawyer and Friedman, or at a local level where a TV news anchor has a strong following. People who develop themselves as brands are unusual, and their incomes reflect how much media consumers value them and what they do.

The Federal Fair Labor Standards Act (FLSA) establishes minimum wage, overtime pay, and child labor standards for full- and part-time workers in the government and private sector. For example, it covers employees at companies having annual minimum revenues of $500,000 or engaging in interstate commerce ("Handy reference," 2010). At the time of publication, the Federal minimum wage was $7.25 per hour. When an employee is subject to both state and federal minimum wage laws, he or she is entitled to the higher minimum wage (U.S. Department of Labor, 2011a). Managers should be aware that not all states have a minimum wage law, and the legal minimum wage varies greatly in the United States and around the world. States having minimum wages higher than the Federal rate include California, Massachusetts, Michigan, and Ohio, while states having minimum wages below the Federal rate include Arkansas, Georgia, Minnesota, and Wyoming (U.S. Department of Labor, 2011b).

Managers should remember that these are legal minimum wages. Companies can pay higher wages and may be forced to do so by their labor markets. The geographic nature of labor markets varies with the type of employee. Journalists work in a national labor market and often move for jobs. An advertising salesperson might move, but local connections with businesses would make a person more valuable.

Managers should be aware of other stipulations in the FLSA. For example, workers covered by the FLSA must be paid overtime at a rate of "not less than one and one-half times their regular rates of pay after 40 hours of work in a work week" ("Handy reference," 2010, p. 1). Some journalists qualify for overtime pay and some do not. General assignment and beat reporters typically qualify, but journalists who conduct investigative journalism, analysis, or commentary are considered professionals and are paid salaries (Lucan, 2004). Overtime can be important because breaking news creates erratic schedules for journalists and results in their working more than 40 hours per week. Violations of wage laws are more likely to happen at small news organizations with correspondingly small staffs and newsroom budgets.

Some employees may try to work overtime without authorization in order to increase their pay. To prevent abuses, publicize in writing and in face-to-face meetings that any overtime work must be authorized in advance by a supervisor. Devise and set a policy for approval of overtime work and make sure supervisors and employees understand it. Make sure the overtime policy is workable when breaking news or other timely events occur. Discipline equally all employees who do not follow directions. A supervisor cannot refuse to pay an employee for unapproved overtime hours but, if warranted, can reprimand, suspend, or eventually terminate an employee.

Develop policies to deal with issues such as unauthorized overtime. *The HR Specialist* provides a sample overtime policy for employers:

> Overtime must be approved by your supervisor in advance and should be included on the time sheet in your total hours worked. (Company) retains sole discretion to determine when employees must work overtime. Working unauthorized overtime hours may lead to discipline under our progressive discipline policy, up to and including termination.
>
> ("Stop off-the-clock work," 2011, p. 1)

Another example of an overtime policy is: "Overtime must be approved by your supervisor in advance and should be included on the time sheet in your total hours worked. (Company) retains sole discretion to determine when employees must work overtime. All nonexempt employees will be paid at one and a half times their base hourly rate for any work performed over 40 hours per week" ("How to discipline," 2011, p. 2).

## DEALING WITH EMPLOYEES AND PREVENTING LEGAL PROBLEMS

The basic guidelines for managers to follow to prevent legal problems include: (a) treat all employees the same; (b) communicate with employees in a respectful manner; (c) remain unemotional on the job; (d) stay proactive and address problems immediately; (e) document conversations, meetings, and/or correspondence regarding discipline, performance evaluations, problems, employee queries regarding employment policies, and any conversations or situations that could be subject to disagreements or legal actions; (f) find a good lawyer who specializes in employment law and follow his or her directions; (g) regularly review, keep current, and publicize employment policies; (h) stay current on federal and state employment laws; (i) train supervisors and employees on employment policies, job tasks, and laws; and (j) promptly heed and investigate reports of discrimination, sexual harassment, and workplace bullying ("Lawsuit-proof," 2011).

### Performance Management and Evaluation

Employees perform better when they have a clear understanding of what is expected on the job. Regular, formal communication from supervisors with their employees about performance is simply good business practice. Standardizing the performance evaluation process helps to create a fair process for all employees and minimizes the idiosyncratic influences of individual managers. Documenting performance problems using factual information supports a firm's legitimate, nondiscriminatory reasons for rewarding, disciplining, or firing employees. If possible, standardize performance criteria and measurement across the organization to enable comparisons between employees in various departments and to demonstrate that standards and procedures are applied consistently ("Lawsuit-proof," 2011).

Develop organizational goals that guide performance assessment, allowing managers, supervisors, and employees to participate in setting them. Notify and educate employees about how to prepare for evaluations long before they occur. Meet with employees to discuss the written goals, performance measurements, and deadlines of evaluations. Explain what rewards may be given for exceptional performance and the penalties for unsatisfactory performance (Fox, 2009; Knight, 2011a; McGrory, 2011; Service & Loudon, 2010).

### Progressive Discipline

Managers must be familiar with appropriate procedures for disciplining and, if necessary, firing employees when unsatisfactory evaluations or behavior occur. Using progressive discipline (or using an oral warning, written warning, final written warning, termination review, then dismissal) gives employees a fair chance to correct performance before termination and provides documentation for employers who must fire employees for legitimate, nondiscriminatory reasons. Wrongful-termination lawsuits may result from a failure to document progressive discipline ("Progressive discipline," 2009).

There are steps to follow when planning and executing discussions to address employee performance problems. When you schedule the meeting, make clear what it is about and what you plan to discuss. Make the employee feel at ease, but avoid too much small talk. Focus on the performance problem in nonjudgmental, concrete terms using specific examples. For example, don't say, "Your work has been sloppy lately," say, "Your last three stories have contained an unacceptable number of factual and grammatical errors." If there is more than one problem, address each one individually. Review the standards expected and ensure they are clear and the employee understands why he or she must meet them. Present a plan for helping the employee improve, allow the employee to suggest additional solutions, and agree on a method and timetable for improvement. Offer to help by providing any training, resources, or other assistance available to achieve the performance goals. Provide accurate information and feedback, tell the employee if you believe he or she can improve, but avoid any positive feedback that is not genuine. If the employee is eventually terminated, he or she might question the "real" reason for the termination if you made inaccurately positive comments just to be kind ("Addressing," 2010).

If the employee does not respond to progressive discipline, his or her direct supervisor should not have the final firing authority. Human resources management and/or other supervisors such as the head of that supervisor's department, the supervisor of all departments, and/or the head of the firm should meet before firing an employee to establish whether progressive discipline was followed fairly and correctly. This protects the employee from being fired unfairly by a biased or incompetent manager and protects the firm against a wrongful termination suit ("Progressive discipline," 2009).

Managers should consider the following types of questions in the meeting to ensure that a termination is fair: What is the employee's overall record? Are there any mitigating factors that might explain or excuse the employee's misconduct or unsatisfactory performance? Are any statutory problems involved (e.g., regarding race, age, gender, etc.)? Does the employee have a contract or any implied contractual rights? Has the worker recently filed a workers' compensation claim? Has the worker complained to a government agency about alleged workplace violations or other action that could make the firing appear to be an unlawful retaliation? Is there a good faith or fair dealing issue involved, especially if firing a long-term employee? Has the employee received progressive discipline? Is the termination justified? Does it fit the offense? ("Progressive discipline," 2009).

Although it is difficult to fire someone without due process, on-the-spot firings are warranted when an employee breaks the law, engages in substance abuse on company property, or engages in illegal conduct, gross insubordination, or negligence. If there is any doubt, a manager can suspend an employee until an investigation of the conduct is completed. This allows time to speak to an attorney versed in labor law. Previous disciplinary actions may also be examined to ensure disciplinary actions are fair.

### Understanding and Preventing Discrimination

Title VII of the amended Civil Rights Act of 1964 proscribes employment discrimination (or treating an employee unfairly or unfavorably) based on race, religion, gender, or national origin. Prohibited actions include refusing to hire employees based on race or gender, providing unequal conditions of employment, and providing unequal pay for the same job. Title VII applies to various employment practices including discipline, termination, promotion, and demotion (Title VII, 2011).

It is important to consider discrimination because managers may harbor unconscious perceptions that can influence performance reviews and decision making. Some managers unconsciously identify with people of their own race, gender, or socioeconomic class. Every manager should watch for warning signs that they may favor certain employees over others. Typical signs of partiality include spending more time with some employees and thinking of ways to enhance their careers, but not doing so for all employees; enjoying talking with certain employees, but not others; dreading conducting evaluations of some employees, but looking forward to other evaluations; and relaxing when you talk to some employees, but feeling tense when you speak to others ("Playing favorites," 2010).

Wu and Izard (2008) found that the number of minority staff members employed by a newspaper was a stronger and more significant indicator of the quantity of coverage of that minority group than the size of that group's population in the geographic area. They found that the more Asian American staff members a newspaper employs, the more stories about Asian Americans it publishes. "This study supports the long-suspected association between the presence of ethnic journalists and both the quantity and attributes of reporting about an ethnic group" (Wu & Izard, 2008, p. 109).

The percentage of African American, Asian, Latino, and Native American journalists employed in print and online newsrooms totaled 12.79% in 2011, declining for the third consecutive year. Yet, minorities represent about 36% of the U.S. population. Minorities are 11% of all newsroom supervisors. Of journalists working online only, about 18.7% were minorities. Women represented about 37% of full-time workers in daily newspapers, while minority females comprised 19.3% of female newsroom staffers ("Newsroom employment," 2011). Ironically, the ASNE or American Society of News Editors, which conducts a survey of newsrooms, pledged in 1978 to achieve racial parity by 2000, a goal which now has been pushed back to 2025 (Newkirk, 2011).

In 2004 there were 14 black print publishers, declining to 9 in 2010. In 2004 there were 13 black top editors, increasing to 18 in 2010. In contrast, there were 17 black managing editors in 2004, declining to 10 in 2010. There were only three cities with African American editors and managing editors: Oakland, California, Shreveport, Louisiana, and Jackson, Mississippi (NABJ Print, 2010).

People of color comprise 12.6% of television newsroom managers.

Out of 815 executive producers, assignment managers, managing editors, assistant news directors, news directors and general managers at the ABC, CBS, Cox, FOX, Gannett, Hearst Argyle, Media General, Meredith, NBC and Tribune stations 713 (87.9%) are White, 64 (7.8%) are African American, 24 (3%) are Hispanic/Latino, 13 (1.6%) are Asian, and only 1 is Native American. The management teams at 82 of the stations are all White.

(NABJ Broadcast, 2010)

The Pew Hispanic Center (2009) study found that only 57 of 34,452 news stories examined focused directly on the lives of U.S. Hispanics. Only 645 of the stories in the 55 U.S. news outlets sampled (including 13 newspapers, 15 cable programs, the 7 broadcast network morning and evening news programs, 12 major news websites, and 9 news radio/talk programs) included substantial references to Hispanics. The public learns about Hispanics through event-driven news stories such as the nomination and confirmation of Supreme Court Justice Sonia Sotomayor or the Mexican drug war. Of the major ethnic or religious groups studied, Muslims received the most coverage (3.7%) in the stories examined, followed by Hispanics (2.9%), Asians (2.4%), and Africans/African Americans (2.2%).

Hollifield and Kimbro (2010) argued that media organizations, specifically local TV stations, have not yet embraced workforce diversity and do not reflect their audience. The primary factors from their study in predicting whether minorities were employed in top-level positions at local television stations were the diversity of the population in the geographic area surrounding a station, the station's goal to target minority audiences, minority ownership of a station, and the size of the market. Whether a station was owned by a group and that group's size were unrelated to greater diversity in hiring. The results suggest that minorities may face more obstacles than nonminorities in obtaining top management positions at major stations and in major markets. They also note that "[i]n an increasingly diverse nation, media managers can expect issues of fairness, economic opportunity, source diversity, understanding, coverage of minority communities, and media reflectivity to remain high-profile media policy issues" (Hollifield & Kimbro, 2010, p. 244).

Newkirk (2011) reports that minority journalists are leaving mainstream media to return to minority media outlets. These journalists said they left mainstream media jobs because of the failure of the mainstream media to embrace diverse viewpoints. Minority employees left because they felt they were bumping up against a glass ceiling regarding promotion, resistance to their story ideas, and supervisors who were suspicious about their ability to be objective when covering their minority group. Others said that the newspaper covered stories in the suburbs where more affluent readers lived rather than the city itself where more minorities lived. The advertising industry is not retaining minority employees either "due to the lack of an encouraging environment," highlighting the need to make the industry more inclusive and attractive to minorities (Bush, 2011, p. 4).

Poindexter, Coleman, and Shader (2010) said that people of color and issues important to them have been underrepresented in the news. Historically, African Americans, Asian Americans, Native Americans, and Latinos have been excluded from stories. African Americans have been stereotyped as sports figures, criminals, and poor in news reports. In a 2010 study, these authors analyzed 620 nonwire-service, stand-alone, slice-of-life newspaper photographs for racial composition. For the 76% of photographs including people where race could be identified, 78% included at least one white person, 18% had at least one African American, 12% had at least one Latino, 5% had at least one Asian, while only one photo included a Native American. About two-thirds or 67% of the photographs included whites only, suggesting that newspapers tend to publish segregated slice-of-life photos. The authors argue that newspapers still visually depict everyday community life as homogenous and segregated, even in the most diverse American cities. In news photographs where the purpose is to "represent a slice of everyday life, the study exposes a seemingly innocuous genre of news in which everyday reality is segregated and people of color are under-represented, even when traditional news criteria do not determine newsworthiness" (Poindexter et al., 2010, p. 87).

Pritchard and Stonbely (2007) found that minority reporters at a Milwaukee newspaper generally wrote about minority issues and white reporters generally did not. Specifically, "reporters and editors alike rationalized the situation by saying reporters were assigned to stories and beats at least in part based on their life experiences, which in a majority-minority city such as Milwaukee are heavily influenced by race." They argued that "racial experience was explicitly valued only in the case of minority journalists . . . none of the journalists we interviewed mentioned the idea that being white might be useful in covering the overwhelmingly white worlds of government and business" (Pritchard & Stonbely, 2007, p. 243). They also said that "[b]y and large, reporters of color covered Local Public Issues of secondary importance to people in the newsroom" (Pritchard & Stonbely, 2007, p. 244).

Lasorsa and Dai (2007) compared the content of 183 deceptive news stories that were fabricated or plagiarized in five major news outlets (including stories by Jayson Blair of the *New York Times* and Stephen Glass at *The New Republic*) to authentic news stories from the same outlets. Lasorsa and Dai (2007) argued that reporters, unless able and motivated not to, are likely to stereotype, especially when events are unfamiliar and hard to understand, or the reporter made no personal observations and thus seeks to make stories "resonate with audience expectations" (p. 281). International news stories that were deceptive included the most stereotypes. "Deceptive reporters often conjure characters" who say and do "the perfectly predictable thing" (Lasorsa & Dai, 2007, p. 291). While Lasorsa and Dai (2007) found little gender, race, or ethnic stereotyping in the authentic news stories in their study, they were surprised by "the large number of stereotypes of occupations and social class." They concluded: "If stereotyping is to be avoided in news coverage, then it will take reporters who have both the ability and motivation to avert it" (Lasorsa & Dai, 2007, p. 293).

According to the Global Media Monitoring Project 2010 (www .whomakesthenews.org), only 24% of people covered in traditional media news are female. Women outnumber men only in two occupational categories in the news, as homemakers and students, and are "virtually invisible as active participants in work outside the home" internationally ("Who Makes—Highlights," 2010, p. 2). Men represented 81% of spokespersons and 80% of experts in the news. Of stories reported on television, radio, and newspapers, 37% were reported by female reporters. Stories by male reporters exceed those reported by females for all topics including politics/government (67% reported by males), crime/violence (65%), and the economy (60%). Only 6% of stories featured issues regarding gender equality or inequality. Internationally, "46% of stories reinforce gender stereotypes, almost eight times higher than stories that challenge such stereotypes (6%)" ("Who Makes—Highlights," 2010, p. 3).

For Internet news, women comprised 23% of the news subjects in stories from 84 international websites. Women reported 36% of the news stories online, compared to 64% by males. While most news stories online, 54%, neither reinforced nor challenged stereotypes, 42% reinforced gender stereotypes and 4% challenged them. The Global Media Monitoring Project 2010 concludes that "Internet news is a format in which gender biases become not only more visible but even more concentrated than in the traditional news media" ("Who Makes—Highlights," 2010, p. 3).

The Global Report on the Status of Women in the News Media (International Women's Media Foundation, 2011) found that women have not achieved full equality with men in most of the newsrooms surveyed. "Women represent only a third (33.3%) of the full-time journalism workforce in the 522 companies surveyed" worldwide (International Women's Media Foundation, 2011, p. 6). Women are "in 26% of the governing and 27% of the top management jobs" (p. 9). "In the United States women are less than a fourth of those in top management and only a third of those in governance level roles. . . . Glass ceilings were especially noticeable in . . . the United States" (p. 11).

The Global Report (International Women's Media Foundation, 2011) found several patterns in women's employment in the national news media worldwide. Women were underrepresented in employment, with 44% of the 59 nations exhibiting this pattern. About a third, or 34%, of nations had a glass ceiling inhibiting women's promotion. In 22% of the nations studied, women had achieved relative parity with men and were employed in fairly similar numbers at the news reporting levels or higher in newsrooms (p. 41).

More than half of the newsrooms surveyed had sexual harassment policies, ranging from 47% in Western Europe to 67% in both Sub-Saharan Africa and Asia and Oceana (International Women's Media Foundation, 2011, p. 40). Common responses to the survey question about harassment policies included that sexual harassment was not a problem in their nation or firm so such policies were unnecessary, or that it was an issue raised by "American (or western) feminists" that was "irrelevant" in their country (p. 37). These comments arose in developing and developed countries in almost all regions surveyed. Ironically, the problem of sexual harassment of women in newsrooms was "well established" internationally before the study was conducted (p. 37).

Companies are subject to national laws on parental leave, which differ for maternity and paternity leave and other benefits such as child care and time for mothers to nurse their infants. Maternity leave policies were adopted by nearly all companies surveyed in all regions. Yet for men, only 37% of companies had paternity policies in the Sub-Saharan region compared to 100% in the Nordic European region, where state-sponsored child care is available to all working parents. Consequently, only 12% of the 32 companies surveyed have child-care provisions for employees. These free community services made it unnecessary to offer such policies. Yet low percentages in regions such as 17% in Asia and Oceana and 19% in Sub-Saharan Africa are problematic for employees where such public policies and services are nonexistent. While the percentages of companies offering these benefits may be similar, the differences in public policy in these regions and countries highlight the importance of understanding the laws, customs, and cultures in countries and their effect on employment policies and practices.

Regarding pay, some news organizations refused to provide salary data, despite assurances of confidentiality and only aggregate reporting of data, "which speaks to the sensitivity of the issue" (International Women's Media Foundation, 2011, p. 7). No salary data was provided in Israel and Zambia, while very limited salary data was available in Australia, China, France, Germany, Norway, and Cameroon, for example. More salary data was obtained from news organizations in the Americas, Eastern Europe, Nordic Europe, Asia, and Oceana (p. 29). Males and females generally earn comparable pay in Eastern Europe (pp. 29–30). Pay inequity persists in the Americas, Asia, and Oceana, with men generally earning more than women. While it has been argued that Nordic nations achieved gender parity, the study found that men generally are paid more. However women in journalism are generally younger and have less time in the profession than their male Nordic counterparts, suggesting that men's greater seniority may explain some of the differences in salary (p. 31).

Of the companies surveyed worldwide, slightly more than half had a company policy on gender equity, ranging from 16% in Eastern European to 69% in Sub-Saharan Africa and Western Europe. In the Americas, 38% of companies had a gender equity policy, yet most of these nations apparently lack a national-level law mandating gender equality in the workplace (International Women's Media Foundation, 2011, p. 35).

Once again, there are factors that explain the differences among regions in the proportion of gender policies. For example, under communism in Eastern Europe, women had access to education and were encouraged to work outside the home. After communism fell, many women entered journalism because the profession prospered and most of these nations have national equality laws. These factors help to explain why in Eastern Europe, only 16% of companies had equity policies and why men and women were represented in about equal numbers in the newsrooms surveyed (International Women's Media Foundation, 2011, p. 34).

Nordic and Western European nations are bound by European Union gender equity legislation. Of the companies surveyed, 57% of Nordic companies and 69% of the Western European companies had gender equality policies. Yet the level of female participation does not necessarily correspond to the presence of an equity policy. While women in Western Europe are near parity with men regarding overall numbers in journalism, a glass ceiling limits their participation "above the senior professional level" (International Women's Media Foundation, 2011, p. 35). Only 27% of surveyed companies had a gender equity policy in North Africa and the Middle East and there are no national laws prohibiting workplace discrimination. The combination of few gender equity policies and national laws likely explains women's low representation in most newsrooms in this region.

Geertsema (2009) examined the implementation of a gender mainstreaming policy in the newsrooms of the global news agency Inter Press Service (IPS). The goal of gender mainstreaming is to "ensure women's inclusion in all areas of organizations, including staffing, program planning and budgeting" (Geertsema, 2009, p. 66). Historically, women were ignored or represented in negative and stereotypical ways in news, nationally and internationally, with women being trivialized, sexualized, and victimized in the news media. Geertsema (2009) argued that, despite the best of intentions, the IPS was not able to mainstream gender into all parts of the organization or news reports. However, comprehensive organizational changes led to the inclusion of female and gender issues. Individual reporters were trained, and a gender-sensitive policy was created for employment and news content. The project resulted in employing more women as permanent staffers and promoting women to senior organizational levels.

Geertsema (2009) made recommendations on how to improve the coverage of women. Top management must be committed to the change by actively supporting such coverage and having a succession plan so that future managers support it as well. Approach the change systematically by continually researching, training, monitoring, and evaluating whether and how well changes are made in the coverage of females or other groups who lack coverage or are stereotyped in reporting.

Managers must create a positive climate conducive to open communications, fair and equitable promotions, productive work environments, and job satisfaction for employees of all colors and genders to encourage diverse employees to remain in media industries and prevent incidents of discrimination. Diversifying a media organization involves good business and ethics, not just law. A company that produces cultural goods such as journalism and entertainment needs to understand the diversity of its audience. This occurs best when the workforce and management include members of the various cultural groups in that audience. Professional media groups agree that representing the range of groups in a society is the right thing to do. With the increasing diversification of the U.S. population, this issue will remain important during the rest of the 21st century.

## Trends in Legal Employment Issues

Managers should examine their policies regarding what employees may post on social media and prohibit only communication that legitimately can be restricted, such as disclosure of confidential company information. While it may not be prudent for an employee to complain about a supervisor or company on Facebook, especially if vulgar words are used, a company may not be able to fire that employee for doing so ("NLRB: Employee Facebook," 2011). In developing company policies regarding social media, employers should treat social media similarly to other forms of employee communications. A company should avoid setting rules that are broad, improperly restricting "employees from discussing their wages, hours and working conditions with co-workers while not at work" ("After the NLRB case," 2011, p. 4). Yet neither do employees "have license to defame, disparage or otherwise trash their company, management, product or co-workers" ("After the NLRB case," 2011, p. 4).

Supervisors also should carefully consider whether to "friend" employees. Managers may learn about an employee's sexual orientation or other private information on Facebook. Even if the supervisor never acts on that information, a fired employee may claim that termination was based on this personal information. The liability risk is increased if the boss initiated the friend request ("Should you ban," 2011).

When employee social communications involve protected topics such as discussing wages and other terms and conditions of employment with fellow employees, what an employee posts on Facebook may be protected. Some social media policies were viewed as overly broad, stating employees were subject to discipline for engaging in inappropriate discussions about the company or management, yet what constituted an inappropriate discussion was not clearly defined in the policy. Social media rules that might inhibit employees from discussing an employer's labor policies or treatment of employees are also questionable. A policy prohibiting employees on their own time from posting anything they would not want their supervisor to see, or that would jeopardize their job, when these types of communications were not defined, were viewed as overly broad (Solomon, 2011).

However, when a reporter posted inappropriate and unprofessional tweets on a work-related Twitter account, and those tweets did not involve protected concerted activity, it was lawful to fire the reporter. In this case, the reporter first posted tweets critical of the paper's copyeditors but there was no evidence he had discussed his concerns with any of his coworkers. The Human Resources Director asked the reporter why he posted his concerns on Twitter rather than discussing them with his coworkers. Next, the reporter was told he was prohibited from commenting about the newspaper or airing his grievances in any public forum. The reporter, who was on the public safety beat, then posted tweets about homicides, with several tweets having sexual content and criticizing an area television station. The reporter was called into a meeting regarding these tweets with the managing editor, the city editor, and his team supervisor. The managing editor discussed the tweet about the television station and asked why he was tweeting about homicides, apparently unrelated to his beat. He was notified that it was not acceptable to make these types of tweets. He was suspended and then fired (Solomon, 2011).

Social media and evolving technologies create evolving legal concerns. Many recruiters and human resources professionals use online searches to investigate job applicants. Managers must consider how to handle issues such as finding unsuitable photos or videos, information about one's age or sexual orientation, concerns about a potential applicant's lifestyle, or other information online. Legal actions can result from making subjective hiring decisions based on discrimination regarding an applicant's age or sexual orientation. If such searches are conducted, employers should search based on established job qualifications, provide the guidelines and sources to use in searching for that information, and have personnel other than those making the final hiring decision conduct and report on the search ("Mobile devices," 2010).

Journalists cannot control when a news story breaks, so new and evolving technologies raise other concerns for managers. For employees, time stamps on e-mails or mobile devices show when work-related, and nonwork-related, activities occurred. The history tab on Explorer, Firefox, or Google Chrome can be used to determine which websites an employee visited. If the employer provides the device but allows its use when the employee is not at work, this can complicate an employer's search of the device. Employers are advised to consider providing and paying for smart or cell phones, laptops, or other devices, and specifying that those devices can only be used for work purposes. This allows an employer to clearly assess whether, how much, and when an employee is working. Employment policies should clearly state that the employer reserves the right to monitor the use of electronic devices and secure the employee's consent when hired or when he or she receives the device.

Smartphones iPads, flash or thumb drives, and other devices may also be used to steal confidential company data ("Mobile devices," 2010), making it difficult to protect company files or difficult for journalists to assess whether a source's information was obtained legally.

## REGULATION

Not all media are created equal before the U.S. Constitution. The Federal Communication Commission (FCC) regulates broadcast communication, including the assignment of broadcast licenses for radio and television stations, the establishment of rules of ownership, the punishment of indecent content, and rules for political communication on broadcast media. Justification for such regulation rests on the physical scarcity of the broadcast spectrum and its pervasive presence in society. As technology developed, Congress extended regulatory power over cable distribution, although the regulation remains at a lower level than with broadcast TV and radio. During the last two decades of the 20th century, the federal government began to deregulate the telecommunication industries, although debate continues about the appropriate degree of deregulation. States also have rules governing electronic communication, but federal rules supersede state regulations.

### Broadcast Television, Cable, and Radio Regulation

The Communication Act of 1934 established the FCC and was the primary regulatory act until the Telecommunications Act of 1996. During the 62 years between, regulations changed periodically as technology developed. Three important areas of regulation are ownership, political communication, and indecency.

*Ownership rules.* The FCC sets limits on the number of broadcast stations a firm or individual can own, and on the common ownership of newspapers and broadcast stations. For example, the number of TV stations an entity owns is not limited; rather, the stations owned collectively cannot reach more than 39% of all U.S. TV households. For radio stations, the number and service (e.g., AM or FM) of stations owned varies by market size. For example, in a market with 45 or more stations, an entity may own up to 8 stations and no more than five may be in the same service (AM or FM). The FCC reviews its ownership rules every 4 years to determine whether such rules continue to be in the public interest, repealing or modifying any rule that does not meet the public interest criteria (Federal Communications Commission, 2011).

The FCC evaluates a proposed cross-ownership combination (the joint ownership of a newspaper and television or radio station in the same market by one entity) on a case-by-case basis to determine whether it would promote the public interest, which includes promoting competition, localism, and diversity. All proposed cross-ownership combinations are reviewed based on the following four factors in the market: (a) the extent to which the combination increases the amount of local news; (b) whether each outlet in the combination exercises independent news judgment; (c) the level of market concentration; and (d) the financial condition or level of distress of the outlets, including whether the owner plans to invest in newsroom operations (Federal Communications Commission, 2011).

*Political communication.* The FCC requires broadcast stations to provide candidates with equal broadcast opportunities rather than simply equal time. A station selling time to one candidate must sell opposing candidates the same amount of time during a daypart when a comparable audience can be reached. For example, an hour of time at 7:00 am on Sunday is not equivalent to one hour at 7:00 pm on Sunday as significantly fewer people watch in the morning vs. primetime. However, broadcasters do not have to provide equal opportunities when candidates appear in regularly scheduled newscasts, news interview programs, or spot coverage of news events where content and editorial decisions are made by network or station personnel, not any candidate (Middleton & Lee, 2011).

Broadcasters have no control over the content of a candidate's political programming and cannot censor a candidate's statements that are racist, vulgar, or defamatory. Therefore, broadcast licensees subject to the equal opportunities rule cannot be held responsible for a candidate's libelous statements. Broadcasters must charge political candidates the station's lowest advertising rates 45 days before a primary and 60 days before a general election (Middleton & Lee, 2011).

*Obscenity and indecency.* Obscenity is "the most graphic form of sexual expression and is banned in all media distributed in the United States" (Middleton & Lee, 2011, p. 409). Obscene material appeals to the prurient interest, is patently offensive, and has no serious social value. To determine whether a work is obscene, an average person applying contemporary community standards would find that the work taken as a whole appeals to the prurient interest or "to a lascivious, shameful or morbid interest in sex" and has no social value when viewed as a whole (Middleton & Lee, 2011, p. 411). Patently offensive material, which features an excess of sexual detail or explicit depictions of "hard-core" pornography, is obscene as well (Middleton & Lee, 2011, p. 418).

Indecency receives some First Amendment protection that varies by medium. The Supreme Court ruled in *FCC v. Pacifica Foundation* that broadcasters can be restricted to airing indecent material only when children are unlikely to be in the audience, between the hours of 10 p.m. and 6 a.m. Yet print and Internet publishers have a First Amendment right to disseminate indecency (Middleton & Lee, 2011, p. 447).

Indecency regulations are analyzed by the courts by considering a medium's technical attributes and the audience's level of effort required to receive messages. For example, the Supreme Court regards the Internet as similar to the highly protected print media because both require affirmative effort by audience members to receive a message. Yet indecency is restricted in broadcasting because it is intrusive and accessible to children, even those who cannot read (Middleton & Lee, 2011, p. 425).

The FCC considers the "serious merit" of a program when determining whether it is indecent (Middleton & Lee, 2011, p. 425). An indecent broadcast includes vulgar language or descriptions of depictions of "sexual or excretory activities or organs in a manner patently offensive by contemporary community standards for the broadcast medium" (Middleton & Lee, 2011, p. 429). Context is important in determining indecency; it includes the "manner in which the words or depictions are portrayed, whether the portrayal is isolated or fleeting, 'the merit' of a program, and whether children might be listening or viewing" (Middleton & Lee, 2011, p. 429). Repeating vulgar content and intentionally trying to shock or pander to the audience makes it more likely the material will be found indecent. Indecent content must be preceded by a warning, whether or not children may be in the audience. The maximum indecency fine the FCC is $325,000. A group owner may pay the fine for each station that aired indecent material where viewers complained to the FCC about it (Middleton and Lee, 2011).

### Advertising Regulation and Self-Regulation

Managers may need to train employees to clear or review advertising to determine whether it is misleading or offends the audience. Sections 5 and 12 of the Federal Trade Commission (FTC) Act of 1914 give the FTC the power to regulate deceptive advertising and other unfair acts or practices. The FTC definition of deception is as follows: (a) there must be a representation, omission, or practice that is likely to mislead the consumer; (b) the representation, omission, or practice is examined from the perspective of a consumer acting reasonably in the circumstances to the consumer's detriment; and (c) the representation, omission, or practice must be a material one (Policy Statement on Deception, 1983, p. 1–2). Deceptive claims or practices include false verbal or written statements, misleading price claims, selling dangerous or defective products without adequate disclosures, not delivering promised services, and failing to meet warranty obligations. The FTC considers whether the entire ad is likely to mislead reasonable consumers, meaning that even if all of an ad's claims are true, if the general impression of the ad is false, it still may be deceptive (Policy Statement on Deception, 1983). Advertisers must have prior substantiation such as competent and reliable scientific evidence that supports any claims made in advertising (Middleton & Lee, 2011). An advertiser injured by a competitor's misleading ad may sue under Section 43(a) of the Lanham Act (Middleton & Lee, 2011).

The FTC said certain practices are not likely to deceive reasonable consumers. For example, misrepresentations about inexpensive products that are evaluated easily and purchased frequently by consumers are of less concern because these advertisers depend on repeat sales for survival. The FTC usually does not pursue cases based on puffery or correctly stated and honestly held opinions about a product, or obvious exaggerations about the product or its qualities (e.g., the "best" or "greatest") ("Policy statement on deception," 1983).

The Advertising Self-Regulatory Council (ASRC), comprised of several voluntary regulatory programs, fosters truth and accuracy in national advertising. One NARC program, the National Advertising Division (NAD) initiates, evaluates, investigates and rules on whether a national advertisement in question is deceptive. The Children's Advertising Review Unit (CARU) does the same, handling deception cases for child-directed advertising and promotional material in all media, as well as online privacy practices. An advertiser may appeal a NAD or CARU decision to the National Advertising Review Board (NARB), which is the appeal division and provides the final review. If the advertiser does not comply with the NAD, CARU, or NARB decision, the case may be referred to the FTC or the appropriate government agency (Middleton & Lee, 2011; ASRC, 2015).

Media managers must expect that the regulation of media industries will dramatically change in the future. As noted earlier, every 4 years, the FCC reviews its ownership rules to determine whether these rules continue to be in the public interest, repealing or modifying any rule that does not meet the public interest criteria ("Review," 2011). Managers must keep abreast of any changes in ownership or cross-ownership rules that could affect their media outlets. Issues regarding children's privacy online (Federal Trade Commission, 2011) and what types of food and beverage advertising should be directed to children (Better Business Bureau, 2011) continue to be of concern to parents and regulators. Such issues will require managers to face decisions pitting the business interests of their owners against the public interest. Such regulatory and self-regulatory concerns will raise thorny ethical issues to be faced by media managers.

## ETHICS

Ethics and law are interrelated. Laws and regulations define what a manager must do, and ethics defines what he or she should do. Laws prevent a manager from stealing trade secrets from a competitor, but laws may not prevent her from lying to gain an advantage. Courts settle disputes over just what a law means, but no formal authority settles disputes about ethics. Some journalists believe that reporting should be fair, balanced, and complete, but others believe that journalists should express their opinions in what they write. Regardless of what they believe, managers of news organizations need to understand that the individual citizens who use media pass judgment on what they feel is ethical journalism. This judgment by the court of public opinion does not require that news organizations do everything their readers, viewers, and listeners want. Not only is it impossible to suit all potential media users in a market, sometimes doing as the audience wants can violate professional ethics. For instance, some readers expect newspapers to run the names of people arrested for crimes. However, many newspapers have a rule that the names of arrested people will not be run until after the people are officially charged by the prosecutor.

Just as there are disagreements as to what are appropriate ethical standards, managers, journalists, and ethicists also disagree on the best way to establish ethics. Most news organizations and professional journalism associations have codes of ethics. Other media organizations, such as those in the information and entertainment businesses, are less likely to have codes. Such codes, however, do not guarantee ethical behavior. Codes can be vague and difficult to follow and enforcement for many is voluntary (Goodwin, 1987). Merrill (1974) argues that media workers must decide whether to be ethical; a code will not cause a journalist or manager to behave according to standards if the individual has not already decided to be ethical. The argument about the relationship between codes and behavior explains the two approaches taken to media ethics. Those who doubt the effectiveness of codes argue that ethics must be established through a rational process that applies general principles to each ethical situation. This "moral reasoning" process makes ethical decision making more flexible than just adhering to a list of rules.

### Ethics Codes

Codes of ethics exist in many media industries. For example, the Society of Professional Journalists (SPJ) has its Code of Ethics (www.spj.org/index. asp) and the Radio Television Digital News Association (RTDNA) has its Code of Ethics and Professional Conduct (www.rtdna.org). The Public

Relations Society of America (PRSA) has a Code of Ethics (www.prsa.org) and encourages members to consult with PRSA's Board of Ethics and Professional Standards when dealing with ethical dilemmas. The Institute for Advertising Ethics has its Principles and Practices for Advertising Ethics (www.aaf.org/institute-advertising-ethics), while the 4As has its Standards of Practice and Creative Code for advertising agencies (www.aaaa.org/about/association/pages/standardsofpractice.aspx).

Codes represent behavior acceptable to employees of a media organization, such as the *Washington Post*, or to members of a professional organization, such as Public Relations Society of America. The codes can take a negative tone by listing behaviors that are unacceptable or a positive tone by listing behaviors that are encouraged. An example of a positive listing is this statement from the Society of Professional Journalists Code of Ethics: "Test the accuracy of information from all sources and exercise care to avoid inadvertent error" (Society of Professional Journalists Code of Ethics, 1996). Examples of negative standards from the same document are: "Never distort the content of news photos or video" and "Never plagiarize."

Most codes represent the position of the organization that created the code. Although it wasn't a code of ethics, the Commission on Freedom of the Press, also called the Hutchins Commission after Chairman Robert Hutchins, undertook an effort in the 1940s to define standards of behavior for a responsible press (Commission on Freedom of the Press, 1947). Reacting to a growing economic concentration of media, the Commission listed five requirements of a press that was responsible to society (Commission on Freedom of the Press, 1947, pp. 20–29):

- A truthful, comprehensive, and intelligent account of the day's events in a context which gives them meaning;
- A forum for the exchange of comment and criticism;
- The projection of a representative picture of the constituent groups in the society;
- The presentation and clarification of the goals and values of society;
- Full access to the day's intelligence.

This was not a code of ethics because it prescribed requirements for the entire media system, not individual organizations. However, the underlying assumption is that individual media organizations should be responsive to the needs of their communities and not just pursue their own self-interest. This assumption, called social responsibility, differs from that of the libertarian approach, which assumes that if news organizations each pursue their own interests, then the system as a whole will supply the diversity of voices and positions a democratic system requires. Most codes of ethics are based either on the social responsibility or libertarian approaches toward journalism.

Codes of ethics have drawbacks. They can be overly general and vague and they can be difficult to enforce. A media organization's code will only be as strong as the individuals in the organization are ethical. However, codes also have the advantage of explicitly communicating to employees what is expected of them. In effect, codes can be a form of programmed decisions that tell employees what can and cannot be done. They force the people within the organization to think about and discuss the values of the organization and the behaviors that promote those values.

Managers need to understand the advantages and disadvantages of codes of ethics. If an organization has an ethics code, management should examine it periodically and include employees in that examination. The assessment should evaluate how well the organization's code fits with professional standards and social norms, how well employees follow the code, and how well the code fits the goals of the organization. If an organization does not have a code, management should consider whether it wants to add one, and if so, what form it would take.

### Moral Reasoning

Moral reasoning concerns how individuals use logic to solve moral and ethical problems (Jaksa & Pritchard, 1988). A consistent process of reasoning allows people to solve problems without relying just on their emotions. The role of reasoning in ethics is central, according to Merrill (1974):

> If there is not a large dose of reason in one's ethical determinations, there can really be little or no consistency and predictability to ethical actions. And, of course, one of the main purposes of ethics is to serve as a reliable and helpful guide to right actions. Such a guide cannot be provided simply by whim or instinct; otherwise we could talk of dogs and cats as being ethically motivated.
>
> (Merrill, 1974, p. 185)

Moral reasoning can be thought of as a process, or a series of processes, by which people evaluate and solve ethical problems. A variety of processes are available to help individuals analyze a problem (Bok, 1989; Goodwin, 1987), but most of these involve a manager or employee asking a series of questions about the impact and benefits of the ethical decision. The following questions are consistent with the various questions used to promote reasoning:

1. What is the goal of the action?
2. Is this the only or best way of accomplishing the goal?
3. Who is harmed by the action?
4. Is the harm justified?
5. Who benefits from the action?
6. Do the benefits outweigh the harm?
7. Will the action be consistent with generally accepted standards in the business?
8. If not, do the benefits demand that the action be taken?

The success of the moral reasoning process revolves around collecting sufficient information about the decision. This is especially true of the potential harms and benefits. Rather than speculating, managers should collect hard data. Another similarity to the decision process is that some ethical decisions can be programmed through ethics codes. For example, at large commercial news organizations, truthful, balanced, fair, and complete reporting should be required regardless of the news story. These types of generally accepted professional behaviors need not be discussed with editors in making individual story decisions. The time managers save can be devoted to solving more controversial ethical issues.

Dealing with ethical problems is central to the management of any business that expects to serve the public. This is particularly true of media organizations. Ethics codes and moral reasoning can help managers cope. The two are not mutually exclusive. Both require that management and employees commit to the idea that businesses have responsibilities beyond what is legal. Such commitment cannot be assumed. Managers should create an environment in which ethics are discussed, encouraged, and used on a daily basis.

### SUMMARY

Understanding U.S. and international law, regulations, and ethics remains central to a media manager's ability to achieve the organization's goals. Laws and regulations constrain an organization's goals and manager's decisions. They are dynamic, changing with political, social, and economic shifts. Ethics also change, but because they carry no formal enforcement process, they constrain decisions less than do laws and regulations. Ethics concern whether decisions met standards of right and wrong. This chapter provides only a surface introduction to the issues related to these areas. Students should access online material and the various sources cited here.

## CASE 9.1 THE AGGRESSIVE LEGAL EXPERT

You are the news director at Fair & Balanced News (FBN), a new news network distributed over cable. In order to gain audience from the existing networks (CNN, Fox, and MSNBC), you have taken an aggressive approach toward your reporting. Some might call it sensational, but you prefer the term "muckraking." One of your stars is Susan Allen, who looks for criminal cases from throughout the country and interviews people connected with the cases. The promotional phrase of the program, called the *Allen Report*, is "Searching for Justice."

The program has been on air for about 6 months and has seen a fairly rapid increase in viewers. It is a close second to Fox for the time slot and does well with the 18 to 49 demographic. This morning, you received a letter from a reporter at *The Daily Tribune* in a medium-sized, Midwest city. The letter addresses a program from last month about a criminal case covered by the reporter.

The letter includes the following information about the case: 6 months ago, John Smith pleaded guilty to aggravated sexual assault of a child and indecency with a child by contact and received a 10 years suspended sentence. Any violation of the conditions in the sentence would result in Smith going to jail for up to 99 years. He has to undergo counseling for sex offenders and, as a registered sex offender, cannot come within 1,500 feet of locations where children congregate. In addition, Smith can never be around the child in the case. As part of the sentence, Smith must complete 500 hours of community service, but because of health problems, the service will be working in a library.

The child is Smith's 8-year-old stepdaughter and the daughter of Smith's former wife. The accusation came to the attention of the prosecutor during the divorce proceedings. The mother had contacted the Child Protection Agency 6 times before the divorce, accusing Smith of sexually abusing her daughter. In each case, doctors examined the child and found no physical evidence of sexual abuse.

The reporter's letter went on to criticize Allen for the program about this case. Allen had the prosecutor on her show as a guest, but constantly cut him off when he tried to make a point that conflicted with Allen's position. At the end of the interview, Allen made a statement that implied the prosecutor had physical evidence of assault, and before the prosecutor could disagree, she closed the interview. At the close of the segment about this case, she accused the judge in the case as being too liberal and called for the removal of the judge.

The letter disagreed with this assessment and explained that the judge is known in the county as a fair and hard-working judge. It also points out that if the case had gone to a jury rather than being plea-bargained, it was unlikely that a conviction would have resulted because there was no confession and no physical evidence of abuse.

The reporter writes that she talked with a producer on the Allen program and was told that the statement about physical evidence was a misunderstanding between the writers and Allen. However, the producer said Allen would not retract the call for the judge's recall.

The reporter's letter ends with: "Susan Allen's call for the judge's resignation was uncalled for and inconsistent with the facts of the case, as was her insinuation that the prosecutor had physical evidence of abuse. The behavior was unethical, and the viewers of the *Allen Report* should know about the story."

### Assignment

As news director of FBN, you need to react to the letter and to discuss the case with Allen and her staff. In doing so, you should think about these questions.

1. Did the story violate journalism ethics? Explain your answer.
2. What should the news director do about this particular story? How will your solution help the network? How might it harm the network?
3. Should the network run these types of programs in the future? Why or why not?
4. Would you change policy in the newsroom? If yes, how? If not, why?

### CASE 9.2 EXPANDING THE WEBSITE

You and a friend started a commercial website in a small, college town in Ohio. You are both graduates of the college and enjoy living in the area. After 2 years, your gross revenues reached $400,000 and you have three part-time employees. The website, YourTown

.com, carries news and features about the college and community. In addition to you, your friend, and the part-time employees, many residents contribute information at no cost.

The publisher and editor of the town's weekly newspaper approaches you and offers to sell you the newspaper because she is planning on retiring. The weekly is the only other news organization in the town, except for a weekly college newspaper. In addition to the publisher/editor, the weekly staff includes two full-time and two part-time employees. The weekly, which is distributed for free in the central portion of the county, has gross income of $450,000 a year.

You and your partner are interested in acquiring the newspaper, but you are not sure how this might affect the way in which business laws apply to your new media company. The acquisition would double your revenues and number of employees, as well as affect competition in the town.

**Assignment**

Use the information in this chapter and gather additional information from the Internet regarding the laws that might affect the creation and running of this new company. Identify the laws and factors you'd have to consider by combining your website and the weekly newspaper. Discuss the impact of the laws and how that might affect your decision to buy the weekly. What information do you need to better evaluate the impact, and why? Would some of the laws have a greater impact than others? Which ones and why?

---

### CASE 9.3 THE BANKER AND LAUNDERING DRUG MONEY

A reporter at KCCR-TV in Muleshoe, Texas, recently received an anonymous message in the mail claiming that the president of the Fifth National Bank is laundering money for illegal drug dealers from Mexico.

According to the note, the banker, James Wilson, has created several fake companies. The dealers send money to the banker, who deposits the money in the account of one of the companies. This company then buys goods from a second company and that second company buys from a third company, until the money has gone through several companies. The note claims that no goods ever change hands. In the end, the money is deposited into an account that belongs to the drug dealers, minus a service charge for the banker. The note said he makes four trips a year to Mexico to meet with the drug dealers.

The reporter talks with his news director, who said she has met the banker on a few occasions at the Rotary Club lunch. However, Wilson is not active in community politics or any other sort of public activities. He lives on a large ranch in a very big house, but that would be expected of a bank president.

The reporter and news director discuss what they can do and identify the following actions:

1. They simply ignore the note because they don't have the resources to investigate this type of story.
2. They send a copy of the note to the Texas Rangers to see if the Rangers would like to investigate. If there is any truth to the note, the station can run the story after the Rangers arrest the banker.
3. They begin discreet inquiries into the banker's background and behavior without mentioning the note to anyone. They would start with finding out whether the banker travels to Mexico on a regular basis.
4. They confront the banker with the note and see how he reacts.

**Assignment**

Put yourself in the place of the news director. Using the material in the chapter and any other relevant information you find, answer the following questions.

1. Can you think of any other options? What?
2. Discuss the legal and ethical implications of each option. Could the option violate the law? How? Is the option unethical? Why?
3. Which option would you pursue and why?

---

### CASE 9.4 THE CASE OF THE POORLY PERFORMING SALESPERSON

Ed Markham, the African American sales manager at WCTV, is considering how to handle a problem with one of his salespersons, Jane Folsom, who is white. Ed was promoted to sales manager 3 months ago after working at WCTV for 2 years. He earned his promotion by exceeding sales goals every month after his first on the job. He developed a research report using secondary data from sources such as MRI and the SRDS Local Market Audience Analyst to analyze the market. His former boss praised the report, gave a copy to all salespersons, and included a summary of it in the rate card. When his former boss left for a new job in a larger market, he recommended Ed as his replacement.

Jane has been a salesperson at WCTV for 2 years. For most of that time, she has exceeded sales quotas about as much as Ed had. For the past 3 months, she had not met sales quotas. After his second month as sales manager, Ed talked to Jane about her performance. She attributed her below-average performance to the closing of a major advertiser, Anthony's Fashions. This local clothing store closed because several major retailers, including JC Penney and Dillard's, had opened at the local mall.

Ed listened to Jane's explanation and then suggested ways to obtain new clients. He asked Jane whether she had set personal sales goals, set up a prospect file of new and inactive advertisers as well as existing businesses that were potential clients, come up with research and data on the market to use in presentations and reports to clients, come up with new ideas or opportunities to advertise for clients, or asked her clients about their needs and goals (Shaver, 1995). Jane said no, she simply telephoned or visited her clients regularly to see if they wanted to run ads.

Ed also asked Jane why several of her clients had not paid their bills. He explained that a salesperson must check out a client's ability to pay before running a schedule. Jane replied that she was not aware of that fact and that no one had ever trained her to sell. She had sold time for a radio station before, but that was all the training she'd had. Ed's predecessor had just hired her and cut her loose.

Ed gave Jane a memo after their first meeting a month ago asking her to focus on sales training for the next month. First, she should read Shaver's (1995) *Making the Sale! How to Sell Media with Marketing*. He gave her a copy, told her to read it, and asked her to contact him if she had any questions. After reading the book, he told her that she should establish written personal sales goals, begin to develop a prospect file (with two new and two inactive clients), and develop three ideas for new advertising opportunities for existing clients. In the memo, Ed told Jane that he would not hold her to sales performance standards that month. He wanted Jane to focus on doing the background work he assigned to help her improve her future sales performance.

At the meeting a month later, Ed discovered Jane had made only a halfhearted attempt at training. For example, she had not developed a prospect file; she told him she had no idea how to do it. Ed asked her why she had not contacted him to set up a meeting to discuss questions she had about the book or completing the assignments, as noted in his memo. She said she had forgotten. When asked specific questions about Shaver's (1995) sales book, she was unable to respond, suggesting she had not read it.

Ed asked Jane to read the book again, and scheduled a meeting with her to discuss the book. He instructed Jane to have a written memo ready for the next meeting that identified the assistance or training she needed to accomplish the tasks he had set for her the previous month. "Base your needs assessment memo on the Shaver book and be prepared to discuss the book fully," he told her. Ed said he would send her a memo about their meeting, outlining what he had verbally asked her to do during the next month as well as the consequences of not completing these tasks. Ed told her, "Jane, if you don't start to make a serious effort in participating in your training, and ultimately improving your sales performance, your job here could be in jeopardy." He followed through and sent the memo, keeping a copy for his files.

Ed's gut feeling was that something else was bothering Jane. He wondered why she had gone from exceeding sales quotas to below-average sales performance. He was surprised an employee would respond half-heartedly to a written notice of unsatisfactory job performance. He wondered if there were another reason she was not responding to his attempts to help her. Ed wanted Jane to succeed because he thought she was a good salesperson despite her apparent lack of formal training and her poor recent performance. He wanted to give her a fair chance to improve, but knew he would have to fire her if she did not take her training seriously and improve her performance. He wondered how to be fair to her while protecting the station. He had never faced this kind of problem before. Welcome to management, he told himself.

**Assignment**

Using information from this and previous chapters, answer the following questions:

1. Have Ed's actions in working with Jane been fair and appropriate thus far? Why or why not?
2. Are there any other steps Ed should take now in dealing with Jane and this situation? If yes, explain them in detail.
3. What do you think may be the reason for Jane's sudden poor performance?
4. How can Ed discover whether there is another reason for Jane's apparent unresponsiveness to his efforts to help her improve her performance without incurring any legal liability? Should he take steps to find out? Why or why not?
5. What steps should Ed take to identify the training Jane may need? Why?
6. How can Ed determine fairly whether Jane simply lacks adequate sales training without opening his station to a wrongful termination or other lawsuit? Explain your answer and provide examples of what Ed should do.
7. How should Ed document the steps he takes to train or, if necessary, discipline Jane? Why?
8. How should Ed respond to today's meeting with Jane? To answer this question, write a sample memo from Ed to Jane about today's meeting.
9. Write a sample memo for Ed assuming that Jane does not respond satisfactorily to the meeting scheduled for one month from now.
10. Write a sample memo for Ed, assuming Jane does respond satisfactorily to the meeting one month from now.
11. What other present or future steps or actions would you recommend to Ed? Why?

**CASE 9.5 REVIEWING AND ANALYZING FOIA RESOURCES AND ISSUES**

Select a state of interest and review information online and use other available sources to discover its information access laws, if any. Conduct a database search of freedom of information in ABI/Inform, ProQuest, EBSCO, and/or Lexis-Nexis Academic to find recent cases or issues regarding access to information in your state of interest, or about other current states' or national freedom of information legislation, issues, cases, or debates. For example, see if any access issues or cases involving national security have arisen. Have there been any abuses of access in the name of protecting national security? Have any other cases involving celebrities or public figures arisen? Is there a new category of access issue that has emerged recently?

Visit the nearest law library to review copies of the access laws in your state of interest. Contact the appropriate government agency or office for more information about access in your area. (If your research into state access-to-information rules becomes too difficult, then research access at the federal government level.)

Conduct an online review of FOIA sites. Check out the SPJ's FOIA Resource Center (www.spj.org/index.asp). Review other sources that may have articles and information on access. For example, try searching the Reporters Committee for Freedom of the Press site (www.rcfp.org), which offers an Open Government Guide providing information on each state's laws (www.rcfp.org/open-government-guide). The RTDNA or Radio Television Digital News Association (www.rtdna.org) has a Freedom of Information page. Also try Cornell University's Legal Information Institute (www.law.cornell.edu).

### Assignment

Develop a report, including but not limited to the following questions, which could be used by reporters or others in the state you selected as a guide to understanding the FOIA, the major issues surrounding it, and the processes for requesting government documents.

1. What laws, if any, are applicable in the state you selected?
2. What are the major contemporary issues regarding access to government information in your state and nationally? Identify and describe each type of issue, both national and state, and provide a description and example of each.
3. What are the general techniques for obtaining documents from the appropriate state government or federal entities?
4. What are common problems or pitfalls to avoid when attempting to gain access to government documents?
5. What other important information or advice did you find in your research? Identify and explain each factor here.

### CASE 9.6 REVIEWING AND ANALYZING INDUSTRY CODES

Read and review the major industry codes of ethics including the (a) SPJ Code of Ethics (www.spj.org/index.asp); (b) RTDNA Code of Ethics and Professional Conduct (www.rtdna.org); (c) PRSA Code of Ethics (www.prsa.org/AboutPRSA/Ethics); (d) Institute for Advertising Ethics Principles and Practices for Advertising Ethics (http://www.aaf.org/institute-advertising-ethics); and/or the (e) 4As Standards of Practice and Creative Code for advertising agencies (www.aaaa.org/about/association/pages/standardsofpractice.aspx). Your professor may assign these and/or other codes to review.

First, identify the major topics or themes that are common to all codes. Second, identify the major topics or themes that are unique to one or a few of the codes. Third, consider how and why those themes are similar or differ from code to code. Fourth, consider the strengths and weaknesses of each code. Fifth, identify other topics or themes that are omitted from one or more of these codes but should be included.

#### Assignment

Once you've completed your review and analysis of the codes, answer the following questions:

1. What topics or themes are common to all codes? Why are those topics or themes important? Why are they included in all or most codes?
2. What are the major topics or themes that only appear in one or a few codes? Why are these topics or themes rarely discussed in other codes?
3. Are there any major topics or themes that are omitted from most or all codes that should be included? What are those major topics or themes? Why should they be included in most or all codes?
4. What other changes should be made in one or most codes? Why?
5. Are these codes too specific or too general? Can they be used, as written, by industry workers to deal effectively with ethical issues when they arise? Why or why not?

6. Select one code and revise it to make it more effective for dealing with ethical issues. To answer this question, you can take one of two approaches: Either select three principles or topics from a code, rewrite them, and explain why your revised version is more effective, or select three topics or themes you identified as lacking from a code, write those three topics or themes in the language of the code you select, and explain why these new statements or sections will be effective and helpful to industry workers in dealing with ethical issues.

# Extended Case Study 1: Changing Leaders and Direction in Dallas/Fort Worth

**TO THE INSTRUCTOR: ABOUT EXTENDED CASE 1**

Effectively facilitating case discussions requires significant preparation by the professor. The professor first selects an appropriate case, or certain questions from a longer case such as the Extended Cases here, to accomplish the learning objectives for each class. Then significant effort and time are devoted to preparing to discuss each case or question. Zbylut, Brunner, Vowels, and Kim (2007, p. 1) noted that instructor preparation requires "(a) building a complete understanding of the case, (b) constructing discussion questions to elicit key points and influence student thought processes, and (c) anticipating potential student statements, misconceptions, and questions that might arise during discussion."

In addition, professors must "orchestrate the discussion in such a way that they spend minimal time lecturing and maximal time soliciting a variety of student perspectives. Moreover, the instructor must be able to manage the group discussion process so that no one student dominates the discussion, less talkative students participate, the discussion stays on topic, differing student opinions do not devolve into destructive confrontations, and students end the discussion more knowledgeable than they were prior to discussion" (Zbylut et al., 2007, p. 1–2).

A number of sources, including those cited in the Introduction, provide background information and ideas for instructors on using the case method. For example, instructors who seek ways to make students comfortable about speaking in class and enhancing case discussion might review Aylesworth (2008). Professors who need assistance in teaching financial concepts, such as profit ratios or cash flow, might use Case Studies—The Role of Financial Analysis (Cenage Learning, 2015). For more information on teaching using the case method see Boehrer and Linsky (1990); Case Method How-Tos (Columbia University, 2015); Christensen (1987); Lundberg (2009); Lundberg and Enz (1993); Lundberg, Rainsford, Shay, and Young (2001); Preparing (2005a, 2005b); and Weber and Kirk (2000).

Extended Case Studies 1 and 2 feature fictitious characters at fictitious media organizations facing fictitious situations. While each case is based on real-life events representing the types of problems and issues media managers face on the job, neither case represents any real-life person or organization. These cases also provide practice in using concepts covered in all chapters of the book.

Both extended cases can be used as major end-of-the-semester assignments, assignments to cover certain course segments, several chapters, or one chapter. The questions indicate which chapters are to be used in formulating answers. One or more questions from the case also can be assigned for in-class discussion or preparation for a major case assignment or exam. For example, if you plan to use Extended Case 1 for your midterm or final, assign Question 1 well before your deadline for an in-class discussion, based on concepts covered in Chapters 6 and 8. That way all students develop an overview of the case and the major problems to be solved. You could use one or more questions this way to prepare students for whatever approach you wish to take with the case.

If you prefer to use a holistic approach and plan to assign a number of questions from an extended case throughout the semester, assign questions to be discussed in class for the day when those chapters are due to be read. Because many questions can be used with more than one chapter, you can revisit those same questions later in the semester to demonstrate how managers' decisions may change when more information about options, or additional facets of a problem, are considered. For example, have students read Chapters 1 through 3 and assign Question 2 for an in-class discussion. Assign Question 2 again after students read Chapter 4 to have them reconsider how the difficulties of entrepreneurship might affect leadership, motivation, and a changing workforce. This method can be used for any question that incorporates multiple chapters.

Some extended case questions allow students to apply the concepts they learn using real-life examples that are readily available online. This helps students to learn to find quality and reliable sources of information to solve problems they'll face on the job. Several questions include Web titles and links where students can use and analyze information to answer the questions. For example, Question 11 provides links for legal advice for nonprofit and for-profit sites or startups. Question 12 includes the links to several codes of ethics to provide examples for students in developing ethics codes and policies for the site they propose. Question 14 has students visit several websites that provide information about how to measure and quantify site audiences.

Have students read the Introduction before they begin work on any cases. It explains why and how the case method is used for teaching managerial concepts and also provides examples of how students should prepare for case discussions in class. One or more questions could be assigned from each extended case only once during the semester. Either or both extended cases also can be used in a holistic and comprehensive approach to dealing with organizational problems. As noted earlier, different questions from one or both cases can be assigned at several points during the semester. Using the holistic approach allows students to see how changes in one area of the firm affect other departments or decisions in that same organization.

Extended Cases 1 and 2 also can be used for individual and/or group assignments so students learn and apply the individual and group decision-making aspects covered in the book. For example, have students work individually on one question in a case. Then have them work in teams on other questions in the same case at midterm. Have teams work on some or all of the case's questions as a final course project. The goal is to provide the most flexibility to professors and students in using the cases to allow for different teaching and learning styles.

Many sources are included in Backgrounder 5, for example, to teach students to locate, assess, and analyze a variety of data. That is why Extended Case 1 allows you to select a major city close to you, if you prefer not to use the market featured in the case. Professors often already have data about nearby cities or media markets to be used for cases. The examples presented in Extended Case 1 provide ideas for sources to find data for the city you assign. That way you can tailor the case to meet your own learning goals and use material you already have.

Students will find the number and types of sources in the extended cases overwhelming if they receive little or no guidance in using them. Professors are therefore urged to examine the sources included in the extended cases before assigning them to students. You can then select the sources most appropriate to your goals and teaching style. Titles are provided to aid searching because some of the Internet addresses in the case will change or disappear after publication.

For example, before assigning Extended Case 1, professors are encouraged to review sources such as the J-Lab's Launching a Nonprofit News site found at www.kcnn.org. This learning module includes 12 steps on all aspects of launching a nonprofit news site, so decide whether to use all or some of the steps when deciding whether to assign the entire case or certain questions from it. Other reports from the J-Lab are available at www.j-lab.org and its how-to site for community journalism at www.j-learning.org/. Poynter's Entrepreneurial Journalism page at www.poynter.org/category/how-tos/ provides various articles. Also see the Tow-Knight Center for Entrepreneurial Journalism's Resource Guide for Local Sites at http://towknight.org/research/, as well as its Resource Guide for Business at http://towknight.org/research/resource-guide/business/. Visit Columbia Journalism Review or CJR's Guide to Online News Startups at www.cjr.org/news_startups_guide/ to examine the various commercial and nonprofit startups around the country (and find out which ones are now defunct). CJR's guide can be useful for students who need ideas about the type of hyperlocal content they might propose, or how an existing startup might be changed to become more profitable. Online Journalism "How-To" Guides are found at www.ojr.org.

You may find additional information about hyperlocal startups at The Citizen Media Law Project's Forming a Business and Getting Online at www.citmedialaw.org/legal-guide/forming-business-and-getting-online, which also addresses legal issues entrepreneurs must consider. Hermes (2012) wrote a detailed guide explaining how news organizations must be structured to obtain federal tax-exempt status as a nonprofit organization. More information about a variety of legal issues pertaining to online publishing can be found at the Digital Media Law Project's (DMLP) searchable Legal Guide at www.dmlp.org/legal-guide. DMLP also has a page on How to Start a Business. If you're a member, the Society of Professional Journalists has the SPJ Freelancers page at www.spj.org/freelance.asp. These are just a few of the resources available online, enabling you to prepare and teach as much or as little as you'd like about the issues and knowledge needed to participate in entrepreneurial journalism.

Once you've decided how to approach Extended Case 1, consider teaching your media management course in a computer lab, even for a short period of time, to allow the class to conduct a Web, database, and library search to locate information to share. Organize an efficient search for the students by assigning different search objectives to different students or teams. For example, have a class discussion to generate an exhaustive list of search objectives and key words or terms to use for searching. Then assign one team to conduct a thorough search in the Lexis-Nexis Academic database, another team in ABI/Inform ProQuest, and a third team to search EBSCO Academic and/or EBSCO Business (or whatever online databases are available through your library). Assign another team to conduct a thorough Internet search using Google or similar search engines. Have another team go to the library to obtain other relevant published information or make an appointment with a Reference Librarian to locate any other available or newer information or publications. Assign another team to find data from Mediamark, Simmons, and/or the SRDS Local Market Audience Analyst, if these resources are available at your library. Assign other teams to search the links or sites listed in Backgrounder 5 (e.g., for Irving, Texas, and the Dallas/Fort Worth metropolitan area). Continue making such assignments until all major information sources available are to be investigated by a team.

Instruct all students to post or e-mail any useful articles or citations they find to the professor. Most online databases have an e-mail function for this purpose. If useful Internet sites are found, those Web addresses could be pasted into an e-mail message and sent to the professor. After the research is conducted, the professor can organize and share the relevant articles and sites to the entire class via e-mail, Blackboard, Google Docs, or a digital dropbox.

By dividing the major search goals, then organizing and sharing what is found, much information to use in working on the case can be obtained quickly. Then the class is assigned to read sources or assigned materials to discuss in the next class or future classes. Breaking up and organizing the case and related tasks this way teaches students how to break major projects into manageable parts, how to organize a strategy of action to obtain quality information quickly, and how to organize and consume information once it's obtained. Such projects will be less overwhelming when students encounter them on the job because they'll already know how to divide projects into manageable steps.

Conducting a market analysis can be a formidable project. It could be bewildering for students to define the geographic and product market, trends in technology, and future demand for media products for a hyperlocal site, for example. Consider having the class as a whole conduct a market analysis together or discuss each major aspect to provide focus and direction. After the class conducts and reads the research you shared with them, use Table 7.1: The Market Analysis Process as an outline to follow when conducting class discussions. Or you might assign groups to report on each major or relevant category of a market analysis, using the research the class as a whole found. Again, students will learn to focus on one part of a project at a time. They'll see how their colleagues present insights and ideas that they did not see, demonstrating the value of a variety of perspectives. Students also learn about group decision making, including its positives and negatives, as they consider different viewpoints and sources when deciding what the best course may be based on the market analysis.

Extended Case 1 provides information and practice in dealing with managing change and entrepreneur journalism. Extended Case 2 provides practice in dealing with diversity, crises, as well as international and cultural issues. Both cases allow students to deal with specific problems in the overall context of the organization and situation. Both involve vexing management situations with no easy or clear answer. Students must consider the managerial, organizational, structural, legal, ethical, and human consequences of the decisions they make.

The first goal in both extended cases is to give students a chance to consider major problems that they are likely to face in their careers. The second goal is to instruct students on how to quickly find good, relevant information to aid in problem solving and decision making. A third goal is to provide a variety of real-life situations where students can apply theory, research, and data analysis. A fourth goal is to give students a better perspective on how smaller problems seemingly unique to one department or situation are interrelated with, and not necessarily independent of, larger, more complex organizational problems. Next, background information is provided to help you in completing these extended cases.

The "Backgrounder" sections provide information on topics covered in the extended cases. These provide some of the context you will need to answer questions regarding each case. These also provide examples of the types of information you may need to find to help you complete case assignments or deal with managerial problems after you graduate.

### BACKGROUNDER 1: CITIZEN JOURNALISM

Citizen journalism, also called participatory or user-centered news production, is news produced by amateurs rather than professional journalists, "often with less editing and less rigor" (Kaufhold, Valenzuela, & Gil de Zuniga, 2010, p. 515). Citizen journalism includes comments in a blog, user-generated photography and video, as well as news stories on digital or social networking sites. Kaufhold et al. (2010, p. 517) identified the differentiating characteristics: citizen journalists are unpaid, have no professional training, typically publish unedited content, use plain language, have distinct story selection and news judgment, access to their content is free and interactive, and typical reporting is on hyperlocal issues.

Citizen journalism is not a new phenomenon, but online digital platforms have made it much more common, as it is far easier now to produce and distribute one's own news. Online citizen journalism first came to prominence when citizens present at breaking news stories such as the London Tube bombings or South Asia tsunami used smartphones or other personal devices to e-mail images or video to news outlets or post them online. Given the global recession, many major news organizations can no longer afford to have reporters and bureaus in as many locations around the world. As a result, "photographs taken by so-called 'street reporters' are finding their way onto the front pages of major news vehicles, including *The New York Times*, *The Guardian* and *Time* magazine" (Citizen Snappers, 2011, p. 15).

Citizen journalists can serve as a powerful force for global change (Garcia, 2011) by sharing photos and videos of breaking news events (Schaffer, 2007) such as the South Asia tsunami or the Arab Spring. Curry (2010, p. 54) said: "cell phones, Twitter, and the Internet allow any daring individual to send messages to the outside world. This action may not stop rulers from brutal repression but does turn it into a globally known event." While governments may ban foreign correspondents to inhibit reporting on repression, it is much more difficult to identify or stop citizen journalists from posting incriminating photos or videos. Repressive regimes may monitor or block Internet access, but hackers often develop programs to circumvent those blocks almost as quickly as they are implemented (Curry, 2010).

A number of sites, apps, and services allow citizen journalists to publish or sell their visuals. For example, citizen journalists can post visuals of breaking news events using CNN's iReport at ireport. cnn.com. Smartphone apps such as Meporter (meporter.com) enable citizen journalists to register and post reports online as well as follow breaking hyperlocal news directed to a particular small town or area of a city. Citizenside.com allows citizen journalists to post images that are shared with other reporters or sold to media outlets. Demotix.com also enables amateurs to post images to be sold to news organizations. Demotix claims to offer global reach to media with "a vast network of local photographers on the ground" who "have a different perspective than Westerners have and can often get access they can't" (Citizen Snappers, 2011, p. 15). For example, citizen journalists offered better access to coverage of the 2009 Iran election protests than professional journalists could (Kaufhold et al., 2010).

Yet there are concerns that compensating citizen journalists might encourage some to fake videos or invent scoops to gain money or attention (Colchester, 2011). Reports posted by citizen journalists on social media or YouTube often include inaccuracies (Grotticelli, 2011). Nichols and McChesney (2010, p. 16) argue that citizen journalism cannot replace great investigative journalism because "you get what you pay for." They argue that a foundation of newsrooms with digital components and professional, adequately paid staff is needed to maintain journalism's watchdog role. Professional journalists can be inaccurate as well, but most media organizations have an established process for correcting errors and distributing the correction, which citizen journalists often do not.

There are a number of other problems associated with citizen journalism sites. These sites tend to be short-lived, focus on personal information and entertainment stories, struggle to gain audiences and advertising, and provide highly specialized topics or areas rather than comprehensive coverage of communities and their public issues. Citizen journalists may have a very limited impact on the news agenda, lacking the influence that professional journalists or outlets have. Therefore, while the journalism industry tends to be overly positive about citizen journalism, its long-term impact and viability appear uncertain (Karlsson, 2011; Kurpius, Metzgar, & Rowley, 2010; Singer et al., 2011).

## BACKGROUNDER 2: HYPERLOCAL AND COMMUNITY JOURNALISM

Given the worldwide growth of citizen journalism, media outlets sought to provide content of local interest to communities to encourage resident engagement with sites. Grabowicz (2012) reported that many newspapers adopted a hyperlocal strategy where they created locally focused sites for individual towns or communities, or areas of a major city, that provide more in-depth, extensive coverage of local issues. Such local sites might have the typical sections found in newspapers, such as crime, education, or health. These sites also offer even more detailed "verticals" or coverage of specific topics of concern to local residents. For example, the health section might post health department inspection reports on local restaurants, supplemented by databases, background information, and/or citizens' reports or comments. Hyperlocal news also includes "when that danged Dunkin' Donuts is finally going to move in. Or why there isn't a stoplight at the intersection where there have been a lot of accidents" (Farhi, 2007, p. 43).

Other independent community news startups, as well as companies with platforms for creating hyperlocal sites, are springing up in local markets. AOL Patch, Yahoo Local, and Facebook Places are platforms for creating hyperlocal sites and attracting local advertising (Grabowicz, 2012). Patch.com is a community-specific news platform intended to provide in-depth, trusted local coverage for individual towns and communities. Patch helps residents stay abreast of news, view local visuals, learn about local businesses, participate in local discussions, and submit visual and verbal content. Patch is managed by local professional journalists who are supported by a team at the New York City headquarters. Patch encourages local residents to comment on stories, share opinions, post visuals, and post events to the community calendar. Business owners may request a listing on the hyperlocal site ("About us," 2012a).

The communities where Patch.com sites are launched are selected based on demographic characteristics of affluence in a local population such as median household income, the level of Internet penetration, and the quality of the school district (Roach, 2012). To build goodwill, Patch sites dedicate space to enable local charities and volunteers to find each other. Free advertising space is donated to local charitable organizations and Patch managers and employees contribute time as volunteers ("About us," 2012a). The Patch.org Foundation seeks to establish Patch sites in inner-city neighborhoods and localities underserved by media with populations of 15,000 to 100,000 around the world that would benefit from having access to local news about government, education, and business (Patch.org, 2012).

Shields (2010) reported that AOL's Patch and MSNBC's Every-Block hyperlocal platforms represent an effort to move into the $15 billion local Web advertising market. Patch and EveryBlock sought to own the void left by the demise or shrinking of daily newspapers. EveryBlock sought to gather and organize information from government agencies to provide block-by-block local news. Patch hired local reporters to cover stories such as the creation of a town's new animal cruelty unit, high school basketball, and the local municipal budget. These companies are trying to take advantage of cheap publishing technology and the ability to hire unemployed journalists and freelancers at low rates.

Patch also offers self-service advertising at each local site, creative Web pages for local businesses, and do-it-yourself advertising platforms. Competition for local advertising dollars comes from firms such as Yodel, ReachLocal, and Local.com, which create banner ads, videos, and search marketing for local advertisers, as well as CityGrid, an extensive local online ad network. Social networking as well as smartphones and apps have spurred local digital advertising (Shields, 2010).

Grabowicz (2012) said hyperlocal sites may fill a void in local or neighborhood coverage when daily newspapers cut staff or fold. Some sites partner with local media such as newspapers to gain financial support and credibility. Major media firms select cities or counties in which to support hyperlocal sites based on factors such as growth rate and affluence. For example, the *Washington Post* selected Loudon County, Virginia, because its median household income of $98,483 is among the highest nationwide (Farhi, 2007).

The hyperlocal site Loudonextra.com was designed to rely on citizen journalists, including bloggers and amateur contributors who live in Loudon County. When introduced, the site planned "podcasts of some local church sermons, real-time accounts of high-school games and highly detailed restaurant guides . . . revealing which restaurants are open after 11:00 pm" (Farhi 2007, p. 43). Yet, raising awareness is difficult and small businesses do not have much money to spend on advertising (Farhi, 2007; Adams, 2008).

Backfence, which folded after about 2 years, provided "microscopic" local news that traditional media did not cover. It included discussions between reporters and residents producing "back and forth exchanges of hundreds of words of passionate prose" that provided "far more detail and nuance on a topic than a traditional news story" (Potts, 2007b, p. 66). Backfence.com had over 400 local advertisers, yet some ads sold for only $50 and advertising revenues did not grow as quickly as planned (Farhi, 2007).

EveryBlock's hyperlocal sites allow the audience to follow neighborhoods and connect with neighbors by creating an account and selecting places to follow, including one's home address, work address, or a particular zip code area. EveryBlock includes local news such as crime reports and public records, neighbors commenting on news reports or having questions about local events, civic information such as restaurant inspections and building permits, media mentions when your selected neighborhood or zip code is named in news coverage, as well as local photos, reviews of local businesses, and lost-and-found postings from Craigslist. EveryBlock sites are available in five cities such as Chicago, Illinois (www.everyblock.com; "About EveryBlock," 2015).

VillageSoup (villagesoup.com) in Maine was another type of hyperlocal site, called a community host. It had a three-column website with traditional news in the left column, user-generated content including bizBriefs and blog entries in the middle column, and advertising in the right column. Local businesses paid $20 weekly to post content, which is not censored by the editors, ranging from the menu of the day to the dangers of oral piercing on bizBriefs. The Knight Foundation gave $885,000 to update the site's software and create an open source version so others could launch similar sites without paying a licensing fee. VillageSoup earned 21% of its advertising revenue online, yet had not recorded a profitable year as of 2010 (Carpenter, 2010).

Potts (2007b) said that newspapers and broadcasters are experimenting with local, user-contributed sites, offering a low-cost way to provide detailed coverage of issues and stories typically uncovered. Crowdsourcing or using amateur contributors to develop staff-directed investigative stories has been tried. For example, the Gannet-owned Florida paper, *The (Fort Myers) News-Press*, used dozens of experts and local citizens to investigate the high cost of local sewer service, resulting in 110 stories about the issue. As a result, a local official resigned and sewer fees were reduced by 30%. The hosted discussion on the sewer rate controversy was the most visited part of the newspaper's website.

Professional journalists must understand certain realities when interacting with citizen journalists. User-generated content is often a forum for sharing and discussing goings-on around town, not reporting in the classic sense. Place safeguards such as profanity filters, moderate discussions, and provide "report abuse" mechanisms so local debates remain civil and informational. Realize that journalists and the audience often care about different issues. Citizen journalists provide insights into what is important to local residents; ideas which often show up a few days later in local newspapers (Potts, 2007a,b).

Potts (2007a,b) also noted that citizen journalists will write about their localities for free because it makes them feel like experts in their community and provides a chance to have their voices heard. Yet citizen journalists do not replace professional journalists; they add to news stories through commentary, providing additional information and giving a voice to the audience. Citizen journalism also gives residents a personalized stake in local print or broadcast outlets that develop sites. With the feedback provided by residents, professional journalists may be freed to cover local stories in more depth.

Citizen journalists are rarely trained journalists, and especially in smaller towns and cities, the work or visuals they post may be of poor quality and require significant editing. Another problem is that reports by professional journalists on hyperlocal sites may be indistinguishable from posts by amateurs. Professional journalists are trained in journalism techniques and standards to avoid bias. The average reader of a hyperlocal site may not realize that some journalists are trained to report objectively, while amateurs may have an agenda or "axe to grind" (Barton, 2011).

Schaffer (2007, pp. 59–60) reported many sites claim they do not need to make money as they use volunteer labor and server space can be as inexpensive as $13 monthly. Consequently, many citizen sites assess their efforts as successful based on community impact such as increasing voter turnout to town meetings and elections, helping localities solve problems, and serving as a local government watchdog. Formerly, few sites used traditional measures of success such as unique visitors to a site, number of page views, or revenues. However, as more site owners and bloggers are seeking revenue, most are measuring readership and related statistics now (Lowrey, Parrott, & Meade, 2011; Schaffer & Polgreen, 2012).

Schaffer (2007, p. 61) reported that hyperlocal site founders said attracting contributors and operating support continue to be "major challenges" and it is unclear "whether sustainable business models will emerge." Schaffer (2007) reported that hyperlocal sites are not generally successful businesses and demand for start-up funding is high. Farhi (2007, p. 40) reported that "few of the estimated 500 or so 'local-local' news sites claim to show a profit, but the overwhelming majority lose money" and "their business models remain deeply uncertain." About half of the 141 respondents to a J-Lab hyperlocal site survey said they did not need to earn revenue to survive due to volunteer labor and self-funding. Also, 80% said that either their sites did not cover operating costs, or they were unsure whether operating costs were covered. Only 10 of 141 hyperlocal sites reported breaking even or earning a profit, and those profits were typically very modest.

Schaffer and Polgreen (2012, p. 7) reported that of the 278 respondents to a national online survey of digital-first news startups, 82% focused on a specific community or geographic region, while about 37% reported on a specific topic such as health or the environment. Almost 97% had original content, 63% aggregated content from other sources, and 62% had advertising. Many were very small as 37% had fewer than 10,000 unique visitors per month, while, overall, about 65% had 50,000 or fewer unique monthly visitors. Only 32% reported having more than 50,000 visitors per month.

Digital news startups tend to have a small staff and are launched by young journalists entering the business, midcareer journalists who lost their jobs, or empty nesters who view online journalism as a way to volunteer locally. About 52% of the respondents at startups were between ages 18 and 44, while 25% were between 18 and 34, and about 48% were 45 and older. Readers were encouraged to comment on the sites or their Facebook pages, subscribe to newsletters, become site fans, and tweet or retweet information to grow the audience that could read their stories. About 91% engaged readers through social media such as Facebook discussions or shared content; 81% encouraged readers to contribute photos, stories, or other content. E-newsletters or listservs were used by 75% to alert readers to content, while 63% used events to increase readership and build relationships. Fewer engagement efforts were directed to advertisers (56%), volunteers (42%), or donors (40%) (Schaffer & Polgreen, 2012).

A digital site's publisher or editor (81% of respondents) was typically responsible for building engagement and 65% worked at least 10 hours weekly on engagement activities. There were few efficient ways to measure engagement; manual counts were used to document donors, volunteers, attendees to an event, or revenues raised. Sometimes website activity was monitored, online registration tools were used, or comments or anecdotes were tracked to follow civic engagement (Schaffer & Polgreen, 2012).

Digital site respondents reported that the unique number of visitors (66%) and page views (55%) were the most important tracking tools. About 91% measured engagement using the number of unique visitors and about 91% used page views. While 79% monitored comments, 76% tracked readers' average time on the site. Only 37% tabulated click-throughs to advertisers. For social media, about 79% monitored the number of Facebook fans and 65% tracked Facebook likes, shares, or comments. About 74% measured the number of Twitter followers, while only 53% tracked Twitter activity (Schaffer & Polgreen, 2012).

About 79% of digital-first respondents did not track whether engagement strategies were converting the audience into content contributors, volunteers, donors, or advertisers. Between 65 to 67% used engagement measurement to develop editorial content, and 63% used it for obtaining feedback. Only 45% tried to recruit more content contributors or social media users through engagement measurement, and 37% used tracking to develop marketing or outreach opportunities (Schaffer & Polgreen, 2012).

Not all journalists are happy with audience measures and feedback in the age of online news. Audience feedback plays a role in news decisions as sites generate articles to match what readers search for or respond to online, a "democracy" some journalists dislike (Singer et al., 2011). Engagement measures have a dark side for reporters who fear that too few views of their stories could cost them their jobs. Comments are posted at the end of articles so all readers can view positive and negative feedback about a reporter's work. One Philadelphia journalist termed his readers "a bunch of boorish jerks" (Schudson & Fink, 2012, p. 63).

## BACKGROUNDER 3: RECESSION AND JOURNALISM

The recession was an important factor in spurring the growth of hyperlocal sites and citizen journalism. MacMillan (2008, p. 1) reported that "[t]he news business is in disarray. Thousands of journalists have been left jobless by deep cuts at *Time* . . . Gannet . . . Viacom and other large media properties." Small publications nationwide shuttered operations, while others limited the number of days they published or eliminated bureaus or printed editions. Many migrated online to pursue advertising revenues. Yet online ad revenues grew too slowly to offset reductions in print advertising. Entrepreneurs and journalism advocates experimented with community-funded online journalism, soliciting donations to pay for the work of professional journalists. To be successful, digital sites also had to rely on grants, advertising, or other institutional donations.

For example, representative journalism, where readers in a community sponsor a reporter to cover local stories, has been attempted. The argument was that 1,000 contributors, perhaps paying $1 to $2 per week, could sponsor a reporter to cover a community or topic of interest, such as endangered species in Florida. Such sites also could seek advertising. For example, in November 2007, *MinnPost* was launched by Joel Klein, the former editor of the Minneapolis *Star Tribune*. The site was supported by $390,000 in Knight Foundation grants, donations from more than 1,000 readers, and some display advertising (MacMillan, 2008; see www.minnpost. com). Propublica.org is another independent, nonprofit journalism site that develops investigative journalism in the public interest. *ProPublica* has 34 working journalists. One of its stories won the 2010 Pulitzer Prize for Investigative Reporting and another series of stories won the 2011 Pulitzer Prize for National Reporting. The Sandler Foundation funded ProPublica's launch and other philanthropic donations, individual contributions, and some advertising help keep the site afloat ("About Us," 2012b).

Major costs may be incurred by such sites. Paul Steiger earned $570,000 in base compensation as president and editor-in-chief of *ProPublica*. The estimated cost to produce an article by Dr. Sheri Fink about the alleged euthanasia of patients in the wake of Hurricane Katrina for *ProPublica* and *The New York Times* cost $394,000. In addition, *Chi-Town Daily News* raised $300,000 in 2008 to support the site, yet it had to lay off reporters and change to a for-profit model because it could not raise sufficient funds ("Hard Numbers," 2009, p. 11).

Nichols and McChesney (2010) said that the recession led media organizations to shrink or cut newsrooms and state, federal, or overseas bureaus. Many large newspapers went bankrupt or made severe cutbacks in staff and resources. A serious consequence is the potential loss of quality, independent journalism. They argue that "a free press [with] the resources to compensate those who gather and analyze information, and to distribute that information widely and in an easily accessible form" is crucial to sustaining our democracy. In addition, "a free people can govern themselves only if they have access to independent information about the issues of the day and the excesses of the powerful" (Nichols & McChesney, 2010, p. 12).

Advertisers once supported the news in order to reach consumers. Major financial problems arose as media corporations came to view newsrooms as profit centers rather than a public good offering an important service to communities or the nation. Now the journalism industry fantasizes "that it is just a matter of time before a new generation of entrepreneurs creates a financially viable model of journalism using digital technologies. . . . There is no business model . . . that will create a journalistic renaissance on the web" (Nichols & McChesney, 2010, p. 13). It is unclear how quality journalism from adequately funded newsrooms with paid staff will survive online as "volunteer labor is insufficient to meet America's journalism needs" (Nichols & McChesney, 2010, p. 16)

Journalists who were laid off during the recession must work for less at hyperlocal sites having hourly deadlines, serving as both writer and photographer, perhaps taking a digital and Flip video camera to every interview or event. Newspaper sites pay from $50 to $200 per article, slightly more than hyperlocal sites. Patch pays by the article, which can total several hundred or $1,000 per month for a freelancer who writes stories for several sites (Walsh, 2011). Professional reporters are often poorly paid by hyperlocal sites, earning only $25 to $50 for a post or story. Without good-paying journalism jobs, experts on politics in city hall cannot be supported (Barton, 2011).

McCracken (2010, p. 10) said that "anyone can launch a Web site and call himself a journalist." In the United States and overseas, traditional news media outlets are struggling and competing with digital startups for advertising and readers. In 2012, Newhouse Newspapers announced that major newspapers including the New Orleans *Times-Picayune* will publish only 3 days a week and emphasize online news coverage. After a similar change at *The Ann Arbor News*, the quality of news reporting suffered. "No offense to its staff, but AnnArbor.com, online at least, is a constantly updated blog, which gives equal play to impaled cyclists and rabid skunks as it does to politics and crime. The printed edition is newspaper-like, but with a different style and less gravitas than its predecessor" (Maynard, 2012).

In addition, due to digital access and the recession, anyone can register to be a source for journalists. For example, HARO or Help a Reporter Out, found at helpareporter.com, aggregates access to person-on-the-street and expert sources for journalists ("So you," 2012). Instead of doing the time-consuming legwork needed to find good sources, reporters post a query on HARO describing the type of person or expert they'd like to talk to for quotes in stories under deadline. The site e-mails the description to potential sources who registered on the site, and those fitting the description respond. Then the reporter selects one or more sources and obtains the desired quotes. Reporters can select sources who say what they want to publish and confirm their instincts, rather than taking the time to contact independent sources directly who may provide opposing viewpoints. HARO's source list may not be representative as "the online universe tends to be whiter, richer, and younger than the general population" (Paskin, 2009, p. 11).

### BACKGROUNDER 4: ENTREPRENEUR JOURNALISM

Given the recession and proliferation of hyperlocal sites, professional journalists who freelance or seek digital work must have a variety of skills. Entrepreneur journalists must know how to write, shoot, and edit digital stories; use digital software and post stories online and on social media; produce and run online digital sites; write business plans; develop funding proposals; pitch ideas for digital startups to investors and foundations; and handle legal, accounting, and personnel matters associated with running a for-profit or nonprofit entity. Cole-Frowe (2011, p. 34) offered this advice to entrepreneur journalists and freelancers on marketing one's services and developing a business plan.

1. Statement of purpose. State your objectives simply and directly, outlining the media you want to write for, how much you must earn and business goals to achieve.
2. Describe your business, products and services. Identify your specialties such as writing for online or science writing. Indicate other skills including editing or whether you are a photographer and/or videographer as well. State the times and days you will work.
3. Target market. Identify your best customers, explain and quantify their characteristics, what they buy, what else you could offer to increase your profits, and what media you could break into.
4. Pricing objectives. Identify the minimum price you must receive to accept a job. Track the time you spend per job to determine how much you should make per hour.
5. Competition. Identify the top five freelancers or competing entrepreneur journalists in your area and indicate whether their business is increasing or decreasing. Make a realistic assessment of performance, both theirs and yours, and compare their abilities and experience versus yours.

Consider whether there are new market niches you could build and exploit.

6. Marketing. Develop your brand. Consider how much to budget to promote yourself and develop a website, Facebook page, Twitter or blog. Develop costs for business cards and other printed material to describe your business and reflect an image. Identify conferences where you could network with other professionals, figure out how much it costs to attend them, and build such costs into the amount you seek to earn each year.

7. Location. Strive to make yourself the go-to freelancer in your area.

A key to successful entrepreneurial journalism is the ability to provide quality content to attract and serve a valuable audience, and then earn enough revenue to sustain digital operations. Collaborating or partnering with those who can provide assistance is key; finding tech help, content providers, sales help, networks of potential advertisers or investors, partners who might offer office space, etc. increases the chances for success. When visiting other successful sites, analyze why and how a site attracted you, as well as what made you visit several pages or return. Then use those insights to develop your own startup idea. For example, *Mashable* started covering social media as Facebook and Twitter began to grow audiences. Now it is a major tech blog, has strict editorial standards, uses innovative technology, and employs dozens of journalists. It turned the business and consumer interest in social media into a how-to site for consumers, adding classified advertising and events to maximize readership and revenues. *Mashable* and other noteworthy startups successfully differentiated their sites from competitors to build a loyal community by fostering audience loyalty and engagement. Then, advertisers pay to appear alongside the quality news coverage targeted to that loyal community (Briggs, 2011).

## BACKGROUNDER 5: FINDING INFORMATION FOR PROBLEM SOLVING AND DECISION MAKING

Media managers must find objective, quality information quickly to make decisions. One cannot make a logical decision unless the problem itself, the context in which it arose, the reasons or factors that led to the problem, and how other individuals and organizations have dealt with that problem are researched and analyzed. Decision making in a vacuum, without context or information, typically wastes precious resources on solutions that cannot work, with serious, negative results for management and employees.

This backgrounder includes examples of the types of sources you'll use to research the Extended Cases and can use later on the job. Online resources to aid in researching and analyzing the Irving and Dallas/Fort Worth, Texas, markets for Extended Case 1 are listed below. These same types of sources can be found and used if you selected a different market for Extended Case 1. They provide ideas for the types of sources available for other markets or cities. Remember these addresses may change after publication, so titles are provided to assist in locating them. Check in your university library or with a reference librarian for other sources of information on your selected city, town, county, or regional area.

Your professor may divide up among individuals or teams in the class the following online sources, as well as other sources found online or in your library. This will teach you how to break major research tasks or projects into manageable pieces, to find and share quality information quickly. This list may seem overwhelming at first, but as you use these sources over time, you'll recognize the varying information needs provided by different sites. Developing your research skills will not be easy and will not happen overnight. But knowing how to find quality, credible information quickly will help you to make better professional and personal decisions for years to come.

### Irving, Texas Sites

City of Irving, Texas: cityofirving.org

City of Irving Demographics: http://cityofirving.org/1564/Demo graphics

City of Irving Demographics Snapshot: http://cityofirving.org/DocumentCenter/View/1254

City of Irving—Think Green Be Green: http://cityofirving.org/

Irving Convention and Visitors Bureau: www.irvingtexas.com www.irvingtexas.com/visitors/things-to-do/

Irving on Facebook: www.facebook.com/thecityofirving

Irving Chamber of Commerce: www.irvingchamber.com/

Irving Chamber of Commerce—Las Colinas:
www.irvingchamber.com/ed_about_las_colinas.html
Las Colinas: www.irvingtexas.com/about-us/las-colinas/
Irving Convention Center at Las Colinas: www.irvingconventioncenter.com/
Irving Police Department: http://cityofirving.org/police/index.asp
Irving Fire Department: http://cityofirving.org/fire/
Irving Parks and Recreation Department: cityofirving.org
Irving Arts Center: www.irvingartscenter.com
Irving Independent School District: http://irvingisd.net
University of Dallas in Irving: www.udallas.edu/
North Lake College in Irving: www.northlakecollege.edu/Pages/default.aspx
HP Byron Nelson Golf Tournament in Irving: www.attbyronnelson.org
Irving at City-Data.com: www.city-data.com/city/Irving-Texas.html
Irving, Texas—Texas State Historical Association:
www.tshaonline.org/handbook/online/articles/hdi01
Irving History—Irving Convention & Visitors Bureau:
www.irvingtexas.com/about-us/irving-history/

## Dallas/Fort Worth, Texas Market

Dallas City Web Portal: www.dallascityhall.com
Dallas Office of Economic Development: www.dallas-ecodev.org/
Dallas Office of Cultural Affairs: www.dallasculture.org
Dallas Independent School District: www.dallasisd.org
Dallas Police Department: www.dallaspolice.net
Dallas Field Office—Federal Bureau of Investigation: www.fbi.gov/dallas/
FBI Uniform Crime Reports: www.fbi.gov/about-us/cjis/ucr/ucr
Federal Reserve Bank of Dallas: www.dallasfed.org
Dallas Black Chamber of Commerce: dallasblackchamber.org
Greater Dallas Hispanic Chamber of Commerce: www.gdhcc.com/
Greater Dallas Asian American Chamber of Commerce: www.gdaacc.com/
Dallas County, Texas: www.dallascounty.org/
Dallas Regional Chamber of Commerce: www.dallaschamber.org/

Fort Worth City: http://fortworthtexas.gov

Fort Worth Independent School District: www.fwisd.org/pages/FWISD

Fort Worth Chamber of Commerce: www.fortworthchamber.com

Fort Worth Hispanic Chamber of Commerce: www.fwhcc.org/

Fort Worth Metropolitan Black Chamber of Commerce: www.fwmbcc.org/

Tarrant County Asian American Chamber of Commerce: www.tcaacc.com/

NCTCOG: North Central Texas Council of Governments: www.nctcog.org/

2012 Texas Metro Market Overview—Dallas/Fort Worth-Arlington:

Real Estate Center at Texas A&M University:
Includes population and ethnic data, maps, locations of universities, Fortune 500 headquarters, top public and private employers, employment and wages by industry, as well as other economic and housing data. http://recenter.tamu.edu/mreports/2012/DallasFWArl.pdf

Dallas Visitors—Stats & Facts: www.visitdallas.com/about/stats

Dallas/Fort Worth International Airport—About: www.dfwairport.com/about/index.php

Dallas Love Field—About: www.dallas-lovefield.com/about.html

About Texas—Texas State Library and Archives Commission:
Provides data on business and industry in Texas, state and local economic data, and labor force statistics at www.tsl.state.tx.us/ref/abouttx/index.html

Economic Development & Tourism—Business Research Data:
Office of the Governor—Greg Abbott: gov.texas.gov/ecodev/business_research

Economic Development & Tourism—Map Room:
Shows where key industries and state economic development programs are located, as well as aspects of the Texas economy, such as where Fortune 500 corporate headquarters are located. http://gov.texas.gov/ecodev/business_research/maproom/

Texas Industry Concentrations—Where the State's Key Sectors Cluster: http://gov.texas.gov/files/ecodev/concentrations.pdf

The Official Website of the State of Texas: www.texas.gov

## Selected Dallas/Fort Worth Media Outlets

*Dallas Morning News*: www.dallasnews.com
*Dallas Observer*: www.dallasobserver.com
Fort Worth *Star-Telegram*: www.star-telegram.com/
KDFW FOX 4: http://www.fox4news.com/
KTVT CBS 11: http://dfw.cbslocal.com/
KXAS NBC 5: www.nbcdfw.com/
WFAA ABC 8: www.wfaa.com/
*Community Impact*—DFW Metro: http://impactnews.com/dfw-metro
*Dallas South News*: www.dallassouthnews.org/
Dig In Dallas/Fort Worth: www.tvguide.com/tvshows/dig-in-dallasfort-worth/437048/

## U.S. Census Bureau

U.S. Census Bureau: www.census.gov
   Use State and County QuickFacts tab to select Texas, then Dallas or Tarrant County. http://quickfacts.census.gov/qfd/index.html
U.S. Census Bureau American Fact Finder:
   Enter Irving city, Texas, or Dallas County, Texas, etc., in the state, county, or place box to find demographic and economic data.
   http://factfinder.census.gov/

## Selected Media Sources

Newspaper Association of America: www.naa.org
Newspaper National Network—Newspaper Association of America Top 50 Newspaper Websites:
   http://www.naa.org/Trends-and-Numbers/Newspaper-Websites/Newspaper-Web-Audience.aspx
   Newspaper Circulation in Top Markets:
   http://www.naa.org/Trends-and-Numbers/Circulation-Volume/Newspaper-Circulation-Volume.aspx
Newspaper Association of Newspaper Digital Audience
   This provides data for newspaper web sites in general—may be useful for providing context for local sites used in the case.
    http://www.naa.org/Trends-and-Numbers/Newspaper-Websites/Newspaper-Web-Audience.aspx

NAA 2012 Newspaper Multiplatform Usage Study:
www.naa.org/~/media/NAACorp/Public%20Files/
TopicsAndTools/Research/multiplatform_usage.ashx
TVB—Television Bureau of Advertising: www.tvb.org
Click on Market & Stations or go to www.tvb.org/
market_stations, choose the Market profile type and choose
Dallas-Ft. Worth
CAB—Video Advertising Bureau: www.thevab.com
Click on the Cable Systems Directory Tab on the right,
select Dallas/Fort Worth for your DMA Rank, click the
arrow, and then you'll obtain the names and websites for
cable operators in DFW.
IAB—Interactive Advertising Bureau: www.iab.net
Click on the Guidelines and Best Practices tab, then click on
Ad Standards and Creative Guidelines to browse the types
of ad units, pop-ups, rich media, and digital video used by
most websites.
Click on Mobile to learn about mobile advertising, etc.
Click on Social Media to learn about advertising, met-
rics, etc.
Mobile Marketing Association: www.mmaglobal.com
Mobile Marketing Best Practice: www.mmaglobal.com/
best-practices
Market Data & Insight: www.mmaglobal.com/research
WOMMA—Word of Mouth Marketing Association: womma.
org/main/
Click on the Resources tab for online resources.
Click on the Ethics tab to find the Ethics Code, Social
Media Disclosure Guide, and other documents related
to using word of mouth marketing ethically.
SPJ—Society of Professional Journalists: www.spj.org
SPJ Code of Ethics: www.spj.org/ethicscode.asp
Journalism.org—Pew Research Center's Project for Excellence in
Journalism: www.journalism.org
Ethics Codes: www.journalism.org/resources/ethics_codes
AAF—American Advertising Federation:
Institute for Advertising Ethics: www.aaf.org/
institute-advertising-ethics
PRSA—Public Relations Society of America: www.prsa.org
Industry Ethics Codes: www.prsa.org/AboutPRSA/Ethics/
Resources/IndustryEthicsCodes

**EXTENDED CASE 1: CHANGING LEADERS AND
DIRECTION IN DALLAS/FORT WORTH**

Maria Rincon sat at her desk and pondered the future of the hyperlocal site she'd just inherited, IrvingIndependent.org. The previous publisher, Dean Bledsoe, had just accepted a job as director of public relations and social media for the Fort Worth mayor's office. Bledsoe had started the hyperlocal site, focusing on stories of interest to African Americans in Irving, as well as local Irving news. He had worked at least 60 hours weekly, posting most of his own stories, video, and photographs. He'd also manned booths at local Irving events, fairs, and shopping malls. He'd post tweets on Twitter and stories and visuals on Facebook several times a day. It seemed that IrvingIndependent.org was a one-man show.

Maria had recently moved to Irving with her husband, who'd accepted a management position at Exxon Mobil Corporation. Maria had previously worked as the chief editor, reporter, and blogger for southsanfrancisco.patch.com, so she understood she'd be multitasking and working long hours. She'd taken a digital camera and Flip video camera to everything she covered. Local online news deadlines were minute-by-minute, unlike preparing stories for newspapers or television, so she was constantly on the go (Walsh, 2011). She knew first-hand that a "great local newspaper or local news site has everything—from trustee meetings to petty theft, from church service times to seemingly trivial society pieces" (Roach, 2012, p. 29).

In her previous job, the workload and scope of responsibilities was staggering. Maria had to post about three to five stories or bits of news and information daily, along with a similar number of Twitter posts and Facebook updates. She was expected to know South San Francisco and attend events as a reporter as well as top manager of the site. She wrote or edited most stories every day, paid freelancers, planned editorial, managed the budget, attended and covered weekend functions and events, as well as numerous other administrative duties.

Patch required publishers or lead editors like Maria to volunteer at least 5 days a year for charities or local nonprofit organizations in the community. She'd lost count of the number of booths she'd manned. In essence, serving as the top manager essentially entailed being everything from a publisher to a reporter. Sixty-hour weeks were the norm, she rarely took a vacation, and when she did, she was always working anyway because she was expected to deal with issues via smartphone, tablet, or laptop.

Privately, Maria and her husband were thinking about starting a family. She wondered whether she could handle this new job if they did decide to have children. Maria knew juggling work and family was a major problem that led to burnout. Her best reporter at southsanfrancisco.patch.com, Evelyn Gruene, had quit due to stress from competing family and work demands. Maria had tried using the freelance budget to hire a replacement reporter whenever Evelyn needed a vacation. She allowed Evelyn to use regional content on the weekends when she needed time off for her family. Evelyn was grateful and stayed on as long as she could, but finally had to quit when her second child was born.

Initially, the goal at southstanfrancisco.patch.com was to have the monthly number of unique site-visitors equal half of South San Francisco's population. Keeping tabs on usage metrics was stressful because she and her two full-time reporters had to keep up with every meeting, event, breaking news story as well as local sports. She had a monthly freelance budget of $2,000 to hire good freelancers who'd been laid off, paying about $50 to $200 per article, depending on its length and breadth. She tried to use that budget to offer niche coverage important to the residents and community, but Patch's mandates often ate up that budget (Walsh, 2011; Roach, 2012).

Maria regularly had to implement content, marketing, or other directives from Patch headquarters. One initiative required her to build engagement so visitors would stay on the site longer and visit often. Patch wanted the local community to be involved, post comments, and provide free content. But Maria quickly learned that volunteers required much supervision and editing if their stories were to be publishable and meet minimum journalistic standards. Most volunteers were unreliable and wouldn't post regularly, rarely more than once. She could quickly burn up all her time in a losing battle, so she found and trained a few good contributors and left it at that.

In another instance, Patch directed its sites to target mothers, setting up advisory boards called "Mom's Councils" to suggest topics and content. Wednesdays must be MomsDays and every site was given five or so pieces of content to use to reach the mother demographic. Maria and other editors were encouraged to set up a local event to offer mothers a break from their kids. Other content directives included developing a weekend calendar of family community events and a shopping bargain column (Roach, 2012). Maria was forced to take much of the $2,000 budget she'd been using to develop a specialty in business reporting and economic development in South San Francisco and use it for targeting mothers.

After Evelyn quit, Maria hired Anthony Jackson, a noted business reporter who'd been laid off by the *San Francisco Examiner*, to offer regular business articles and a weekly column. She'd talked to her supervisors at Patch about hiring Anthony full-time because the business niche was catching on. She knew it was engaging readers; she'd received e-mails asking why business coverage was declining when the mother-directed content began appearing. She pointed this out to her supervisors at Patch, but to no avail.

When Maria and her husband agreed he should take the job at Exxon Mobil, she resigned, gave 2-weeks, notice, and requested an exit interview with her supervisors at Patch. In that Skype meeting, she kindly but firmly pointed out why Anthony should be hired as her replacement, why the site should build its business content, and how the mandates could be affecting each local Patch site. She felt she'd left on good terms, but wondered whether her supervisors at Patch would act on any of her suggestions regarding local site content and operations. She also held a confidential, one-on-one meeting with Anthony, who was hired as her successor, to point out such potential issues, the workload to expect, and ways she'd learned to maximize time, effort, and resources. Anthony had many questions during their two-hour meeting, which she answered in a positive but truthful manner, while making it clear and receiving Anthony's assurances that all they discussed would be held in confidence.

When she arrived in Irving, Dean Bledsoe was cooperative but could only meet for about half an hour during his last few days on the job. Maria could immediately see why Dean was so well liked and respected. He was a dynamic and forthright person, providing his positive, yet candid assessment of the strengths and weaknesses of IrvingIndependent.org. She learned that Dean's salary and operating expenses were donated by a wealthy childhood friend, who believed it was important to have an African American news voice in Irving.

Dean did not have a mission statement, goals, organizational charts, or job descriptions for the hyperlocal site. He had no marketing or promotions plans and had recruited advertisers and sponsors himself when he had time. The site had grown on the fly and Bledsoe preferred to handle everything himself. He acknowledged that the site might need to change its editorial focus and audience, develop goals, change its way of operating, and perhaps even change its name.

Maria would have to start from scratch, generating her own resources and revenues after 6 months. Dean arranged for his sponsor to provide funding for 6 months, which included Maria's salary and little else. Maria knew that after 6 months, she'd either have to make the site viable, run and support it herself, or shut it down.

Maria considered various ways to obtain funding. She wondered whether to apply for a grant from a source such as the Knight Foundation at www.knightfoundation.org/apply/. Perhaps she should research what content would be of interest to important segments of Irving residents and seek funding through a digital fundraising site. Should she develop a proposal for Kickstarter.com? Or develop a proposal for seeking local Irving investors? Should she try to obtain funding after the 6-month period from Bledsoe's childhood friend? How could she develop a list of potential advertisers or sponsors? Or some combination of funding sources?

Maria knew that successful hyperlocal sites had a combination of funding sources including grants from foundations, advertising, sponsorships, subscriptions, membership campaigns, and/or special events. She also knew developing partnerships with existing local media outlets could be a key to survival (Remez, 2012). She periodically checked the blog of Mark Briggs at www.journalism20.com/blog/ to find ideas for funding.

While Maria expected to face many problems and issues trying to keep IrvingIndependent.org afloat, she realized that she wasn't a local institution like Dean Bledsoe. She'd either have to hire another respected local journalist or entrepreneur like Dean, which she couldn't yet afford, and/or figure out a new content focus for the site. She accepted the job because the site was independent; she wouldn't have to deal with content and marketing mandates from supervisors who didn't understand the stresses and problems managers at hyperlocal sites face. And the site had occasionally earned minimal profits through advertising and sponsorships.

Maria suspected IrvingIndependent.org survived because of interest in Bledsoe's blog. The site itself had about 15,000 unique monthly visitors; Dean's blog page on the site had 35,000. He was well respected in Irving and throughout the Dallas/Fort Worth area; that's why the Dallas mayor had hired him. She wondered whether to ask Dean to continue blogging weekly or even monthly on the site.

While Bledsoe had tailored his blog and site to African Americans, Maria discovered that the demographics of Irving appeared to be changing. According to the 2010 Census, the population of Irving had increased by 24,679 (or by 12.9%) to 216,290 since the last census. The estimated population in 2012 was 218,850. The African American population grew by 35.1% and the Asian non-Hispanic population grew by 94.6%. The Hispanic population grew by 48.4%, while the white non-Hispanic population decreased by 28.0%. According to the 2010 Census, 69.9% of Irving's population was now represented by minorities, compared to 51.8% in 2000 (Snapshot, 2012).

Maria planned to conduct a market analysis in Irving to help her decide whether and how to change the editorial focus and target audience of the site. Perhaps she could find a local African American journalist or leader and encourage him or her to develop a new, unique voice to maintain the African American voice and community. Maria also felt she should look for ways to reach other major groups and constituencies in Irving, selecting at least one or two to start. Perhaps she'd need to take another focus that wasn't based on race or gender, such as a specialty in business reporting, based on Irving's characteristics. She also wondered whether some combination of targeting and specialty content would be best. A market analysis would help to determine the answer.

Maria's initial research revealed that Irving was the third largest city in Dallas County, the 13th largest city in Texas, and the 94th largest in the nation. The median family income was $50,609, with a 6.8% unemployment rate. The education level attained by adults aged 25 and over included 20.4% with a Bachelor's degree and 12.1% with a graduate or professional degree. The top 10 private employers in Irving included CITI with 7,500 employees, Verizon with 3,260, Nokia with 1,700, Allstate with 1,650, NEC Corporation with 1,515, Microsoft with 1,351, and Zale Corporation with 1,250 employees. Irving is the global headquarters for four Fortune 500 companies (Snapsot 2012, Irving Convention Center, 2012).

The DART Orange Line was part of a regional rail expansion to include routes through Irving and to the Dallas/Fort Worth International Airport. Irving's Orange line stops would include the University of Dallas, the Las Colinas Urban Center, and the Irving Convention Center. The Orange Line was scheduled to connect the Las Colinas Urban Center and the Irving Convention Center with the city of Dallas, Love Field Airport, and surrounding cities by July 2012, and DFW Airport by 2014 (DART 2012a, 2012b; Irving Convention Center 2012).

While new NFL stadiums are often built adjacent to old ones, the city of Arlington lured Cowboys owner Jerry Jones away from Irving with incentives to build the new $1.2 billion Dallas Cowboys stadium there (Hudson, 2010). The Las Colinas Urban Center, a master-planned community comprising 12,000 acres, helped to replace the stadium in Irving's economy. The Irving Convention Center is located at Las Colinas, as well as Texas's only five diamond resort called the Four Seasons Las Colinas, which is home to the PGA Tour's HP Byron Nelson Championship. Las Colinas houses 2,000 corporations and 400 corporate headquarters. More than 10,000 conventions and meetings are held in Irving annually (Quick Reference, 2012).

The Irving Convention Center at Las Colinas was designed so that several different types of events can be hosted concurrently. It is a 275,000-square foot multifunctional building, with a 50,000-square foot exhibit hall, a 20,000-square foot ballroom, and 20,000 square feet of meeting space. The Dallas/Fort Worth International Airport is adjacent to the city and is only 6 miles west of the Irving Convention Center.

Whatever Maria decided to do with the site, she wondered how Dean and Irving's African American community would respond if she changed the focus and audience. She thought about ways to communicate and handle the change effectively. She requested another meeting with Dean, who said he'd be happy to meet with

her once things settled down a bit in his new job. Dean had asked
Maria to contact him in about a month to set up a meeting.


### Assignment

Use Irving, Texas, select another community, or select an existing
hyperlocal site to use for this case. Conduct a market analysis and
consider whether IrvingIndependent.org or your site should change
its content focus and target audience, offering new media content.
Develop a mission statement and goals, and figure out how to organize the site's structure, culture, communication, community relations, as well as its legal and personnel documents. Also figure out
how to obtain funding or investors.

Revamping an existing hyperlocal site requires extensive
research and planning. By carefully planning and considering
many factors before these changes are implemented, executing
those changes should be easier to manage when the process starts.
Remember you must develop a new mission statement and goals,
select new content niches to develop, develop target audiences for
those content niches, and explain why they are viable.

Before you begin your market analysis, try to find by the most
recent market profile of Dallas/Fort Worth (Bachman, 2010), or go
to the TVB's Market Profiles page at www.tvb.org/market_profiles
and select a Market Profile for Dallas/Fort Worth or your market. If
you selected an existing site for Extended Case 1, conduct research
on the site and how it's been covered in local and competing media.
Use the sources and suggestions provided in Backgrounder 5: Finding
Information for Problem Solving and Decision Making to research
the market and conduct your market analysis. Obtain as much information as you can and analyze the demographics, psychographics,
and other characteristics of Dallas/Fort Worth, Irving, or your city's
residents. If available in your library, review the SRDS Local Market
Audience Analyst, Mediamark, or Simmons reports on your market.
Use the information and data obtained from all sources and the text
to answer the following questions:

1. What do you see as the major problems facing
   IrvingIndependent.org? Identify and describe each
   problem in concise detail, ranking them from most to least

important. Review Chapters 6 and 8 before answering this question.

2. Identify Maria Rincon's leadership style. What is positive about how she leads? What is negative about how she leads? Review Chapters 1, 2, 3, and 8 before answering this question.

3. Identify and describe in concise detail the culture of southsanfrancisco.patch.com and IrvingIndependent.org. Compare and contrast the cultures, describing how they are similar and different. Review chapters 1, 2, 3, and 6 before answering this question.

4. Identify and describe the motives and stressors that Maria Rincon is facing and explain how she should plan for or deal with them. What motivates Maria Rincon? What motivates Dean Bledsoe? Discuss the factors that seem to drive or motivate each manager, highlighting their similarities and differences. What are the primary stressors Rincon is presently facing? What other stressors will Rincon face over the next 6 months? How should she best deal with these stresses? Review Chapters 1 and 2 before answering this question.

5. Conduct research and a market analysis. Try to identify content niches and target audiences that are not served adequately in Irving or Dallas/Fort Worth. Then identify and describe in concise detail the content focus and editorial content areas on which IrvingIndependent.org should focus. In other words, based on research and the market analysis, what should the mission of the site be? What are the major content area(s), topic(s), issues, and/or focus of the site? For ideas on types of hyperlocal sites, visit Columbia Journalism Review's Guide to Online News Startups at www.cjr.org/news_startups_guide/. Review Chapters 5, 6, 7, and 8 before answering this question.

6. Identify, quantify, and describe in detail at least one primary and secondary target audience or target market for the content focus you identify in Question 5. Describe the number in the target audience, its demographics, psychographics, and other characteristics in detail. Explain how and why the content focus will appeal to your primary and secondary audiences. Review Chapters 5 and 7 before answering this question.

7. Identify and describe in concise detail the mission
statement, short- and long-term goals, content sections,
types of topics, types of stories, types of images to be
included on the site based on the market analysis. In other
words, what is the overall mission of the site? What are
the major content areas, types of topics, and stories to be
reported regularly? What are the major sections and design
aspects of site? What other information is needed on the
site? Identify and describe any links to other city, state, or
national online reports; data or information to aggregate
on the site; or other ways of making the site more
useful and interactive for the intended audience. Review
Chapter 7 before answering this question.

8. Indicate whether the site should be nonprofit or for-profit
and explain why. Then report in concise detail on the major
business and financial information and decisions that
apply to your type of site (either nonprofit or for-profit).
Ask your professor for the types of information to include
in your answer. For examples of nonprofit and for-profit
sites, visit Columbia Journalism Review or CJR's Guide to
Online News Startups at www.cjr.org/news_startups_guide/
to examine the various commercial and nonprofit startups
around the country (and find out which ones are still
publishing online). Also review the Digital Media Law
Project's Creating a Business page at http://www.dmlp.org/
legal-guide/creating-business and especially the Choosing
A Business Form to help you decide between the types
of for-profit and nonprofit forms. Also read the Business
Form Comparison Chart at www.http://www.dmlp.org/
sites/citmedialaw.org/files/Business%20Comparison%20
Chart_1.pdf.

In addition to the sources listed above, here are examples of
sources you may use to report on business and financial information
and decisions for a nonprofit site. Consult sources such as Launching a Nonprofit News Site—Step Four: Filing Documents to Create
Your Organization at www.jlab.org, Step Six: Bringing in Revenue,
Budgets and Business Plans at www.j-lab.org/tools/launchingnon-
profit/6, How Does the IRS interpret Section 501(c)(3)? at http://
www.dmlp.org/irs/section-501c3, the Interactive Guide to the IRS
Decision-Making Process under Section 501(c)(3) for Journalism

and Publishing Non-Profits at http://www.dmlp.org/irs/home, the IRS: Tax Information for Charities & Other Non-Profits at http://www.irs.gov/Charities-&-Non-Profits, or the Compliance Guide for 501(c)(3) Public Charities at www.irs.gov/pub/irs-pdf/p4221pc.pdf.

In addition to the sources listed at the beginning of this question, sources you might use for reporting on business and financial information and decisions for a for-profit site include Promote It! at http://j-learning.org/ and the various links listed there. Review Advertising Your Site at http://j-learning.org/promote-it/advertising-and-marketing/. See whether any relevant articles have been posted on Poynter's How To's page at http://www.poynter.org/category/how-tos/. See whether there are current articles on the topic on the Digital Content Next site at http://digitalcontentnext.org/

9. Develop a business plan for the site. Review Chapter 8 before answering this question and model your plan based on a business plan provided by your professor or one of the examples cited at the end of Chapter 8.
10. Identify and describe in concise detail a minimum of three categories of funding sources (e.g., advertisers, foundations, etc., depending on whether you propose a nonprofit or for-profit site) and five examples of each category (e.g., at least five major advertisers who might buy ads on the site). In other words, consider the following questions. How should funding be raised for the site? What types of funding should be targeted? Why? What type of funding sources should be developed? Then select a minimum of three categories of funding sources, and identify and describe at least five examples of potential donors, sponsors or advertisers, etc., for each category. Explain in detail why these are good potential funding sources and why these potential advertisers or donors are good prospects. In addition, discuss the negative consequences or downside of using each type of potential donor you recommend. Identify what managerial or organizational resources may be needed to manage each different type of funding source. Review Chapter 8 before answering this question.

11. Identify and discuss in concise detail the major types of legal issues managers at for-profit or nonprofit sites might face. Recommend how the site should be structured or developed in order to minimize legal programs or threats. Be sure to consider what types of intellectual property rights you will expect contributors to assign to your site when they contribute. Review Chapter 9 before answering this question.

For more information, review sources such as Dealing with Legal Threats and Risks at at http://www.dmlp.org/legal-guide/. Newsgathering and Privacy at http://www.dmlp.org/legal-guide/newsgathering-and-privacy, as well as, Access to Government Information at, Intellectual Property Risks Associated With Publication at www.citmedialaw.org/legal-guide/risks-associated-publication, Unique Content: Special Risks, Other Business Formation and Governance Issues and Guides and Resources.

12. Develop a code of ethics or ethical policies for managers, journalists, and/or freelancers who work for your site to follow. Include concise yet detailed sections on topics such as conflict of interest, ethics, fundraising or advertising, code of conduct, fact-checking, and/or any other topics your professor assigns. Review Chapter 9 before answering this question. For background information on what to include in an ethics code, review Launching a Nonprofit News Site—Step Five: Establishing Sound Policies at www.j-lab.org/tools/launchingnonprofit/5. Also review the Society of Professional Journalists' SPJ Code of Ethics at www.spj.org/ethicscode.asp and the Pew Research Center's Project for Excellence in Journalism Ethics Codes page at www.journalism.org/resources/ethics-codes.

13. Identify the social media to be used to reach the site's targeted audience, and explain how and why to do so. Which social media should be used? Why? How? What types of posts or messages are to be disseminated for the major content areas on the site? Review sources such as Mashable's The Facebook Guide Book at http://mashable.com/guidebook/facebook/, The Twitter Guide Book at http://mashable.com/guidebook/twitter/, or its Social

Media page at http://mashable.com/social-media/, or review sources such as IAB's Social Media page at www. iab.net/guidelines/508676/801817 for information. http:// kcnn.org/learning-modules/likes-and-tweets/.

14. Identify and describe in concise detail at least three methods of measuring engagement and usage of your site. Explain why each measurement method or metric is best to use. In other words, write a report where you recommend a minimum of three measures (where at least one of these three measures site traffic in some way and at least one measures engagement). Review examples of measures used in the industry in sources such as those listed below. You may recommend more than three measures and additional types of measures in addition to those listed above. If you have already developed a mission statement and goals for the site, be sure to use your mission and goals to select appropriate measures to assess them.

Review Chapter 5 before answering this question. For ideas on the types of measures available, visit quantcast.com and enter the name of a site (such as star-telegram.com or a site in your area). Review the data using the quantcast.com Reading Our Reports page at https://www.quantcast.com/help/how-to-read-our-reports. For additional background information on measurement, review Chapter 8. Also read sources such as Tracking Services at http://j-learning. org and Understanding Traffic at http://j-learning.org and Making the Most of Metrics at www.kcnn.org. You might download the Engaging Audiences: Measuring Interactions, Engagement and Conversions report at http://www.j-lab.org/_uploads/publications/ engaging-audiences/EngagementReport_web.pdf. Be sure to review the list of Popular Engagement Trackers on page 34.

15. Should a partnership be developed with any other local, national, or international media outlets or other entities? Why or why not? Even if you recommend against partnering with another organization, identify at least three other organizations or outlets for potential partnerships and explain why and how the partnership might work. Include information such as the role and content of the site and each potential partner. Explain how the partnership might help to increase revenue

streams and why. Provide any other data or information that explains why the partnership is recommended. Review Chapters 5 and 7 before answering this question.

16. Develop a plan for piloting and launching the site. How will it be developed and posted online? What resources and expertise are needed to produce it? How will audience feedback mechanisms be designed into the site to ensure you can respond accordingly to audience feedback? How can social media be used to facilitate audience feedback and adjust the site as needed? What else must be considered or done to pilot and launch the site?

# Extended Case Study 2: Solving Crises at South Asian Entertainment

phones of celebrities and a murder victim became public knowledge. Thus, the actions of employees and managers at one firm in a conglomerate can seriously harm the reputation of other firms and owners of the conglomerate.

You might take part of a class one day to teach your students about major media conglomerates and the firms they own. Columbia Journalism Review has a "Who Owns What" tab to examine conglomerates such as Bertelsmann (www.bertelsmann.com/), Disney (http://thewaltdisneycompany.com/disney-companies), News Corporation (www.newscorp.com/), and Time Warner (www.cjr.org/resources/). You might review and then select major media companies in India (e.g., Sahara India Pariwar at www.sahara.in/media.html) or Argentina (Grupo Clarin at www.grupoclarin.com.ar/—use the translation feature in your browser) for your students to review. The Federal Communication Commission provides information on media ownership rules in the United States including www.fcc.gov/ownership/ or www.fcc.gov/guides/review-broadcast-ownership-rules.

Critics argue that central ownership and consolidation of media properties limits the diversity of viewpoints presented in news and entertainment. Control of information arguably rests in the hands of a few owners. Critics also argue that owners may discourage coverage of topics unpopular to them or unfavorable to their businesses. The advocacy group FreePress has a "Who Owns the Media" page at www.freepress.net/ownership/chart/ and a Media Consolidation page at www.freepress.net/media-consolidation. Use these and other sources to obtain current information on issues regarding U.S. and international media ownership.

A number of copyright and intellectual property links are provided in Backgrounder 6: International Copyright. It is imperative that you review these sources carefully before assigning students to use them. There is a lot of information, some of which is likely beyond what you need to assign to students. Students will be very confused and frustrated if they are not given guidance on using these sources and directed to those to use for class. You are strongly encouraged to review these links beforehand to select the sources that are appropriate for your class.

Consider taking a class day to cover the culture and customs, ways of conducting business, etc., in Argentina, India, and South

Korea. Select the U.S. State Department, Kwintessential, and/or country links provided in Extended Case 2 to assign your students. Ask students to be prepared to discuss in class the similarities and differences in the cultures and business approaches for each country. Then, after this discussion, when the students read the case, they'll be able to recognize nuances they might not see otherwise. For example, the primary manager in the case, Dhavan Bannerjee, apparently comes from a high caste in India. Ask students how this affects his relationships with employees and managers who work for him in India. Have students consider how Kruti Khan's advocacy of access to water and sewer services for the poor might be viewed in some circles in India. Review these State Department and Kwintessential links to look for other nuances like this before assigning the case.

Consider looking for examples to help educate students about cultural ignorance and stereotyping. Critics argue that the Harold and Kumar movies promote racism and stereotyping. In another example from May 2012, a Popchips advertisement featuring Ashton Kutcher in the role of Raj, a Bollywood producer, was criticized and pulled from the air, resulting in an apology from the advertiser. Specifically, the complaint was this: "Dressed in a shiny blue sherwani, with a brown Indian accent and brown face makeup, Kutcher, as Raj, describes his perfect woman (Kim Kardashian, he says in his accent). . . . Blogs have called Kutcher and the company racist . . . (and) . . . 'made a racist ad because they are so steeped in our (US) culture's racism that they didn't even realise [sic] they were doing it.' . . . 'Asians and Indians are the new clownable minority . . . just people that have accents and fix computers'" (Kumaraswami, 2012). Videos about this Popchips ad to use in class were still available on YouTube at the time of publication.

Be sure to prepare thoroughly and carefully before assigning the online reports and the case. It is important to prepare for and understand that even discussing these issues might be offensive to some of your students. These discussions could reveal prejudices and/or the political or cultural views of you and/or your students (or even the inadvertent prejudices of the author). Managers must understand that even those who care for and respect other cultures can sometimes be unaware or inadvertently offend.

Check to see whether diversity and prejudice training is available at your college or university. Invite an expert to speak to your class and, if possible, hold a session on diversity training and prejudice awareness. Extended Case 2 provides the opportunity to learn a great deal about diversity and various cultures.

Extended Case 2 also provides a chance to learn about developing and revising social media policies. A survey conducted by Deloitte found that 22% of employees report that they use some form of social networking five or more times per week, and 15% of employees admit they access social media at work for personal reasons. Only 22% of companies report having a policy regarding the use of social media at work. Yet 74% of U.S. employees surveyed believe it is easy to harm a brand's reputation via social media such as Facebook, Twitter, and YouTube ("After the NLRB," 2011; Deloitte, 2009).

Check the National Labor Relations Board (NLRB) website to find the most recent advice regarding social media policies before you assign Extended Case 2. For example, on May 30, 2012, the NLRB issued Memorandum OM (Operations Management) 12–59: Report of the Acting General Counsel Concerning Social Media Cases available at www.nlrb.gov. The NLRB had previously released memos on social media policies in August 2011 and January 2012. The NLRB had previously released memos on social media policies in August 2011 and January 2012.)

The NLRB's Memorandum OM 12–59 includes examples from social media policies that were found overbroad or unlawful, as well as a complete example of a lawful social media policy (starting on page 22). You can use this complete policy as an example for a discussion in class. As new advisories and updated social media policies are posted by the NLRB, you can compare this complete policy from 2012 to any more recent policy the NLRB issues to show how such policies evolve. These NLRB memos provide examples of problems arising from the policies of specific companies, so they include good examples to use in class. Social media policies often include sections or rules on the use of social media and electric technologies, intellectual property, privacy, confidentiality, protection of employer information, and contacts with the media and government agencies (National Labor Relations Board, 2012;

Smith, 2012). Check each semester before you cover this topic to see whether the NLRB has issued an updated example of an appropriate social media policy.

---

## TO STUDENTS AND INSTRUCTORS: ABOUT EXTENDED CASE 2

Extended Case 2 teaches you about the importance of learning about a different country before conducting business there. It also teaches you about different cultures and how assumptions and behaviors may vary, depending on a manager's native country. A manager never assumes that the way he or she does business in one country is appropriate for a colleague, client, or business relationship in another country. Read the U.S. State Department and Kwintessential online reports on Argentina, India, and South Korea before reading and working on Extended Case 2. The information in these online reports will help you consider in a different light and better understand the issues presented and the behavior of managers in the case.

Understanding and genuinely appreciating and embracing diversity is crucial for managers. The ethnic composition of the United States and other countries is changing. Managers must understand that there are differences in cultures when conducting business within nations, including the United States. Countries such as India and China have major, growing economies that are important to many other nations. Managers must understand and respect other cultures and understand how to conduct business and avoid offending business associates worldwide.

Managers must also understand that the higher they progress in management, the more serious the problems they face. Extended Case 2 reveals only the tip of the iceberg of the types of serious issues faced in upper international management. A top manager in some media firms might not have to face the prospect of a journalist or employee and/or one or more of their family members being murdered or kidnapped for reporting on corruption or criminal activity. Top managers in some countries might not have to worry about their own children or the children of their employees being kidnapped. Yet these are real problems in some parts of the world and managers in many media companies will likely prepare for or face these dangers. Equally important to keep in mind, where these dangers may occur is likely to change in the future. In every country, media managers must also consider and review security to minimize any terrorism or other threats that may arise.

### BACKGROUNDER 6: INTERNATIONAL COPYRIGHT

Online resources are provided in this section to help you learn more about international copyright protection and issues. Be sure to ask your professor about which resources to use before you begin research on international copyright protection and issues. These resources offer a great deal of detail and you must have guidance from your professor before you use them.

Review the Priority Watch List and Watch List regarding intellectual property protection and enforcement at the Office of the United States Trade Representative (USTR) online at www.ustr.gov. For example, in 2012, Argentina remained on the Priority Watch List due to the widespread availability in that country of counterfeit and pirated goods, including Internet piracy. India remained on the Priority Watch List for copyright as well, due to Internet piracy, pirated music and movies, as well as other concerns. Also look for topics such as "Trends in Trademark Counterfeiting and Copyright Piracy" and "Piracy over the Internet and Digital Piracy" to learn about current issues worldwide related to intellectual properties from the viewpoint of the Office of the United States Trade Representative (Kirk, 2012).

Look for and review the most recent version of the U.S. Copyright Office Circular 38A entitled International Copyright Relations of the United States at www.copyright.gov/circs/. Specifically, read the background information and all descriptions of the various conventions or relations (e.g., Berne, etc.). Identify the conventions or relations that currently apply to Argentina, India, and South Korea. Review any other relevant copyright information available on the U.S. Copyright Office's home page (www.copyright.gov/), such as the most recent version of the International Copyright page.

Look for the copyright offices in other nations. For example, see the Government of India Copyright Office page at copyright. gov.in. Look for the most recent version of the Indian government's Hand Book of Copyright Law at http://copyright.gov.in/Documents/handbook.html. However, be aware that many countries publish copyright pages in their native languages, not English. If available, use your browser's translate feature or find other sources of information.

The World Trade Organization (WTO) has an Intellectual property: protection and enforcement page at www.wto.org/english/thewto_e/whatis_e/tif_e/agrm7_e.htm. WTO also has a TRIPS (Trade-Related Aspects of Intellectual Property Rights) page at www.wto.org/english/tratop_e/trips_e/trips_e.htm.

Visit the World Intellectual Property Organization (WIPO) website to find information about specific conventions or agreements. For example, information about the Berne Convention is found at www.wipo.int/treaties/en/ip/berne/. More information about the WIPO Convention is found at www.wipo.int/treaties/en/convention/. Information about specific international treaties and conventions regarding intellectual property may be found in Chapter 5 of the WIPO's Intellectual Property Handbook at www. wipo.int/export/sites/www/about-ip/en/iprm/pdf/ch5.pdf or www. wipo.int/about-ip/en/iprm/. The WIPO also has a Directory of Intellectual Property Offices at www.wipo.int/directory/en/urls.jsp and Information by Country at www.wipo.int/directory/en/index. jsp where you can find information about various countries. Also visit the World Trade Organization's Agreement on Trade-Related Aspects of Intellectual Property Rights at http://www.wipo.int/directory/en/.

Your professor may invite an expert in intellectual property or copyright law related to media organizations to speak to the class. Also ask your professor for other sources of information to aid in completing this case. Ask your law or reference librarian for good sources of information. Conduct a search on an online library database such as ProQuest, EBSCO, or Lexis-Nexis to find recent articles regarding positive or negative developments, problems, costs, issues, etc. regarding copyright, intellectual property, theft, piracy, and related topics in the countries included in Extended Case 2.

## EXTENDED CASE 2: FACING INTERNATIONAL CRISES AT SOUTH ASIAN ENTERTAINMENT

Dhavan Banerjee, a native of India, has served for 5 years as the CEO of South Asian Entertainment based in Mumbai, India. (The World Bank identifies the South Asia region to include Afghanistan, Bangladesh, Bhutan, India, Maldives, Nepal, Pakistan, and Sri Lanka [World Bank, 2012].) South Asian Entertainment is a subsidiary of Vizcacha International, a media conglomerate. Roberto Vizcacha is the founder, Chairman, and CEO of Vizcacha International, which was started when he inherited Argentina's top daily newspaper, *Buenos Aries Noticias*. He took the profits earned from that paper and began purchasing media-related firms and outlets to expand over time through international acquisitions including newspapers, television stations and networks, cable networks, digital and mobile media, film and television studios, theme parks, and an international publisher. At times, he'd used profitable firms or outlets he'd purchased as collateral to borrow to buy desirable entities. Then he would merge firms and implement reorganization and layoffs to cut costs and pay off the debt. Vizcacha established corporate headquarters in New York City when the corporation went public about 30 years earlier, but the Vizcacha family retained primary ownership of the firm.

South Asian Entertainment owns Anokhi, a magazine, digital, and television brand also based in Mumbai, as well as all Indian properties owned by Vizcacha International. When Dhavan took over South Asian Entertainment, it was mired in debt from acquiring Anokhi magazine and its fledgling Internet and mobile editions, as well as a film and TV production firm in Mumbai. Dhavan reorganized all operations in India under South Asian Entertainment, which led to layoffs among management and staff of the various firms Vizcacha had acquired. Dhavan then held many organizational and planning meetings with a few top managers from each firm or outlet owned by South Asian to develop plans and strategies for growth.

As a result of these meetings, Dhavan and his managers had major stars and the casts of successful movies and television programs produced by South Asian Entertainment featured in Anokhi and Vizcacha's other regional media properties. The film and TV studios produced YouTube videos, video press releases, and other entertainment news or features highlighting the firm's major celebrities, productions, or outlets. This built circulation and profits for Anokhi and its digital offerings. Dhavan also encouraged his managers at various Vizcacha studios and outlets to feature successful actors, actresses, and other celebrities from successful films and TV programs produced by competing studios. As a result, Anokhi became the leading entertainment news and lifestyle brand in South Asia. However, South Asian Entertainment was having difficulty with social media efforts. For example, Facebook only had 3.5% penetration in India, yet a campaign featuring a Bollywood star helped the automaker Nissan gain 500,000 Indian fans (Pathak, 2012).

When he first took over at South Asian, Dhavan also met with Sanjay Kulkarni, the head of communications and public relations, and Anushka Choudhary, head legal counsel and director of legal operations. He was very impressed by both managers. He worked with Kulkarni to establish regular and emergency communication policies, and enabled all managers and employees to notify Kulkarni's office of positive news or developments. News of such developments would be screened and, if appropriate, included in individual company or South Asian company monthly e-mail newsletters. The e-mail newsletters were positively received as most employees enjoyed seeing positive developments in their own or other divisions or companies in the newsletters. Many managers and employees said they didn't know before what was going on in other parts of their companies, other South Asian companies, or at South Asian Entertainment as a whole. Sanjay and Dhavan often visited different companies and offices to build good relationships with managers and employees throughout South Asian. He featured celebrities and other employees who had served their communities in the newsletter as well, which encouraged more good works throughout the company and built good feelings among the South Asian companies and communities where they were located.

A number of popular South Asian film and television stars, such as Kruti Khan, a leading female Bollywood star, also volunteered for established local charities. The stars had their pictures taken with other South Asian volunteers to appear in the company newsletters. Dhavan sent a thank-you note to each celebrity who did so, placing a copy in their employment files to document their consideration for the company. He awarded annually a small bonus or other reward for noncelebrity employees who had served in this way. Dhavan also paid stars a fee to appear at company annual meetings, giving many employees the chance to see them in person, or get an autograph. After a few years, a feeling of family and unified purpose developed throughout South Asian Entertainment.

Anushka Choudhary had been hired 2 years before Dhavan. She had reviewed, updated and/or established legal policies, holding regular meetings and soliciting feedback throughout the process to ensure employees and managers had a say in policy development. Anushka had significantly revised the performance evaluation and progressive discipline policies to ensure they were consistent across units and, where appropriate, across firms. She hired a staff of specialists to cover the major types of legal issues a firm like South Asian Entertainment typically faced. By the time Dhavan was hired, the legal office was a well-oiled machine, working closely with other units and managers as needed to ensure contracts and policies were thorough and followed.

Dhavan's head of security, Emraan Bhagat, had formerly served as a police administrator and bodyguard to national government ministers. He was trusted and respected by those he guarded, but Dhavan had recruited Bhagat with a lucrative compensation package. Dhavan had hired him a few months after taking over at South Asian due to the history of crimes in the region involving journalists, celebrities, and sometimes their families. The Committee to Protect Journalists reported 17 journalists had been murdered in India since 1992. As was the practice worldwide, Indian celebrities and wealthy families hired bodyguards for themselves and their families as kidnap attempts occasionally occurred.

Dhavan was contacted to schedule a meeting with Vizcacha and Charles Archer, the new CEO of Vizcacha International. Archer's office contacted Dhavan to inform him a meeting was needed to discuss where and how Dhavan could best serve Vizcacha International in the future. Dhavan was told that Vizcacha and Archer wanted to hear his thoughts on how and where he could best serve the company, as well as his long-term career goals and goals for the conglomerate. They also wanted to discuss the major issues and problems Dhavan had dealt with over the past few months.

Dhavan also had received official notification of Vizcacha's long-term plans through an annual report and letter addressed to him (and other top managers, he found out) outlining goals to grow the company faster by making it more digital and international. In the letter, signed by Archer, the company sought to strengthen its portfolio by selling off less profitable branches and/or consolidating existing properties. A second goal was to build upon existing successful print and broadcast entities or brands by taking them digital and/or creating new digital outlets based on these successful entities. Vizcacha International's long-term goals also included "establishing new growth platforms," to be developed from consultations with certain directors and managers throughout the firm. Finally, a major growth goal was to expand into new geographic growth regions.

This was a new direction for the firm, as details about long-term goals and plans had rarely been shared with top managers at all company-owned firms and outlets. As Roberto Vizcacha was in his early 70s, he'd hired Charles Archer to replace him as CEO, to be based at corporate headquarters in New York City. Roberto often traveled between Buenos Aries and New York City and was getting tired of traveling so much. Archer, who was 47 years old, had been a president of finance and then operations at News Corporation for 10 years. Yet Archer had no hope of promotion there because Rupert Murdoch reportedly planned to place his son in charge. Vizcacha recognized that he was losing ground to firms such as Bertelsmann and News Corporation, so he wanted to adapt and ensure profitability well into the future, on his family's behalf.

Rumor was that Archer accepted the CEO position because it was common knowledge Vizcacha's children had no interest in running the conglomerate or its companies. His younger son and daughter lived in Argentina, were totally uninvolved, and had no interest in the company, just their share of the profits and inheritance. His eldest daughter Maria had stepped into the role of her father's advisor after her mother had died. Maria had been encouraging her father to find a CEO with experience running a media conglomerate as Roberto had recently had a mild heart attack. With Maria's help, Roberto had recovered fully and made changes in his diet and exercise habits, as he was not yet ready to retire. Yet these health concerns made him appreciate the need to identify and hire a successor for the long-term good of the conglomerate. Maria lived in Buenos Aries, but was involved in and approved of Archer's hiring, shuttling back and forth to New York during the process. Archer had been friendly with the Vizcacha family for many years, as was Rupert Murdoch and his family. When Archer was hired, there had been some strain on the friendship between the Vizcacha and Murdoch families.

Roberto became chairman of the board when Archer was hired as CEO. Roberto planned to retire from the board in 2 years, when Maria would take his place for at least 5 years. Maria indicated she wanted to step back from advising her father over the next few years, once Archer was settled in. She saw her future role as board chair as primarily protecting the family's interests. Her siblings were not comfortable passing the mantle to someone outside the family unless Maria served as board chair for at least 5 years, possibly longer. Roberto simply wanted to ensure the conglomerate was financially sound over the long term and had the ability to adapt and grow to ensure his family's security after he retired or died. Dhavan knew of Archer's stellar reputation and felt he was the perfect hire to achieve that transition and lead the firm into the future. Dhavan was surprised that Archer had been lured away from News Corporation. Dhavan had met Maria a few times at company functions and felt she also had the company's best interests at heart.

Dhavan heard through the grapevine that Vizcacha and Archer were pleased with how he'd streamlined operations and turned South Asian Entertainment and its properties into successful and profitable ventures. They also liked how Dhavan had recommended using the firm's major celebrities to help build relationships within the companies and publicity for all South Asian properties. Dhavan had received strong and positive performance reviews over the past 5 years and substantial raises and profit-sharing incentives. Yet Dhavan made sure to praise Bhagat, Choudhary, and Kulkarni to Archer, pointing out how and why they were a big part of the success of South Asian Entertainment. He also praised other media outlet managers under the South Asian International umbrella when they performed well. Dhavan felt he and his top managers would continue to be employed in some capacity by the conglomerate. If possible, he hoped to recruit one or more of them to move up with him, if he was, indeed, promoted.

However Dhavan heard rumors from his manager of the film studio in Mumbai that Roberto Vizcacha did not like that interracial couples were sometimes featured in South Asian Entertainment films and programs. Apparently Maria had read her father the riot act over these attitudes, pointing out such statements were discriminatory and inappropriate. This rumor troubled Dhavan, who was Indian, but his Caucasian wife, Ingrid Nielsen, was a United States citizen who grew up in Minneapolis, Minnesota.

Dhavan also heard about Vizcacha's attitudes from his meeting with Kruti Khan, the major Bollywood star from India who was in a serious relationship with Juan Varela, an internationally famous tennis star from London whose family had immigrated to the United Kingdom from Argentina in 1945. Varela's family had been close friends with the Vizcacha family before and after emigrating due to political disagreements with Juan Peron and the Peronists. The Varela family left because they feared repercussions from Peron for opposing him. They emigrated before Peron was elected president of Argentina in 1946.

Kruti told Dhavan privately that while at a family party on Vizcacha's yacht, Juan told Roberto that he was secretly engaged to Kruti. Juan was taken aback when Roberto told him he shouldn't marry Kruti because it was wrong for people of different races to marry. Juan said Maria apparently heard the conversation, and gently steered Vizcacha away from Juan to sit nearby with Archer. Archer and Maria whispered together for a few moments, then Archer came directly to Juan, apologized, and told him Roberto's outdated views were not representative of Archer's views, Maria's, or the conglomerate's. While completely wrong and misguided, Archer told Juan that he knew Roberto did not mean to offend Juan or Kruti. Archer told Juan that his private life was not the company's concern as long as all contractual obligations were met. He told Juan that Archer himself and Maria were delighted to hear the news about him and Kruti, were proud of them, valued them both, and had absolutely no problems with their relationship. Archer said Vizcacha International would be honored to feature their engagement and wedding prominently in Vizcacha properties, if, how, and when they wished. Archer said to feel free to contact him if Juan had any other concerns. If this rumor were true, Dhavan was astonished to think that Vizcacha would say something like that to Varela. Dhavan couldn't help but wonder whether Vizcacha felt the same way about his own marriage.

Then there were the public relations and security problems Dhavan had dealt with over the past year. Bollywood stars at other companies had begun advocating political or social stances. For example, Salman Khan, a major star who worked for a different studio, asked the people of Pakistan to support him in efforts to free an Indian who had been held in a Pakistan prison for the past 30 years. Khan appeared regularly in South Asian Entertainment's vehicles, and Dhavan heard from his managers at those vehicles that readers and advertisers were complaining about entertainers taking political stands. At that point Dhavan directed Choudhary to remind all South Asian Entertainment celebrities that political advocacy was banned in their contracts and all work with charities or nonprofits must be preapproved by the lead counsel.

Yet Salman's stance was nothing compared to Kruti Khan's. Kruti apparently ignored the reminder and created a media firestorm in India when she said how political corruption made access to water and sanitation difficult for the poor. She argued that "access to water and the location of public toilet blocks are frequently linked to political patronage in slums, especially where 'payment for use' arrangements generate large sums of cash for the politicians that control them" (Jewitt, 2011, p. 619). Via social media and then through media coverage, Kruti asked her countrymen to donate to a fund to help the destitute obtain inexpensive access to water and sanitation. Dhavan, his communications, legal, and security officers were dealing with numerous complaints and angry recriminations from the public, the media, as well as management in several South Asian Entertainment companies.

Following company policy, Dhavan immediately called a meeting with Kruti, reminding her that there was a "no political advocacy" clause in her contract and all employees must have any charity they wanted to represent preapproved by the South Asian head of legal counsel. Kruti had failed to follow these policies even though she'd recently been notified of them. Dhavan informed her of these violations verbally and in a letter he gave her at the end of their meeting.

Kruti was apologetic at first, said she did not realize there was a nonadvocacy clause in her contract and truly did not expect the firestorm she created. Then she said she had the right to speak her mind and didn't understand how this violated any policies. South Asian

Entertainment celebrities had been working for charitable causes, supported by company policies and rewards. Dhavan reminded her that employees had to have the charities they worked for preapproved. South Asian's communications policy also included clauses prohibiting political advocacy, and sanctions could be imposed when an employee created negative publicity that harmed the image of any of the conglomerate's firms. Vizcacha's corporate counsel would handle her case because several South Asian companies or outlets were reporting public relations damage from her actions. Dhavan told her how her case would be handled, and politely but firmly told Kruti she was being warned through the meeting and letter that she must meet all contractual obligations and follow all company policies. Any future violations could result in sanctions or dismissal.

He also told her verbally and in the letter that she was requested to first meet with her own attorney to review her contract and develop a written response, if she wished or was advised by her attorney to do so. Then she was required to meet with Vizcacha's lead counsel and primary contract counsel to fully review the terms of her contract and company policies. She also would meet with Choudhary and South Asian's contract specialist. Dhavan told her she was a valued member of the South Asian family, and she would not be sanctioned for this first violation. However he stressed that she was being warned in the meeting and letter that any future violations could result in serious sanctions including dismissal.

Dhavan then told her that he was hiring additional security to protect her as some of the complaints reported to him were borderline threats. He would take no chances with her safety. Kruti became upset and initially threatened to go public with the story of what Vizcacha allegedly said to Valera. Then she quickly relented, saying she was sorry and would not go public with Valera's comments, appreciated Dhavan's concerns for her career and safety, and planned to comply with the letter and her contract. When Kruti left, Dhavan had ensured that two security officers were there to escort her home. He'd arranged for around-the-clock protection at work and home for Kruti, with two security officers always present. After the meeting, Dhavan immediately called Archer's office to schedule an important phone conversation as soon as possible.

About 30 minutes after Kruti left, and after placing the call to Archer, Dhavan met with his public relations director Kulkarni, lead counsel Choudhary, and security officer Bhagat, as planned and scheduled beforehand, to discuss how the meeting with Kruti went and address whatever actions were needed. They all agreed security measures should be taken on Kruti's behalf until further notice. They agreed all company communications and social media policies should be reviewed and updated if needed. They also agreed all celebrities, on-air talent, and other employees should be reminded again via letter that they were responsible for being educated about and following all contractual obligations and company policies, directing them to schedule meetings with their firm's lead counsel's office if they had any questions or concerns about their contracts. Dhavan did not tell them about what Roberto allegedly said to Juan or Kruti's threat to go public with that rumor.

The next morning when Archer returned his call, Dhavan verbally informed him of Kruti's contract violations and the public relations issue, what Kruti alleged Roberto had said to Juan, and Kruti's threat to go public with the rumor. Archer thanked Dhavan for telling him and said that all types of discrimination were prohibited by Vizcacha International and its companies. Archer told him that Roberto himself had directed and ensured that nondiscrimination policies were established at all his companies well before it became common in media industries. Archer pointed out that it was company policy when an employee violated a contract or caused negative publicity for more than one Vizcaya company, corporate headquarters was responsible for dealing with the employee. Did Dhavan object or have any concerns with following company policy in this case?

Dhavan thought for a few moments and then said, "Both as a CEO and as a person, I want to be sure that discrimination is not tolerated, no matter which entity or member of the Vizcacha corporate family is involved. I have no idea whether this rumor is true. If you give me your word that discrimination will not be tolerated no matter who is involved, and if you give me your word that Kruti will be treated the same as any other employee would in this situation, I have no objections to following company policy in this case. If you feel it is best to have an independent, trusted third party handle Kruti's case, then that would be acceptable to me as well."

Archer replied, "I can assure you, as the CEO of Vizcacha International and as a person, discrimination will never be tolerated, no matter who in the Vizcacha corporate family is involved. Kruti will be treated just as any other employee would in this case. I agree with your approach; I feel it is best to warn her at this point. She has been a good employee and this is her first violation of any kind. I agree with what you have done and that no sanctions should yet be imposed. I have no doubt that she will be treated fairly and equitably by our corporate lead counsel, who is unaware of this rumor. If acceptable to you, I propose we follow company policy in Kruti's case." Dhavan replied, "It is acceptable to me in Kruti's case. If you have no objections, I plan to follow company policy and schedule a follow up meeting with Kruti in about a month to be sure she has followed through with company requirements and is informed about her contractual and policy obligations. I also want to be sure Kruti is comfortable with me and comfortable representing South Asian." Archer replied, "That's absolutely fine with me. Let's follow company policy."

A month later, Dhavan met with Kruti, who told him that she had met with the lead counsel and head contract attorney at Vizcacha International, as well as Choudhary and South Asian's lead contract counsel, and had carefully reviewed contractual and policy requirements in both meetings. Kruti told Dhavan she was satisfied and had been treated fairly by all concerned, and was comfortable with him and with representing South Asian Entertainment and Viscacha International. She told Dhavan she was now officially engaged to Juan. He congratulated her warmly, and offered to feature their engagement and wedding in Vizcacha International properties, only if and how they wished. Kruti added she would no longer engage in political advocacy. As a result, the negative publicity and complaints died down quickly. After a month, Kruti asked Dhavan to remove the extra security and, after first consulting with Archer, Vizcacha's head of security, Bhagat, and Choudhary, he complied.

Yet this was not the most difficult problem Dhavan had encountered as CEO of South Asian International. Three months before his first meeting with Kruti, one of the journalists from Anokhi had been murdered. The journalist, Vikas Mishra, wrote about crime in the Bollywood industry, reporting in print and digital editions how management in several film and TV production companies, including one owned by Vizcacha International, had allegedly taken bribes to ignore when counterfeit copies of films and programs were made on site and then sold illegally. Rumors were flying that Mishra's reporting had angered the organized crime syndicate that earned significant profits from the operation. Mishra was killed in a drive-by shooting when leaving Anokhi's offices in Mumbai one evening.

About 6 weeks before the murder, Anokhi CEO Kangna Shankar notified Dhavan at about noon Mumbai time that an anonymous caller had just threatened to kill Mishra and blow up Anokhi headquarters unless the stories on the illegal sales of counterfeit programs and films were stopped. Shankar wanted to temporarily suspend coverage of the story until security was in place and the police investigation was complete. On the spot, Dhavan immediately authorized Shankar to hire security to escort Mishra to and from work, and to place a 24-hour guard at the Anokhi office and at Mishra's home until further notice. He authorized Shankar to arrange any other security that was needed for any employee and/or their families. Dhavan made it clear that he would cover all security expenses; safety was of primary importance. He agreed that the stories could be temporarily suspended but felt they should not be canceled. Dhavan then told Bhagat to contact Shankar and provide additional security advice or assistance, immediately notify security at all South Asian Entertainment companies, take all necessary security precautions at South Asian Entertainment headquarters and firms, and put into action the plan to ensure notification of all branches of the firm.

Following company policy, next Dhavan called Vizcacha's headquarters, notifying Archer's assistant that the call must be taken now, and was put through immediately. Archer agreed that employee safety was paramount and all security expenses would be covered. Archer also agreed and authorized Dhavan to take whatever security precautions might be needed at all South Asian Entertainment properties. Archer would notify Roberto Vizcacha, the board, and any other person or property that corporate headquarters should inform. Dhavan and Shankar should act as needed, but keep Archer informed per company policy, submitting daily reports by telephone, or immediately, if any emergency or threat occurred or anything else was needed. Archer said the head counsel for

Vizcacha International and the corporate legal office would work with Dhavan and Shankar to ensure all appropriate measures were taken and policies and procedures were followed. Archer told Dhavan to provide security for himself and his family, including his wife in India and, if needed, for his son and daughter attending college in the United States. Archer closed the conversation by stressing that the protection of everyone in the Vizcacha International family was paramount among all other considerations.

Dhavan's next step was to follow up to ensure security precautions were being implemented for Mishra, Shankar, Anokhi employees and offices, and other South Asian Entertainment firms. As stated in South Asian's emergency policy, Dhavan or other top security and communications managers were each assigned a South Asian firm top manager to notify and provide with initial instructions in the event of an emergency. Once those initial calls were made, Dhavan placed follow-up calls until he personally spoke to the top manager of all firms he supervised, reiterated that the safety of all employees and offices was paramount, reiterated that he authorized extra security expenses, informing them to stay in touch with him, and South Asian's legal, security, and communications officers as needed. Dhavan reminded them of the precautions to take immediately to protect employees and how to respond, and that all employees must read the security e-mail that would arrive within the hour. Each top manager was personally responsible for scheduling meetings to ensure all employees were informed, prepared, and read the security e-mail.

Next, still within an hour of the threat, Dhavan informed all managers and employees at all South Asian Entertainment companies via the security e-mail of the threat and directed them to take all necessary safety precautions immediately. Dhavan and his lead counsel had quickly composed the message, based on several drafts prepared in advance, just in case. Copies of South Asian Entertainment's overall safety policies were attached, and the e-mail message included the links for all other company safety policies, directions on what to do if a threat were made, what to do if any hostile or threatening actions occurred at work, and information on how to minimize their exposure to danger at or away from work. All employees were notified that meetings would be held at their offices to provide information and answer their questions. Employees were told they must check in and out with the security detail set up in the lobby of the primary entrance of each office in the company until notified otherwise by the South Asian International head of security via e-mail. No employee was to wait outside to be checked in. Any threatened or fearful employee could be escorted to their vehicles or home.

All managers and employees were also directed to contact South Asian Entertainment's head of security immediately if they had been threatened, or at any future time were threatened, and/or needed additional individual security protection. Dhavan or his authorized manager would relay any additional threats of information to Archer or the appropriate manager at Vizcacha International, as noted in company policies.

Dhavan directed all top South Asian Entertainment managers at all companies and outlets to provide a written report of all immediate and future actions to be taken to ensure security as soon as possible, but no later than 24 hours after the threat was made. This report must include a schedule of, and report on, all meetings held at each office to inform all managers and employees in person about the threat, the security e-mail and policies, as well as answer questions and provide reassurance. After taking security precautions at their offices, all top managers were directed to review all relevant company policies, ask Dhavan if they had questions, and follow the policies. All top managers also were directed to contact Dhavan and lead counsel immediately if any other threats were made, if they needed assistance in ensuring security, and if they had any other questions.

Within 2 hours of the threat, Dhavan held meetings with South Asian's head of security, lead counsel, communications/public relations officer, and other management involved in security, legal issues, and communications. They planned strategy and reviewed the company policies regarding security and safety, which had been developed 5 years earlier when Dhavan became CEO. Choudhary also said, "Later we've got to reexamine copyright laws and conventions to see if there's anything else we can do." Bhagat said, "We've got to figure out whether any employees in any of our companies are involved in this or are taking bribes."

At 4:00 a.m. the next morning, Dhavan and these same senior managers reviewed the 24-hour security reports and responses taken by all top managers, who had already submitted them well before the 24-hour deadline. Dhavan added security where he felt enough had not been implemented, and ensured that comparable, yet appropriate, security measures were taken at every firm. In no case was the level of security authorized by a top manager reduced. Dhavan also sent e-mail memos, followed up by printed versions delivered via courier with confirmed receipt, to every manager at every firm requiring them to hold a meeting with all employees they supervised, review all policies and procedures regarding security, and answer all questions. All managers also were directed to ensure all employees knew updates would regularly be sent via e-mail, so to check e-mail often. Each manager was personally directed to contact and confirm that any employee on vacation or out of the office was informed of everything as well. Each manager was required to send a written report about each meeting held to Dhavan, South Asian's head of security, and head of communications/public relations, and to share questions raised by employees.

Communications/PR officer Kulkarni wanted to send out special newsletter issues answering the questions many employees had and reiterating the information in the first security e-mail. Kulkarni also directed his PR officers at each unit to send e-newsletters reminding employees what to do and where to go if their offices were attacked, providing basic first aid treatment advice, listing the names and numbers of each unit's nurse, providing emergency phone numbers for local hospitals and ambulance companies, and anything else that employees asked about. He asked each firm to hold informational meetings to review these safety and first aid techniques as well. Kulkarni also asked each firm's PR officer to ask and report on any other information employees needed or other questions or concerns that needed to be addressed in newsletters or another form.

A week after the threat, managers and employees throughout South Asian Entertainment were sent via e-mail another copy of the company's safety policies and reminders about what to do if a threat were made, what to do if any hostile or threatening actions occurred at work, how to protect themselves and minimize their exposure to danger, and the need to check in and out with security until further notice, with the option of requesting escort home or to their vehicles, if needed. They also were reminded to check e-mail regularly for updates and e-newsletters with additional information. All employees who were threatened were required to have guards at home and to be escorted to and from work, even if they did not wish to have an escort. All managers and employees were directed to contact South Asian's lead counsel if they were threatened and/or felt they needed additional individual security protection. This reminder message and copies of all policies were e-mailed again one month after the threat to all South Asian managers and employees.

Dhavan was frustrated with Mishra's attempts to circumvent security. Mishra was angry that coverage was temporarily suspended. "These thugs will be emboldened if we don't keep running my stories. You, Shankar, and Dhavan don't have the guts to stand up to these thugs. I can't do my job if security guys are following me everywhere," he complained to his immediate supervisor, Vijay Mirza, who replied, "You can't do your job if you're dead either. You are ordered to follow all security measures and have your designated security officer with you at all times." Mishra called Dhavan to complain about Shankar, Mirza's comments, and the safety requirements. Dhavan told Mishra he would discuss his concerns with Shankar and Mirza. But Dhavan also made it clear that Mishra must follow all security directives: He must have one or more security officers with him at all times, he must always check in and out at work, all security measures would continue, and there was no negotiation where his security was concerned. "I think you're all wrong; these crooks are just trying to scare us, they won't do anything," Mishra said. "We can't take that chance," Dhavan replied. "You know journalists have been killed in the past. You must comply with all security measures for your own safety and the safety of your family."

Mishra said he would comply and hung up. Dhavan immediately called Shankar and Mirza and told them to have security watch Mishra carefully. He also called the Anokhi head of security, Ashkay Hashmi, and told him Mishra had been trying to circumvent security, commanding him to watch Mishra carefully, and telling him to ensure that all safety precautions and procedures for Mishra were followed at all times. Dhavan told Hashmi that he must ensure that at least one security guard was with Mishra at all times. Dhavan also sent Mishra, Shankar, Mirza, Hashmi, and Bhagat an e-mail reiterating that all security precautions and procedures must be continued and followed.

Then, a week later, Mishra slipped away from his security officer, apparently going to meet an anonymous source who had information about how digital HD copies of programs and films were being stolen, and where they were being sold. Mishra called his wife and told her he was going to this meeting. She immediately called Mirza to try and stop him, who reached Mishra's security officer while he was in the bathroom. Mishra had checked out, but was not stopped for leaving without his security officer. Mirza then called Hashmi, who wasn't in his office. Mishra made it out of the building, went halfway down the block, and then was killed.

Mirza called Dhavan, who immediately confirmed Mirza had called the police, told him to allow no one to enter or leave the building, detain Hashmi, detain the security guard who had gone to the bathroom instead of guarding Mishra, and detain the officers who let Mishra out of the building. Then Mirza was to call Mishra's wife. Dhavan then called Shankar immediately and directed her to do the same.

Next Dhavan called Bhagat, who immediately left to ensure the Anokhi security chief and personnel were detained and to assist the police in the investigation. Bhagat told him, "This smells like an inside job to me. Somebody infiltrated and bribed someone." Dhavan said, "Keep that between us for now. Provide all assistance to the police but keep your eyes open and report back to me. Talk to Hashmi and all the officers and guards involved, as well as others who weren't involved." Dhavan immediately placed an emergency call to Archer, who said he would contact Mishra's wife, see about providing Mishra's pension to his family, and send a corporate security representative to aid in assisting the police and the investigation. Dhavan said he'd contact Mishra's wife later, too, to offer his condolences and reiterate what Archer would tell her. Late that night when Dhavan went home, he told Ingrid, "I'll live with this for the rest of my life. I'll always wonder if there's anything else I could have done, or done better, to prevent this murder."

Dhavan had been thinking about all the events and conversations of the past few months in preparation for his meeting with Archer and Vizcacha. He thought about how much he trusted and believed in Bhagat, Choudhary, and Kulkarni and how to help advance their careers. He liked the conglomerate and company and considered what he wanted to do next, including where he and his wife would live. "It would certainly be nice to be closer to, or live in the U.S.," Ingrid told him. "We could see the children and my family more often. Mom and Dad are in their late 70s now. They've been doing pretty well, but who knows when they'll get sick and need care?" His parents had already died, so it was easier to move away from India now. But he suspected he might be asked to move to Korea because Vizcacha International was trying to expand there. An Indian film festival had been held in Seoul, and additional Bollywood films would be opening there soon. He also needed to consider that the meeting might be unpleasant. What failures or errors would he have to answer for? What could he have done differently where Kruti Khan and Vikas Mishra were concerned? "You've always got to prepare for all possibilities," he reminded himself. Dhavan prepared a list of possible topics and issues to research to prepare for his meeting with Archer and Vizcacha.

**Assignment**

Before answering the following questions, you must educate yourself on India, South Korea, and Argentina, as well as customs and etiquette. Read the most current versions of these and other reports assigned by your professor.

Read these reports for Argentina:

The U.S. State Department Background Note: Argentina—Profile at www.state.gov/r/pa/ei/bgn/26516.htm:

Kwintessential Argentina—Language, Culture, Customs and Etiquette at Customs and Etiquette: www.kwintessential.co.uk/resources/global-etiquette/argentina.html

Kwintessential's Doing Business page for Argentina at www.kwintessential.co.uk/etiquette/doing-business-argentina.html

Argentina Web page: http://translate.google.com/translate?hl=en&sl=es&u=http://www.argentina.gob.ar/&prev=search

Read these reports for India:

The U.S. State Department Background Note: India—Profile at www.state.gov/r/pa/ei/bgn/3454.htm

Kwintessential India—Language, Culture, Customs and Etiquette at Customs and Etiquette: www.kwintessential.co.uk/resources/global-etiquette/india-country-profile.html
Kwintessential's Doing Business page for India at www.kwintessential.co.uk/etiquette/doing-business-india.html
India web page: www.india.gov.in

Read these reports for the Republic of Korea or South Korea:

The U.S. State Department Background Note: South Korea—Profile at www.state.gov/r/pa/ei/bgn/2800.htm
Kwintessential South Korea—Language, Culture, Customs and Etiquette at Customs and Etiquette: www.kwintessential.co.uk/resources/global-etiquette/south-korea-country-profile.html/
Kwintessential's Doing Business page for South Korea at www.kwintessential.co.uk/etiquette/doing-business-southkorea.html
Republic of Korea's web page: www.korea.net/

Answer the following questions:

1. Develop a list of topics and issues that Dhavan should research to prepare for his meeting with Archer and Vazcacha. Provide a concise yet detailed summary of each topic or issue.
2. What are the advantages and disadvantages of having Dhavan Banerjee serve as the new top manager at a Vizcacha International media company in the Republic of Korea or South Korea? Would Dhavan be a good choice to run a company for Vizcacha International in South Korea? Why or why not? Answer yes or no and provide a detailed yet concise answer based on the reports you were assigned to read for South Korea and India. Also discuss whether it is better to have an expatriate top manager, or hire a top manager from South Korea. Review Chapter 5 before answering this question.
3. Should Dhavan have raised the issue of interracial relationships with Archer? In other words, should he have discussed with Archer what Kruti said her fiancé told her Roberto Vizcacha said about their relationship? Why or why not?
4. What other ways could Dhavan have handled the rumor involving interracial relationships? Explain your answer in concise detail.

5. If the topic of the rumor about interracial relationships comes up in his meeting with Vizcacha and Archer, what should Dhavan say? Why?

6. Should Dhavan have handled the situation with Kruti Khan differently? Identify the responses Dhavan made that you thought were good or appropriate, as well as the responses you felt were not appropriate. Also identify any responses or actions he failed to take (but should have taken). Explain your rationale in concise detail for each response or action Dhavan took or failed to take.

7. Should Dhavan have handled the situation with Vikas Mishra differently? Identify the responses Dhavan made that you thought were good or appropriate, as well as the responses you felt were not appropriate. Also identify any actions he failed to take (but should have taken). Explain your rationale in concise detail for each response or action Dhavan took or failed to take.

8. How can Dhavan best discover whether any of his employees were involved in the murder of Vikas Mishra or were taking bribes? What should he do to find out whether employees such as Hashmi, the Anokhi head of security, or the South Asian head of security, Bhagat, were not involved? How does he do so without risking his own, his family's, or his employees' security at South Asian International and Anokhi?

9. What other security measures should Dhavan have taken for Vikas Mishra, if any? Why? Explain your answer in concise detail.

10. What could be done at South Asian International to minimize the chances that employees will be involved in counterfeiting, piracy, or accepting bribes in the future?

11. What other security measures should Dhavan have taken for Kruti Khan, if any? Why? Explain your answer in concise detail.

12. Your professor will assign copyright sites or information to read about India. Your professor also may assign you and/or your team to research information about copyright protection in India. Once you've conducted the research and/or read the copyright information you've been assigned, answer questions 12 a–e, or the parts of the question your professor assigns.

a. Is India on the U.S. Trade Representative's Priority Watch List or Watch List? If yes, identify and describe in concise detail the problems or examples related to programming or media-related copyright or intellectual property violations, piracy, theft, or other media-related problems in India.

b. Identify and describe in concise detail any other media industry-related major copyright or intellectual property problems in India that are important or related to South Asian International and Anokhi. These would include problems or issues you found in conducting research or reading information provided by your professor.

c. Identify and describe in concise detail the laws, conventions, relations, or agreements (e.g., Berne) in India found in the U.S. Copyright Office Circular 38A entitled International Copyright Relations of the United States (reviewed in 11/2010, or a more recent version available online at www.copyright.gov/circs/circ38a.pdf). Use any other sources you find while conducting research or assigned by your professor to answer this question as well.

d. Based on the laws, conventions, relations, or agreements for copyright that you discussed in Question 12c, summarize the major protections, duration of protection, etc. in India. In other words, summarize the major protection, or lack thereof, offered by all conventions, relations, and agreements in India. If there is no or little protection, or there are serious problems regarding protection, state that and explain why in as much detail as possible.

e. Based on your answers to Questions 12 a–d, discuss the pros and cons of selling film, digital, and television programming in India. Recommend what courses of action South Asian International and Anokhi might take to protect intellectual property in India.

13. Based on what you learn about copyright in India from Question 12, is there anything else South Asian International and Anokhi can do to minimize the problems of counterfeiting programs and piracy?

14. Based on what you learn about copyright in India, should South Asian International and Anokhi each develop a company policy about copyright? Why or why not? If

yes, identify and describe in concise detail the principles, topics, rules, and/or guidelines that should be included in each copyright policy you recommend for development.

15. Develop a social media policy for South Asian International. Include the topics that are typically included in such policies. Be sure to include rules or guidelines that address what and how employees can communicate using social media.

16. Develop a policy for dealing with public relations issues (such as the negative publicity resulting from Kruti's advocacy of water and sewer issues for the poor, or tragedies such as Mishra's murder) at South Asian Entertainment in the future. Be sure to include the steps to be taken in the future when such public relations issues occur, as well as rules or guidelines about major topics related to crisis communication.

17. Should the contracts of South Asian International celebrities such as Kruti Khan be changed? If yes, how and why should the contracts be changed? If no, why not?

18. Propose a new diversity policy for Vizcacha International to include standards and guidelines that should be used at all of its companies and outlets worldwide. Identify and describe in concise detail the diversity rules, guidelines, and/or principles that would be appropriate to include in a conglomerate-wide policy.

19. Propose a new diversity policy for South Asian International to include standards and guidelines that should be used at all of its companies and outlets in the region. Identify and describe in concise detail the diversity rules, guidelines, and/or principles that would be appropriate to include in a policy for all of South Asian's companies and outlets.

20. Propose a new diversity policy for Anokhi to include standards and guidelines that should be used at all of its print and digital outlets in Mumbai. Identify and describe in concise detail the diversity rules, guidelines, and/or principles that would be appropriate to include in a policy for all Anokhi brands and outlets.

21. If Vizcacha International does start or buy a media company in South Korea, where should it be located? Why? Explain your answer in concise detail. You may conduct research to answer this question.

22. What type of media company or companies should Vizcacha International start or buy in South Korea? Explain your answer in concise detail. You may conduct research to answer this question.

23. What other major issues are found in this case? In other words, what are other major problems identified or implied in the case that are not covered in a previous question? Identify any other major problems, discuss each problem in concise detail, and explain how and why the problem is occurring. Identify the major causes, symptoms, and characteristics of each problem.

24. Describe in concise detail which manager from Vizcacha International, South Asian, and/or Anokhi is the best choice to solve each problem you identify in Question 23. Explain why each manager is best, or explain why a particular set of managers you identify are best to work together to solve each problem.

25. Explain in concise detail how each problem you identify and discuss in Questions 23 and 24 might be solved. Provide specific suggestions and details.

26. After completing other questions from this case, and reading all background links given in the case for the three countries, identify the similarities and differences between working in Argentina, India, and South Korea. What are important things to do or remember when working in each country? What are important things to do or remember that would be appropriate in each country? Explain your answers and suggestions in concise detail. You may conduct additional research to answer this question.

27. What are other ways to find out information to help you live and work effectively and appropriately in a different, nonnative country? Identify and describe in concise detail other specific sources of information to use to learn about another country and doing business there. Identify and describe in concise detail other sources or ways of finding out about another country's culture, customs, and ways of doing business. You may conduct additional research to answer this question.

# REFERENCES

About EveryBlock. (2015). Retrieved from http://www.everyblock.com/about/

About Us. (2012a). Patch. Retrieved from www.patch.com

About Us. (2012b). ProPublica: Journalism in the Public Interest. Retrieved from http://www.propublica.org/about/

Achtenhagen, L., & Raviola, E. (2007). Organizing internal tension: Duality management of media companies. In L. Achtenhagen (Ed.), *Organizing media: Mastering the challenges of organizational change* (pp. 127–145). Jönköping, Sweden: Jönköping International Business School.

Acs, Z.J., & Audretsch, D.B. (2009). Knowledge spillover theory of entrepreneurship. *Small Business Economics, 32*, 15–30.

Adams, J.S. (1963). Toward an understanding of inequity. *Journal of Abnormal and Social Psychology, 67*, 422–436.

Adams, J.W. (2008). Innovation management and U.S. weekly newspaper Web sites: An examination of newspaper managers and emerging technology. *The International Journal on Media Management 10*(2): 64–73.

Addressing employee performance problems: 7 steps to success. (2010). *North Carolina Employment Law*, (January): 6.

ARF. (2003, August). *Advertising Research Foundation's Guidelines for Market Research*. New York, NY: ARF Board of Directors. Retrieved from www.thearf.org

After the NLRB case, can employees really trash your company on Facebook? (2011). *The HR Specialist: Employment Law, 41*(5): 4.

Albarran, A.B. (1996). *Media economics: Understanding markets, industries and concepts*. Ames, IA: Iowa State University Press.

Albarran, A.B. (2010). *The media economy*. New York, NY: Routledge.

Alderfer, C.P. (1972). *Existence, relatedness, and growth*. New York, NY: Free Press.

Aldrich, H.E., & Ruef, M. (2007). *Organizations evolving*. Los Angeles, CA: Sage.

Ali, A., & Seiders, K. (2004). Entrepreneurial marketing. In W.D. Bygrave & A. Zacharakis (Eds.), *The portable MBA in entrepreneurship* (pp. 71–105). Hoboken, NJ: John Wiley and Sons.

AMA board approves new marketing definition. (1985, March 1). *Marketing News*.

American Advertising Federation. (2011). Institute for Advertising Ethics Principles and Practices for Advertising Ethics. Retrieved from http://www.aaf.org/default.asp?id=1236

American Association for Public Opinion Research. (2011). AAPOR standards and ethics. Retrieved from http://www.aapor.org/Standards_and_Ethics/4260.htm

American Society of News Editors. (2010, April 11). Decline in newsroom jobs slows. Retrieved from http://asne.org/article_view/articleid/763/decline-in-newsroom-jobs-slows.aspx

American Society of News Editors. (2011, April 7). Individual minority percentages of respondees. Retrieved from http://asne.org

American Society of News Editors. (2014). 2014 Census. Retrieved from http://asne.org/content .asp?pl=121&sl=387&contentid=387

Andrews, R., Boyne, G.A., Law, J., & Walker, R.M. (2009). Centralization, organizational strategy, and public service performance. *Journal of Public Administration Research & Theory, 19*(1): 57–80.

Andriessen, J.H.E. (1994). Conditions for successful adoption and implementation of telematics in user organizations. In J.H.E. Andriessen, and R. Roe (Eds.), *Telematics and work* (pp. 11–439). Hillsdale, NJ: Lawrence Erlbaum Associates.

Argyris, C. (1962). *Interpersonal competence and organizational effectiveness.* Homewood, IL: Dorsey.

Argyris, C., & Schön, D.A. (1974). *Theory in practice: Increasing professional effectiveness.* San Francisco, CA: Jossey-Bass.

Arnold, M., & Nesbitt, M. (2006). *Women in media 2006: Finding the leader in you.* Evanston, IL: Media Management Center, Northwestern University.

ASRC Advertising Self-Regulatory Council (2015). Retrieved from http://www.asrcreviews.org.

Associated Press (AP). (2011). *Associated Press Stylebook and Briefing on Media Law* (46th ed.). New York, NY: Basic Books & Associated Press.

*Associated Press v. U.S.* (1945). Dist. Court, 705 F.2d 1143.

Aylesworth, A. (2008). Improving case discussion with an improv mind-set. *Journal of Marketing Education, 30*(2): 106–115.

Bachman, K. (2010). Dallas/Fort Worth. *Adweek, 51*(3): 28.

Bailyn, L. (1985). Autonomy in the industrial R&D laboratory. *Human Resource Management 24*(2): 129–146.

Bandura, A. (1997). *Self-efficacy: The exercise of control.* New York, NY: Freeman.

Barkin, S. (2001, September). Satellite extravaganza. *American Journalism Review 23*(7): 48–51.

Barney, J.B., & Hesterly, W. (2001). Organizational economics: Understanding the relationship between organizations and economic analysis. In S.R. Clegg, C. Hardy, W.R. Nord (Eds.), *Handbook of Organization Studies* (pp. 115–147. London, England: Sage Publications.

Barton, D.W. (2011, November 17). What I saw at the hyperlocal revolution. *Columbia Journalism Review.* Retrieved from http://www.cjr.org/the_news_frontier/what_i_saw_at_ the_hyperlocal_revolution.php?page=all

Batsell, J. (2012). Friday night bytes. *Columbia Journalism Review 50*(5, January/February): 39–41.

Baum, J.A.C. (2001). Organizational ecology. In S.R. Clegg, C. Hardy, & W.R. Nord (Eds.), *Handbook of organization studies* (pp. 7–14). London, England: Sage.

Beam, R.A. (2006). Organizational goals and priorities and the job satisfaction of U.S journalists. *Journalism & Mass Communication Quarterly 83*(1): 169–185.

Beam, R.A. & Meeks, L. (2011). So many stories, so little time. In W. Lowrey & P.J. Gade (Eds.), *Changing the news: The forces shaping journalism in uncertain times* (pp. 230–248). New York, NY: Routledge.

Beaver, G. (2003). Small firms: Owners and entrepreneurs. *Strategic Change, 12*: 177–183.

Becker, L.B., Hollifield, C.A., Jacobsson, A., Jacobsson, E.M., & Vlad, T. (2009). Is more always better? Examining the adverse effects of competition on media performance. *Journalism Studies 10*(3): 368–385.

Becker, L.B., Lauf, E., & Lowrey, W. (1999). Differential employment rates in the journalism and mass communication labor force based on gender, race and ethnicity: Exploring the impact of affirmative action. *Journalism & Mass Communication Quarterly, 76*: 631–645.

Becker, L.B. & Vlad, T. (2011). Where professionalism begins. In W. Lowrey & P.J. Gade (Eds.), *Changing the news: The forces shaping journalism in uncertain times* (pp. 249–269). New York, NY: Routledge.

Becker, L. B., Vlad, T., Daniels, G., & Martin, H. J. (2007). The impact of internal labor markets on newspaper industry personnel practices. *International Journal on Media Management 9*: 59–69.

Becker, L.B., Vlad, T., & Simpson, H.A. (2013). Report of the 2012 Annual Survey of Journalism & Mass Communication Graduates. Presented to the Association for Education in Journalism and Mass Communication

Beckhard, R., & Harris, R. (1987). *Organizational transitions: Managing complex change.* Reading, MA: Addison-Wesley.

Bendick, M. Jr., & Egan, M.L. (2009, January). Research perspectives on race and employment in the Advertising Industry. Retrieved from http://www.bendickegan.com

Bergen, L.A., & Weaver, D. (1988). Job satisfaction of daily newspaper journalists and organization size. *Newspaper Research Journal, 9*(2): 1–13.

Bertlesmann, S.E. & Co. KGaA. (2013). Annual Report. Retrieved from http://www.bertelsmann. com/media/investor-relations/annual-reports/bertelsmann-annual-report-2013.pdf

Better Business Bureau. (2011). Children's food and beverage advertising initiative. Retrieved from https://www.bbb.org/council/the-national-partner-program/national-advertising-review-services/childrens-food-and-beverage-advertising-initiative/

Bielby, W.T., & Baron, J.N. (1986). Men and women at work: Sex segregation and statistical discrimination. *American Journal of Sociology, 91*: 759–799.

Blackler, F., and Brown, C. (1985). Evaluation and the impact of information technologies on people in organizations. *Human Relations, 38*(3): 213–231.

Boehrer, J., & Linsky, M. (1990). Teaching with cases: Learning to question. In M.D. Svinicki (ed.), *The changing face of college teaching. New directions for teaching and learning, no. 42.* San Francisco: Josey-Bass. Related materials may be retrieved from http://www .soc.ucsb.edu/projects/casemethod/teaching.html

Bok, S. (1989). *Lying: Moral choice in public and private life.* New York, NY: Random House.

Bond, P. (2012, May 3). NBC fires third employee over doctored 911 call in Trayvon Martin controversy. *Hollywood Reporter.* Retrieved from http://www.hollywoodreporter.com/news/trayvon-martin-nbc-news-fires-third-employee-319991

Bormann, E.G., & Bormann, N.C. (1992). *Effective small group communication* (5th ed.). Edina, MN: Burgess International Group.

Bourgeon, L. (2002). Temporal context of organizational learning in new product development projects. *Creativity and Innovation Management, 11*(3): 175–183.

Bracken, J., & Frisby-Greenwood, D. (2012, January 5). Three tech firms picked for Philadelphia media innovation incubator [Web log post]. *Knight Blog.* Retrieved from http://www.knightfoundation.org/blogs/knightblog/2012/1/5/three-tech-firms-picke d-philadelphia-media-innovation-incubator/

Briggs, M. (2011). What makes a successful news startup? *Quill,* (November/December): 26–30.

Briggs, M. (2012). *Entrepreneurial journalism: How to build what's next for news.* Los Angeles, CA: Sage.

Brockner, J., Grover, S., Reed, T., DeWitt, R., & O'Malley, M. (1987). Survivors' reaction to layoffs: We get by with a little help from our friends. *Administrative Sciences Quarterly, 32*: 526–541.

Brown, S.L., & Eisenhardt, K.M. (1998). *Competing on the edge: Strategy as structured chaos.* Boston, MA: Harvard Business School Press.

Bureau of Competition. Federal Trade Commission. (2008). An FTC guide to the antitrust laws. Retrieved from https://www.ftc.gov/tips-advice/competition-guidance/guide-antitrust-laws

Bureau of Competition. Federal Trade Commission. (2010). Competition counts. Retrieved from http://www.ftc.gov/bc/edu/pubs/consumer/general/zgen01.pdf

Bureau of Labor Statistics. (2000). Current Population Survey. Retrieved from http://www.bls. gov/cps/tables.htm

Bureau of Labor Statistics. (2005). Occupational employment statistics tables. Retrieved from http://www.bls.gov/oes/#tables

Bureau of Labor Statistics. (2013a). Current Population Survey. Retrieved from http://www.bls. gov/cps/tables.htm

Bureau of Labor Statistics. (2013b). Workforce in advertising/agencies. Retrieved from http:// www.bls.gov/oes/current/naics4_541800.htm

Bush, M. (2011). Sorry state of diversity in advertising is not just hiring, but culture problem. *Advertising Age, 82*(January 31): 4–5.

Bygrave, W.D. & Zacharakis, A. (2004). *The portable MBA in entrepreneurship.* Hoboken, NJ: John Wiley & Sons, Inc.

Calder, B.J., & Malthouse, E.C. (2008). Media brands and consumer experiences. In M. Ots (Ed.), *Media brands and branding* (pp. 89–93). Jönköping, Sweden: Jönköping International Business School.

Campbell, C.A. (1992). A decision theory model for entrepreneurial acts. *Entrepreneurial Theory and Practice,* 21–27.

Campbell, C.P. (1995). *Race, myth and the news.* Thousand Oaks, CA: Sage.

Carpenter, M. (2010). A Success Story. *Columbia Journalism Review*, 48(6): 17–18.

Cengage Learning. (2015). Case studies. The role of financial analysis. Retrieved from: http://college.cengage.com/business/resources/casestudies/students/financial.htm

*Central Hudson Gas & Electric v. Public Service Commission of New York*. (1980). 447 U.S. 557.

Chandy, K.T. (2004). Case writing guide. Retrieved from http://bingweb.binghamton.edu/~) tchandy/Mgmt411/case_guide.html

Chang, A. (2012, May 8). Yahoo CEO apologizes in resume flap; Board member Patti Hart to depart. *Los Angeles Times*. Retrieved from http://www.latimes.com/business/technology/la-fi-tn-yahoo-scott-thompson-20120508,0,3648236.story

Chang, B.-H., & Chan-Olmsted, S.M. (2010). *Journal of Broadcasting & Electronic Media*, 54(4): 641–656.

Chan-Olmsted, S.M. (2003). Fundamental issues and trends in media strategy research. *Journal of Media Economics & Culture*, 1(1): 9–35.

Chan-Olmstead, S.M. (2006). Issues in strategic management. In A.B. Albarran, S.M. Chan-Olmsted, & M.O. Wirth (Eds.), *Handbook of media management and Economics* (pp. 161–180). Mahwah, NJ: Erlbaum Associates.

Chan-Olmsted, S.M., & Guo, M. (2011). Strategic bundling of telecommunications services: Triple-play strategies in the cable TV and telephone industries. *Journal of Media Business Studies*, 8(2): 63–81.

Chell, E. (2007). Social enterprise and entrepreneurship: Towards a convergent theory of entrepreneurial process. *International Small Business Journal*, 25: 5–26.

Christensen, C.R. (1987). *Teaching and the case method: Text, cases, and readings*. With Abby J. Hansen. Boston, MA: Harvard Business School.

Chyi, H.I., & Sylvie, G. (1998). Competing with whom? Where? And how? A structural analysis of the electronic newspaper market. *Journal of Media Economics*, 11(2): 1–18.

Chyi, H.I., & Sylvie, G. (2000). Online newspapers in the U.S.—Perceptions of markets, products, revenues and competition. *The International Journal of Media Management*, 2(2): 69–77.

Chyi, H.I., & Yang, M.J. (2009). Is online news an inferior good? Examining the economic nature of online news among users. *Journalism & Mass Communication Quarterly*, 86(3): 594–612.

Citizen Snappers. (2011). *Design Week*, 26(5): 15.

Cleary, J. (2005, August). "Walking the walk?": The disconnect over minority professional development in the newsroom. Presented at the meeting of the Association for Education in Journalism and Mass Communication, San Antonio, TX.

Cleland, D.I., & Ireland L.R. (2002). *Project management: Strategic design and implementation*. New York, NY: McGraw-Hill.

Coffey, A.J. (2007). Linguistic market segmentation and audience valuation by U.S. television advertisers. Dissertation. University of Georgia.

Colchester, M. (2011). Websites scour to find, sell video scoops. *Wall Street Journal*, (March 18): B6.

Cole-Frowe, C. (2011). Want freelance success? Here's the plan. *Quill*, (May/June): 34.

Collins, B., & Guetzkow, H. (1964). *Social psychology of group processes for decision making*. New York, NY: Wiley.

Columbia Journalism Review. (2014). CJR's guide to online news startups. Retrieved from http://www.cjr.org/news_startups_guide/

Columbia University. (2015). Case method how-to's. Retrieved from https://casestudies.jrn.columbia.edu/casestudy/www/case_method.asp?nid=3

Commission on Freedom of the Press. (1947). *A free and responsible press: A general report on mass communication: Newspapers, radio, motion pictures, magazines, and books.* Chicago, IL: The University of Chicago Press.

Compaine, B., & Gomery, D. (2000). *Who owns the media?* (3rd ed.). Mahwah, NJ: Lawrence Erlbaum Associates.

Consoli, J. (2007). Rino Scanzoni. *MediaWeek*, 17(November 12, 2007): SR4–SR6.

Copyright Basics. (2011). U.S. Government Printing Office. Circular 1. Reviewed 8/2011. Retrieved from http://www.copyright.gov/circs/circ01.pdf

Copyright Law of the United States and Related Laws Contained in Title 17 of the United States Code. (2011). Retrieved from http://copyright.gov/title17/

Covington, W. G., Jr. (1997). *Systems theory applied to television station management in the competitive marketplace.* Lanham, MD: University Press of America.

Cummings, D. G., & Worley, C. (1993). *Organization development and change.* New York, NY: West Publishing.

Curry, J. (2010). Revolutionary Reporting. *Harvard International Review,* (Fall): 53–57.

Dailey, K. (2011, October 10). Why are Americans leaving good jobs to go solo? *BBC News Magazine.* Retrieved from http://www.bbc.co.uk/news/world-us-canada-15082998

Dailey, L., Demo, L., & Spillman, M. (2009). Newspaper survey suggests TV partnerships in jeopardy. *Newspaper Research Journal, 30*(4): 22–36.

Daniels, G., & Hollifield, C.A. (2002). Times of turmoil: Short- and long-term effects of organizational change on newsroom employees. *Journalism and Mass Communication Quarterly, 79*: 661–680.

DART (2012a). Fact Sheets—Facts: Orange Line. Retrieved from http://www.dart.org/factsheet/orangeline/default.asp

DART (2012b). Orange Line Expansion. Retrieved from http://www.dart.org/about/expansion/orangeline.asp

Day, G.S. (1981). Strategic market analysis: An integrated approach. *Strategic Management Journal, 17*(1), 281–299.

Day, G.S., & Schoemaker, P.J.H. (2000). A different game. In G.S. Day, P.J.H. Schoemaker, & R.E. Gunther (Eds.), *Wharton on managing emerging technologies* (pp. 1–23). New York, NY: John Wiley & Sons.

De Clercq, D., & Voronov, M. (2009). The role of domination in newcomers' legitimation as entrepreneurs. *Organization, 16*: 799–827.

Deggans, E. (2006, May 24). TV reporter painted into a corner. *St. Petersburg (FL) Times Online.* Retrieved from http://www.sptimes.com/2006/05/24/Tampabay/TV_reporter_painted_i.shtml

Deloitte LLP (2009). Deloitte—social networking and reputational risk in the workplace. Ethics & workplace survey results. Retrieved from http://www.deloitte.com/assets/Dcom-UnitedStates/Local%20Assets/Documents/us_2009_ethics_workplace_survey_220509

*Demographics USA—County edition.* (2005). Survey of buying power demographics. New York, NY: Market Statistics.

Denison, D.R. (1990). *Corporate culture and organizational effectiveness.* New York, NY: Wiley.

Deutsch, M. (1949). A theory of cooperation and competition. *Human Relations, 2*(February): 129–152.

Deuze, M. (2001). Online journalism: Modeling the first generation of news media on the World Wide Web. *First Monday 6*(10). Retrieved from http://firstmonday.org/ojs/index.php/fm/article/view/893/802

Deuze, M. (2007). *MediaWork.* Cambridge, England: Polity Press.

Digital Media Law Project. (2014). Retrieved from http://www.dmlp.org/

Doctor, K. (2010). *Newsonomics: Twelve trends that will shape the news you get.* New York, NY: St. Martin's Press.

Donaldson, L. (2001). The normal science of structural contingency theory. In S.R. Clegg, C. Hardy, & W.R. Nord (Eds.), *Handbook of organization studies* (pp. 57–76). London, England: Sage.

Drucker, P.F. (2001). *The essential Drucker: Management, the individual and society.* London, England: Routledge.

Dubini, P., & Provera, B. (2008). Chart success and innovation in the music industry: Does organizational form matter? *Journal of Media Business Studies, 5*: 41–65.

Dupagne, M., & Garrison, B. (2006). The meaning and influence of convergence: A qualitative case study of newsroom work at the Tampa News Center. *Journalism Studies, 7*(2): 237–255.

Eastman, S.T., Ferguson, D.A., & Klein, R.A. (2006). Promoting the media: Scope and goals. In S.T. Eastman, D.A. Ferguson, & R.A. Klein (Eds.), *Media promotion and marketing for broadcasting, cable, and the Internet* (pp. 1–29). New York, NY: Focal Press.

Edmonds, R., Guskin, E., & Rosenstiel, T. (2011). Newspapers: Missed the 2010 media rally. *State of the news media 2011.* Retrieved from http://stateofthemedia.org/2011/newspapers-essay/

Ellis, J. [stanfordbusiness]. (2009, July 28). The business plan [Video file]. Retrieved from http://www.youtube.com/watch?v=yG6_6UbprFw

Emling, S. (2002). DVDs ejecting VCRs from the scene. *The Austin-American Statesman*, (July 7): J1, J6.

Equal Employment Opportunity Commission. (2012). Job patterns for minorities and women in private industry (EEO-1). Retrieved from http://www.eeoc.gov/eeoc/statistics/employment/index.cfm

ESA (Entertainment Software Association). (2011). 2011 Essential facts about the computer and video game industry. Retrieved from http://www.theesa.com/facts/pdfs/ESA_EF_2011.pdf

Eskenazi, G. (1989, September 18). The media business: ESPN's 10-year journey to the top. *New York Times*. Retrieved from http://www.nytimes.com/1989/09/18/business/the-media-business-espn-s-10-year-journey-to-the-top.html

Ettema, J.S., Whitney, D.C., & Wackman, D.B. (1987). Professional mass communicators. In C.R. Berger & S.H. Chaffee (Eds.), *Handbook of communication science* (pp. 747–780). Newbury Park, CA: Sage.

European Industrial Relations Observatory. (2011). *Annual reports of European Industrial Relations Observatory*. Dordrecht, Netherlands: Springer.

Evans, M.G. (1970). The effects of supervisory behavior on the path-goal relationship. *Organizational Behavior and Human Performance, 5*: 277–298.

Fabrikant, G. (1985, December 1). A media giant loses its swagger. *New York Times*. Retrieved from http://www.nytimes.com/1985/12/01/business/a-media-giant-loses-its-swagger.html

Farhi, P. (2007). Rolling the dice. *American Journalism Review*, 29(3): 40–43.

Federal Communications Commission. (2011). Review of the broadcast ownership rules. Retrieved from http://www.fcc.gov/guides/review-broadcast-ownership-rules

Federal Trade Commission Bureau of Consumer Protection Business Center. (2011). Children's Privacy. Retrieved from http://business.ftc.gov/privacy-and-security/children's-privacy

Fedler, F. (2004). Insiders' stories: Coping with newsroom stress: An historical perspective. *American Journalism, 21*(3): 77–106.

Fee, F., Jr. (2007). Firestorm in the newsroom: Cultural issues in altering media organizations. In L. Achtenhagen (Ed.), *Organizing media: Mastering the challenges of organizational change* (pp. 65–87). Jönköping, Sweden: Jönköping International Business School.

Fiedler, F.E. (1967). *A theory of leadership effectiveness*. New York, NY: McGraw-Hill.

Filak, V.F. (2004). Cultural convergence: Intergroup bias among journalists and its impact on convergence. *Atlantic Journal of Communication, 12*(4): 216–232.

Fink, S.L. (1993). Managing individual behavior: Bringing out the best in people. In A.R. Cohen (Ed.), *The portable MBA in management* (pp. 71–112). New York, NY: Wiley.

Fisher, R., Ury, W.L., & Patton, B. (1991). *Getting to yes: Negotiating agreement without giving in* (2nd ed.). London, England: Penguin Books.

Flores, C. (2011, February 3). What a deal! 50% off your job prospects! *Chicago Reader*. Retrieved from http://www.chicagoreader.com/chicago/groupon-noncompete-clause-prospective-writers/Content?oid=3184622

Folkerts, J., & Lacy, S. (2004). *The media in your life* (3rd ed.). Boston, MA: Allyn & Bacon.

Foran, J. (2002). University of California–Santa Barbara case method—Student guidelines. Retrieved from http://www.soc.ucsb.edu/projects/casemethod/guidelines.html.

4As Standards of Practice and Creative Code. (2011). Retrieved from http://www.aaaa.org/about/association/pages/standardsofpractice.aspx

Fox, A. (2009). Curing what ails performance reviews. *HR Magazine*, 54(1, January): 52–56.

Freeland, C. (2010). The rise of private news. *Columbia Journalism Review,* 49(July/August): 36–38.

Gade, P. (2004). Newspapers and organizational development: Management and journalist perceptions of newsroom cultural change. *Journalism & Communication Monographs,* 6: 1–55.

Gade, P. (2005, August). Journalism guardians in a sea of change: U.S. newspaper editors' perceptions of their organizational roles, organizational integration and perceived organizational support. Presented at the meeting of the Association for Education in Journalism and Mass Communication, San Antonio, TX.

Gade, P.J. (2008). Journalism guardians in a time of great change: Newspaper editors' perceived influence in integrated news organizations. *Journalism & Mass Communication Quarterly,* 85(2): 371–392.

Garcia, B. (2011, May 24). Citizens, audiences part of media revolution shaping the world. *Kuwait Times*. Retrieved from http://tl-ph.facebook.com/notes/kuwait-times/citizens-audiences-part-of-media-revolution-shaping-the-world/156607967738139

Geertsema, M. (2009). Gender mainstreaming in international news: A case study of the Inter Press Service. *Journalism and Mass Communication Quarterly, 86*(1): 65–84.

Geisler, J. (2011, March 2). Out of balance: Poynter survey reveals journalists' pressure points. Retrieved at http://www.poynter.org/uncategorized/32679/out-of-balance-poynter-survey-reveals-journalists-pressure-points/

Geron, T. (2011). Zynga says no to ads, yes to in-game promotions. *Forbes*, (April 12, 2011): 55.

Gershon, R.A. (2001). *Telecommunications management: Industry structures and planning strategies*. Mahwah, NJ: Lawrence Erlbaum Associates.

Ghanem, S., & Selber, K. (2009). An analysis of slogans used to "sell the news." *Newspaper Research Journal, 30*(2): 16–29.

Goodwin, H.E. (1987). *Groping for ethics in journalism* (2nd ed.). Ames, IA: Iowa State University.

Grabowicz, P. (2012). The transition to digital journalism: Local. Knight Digital Media Center—University of California Berkeley Graduate School of Journalism. Updated May 28, 2012. Retrieved from http://multimedia.journalism.berkeley.edu/tutorials/digital-transform/hyperlocal/

Gray, C.F., & Larson, E.W. (2000). *Project management: The managerial process*. New York, NY: Irwin/McGraw-Hill.

Greene, C.N. (1972). The satisfaction-performance controversy. *Business Horizons*, (October): 32–40.

Greer, C.F., & Ferguson, D.A. (2011). Using Twitter for promotion and branding: A content analysis of local television Twitter sites. *Journal of Broadcasting & Electronic Media, 55*(2): 198–214.

Gregson, K.S. (2008). Missed opportunities: Use of the Web to promote the local television newscast. *Journal of Web Promotion, 3*(1/2): 102–117.

Griffin, R.W., & Moorhead, G. (1986). *Organizational behavior*. Boston, MA: Houghton-Mifflin.

Grimm, J. (2011, March 3). Will no-compete clause freeze me out? Poynter.org. Retrieved from http://www.poynter.org/how-tos/career-development/ask-the-recruiter/83561/will-no-compete-clause-freeze-me-out/

Grotticelli, M. (2011, April 28). Storify helps newsrooms filter citizen journalism. BroadcastEngineering.com. Retrieved from http://www.tvtechnology.com/news/0086/storify-helps-newsrooms-filter-citizen-journalism/249777

Guskin, E., & Rosenstiel, T. (2012). Network news: The pace of change accelerates. *The State of the News Media 2012*. Retrieved from http://stateofthemedia.org/2012/network-news-the-pace-of-change-accelerates/

Guskin, E., Rosenstiel, T., & Moore, P. (2011). Network news: Durability and decline. *State of the news media 2011*. Retrieved from http://stateofthemedia.org/2011/network-essay/

Haidt, J. (2006). *The happiness hypothesis: Finding modern truth in ancient wisdom*. New York, NY: Basic Books.

Hallen, B.L. (2008). The causes and consequences of initial network positions of new organizations: From whom do entrepreneurs receive investments? *Administrative Science Quarterly, 53*: 685–718.

Handy Reference Guide to the Fair Labor Standards Act. (2010). U.S. Department of Labor: Wage and Hour Division. WH Publication 1282 —Revised September 2010.

Hard Numbers. (2009). *Columbia Journalism Review*, 48(4, November/December): 11

Harris, T.E. (2002). *Applied organizational communication: principles and pragmatics for future practice*. (2nd ed) Mahwah, NJ: Lawrence Earlbaum.

Hay Group. (2011). Executive benefits survey: Results of the 2011 executive retirement benefits & perquisites survey. Retrieved from http://www.haygroup.com/downloads/us/2011_Hay_Group_Executive_Benefits_Survey_Findings_with_brand_cover_(2).pdf

Heath, C., & Heath, D. (2010). *Switch: How to change things when change is hard*. New York, NY: Broadway Books.

Hedlund, M. (2011, April). Why Wesabe lost to Mint. Retrieved from http://blog.precipice.org/why-wesabe-lost-to-mint

Hemmingway, E. (2008). *Into the newsroom: Exploring the digital production of regional television news*. London, England: Routledge.

Hermes, J.P. (2012). Guide to the Internal Revenue Service decision-making process under 501(c)(3) for journalism and publishing non-profit organizations. Research publication no. 2012–8 March 2012. The Berkman Center for Internet & Society at Harvard University. Retrieved from http://cyber.law.harvard.edu/publications/2012/guide_to_IRS_decision_making_process

Herrenkohl, E. (2011). Recruiting strategies: Becoming recruiter-in-chief for your business. Monster.com. Retrieved from http://hiring.monster.com/hr/hr-best-practices/recruiting-hiring-advice/acquiring-job-candidates/recruiting-strategies.aspx

Hersey, P., & Blanchard, K.H. (1969). Life cycle theory of leadership. *Training and Development Journal, 23*(6): 26–34.

Herzberg, F., Mausner, B., & Snyderman, B. (1968). *The motivation to work*. New York, NY: Wiley.

Hickson, M.L., & Stacks, D.W. (1985). *Nonverbal communication: Studies and applications*. Dubuque, IA: Brown.

Hillson, D. (2011). Risk management in practice. In P.C. Dinsmore & J. Cabanis-Brewin (Eds.), *The AMA handbook of project management* (3rd ed., pp. 193–204). New York, NY: American Management Association.

Hinsley, A. (2012). Managing work identities in the "new" newsrooms. In G. Sylvie (Ed.), *Media management decision-making: Under new management* (Chapter 5). Lisbon: Media XXI.

Hitt, M.A., Keats, B.W., & DeMarie, S.M. (1998). Navigating in the new competitive landscape: Building strategic flexiblity and competitive advantage in the 21st Century. *Academy of Management Executive, 12*(4): 22–42.

Hoag, A., Brickley, D.J., & Cawley, J.M. (2001). Media management education and the case method. *Journalism & Mass Communication Educator, 55*: 49–59.

Hof, R.D. (2009, February 18). Ad networks are transforming online advertising. *Bloomberg Businessweek*. Retrieved from http://www.bloomberg.com/bw/stories/2009-02-18/ad-networks-are-transforming-online-advertisinghttp://www.bloomberg.com/bw/stories/2009-02-18/ad-networks-are-transforming-online-advertising

Hofstede, G. (1980). *Culture's consequences*. Newbury Park, CA: Sage.

Holcomb, J., Mitchell, A., & Rosenstiel, T. (2011). Cable: Audience vs. economics. *State of the news media 2011*. Retrieved from http://stateofthemedia.org/2011/cable-essay/

Hollifield, C.A. (2006). News media performance in hypercompetitive markets: An extended model of effects. *The International Journal on Media Management, 8*: 60–69.

Hollifield, C, A, Vlad, T., & Becker, L.B. (2003). The effects of international copyright laws on national economic development. In L.B. Becker & T. Vlad (Eds.), *Copyright & consequences: Central European and U.S. perspectives* (pp. 163–202). Cresskill, NJ: Hampton Press.

Hollifield, C.A., Vlad, T., & Becker, L.B. (2004). Market, organizational, and strategic factors affecting media entrepreneurs in emerging economies. In R. Picard (Ed.), *Proceedings from the International Conference on Strategic Responses to Media Market Changes* (pp. 133–153). Jönköping, Sweden: Media Management and Transformation Centre, Jönköping International Business School, Jönköping University, Sweden

Hollifield, C.A., Becker, L.B., & Vlad, T. (2006, July). The effects of political, economic and organizational factors on the performance of broadcast media in developing countries. Presented to the meeting of the International Association for Media and Communication Research, Cairo, Egypt.

Hollifield, C.A., & Kimbro, C.W. (2010). Understanding media diversity: Structural and organizational factors in influencing minority employment in local commercial television. *Journal of Broadcasting & Electronic Media, 54*(2): 228–247.

Hollifield, C, A, Vlad, T., & Becker, L.B. (2003). The effects of international copyright laws on national economic development. In L.B. Becker & T. Vlad (Eds.), *Copyright & consequences: Central European and U.S. perspectives* (pp. 163–202). Cresskill, NJ: Hampton Press.

Hollifield, C.A., Vlad, T., & Becker, L.B. (2004). Market, organizational, and strategic factors affecting media entrepreneurs in emerging economies. In R. Picard (Ed.), *Proceedings from the International Conference on Strategic Responses to Media Market Changes* (pp. 133–153). Jönköping, Sweden: Media Management and Transformation Centre, Jönköping International Business School, Jönköping University, Sweden

Hoskins, C., McFadyen, S.M., & Finn, A. (2004). *Media economics: Applying economics to new and traditional media*. Thousand Oaks, CA: Sage Publications.

House, R.J., & Dessler, G. (1974). The path-goal theory of leadership: Some posthoc and a priori tests. In J.G. Hunt & L.L. Larson (Eds.), *Contingency approaches to leadership* (pp. 29–55). Carbondale, IL: Southern Illinois University Press.

How to discipline employees for working unauthorized OT. (2011). *The HR Specialist. Employment Law* (April): 2.

Hudson, K. (2010). Cowboys gone, Irving officials call an audible. *Wall Street Journal*, (March 31): C.6.

Hughes, R.L., Ginnett, R.C., & Curphy, G.J. (1999). *Leadership: Enhancing the lessons of experience* (3rd ed.). Boston, MA: Irwin McGraw Hill.

Humphreys, J.M. (2009). The multicultural economy 2009. *Georgia Business and Economic Conditions*, 69(3). Retrieved from http://www.terry.uga.edu/media/documents/selig/GBEC0903q.pdf

Hyman, G. (2011, June 28). ESPN's Carol Kruse on the challenges of legacy branding. *iMedia Connection*. Retrieved from http://blogs.imediaconnection.com/blog/2011/06/28/espns-carole-kruse-on-the-challenges-of-legacy-branding/

International Women's Media Foundation. (2011). Global Report on the Status of Women in the News Media. Author. C.M. Byerly, Principal Investigator. Retrieved from http://iwmf.org/pdfs/IWMF-Global-Report.pdf

Irving Convention Center at Las Colinas (2012). http://www.irvingconventioncenter.com/includes/content/docs/media/Meeting_Planner_Guide.pdf

Irwin, M.J. (2008). Indie game developers rise up. *Forbes.com*. Retrieved from http://www.forbes.com/2008/11/20/games-indie-developers-tech-ebiz-cx_mji_1120indiegames.html

Isaacson, W. (2012, April). The real leadership lessons of Steve Jobs. *Harvard Business Review*. Retrieved from http://hbr.org/2012/04/the-real-leadership-lessons-of-steve-jobs/ar/1

Islam, R. (2002). *The right to tell. The role of mass media in economic development*. Washington, DC: World Bank Institute.

Israely, J. (2011, December 12). Jeff Israely: For a news startup, fundraising isn't just paying the bills: It's how strategy gets built. Nieman Journalism Lab. Retrieved from http://www.niemanlab.org/2011/12/jeff-israely-for-a-news-startup-fundraising-isnt-just-paying-the-bills-its-how-strategy-gets-built/

Jacobsson, A., & Jacobsson, E.M. (2003). Freedom of the press, economic development and market. Dissertation in Economics. Stockholm University.

Jaksa, J.A., & Pritchard, M.S. (1988). *Communication ethics: Methods of analysis*. Belmont, CA: Wadsworth.

Janis, I.L. (1982). *Groupthink*. (2nd ed.). Boston, MA: Houghton Mifflin.

Jewitt, S. (2011). Geographies of shit: Spatial and temporal variations in attitudes towards human waste. *Progress in Human Geography, 35*(5): 608–626.

Johnson, L.K. (2004, December). Execute your strategy without killing it. *Harvard Management Update*. Cambridge, MA: Harvard Business School Publishing Corp. Retrieved from https://hbr.org/2008/02/execute-your-strategy-without-1.html

Johnson, S.D., & Bechler, C. (1998). Examining the relationship between listening effectiveness and leadership emergence—Perceptions, behaviors, and recall. *Small Group Research, 29*(4): 452–471.

Kahn, A.M.Z. (2005). The influence of personality traits on journalists' work behavior: An exploratory study examining a Bangladeshi sample. *Asian Journal of Communication, 15*(1): 72–84.

Karlsson, M. (2011). Flourishing but restrained: The evolution of participatory journalism in Swedish online news, 2005–2009. *Journalism Practice, 5*(1): 68–84.

Katz, D., & Kahn R.L. (1978). *The social psychology of organizations*. New York, NY: Wiley.

Kaufhold, K., Valenzuela, S., & Gil de Zuniga, H. (2010). Citizen journalism and democracy: How user-generated news use relates to political knowledge and participation. *Journalism and Mass Communication Quarterly, 87*(3/4): 515–529.

Kaushik, A. (2009). *Web analytics 2.0: The art of online accountability and science of customer centricity*. New York, NY: John Wiley & Sons.

Keller, K.L. (2008). *Strategic brand management: Building, measuring and managing brand equity*. Upper Saddle River, NJ: Prentice Hall.

Kelley, L.D., Jugenheimer, D.W., & Sheehan, K.B. (2012). *Advertising media planning: A brand management approach* (3rd ed.). Armonk, NY: M.E. Sharpe.

Kerr, N.L. (1983). Motivation losses in small groups: A social dilemma analysis. *Journal of Personality and Social Psychology, 45*(4): 819–828.

Khaire, M. (2005, August). Great oaks from little acorns grow: Strategies for new venture growth. *Best Paper Proceedings of the Academy of Management*.

Kiesler, C.A., & Kiesler, S.B. (1969). *Conformity*. Reading, MA: Addison-Wesley.

Killebrew, K.C. (2003). Culture, creativity and convergence: Managing journalists in a changing information workplace. *The International Journal on Media Management, 5* (1): 39–46.

Kirk, R. (2011, April). 2011 Special 301 Report. Office of the United States Trade Representative. Retrieved from https://ustr.gov/about-us/policy-offices/press-office/reports-and-publications/2011/2011-special-301-report

Kirk, R. (2012, April). 2012 Special 301 Report. Ambassador Ronald Kirk. Office of the United States Trade Representative. Executive Office of the President of the United States. Retrieved from http://www.ustr.gov/sites/default/files/2012%20Special%20301%20Report_0.pdf

Klein, J.S., & Vázquez, M.J. (2011). The jury is still out: The *Long Beach Post* and online local news. *Knight Case Studies Initiative*. Retrieved from https://casestudies.jrn.columbia.edu/casestudy/www/casestudy_collection.asp?nid=2

Knight, R. (2011a). Delivering an effective performance review. HBR Blog Network—Best practices. Retrieved from http://blogs.hbr.org/hmu/2011/11/delivering-an-effective-perfor.html

Knight, R. (2011b). Women make great strides in PR. [Web log post]. Retrieved from http://blogs.ft.com/women-at-the-top/2011/09/05/women-make-great-strides-in-pr/#axzz1jevIMBZ6

Knight Community News Network. (2014). Directory of community news sites. Retrieved from http://kcnn.org/resources/

Kodrich, K.P., & Beam, R.A. (1997, August). Job satisfaction among journalists at daily newspapers: Does size of organization make a difference? Presented at the meeting of Association for Education in Journalism and Mass Communication, Chicago, IL.

Kogut, B. (1989). The stability of joint ventures: Reciprocity and competitive rivalry. *The Journal of Industrial Economics, 38*: 183–198.

Kolo, C., & Vogt, P. (2003). Strategies for growth in the media and communications industry: Does size really matter? *International Journal on Media Management, 5*(4): 251–261.

Kolodny, H., & Stjernberg, T. (1993). Self-managing teams: The new organization of work. In A.R. Cohen (Ed.), *The portable MBA in management* (pp. 279–314). New York, NY: Wiley.

Koontz, H., & O'Donnell, C. (1964). *Management: A book of readings*. New York, NY: McGraw-Hill.

Krumsvik, A.H. (2008). The role of journalists in a digital age: Strategy and structure for online news production. Presented to The International Symposium on Online Journalism, Austin, TX.

Kruse, K. (2012, October 16). 100 best quotes on leadership. *Forbes*. Retrieved from http://www.forbes.com/sites/kevinkruse/2012/10/16/quotes-on-leadership/

Kuchera, B. (2011, September). Feral developers: Why game industry talent is going indie. *Ars Technica*. Retrieved from http://arstechnica.com/gaming/news/2011/08/experience-going-indie.ars

Kuhn, T.S. (1996). *The structure of scientific revolutions*. Chicago, IL: University of Chicago Press.

Kumaraswami, L. (2012). NetFlux: Racist chips anyone? *India Today*. Retrieved from http://indiatoday.intoday.in/story/fanmous-videos-and-apps-from-the-world-of-web/1/188380.html

Kunelius, R., & Ruusunoksa, L. (2008). Mapping professional imagination: On the potential of professional culture in the newspapers of the future. *Journalism Studies, 9*(5): 662–678.

Küng, L. (2004). What makes media firms tick? Exploring the hidden drivers of performance. In R. Picard (Ed.), *Proceedings from the international conference on strategic responses to media market changes* (pp. 65–82). Jönköping, Sweden: Media Management and Transformation Centre, Jönköping International Business School, Jönköping University, Sweden

Küng, L. (2007). *When innovation fails to disrupt.* Jönköping, Sweden: Jönköping International Business School.

Küng, L. (2008). *Strategic management in the media: Theory to practice.* London, England: Sage.

Küng, L., Leandros, N., Picard, R.G., Schroeder, R., & van der Wurff, R. (2008). The impact of the Internet on media organization strategies and structures. In L. Küng, R.G. Picard, & R. Towse (Eds.), *The Internet and the mass media* (pp. 125–148). London, England: Sage.

Kurien, D.N. (2010). Body language: Silent communicator in the workplace. *IUP Journal of Soft Skills, 4*(1/2): 29–36.

Kurpius, D.D., Metzgar, E.T., & Rowley, K.M. (2010). Sustaining hyperlocal media: In search of funding models. *Journalism Studies, 11*(3): 359–376.

Lacy, S., Duffy, M., Riffe, D., Thorson, E., & Fleming, K. (2010). Citizen journalism web sites complement newspapers. *Newspaper Research Journal, 31*(2): 34–46.

Lacy, S., & Martin, H.J. (2005). Circulation and advertising competition: Implications of research. *Newspaper Research Journal, 25*: 18–39.

Lacy, S., & Simon, T. (1993). *The economics and regulation of United States newspapers.* Norwood, NJ: Ablex.

Lang, A. (2000). The limited capacity model of mediated message processing. *Journal of Communication, 50*: 46–70.

Lasorsa, D., & Dai, J. (2007). When news reporters deceive: The production of stereotypes. *Journalism and Mass Communication Quarterly, 84*(2): 281–298.

Lawson-Borders, G. (2003). Integrating new media and old media: Seven observations of convergence as a strategy for best practices in media organizations. *International Journal on Media Management, 5*(2): 91–99.

Lawsuit-proof your company. (2011). *The HR Specialist*, (January): 8.

Lewin, T. (2011, November 2). College graduates' debt burden grew, yet again, in 2010. *New York Times.* Retrieved from http://www.nytimes.com/2011/11/03/education/average-student-loan-debt-grew-by-5-percent-in-2010.html

Lewis, S. (2011). Journalism innovation and participation: An analysis of the Knight News Challenge. *International Journal of Communication, 5*: 1623–1648.

Lippmann, W. (1922). *Public opinion.* New Brunswick, NJ: Transaction Publishers.

Liu, F., & Chan-Olmsted, S.M. (2003). Partnership between the old and the new: Examining the strategic alliances between broadcast television networks and Internet firms in the context of convergence. *The International Journal on Media Management, 5*(1): 47–56.

Locke, E.A. (1968). Toward a theory of task motivation and incentives. *Organizational Behavior and Human Performance, 3*: 157–189.

Lowrey, W. (2005). Commitment to newspaper-TV partnering: A test of the impact of institutional isomorphism. *Journalism & Mass Communication Quarterly, 82*(3): 495–515.

Lowrey, W. (2006). Cognitive shortcuts, the constraints of commitment, and managers' attitudes about newspaper-TV partnerships. *Journal of Media Economics, 19*(4): 241–258.

Lowrey, W. (2009). Institutional roadblocks: Assessing journalism's response to changing audiences. In Z. Papacharissi (Ed.), *Journalism and citizenship: New agendas in communication* (pp. 44–68). New York, NY: Routledge.

Lowrey, W. (2011). News: Once and future institution? In W. Lowrey & P. Gade (Eds.), *Changing the news: The forces shaping journalism in uncertain times* (pp. 136–155). New York, NY: Routledge.

Lowrey, W (2012). Journalism innovation and the ecology of news production: Institutional tendencies. *Journalism & Communication Monographs, 14*(4): 214–287.

Lowrey, W., & Gade, P. (2011). Complexity, uncertainty, and journalistic change. In W. Lowrey & P. Gade (Eds.), *Changing the news: The forces shaping journalism in uncertain times* (pp. 3–21). New York, NY: Routledge.

Lowrey, W., Parrott, S., & Meade, T. (2011). When blogs become organizations. *Journalism, 12*(3): 243–259.

Lublin, J.S., & Mattioli, D. (2010, January 25). Strategic plans lose favor: Slump showed bosses value of flexibility, quick decisions. *Wall Street Journal.* Retrieved from http://www.wsj.com/articles/SB10001424052748703822404575019283591121478

Lucan, A.N. (2004, September). Overtime for journalists? It depends. Association of Alternative Newsweeklies. Retrieved from http://aan.org/gyrobase/Aan/viewArticle?oid=138697

Lund, A.B. (2008). Diffusion of innovation in news organizations: Action research of middle managers in Danish mass media. In C. Dal Zotto & H. van Kranenburg, (Eds.), *Management and innovation in the media industry* (pp. 199–214). Cheltenham, England: Edward Elgar.

Lundberg, C.C., & Enz, E. (1993). A framework for student case preparation. *Case Research Journal, 13*(Summer): 133.

Lundberg, C.C., Rainsford, P.S., Shay, J.P., & Young, C.A. (2001). Case writing reconsidered. *Journal of Management Education, 25*(4): 450–463.

Lundberg, K. (2009). Use a "teaching" case study in your classroom. *The Journalism School—Knight Case Studies Initiative.* CSJ-09–0024.0. New York, NY: Columbia University. Retrieved from https://casestudies.jrn.columbia.edu/casestudy/www/docs/case_method_10_easy_steps.pdf

MacGregor, P. (2007). Tracking the online audience: Metric data start a subtle revolution. *Journalism Studies, 8*(2): 280–298.

MacMillan, D. (2008, December 24). Online journalism: Donations accepted. *BusinessWeek Online.* Retrieved from http://www.bloomberg.com/bw/stories/2008-12-24/online-journalism-donations-acceptedbusinessweek-business-news-st ock-market-and-financial-advice

Malandro, L.A., & Barker, L. (1983). *Nonverbal communication.* Reading, MA: Addison-Wesley.

Malone, M. (2007). New day at WOIO. *Broadcasting & Cable, 137*(March 26): 17.

Malone, T.W., Laubacher, R.J., & Johns, T. (2011). The age of hyperspecialization. *Harvard Business Review, 89*(7/8): 56–65.

Mandel, R.P. (2004). Legal and tax issues. In W.D. Bygrave & A. Zacharakis (Eds.), *The portable MBA in entrepreneurship* (pp. 267–309). Hoboken, NJ: John Wiley and Sons.

Markel, M. (2009). Anti-employer blogging: An overview of legal and ethical issues. *Technical Writing and Communication, 39*: 123–139.

Marshall, J.L. (2005). How to build a fruitful relationship with the boss. *Fusion,* (Winter): 10–11.

Maslow, A.H. (1954). *Motivation and personality.* New York, NY: Harper & Row.

Massey, B.L., & Elmore, C.J. (2011). Happier working for themselves?: Job satisfaction and women freelance journalists. *Journalism Practice, 5*(6): 672–686.

Matsa, K-E., Rosenstiel, T., & Moore, P. (2011). Magazines: A shake-out for news weeklies. *State of the news media 2011.* Retrieved from http://stateofthemedia.org/2011/magazines-essay/

Maynard, M. (2012, May 24). What New Orleans can expect when its newspaper goes away. *Forbes.com.* Retrieved from http://www.forbes.com/sites/michelinemaynard/2012/05/24/what-new-orleans-can-expect-when-its-newspaper-goes-away/

McClelland, D. (1961). *The achieving society.* Princeton, NJ: Van Nostrand.

McCracken, P. (2010, September/October). Coffee, tea . . . and a scoop. *Columbia Journalism Review.* Retrieved from http://www.cjr.org/currents/coffee_teaand_a_scoop.php

McDowell, W.S. (2011). The brand management crisis facing the business of journalism. *The International Journal on Media Management, 13*(1): 37–51.

McGinley, M. (2008, November/December). A little something for your trouble: Buyout packages at papers around the country. *Columbia Journalism Review.* Retrieved from http://www.cjr.org/currents/a_little_something_for_your_tr.php

McGregor, D. (1960). *The human side of enterprise.* New York, NY: McGraw-Hill Book Company, Inc.

McGregor, D. (2006). *The human side of enterprise: Annotated edition; Updated and with a new commentary by Joel Cutcher-Gershenfeld.* New York, NY: McGraw Hill.

McGrory, A. (2011, October 5). How to conduct an effective employee evaluation. BenefitsPro. Retrieved from http://www.benefitspro.com/2011/10/05/how-to-conduct-a n-effective-employee-evaluation

Mcilroy, M., & Wentz, L. (2008). Will new shake-ups stir Aegis? *Advertising Age, 79*(May 12): 6.

McKelvie, A., & Picard, R. (2008). The growth and development of young media firms. *Journal of Media Business Studies, 5*: 1–8.

McLellan, M., and Porter, T. (2007). *News improved: How America's newsrooms are learning to change.* Washington, DC: CQ Press.

McQuail, D. (2010). *McQuail's mass communication theory.* London, England: Sage.

Merriam-Webster Online: Dictionary and Thesaurus. (2012). Retrieved from http://www. merriam-webster.com/

Merrill, J.C. (1974). *The imperative of freedom: A philosophy of journalism autonomy*. New York, NY: Hastings House, Publishers.

Meyer, P. (2004). *The vanishing newspaper: Saving journalism in the information age*. Columbia, MO: University of Missouri Press.

Middleton, K.R., & Lee, W.E. (2011). *The law of public communication* (8th ed.). Boston, MA: Allyn & Bacon.

Mierzejewska, I., & Hollifield, C.A.(2006). Media management theory. In A. Albarran, S. Chan-Olmsted, & M.O. Wirth (Eds.), *Handbook of media economics and management* (pp. 37–66). Mahwah, NJ: Lawrence Earlbaum.

Miller, K.I., & Monge, P.R. (1985). Social information and employee anxiety about organizational change. *Human Communication Research, 11*: 365–386.

*Miller v. California*. (1973). 413 U.S. 22.

Mitchell, A., & Rosenstiel, T. (2012). Overview. State of the news media 2012. Retrieved from http://stateofthemedia.org/2012/overview-4/

Mitchell, R.R., Smyser, C.M., & Weed, S.E. (1975). Locus of control: Supervision and work satisfaction. *Academy of Management Journal, 18*: 623–631.

Mobile devices suggest need for policy reviews, speakers assert. (2010). *HR Focus, 87* (July): 6–8.

Moos, J. (2011, November 8). Census: Journalism majors make about $50,000. Poynter.org. Retrieved from http://www.poynter.org/latest-news/mediawire/152394/census-journalis m-majors-make-about-50k/

Morris, B. (2008). Steve Jobs speaks out. *Fortune*. Retrieved from http://archive.fortune.com/ galleries/2008/fortune/0803/gallery.jobsqna.fortune/5.html

Motion Picture Association of America. (2011). The cost of content theft by the numbers: Motion Picture Association of America Fact Sheet. Retrieved from http://www.mpaa.org/ Resources/8c33fb87–1ceb-456f-9a6e-f897759b9b44.pdf

MRI User Guide Definitions. (2011). GfK MRI. Retrieved from http://www.gfkmri.com/ Shortcuts/ClientService/GfKMRIUserGuideDefinitions.aspx

Munk, N. (2002). Power failure. *Vanity Fair, 503*(July): 128–131,167–170.

Mutter, A.D. (2011, February 24). Hyperlocals like TBD: More hype than hope. Retrieved from http://newsosaur.blogspot.com/2011/02/hyperlocals-like-tbd-mor e-hype-than.html

NABJ Broadcast News Survey: Diversity STILL lags in TV management. (2010). Retrieved from http://www.nabj.org/news/48802/Industry-News-NABJ-Broadcast-News-Surve y-Diversity-STILL-Lags-in-TV-Ma.htm

NABJ Print Census of Newsroom Managers. (2010, November 11). Retrieved from http://www. nabj.org/news/news.asp?id=49809&hhSearchTerms=Print

Nadler, D.A. (1987). The effective management of organizational change. In J. Lorsch (Ed.), *Handbook of organizational behavior* (pp. 358–369). Englewood Cliffs, NJ: Prentice Hall.

Nanus, B. (1992). *Visionary leadership*. San Francisco, CA: Jossey-Bass.

Napoli, P.M. (2003). *Audience economics: Media institutions and the audience marketplace*. New York, NY: Columbia University Press.

National Labor Relations Board. (2012). Acting General Counsel releases report on employer social media policies. Retrieved from http://www.nlrb.gov/news/acting-genera l-counsel-releases-report-employer-social-media-policies

Nelson, B., & Economy, P. (1996). *Managing for dummies*. New York, NY: Wiley Publishing.

Newkirk, P. (2011). The not-so-great migration. *Columbia Journalism Review, 50*(1, May/June): 40–43.

*New York Times v. Sullivan*. (1964). 376 U.S. 254.

Newspaper Association of America. (2014). Newspaper circulation volume. Retrieved from http://www.naa.org/Trends-and-Numbers/Circulation-Volume/Newspaper-Circulation-Volume.aspx

Newsroom employment up slightly, minority numbers plunge for third year. (2011). 2011 Census—ASNE. Retrieved from http://asne.org/content.asp?pl=121&sl=148&conten tid=148

Nichols, J., & McChesney, R. (2010). How to save journalism. *The Nation, 290*(3): 12–14, 16.

Niederhoffer, K., Mooth, R., Wiesenfeld, D., & Gordon, J. (2007). The origin and impact of CPG new-product buzz: Emerging trends and implications. *Journal of Advertising Research, 47*: 420–426.

Nielsen Co., A.C. (2012, January 6). *State of the media: Consumer usage report 2011*. Retrieved from http://blog.nielsen.com/nielsenwire/mediauniverse/

Nielsen Wire: 40% of tablet and smartphone owners use them while watching TV. (2011). Retrieved from http://www.nielsen.com/us/en/insights/news/2011/40-of-tablet-and-smartphone-owners-use-them-while-watching-tv.html

NLRB: Employee Facebook posts are protected. (2011). *HR Specialist*, Florida Employment Law (April): 5.

Noon, M. (1994). From apathy to alacrity: Managers and new technology in provincial newspapers. *Journal of Management Studies, 31*(1): 19–32.

Northouse, P.G. (2010). *Leadership: Theory and practice* (5th ed.). Thousand Oaks, CA: Sage.

O'Guinn, T. C., Allen, C. T., & Semenik, R. J. (2009). Advertising and Integrated Brand Promotion (5th edition—Instructor's edition). Mason, OH: South-Western Cengage Learning.

Olmstead, K., Mitchell, A., & Rosenstiel, T. (2011). Audio: Medium on the brink of major change. *State of the news media 2011*. Retrieved from http://stateofthemedia.org/2011/audio-essay/

Olson, M. (1965). *The logic of collective action*. Cambridge, MA: Harvard University Press.

Ouchi, W.G. (1981). *Theory Z*. Reading, MA: Addison-Wesley.

Ouchi, W. G., & Dowling, J. (1974). Defining span of control. *Administrative Sciences Quarterly, 19*(3): 257–365.

Packer, C., & Cleary, J. (2007). Rediscovering the public interest: An analysis of the common law governing post-employment non-compete contracts for media employees. *Cardozo Arts & Entertainment Law Journal, 24*: 1073–1120.

Paley, N. (2004). *Successful business planning: Energizing your company's potential*. London, England: Thorogood.

Papacharissi, Z. (Ed.) (2009). *Journalism and citizenship: New agendas in communication*. New York, NY: Routledge.

Parpis, E. (2011). Super Bowl crashers up close. *Adweek, 52*(1): 10–11.

Parr, B. (2011, February 6). AOL acquires Huffington Post for $315 million. *Mashable*. Retrieved from http://mashable.com/2011/02/07/breaking-aol-acquires-huffington-post-for-315-million/

Parry, K.W., & Bryman, A. (2006). Leadership in organizations. In S.R. Clegg, C. Hardy, T.B. Lawrence, & W.R. Nord (Eds.) *The Sage handbook of organization studies* (2nd ed., pp. 447–468). London, England: Sage Publications.

Paskin, J. (2009). Man on the (digital) street. *Columbia Journalism Review, 48*(4, November/December): 10–11.

Patch.org (2012). Retrieved from http://www.patch.com

Pathak, S. (2012). East meets West in Nissan social media-B-wood link. *Advertising Age, 83*(15, April 9): 12.

Pearce II, J.A., & David, F. (1987). Corporate mission statements: The bottom line. *Academy of Management Executive, 1*(2): 109–116.

Pearce, J.A., & Robinson, R.B. (1997). *Strategic management: Formulation, implementation and control*, (6th ed.). Boston, MA: Irwin McGraw-Hill.

Petner, T. (2009, September 2). Twitter alights in TV newsrooms. *TVNewsCheck*. Retrievedfrom http://www.tvnewscheck.com/article/2009/09/02/35207/twitter-alights-in-tv-newsrooms

Pew Hispanic Center. Project for Excellence in Journalism. (2009). Hispanics in the news: Events drive the narrative. Retrieved from www.pewhispanic.org

Pfeiffer, J.W. (Ed.). (1991). *Strategic planning: Selected readings*. San Diego, CA: Pfeiffer & Company.

Picard, R.G. (2006). *Journalism, value creation, and the future of news organizations*. Cambridge, MA: Joan Shorenstein Center on the Press, Politics, and Public Policy.

Picard, R.G. (2009, May 19). Why journalists deserve low pay. *The Christian Science Monitor*. Retrieved from http://www.csmonitor.com/Commentary/Opinion/2009/0519/p09s02-coop.html

Picard, R.G. (2011). *The economics and financing of media companies* (2nd ed.). New York, NY: Fordham University Press.

Playing favorites: How to avoid unintended partiality in decisions, reviews. (2010). *North Carolina Employment Law*, (January): 6

Poindexter, P.M., Coleman, R., & Shader, M. (2010). Stand-alone news photographs portray less diverse, more segregated communities. *Newspaper Research Journal, 31*(3, Summer): 83–88.

Policy Statement on Deception. (1983, October 14). Letter from then Federal Trade Commission Chairman James C. Miller III to Congressman John D. Dingell. Reprinted as an appendix to Cliffdale, 103 FTC 110 at 174 (1984).

Porter, M.E. (1985). *Competitive advantage: Creating and sustaining superior performance.* New York, NY: The Free Press.

Potter, D., Matsa, K-E., & Mitchell, A. (2011). Local TV: Good news after the fall. *State of the news media 2011.* Retrieved from http://stateofthemedia.org/2011/local-tv-essay/

Potts, M. (2007a, July 15). Backfence: Lessons learned. Retrieved from http:// recoveringjournalist.typepad.com/recovering_journalist/2007/07/backfence-lesso.html

Potts, M. (2007b). Journalism: Its intersection with hyperlocal web sites. *Nieman Reports, 61*(4, Winter): 66–67. Retrieved from http://niemanreports.org/articles/journalism-it s-intersection-with-hyperlocal-web-sites/

Powers, A. (2006). An exploratory study of the impact of leadership behavior on levels of news convergence and job satisfaction. In L. Küng (Ed.), *Leadership in the media industries: Changing context, emerging challenges* (pp. 11–28). Jönköping, Sweden: Jönköping International Business School.

Preparing an effective case analysis. (2005a). Belmont, CA: South-Western College Publishing. Retrieved from http://www.swlearning.com/management/hitt/hitt_student/case_analysis. html

Preparing an effective case analysis. (2005b). Belmont, CA: South-Western College Publishing. Retrieved from http://www.swlearning.com/management/hitt/sm6e/case_analysis/case_ analysis_2.html

Priest, W.C. (1994). An information framework for the planning and design of "information highways." Retrieved from https://w2.eff.org/Infrastructure/Govt_docs/cits_nii_ framework_ota.report

Pritchard, D., & Stonbely, S. (2007). Racial profiling in the newsroom. *Journalism and Mass Communication Quarterly, 84*(2, Summer): 231–248.

Progressive discipline keeps staff on track—And you out of court. (2009). *Florida Employment Law*, (October): 4.

Project Management Institute. (2008). *A guide to project management body of knowledge.* Newtown Square, PA: Author.

PRSA Public Relations Society of America Code of Ethics. (2000). Retrieved from (www.prsa.org)

Quick Reference Guide for Meeting & Event Professionals—Irving, Texas (2012). Irving Convention & Visitors Bureau. Retrieved from http://planyourmeetings.com/wp-content/ uploads/2012/12/Irving-CVB-quick-reference-guide.pdf

Rajagopalan, N., Rasheed, A., & Datta, D.K. (1994). Strategic decision processes: An integrative framework and future directions. In P. Lorange (Ed.), *Strategic planning process* (pp. 327–365). Brookfield, VT.: Dartmouth Publishing Company.

Reading, C. (2002). *Strategic business planning: A dynamic system for improving performance and competitive advantage.* London, England: Kogan.

Reca, A.A. (2006). Issues in media product management. In A.B. Albarran, S.M. Chan-Olmsted, & M.O. Wirth (Eds.), *Handbook of Media Management and Economics* (pp. 181–201). Mahwah, NJ: Lawrence Erlbaum Publishers.

Redmond, J., & Trager, R. (2004). *Balancing on the wire: The art of managing media organizations* (2nd ed.). Cincinnati, OH: Atomic Dog.

Reinardy, S. (2009a). Beyond satisfaction: Journalists doubt career intentions as organizational support diminishes and job satisfaction declines. *Atlantic Journal of Communication, 17*(3): 126–139.

Reinardy, S. (2009b). Female journalists more likely to leave newspapers. *Newspaper Research Journal, 30*(3): 42–57.

Reinardy, S. (2010). Downsizing effects on personnel: The case of layoff survivors in U.S. newspapers. *Journal of Media Business Studies, 7*: 1–19.

Reinardy, S. (2011a). Journalism's layoff survivors tap resources to remain satisfied. *Atlantic Journal of Communication, 19*(5): 285–298.

Reinardy, S. (2011b). Newspaper journalism in crisis: Burnout on the rise, eroding young journalists' career commitment. *Journalism: Theory, Practice and Criticism, 12*: 33–50.

Remez, M. (2012). How community news is faring. In The Pew Research Center's Project for Excellence in Journalism (Ed.), *The State of the News Media 2012*. Retrieved from http://stateofthemedia.org/2012/mobile-devices-and-news-consumption-some-goo d-signs-for-journalism/how-community-news-is-faring/

Richmond, V.P., McCroskey, J.C., & Payne, S.K. (1987). *Nonverbal behavior in interpersonal relations*. Englewood Cliffs, NJ: Prentice-Hall.

Rizzo, J.R., House, R.J., & Lirtzman, S.I. (1970). Role conflict and ambiguity in complex organizations. *Administrative Science Quarterly, 15*(2): 150–163.

Roach, S. (2012). The constant gardener. *Columbia Journalism Review, 50*(6, March/April): 24–29.

Roderick, K. (2012, July 13). *Daily Journal* lays off photographers, will give cameras to reporters. *LA Observed*. Retrieved from http://www.laobserved.com/archive/2012/07/ daily_journal_lays_off_ph.php

Rogers, E. (1983). *Diffusion of innovation* (3rd ed.). New York, NY: Free Press.

Roose, K. (2012, May 3). Loeb accuses Yahoo officials of resume padding. *New York Times*. Retrieved from http://dealbook.nytimes.com/2012/05/03/loeb-accuses-yahoo-official s-of-resume-padding/

Rossheim, J. (2011). Social Networking: The art of social media recruiting. Monster.com. Retrieved from http://hiring.monster.com/hr/hr-best-practices/recruiting-hiring-advice/ job-screening-techniques/recruiting-using-social-media.aspx

Rossow, M.D. (2009). Connecting with the community: Hiring the right 'face' for the newspaper. *Grassroots Editor, 50*: 5–9.

*Roth v. U.S.* (1957). 354 U.S. 476.

Rubb, S. (2013). Overeducation, undereducation and asymmetric information in occupational mobility. *Applied Economics, 45*: 741–751.

Russial, J.T. (1997). Topic-team performance: A content study. *Newspaper Research Journal, 18*(1–2): 126–144.

Ryan, K.M. (2009). The performative journalist: Job satisfaction, temporary workers and American television news. *Journalism, 10*(5): 647–664.

Sabbagh, D., & Halliday, J. (2012, May 1). Rupert Murdoch 'not fit to lead' major international company, MPs conclude. *The Guardian*. Retrieved from http://www.guardian.co.uk/ media/2012/may/01/rupert-murdoch-not-fit-select-committee

Saksena, S., & Hollifield, C.A. (2002). U.S. newspapers and the development of online editions. *International Journal on Media Management, 4*: 75–84.

Sánchez-Tabernero, A. (2004). The future of media companies: Strategies for an unpredictable world. In R.G. Picard (Ed.), *Strategic responses to media market changes* (pp. 19–34). Jönköping, Sweden: Jönköping International Business School.

Sandstrom, C. (2008, November 2). Disruptive innovation and the bankruptcy of Polaroid. Retrieved from http://www.slideshare.net/Christiansandstrom/disruptive-innovatio n-and-the-bankruptcy-of-polaroid-presentation

Sashkin, M. (1989). The visionary leader. In R.L. Taylor & W.E. Rosenbach (Eds.), *Leadership: Challenges for today's manager* (pp. 45–52). New York, NY: Nichols.

Schaffer, J. (2007). When community residents commit "random acts of journalism." *Nieman Reports, 61*(4, Winter): 59–61. This article includes a section called "Tips about starting a hyperlocal web site."

Schaffer, J., & Polgreen, E. (2012, May). Engaging audiences: Measuring interactions, engagement and conversion—A survey of "digital-first" news sites. J-Lab: The Institute for Interactive Journalism. Retrieved from http://www.j-lab.org/_uploads/publications/ engaging-audiences/EngagementReport_web.pdf

Schein, E.H. (1985). *Career survival*. San Francisco, CA: Jossey-Bass.

Schein, E.H. (2004). *Organizational culture and leadership*. San Francisco, CA: Jossey-Bass.

Schmitz Weiss, A. (2007) Online journalism: Three new research paradigms for exploration. Proceedings of the 5th International Symposium on Communication in the Millennium, Bloomington, IN.

Schmitz Weiss, A. (2008). *The transformation of the newsroom: The collaborative dynamics of journalists' work*. Unpublished dissertation. University of Texas at Austin.

Schmitz Weiss, A., & Domingo, D. (2010). Innovation processes in online newsrooms as actor-networks and communities of practice. *New Media & Society, 12*(7): 1156–1171.

Schudson, M., & Fink, K. (2012). The algorithm method. *Columbia Journalism Review, 50*(5, January/February): 63.

Schumpeter, J. (1950). *Capitalism, socialism and democracy* (3rd ed.). New York, NY: Harper and Row.

Service, R.W., & Loudon, D.L. (2010). The "is" versus the "should be" of performance appraisals: Don't confuse them. *Business Renaissance Quarterly, 5*(3; Fall): 63–84.

Severin, W.J., & Tankard, J.W., Jr. (1992). *Communication theories: Origins, methods, and uses in mass media* (3rd ed.). New York, NY: Longman.

Shane, S., & Venkataraman, S. (2000). The promise of entrepreneurship as a field of research. *The Academy of Management Review, 25*: 217–226.

Shane, S.A. (2008). *The illusions of entrepreneurship: The costly myths that entrepreneurs, investors and policy makers live by*. New Haven, CT: Yale University Press.

Sharma, S. (2009, Fall). Reading ESPN against niches. *Mediascape: UCLA's Journal of Cinema and Media Studies*. Retrieved from http://www.tft.ucla.edu/mediascape/Fall09_Sharma.pdf

Shaver, D., & Shaver, M.A. (2006). Credentials, strategy and style: The relationship between leadership characteristics and strategic direction in media companies. In L. Küng (Ed.), *Leadership in the media industry: Changing contexts, emerging challenges* (JIBS Research Reports No. 2006–1, pp.123–136). Jonskoping, Sweden: Media Management and Transformation Centre, Jonskoping International Business School, Jonskoping University.

Shaver, D., & Shaver, M.A. (2008). Generating audience loyalty to Internet news providers through branding. In M. Ots (Ed.), *Media brands and branding* (pp. 79–86). Jönköping, Sweden: Jönköping International Business School.

Shaver, M. (1995). *Making the sale! How to sell media with marketing*. Chicago, IL: Copy Workshop.

Sherif, M. (1962). *Intergroup relations and leadership*. New York, NY: Wiley.

Shields, M. (2010). A new zip code. *Brandweek, 51*(7, February 15): 13.

Should you ban bosses from "friending" staff? (2011). *The HR Specialist, 9*(4, April): 1–2.

Siegelman, R. [stanfordbusiness]. (2010, May 12). Evaluating a business idea [Video file]. Retrieved from http://www.youtube.com/watch?v=y9ClKzMq3n0&feature=relmfu

Siegert, G., Gerth, M.A., & Rademacher, P. (2011). Brand identity-driven decision making by journalists and media managers: The MBAC model as a theoretical framework. *The International Journal on Media Management, 13*(1): 53–70.

Silcock, B.W., & Keith, S. (2006). Translating the Tower of Babel?: Issues of definition, language and culture in converged newsrooms. *Journalism Studies, 7*(4): 610–627.

Singer, J.B. (2003). Who are these guys? The online challenge to the notion of journalistic professionalism. *Journalism, 4*: 139–163.

Singer, J.B. (2004a). More than ink-stained wretches: The resocialization of print journalists in converged newsrooms. *Journalism & Mass Communication Quarterly, 81*(4): 838–856.

Singer, J.B. (2004b). Strange bedfellows? The diffusion of convergence in four news organizations. *Journalism Studies, 5*(1): 3–18.

Singer, J. (2006). Parternships and public service: Normative issues for journalists in converged newsrooms. *Journal of Mass Media Ethics, 21*(1): 30–53.

Singer, J.B. (2008). Five Ws and an H: Digital challenges in newspaper newsrooms and boardrooms. *The International Journal on Media Management, 10*(3): 122–129.

Singer, J. (2011). Journalism and digital technologies. In W. Lowrey & P.J. Gade (Eds.), *Changing the news: The forces shaping journalism in uncertain times*. (pp. 213–229). New York: Routledge.

Singer, J.B., Domingo, D., Heinonen, A., Hermida, A., Paulussen, S., Quandt, T., Reich, Z., & Vujnovic, M. (2011). *Participatory Journalism*. West Sussex, England: Wiley-Blackwell.

Skinner, B.F. (1971). *Beyond freedom and dignity*. New York, NY: Alfred A. Knopf.

Smith, A. (1776). *The Wealth of Nations*. Hollywood, FL: Simon and Brown.

Smith, A. (2012). NLRB takes sledgehammer to social media policies. Society for Human Resources Management. Retrieved from http://www.shrm.org/legalissues/federalresources/pages/nlrbsocialmediapolicies.aspx

Smith, J.A., Boyle, B.A., & Cannon, H.M. (2010). Survey-based targeting fine tunes television media planning: A case for accuracy and cost efficiency. *Journal of Advertising Research, 50*(4): 429–439.

Smith, S. (2011). Steve Smith's eye on digital media: Quarterly app review. *Media Industry Newsletter, 64*(40): 1, 7–12.

Snapshot. (2012). City of Irving Demographics Snapshot. http://cityofirving.org/1564/ Demographics

So you want to know more about us, huh? (2012). HARO—Help A Reporter Out. Retrieved from http://www.helpareporter.com/about-haro

Society of Professional Journalists Code of Ethics. (1996). In J. Folkerts & S. Lacy. (Eds.), *The media in your life* (3rd ed., p. 353). Boston, MA: Allyn & Bacon.

Solomon, L.E. (2011, August 18). Report of the General Counsel on social media cases. National Labor Relations Board. Memorandum OM 11–74. Retrieved from https://www.nlrb.gov/news/acting-general-counsel-releases-report-social-media-cases

Stelter, B. (2012, April 6). NBC fires producer of misleading Zimmerman tape. Media Decoder, *New York Times.* Retrieved from http://mediadecoder.blogs.nytimes.com/2012/04/06/nbc-fires-producer-of-misleading-zimmerman-tape/

Stelter, B. (2013, May 12). As TV ratings and profits fall, networks face a cliffhanger *New York Times.* Retrieved from http://www.nytimes.com/2013/05/13/business/media/tv-network s-face-falling-ratings-and-new-rivals.html?pagewanted=all

Stepp, C.S. (2007). Caught in the contradiction. *American Journalism Review, 29*(April/May): 34–39.

Stevens, R.E., Sherwood, P.K., & Dunn, P. (1993). *Market analysis: Assessing your business opportunities.* New York, NY: Haworth Press.

Steyn, E., & Steyn, D. (2009). The challenge to incorporate teamwork as a managerial competency: The case of mainstream South African newsrooms. *Journal of Media Business Studies, 6*(2): 47–65.

Stigler, G.J. (1952). *The theory of price* (rev. ed.). New York, NY: Macmillan.

Stinchcombe, A.L. (1959). Bureaucratic and craft administration of production: A comparative study. *Administrative Science Quarterly, 4*: 168–187.

Stogdill, R.M. (1974). *Handbook of leadership: A survey of theory and research.* New York, NY: The Free Press.

Stop off-the-clock work with strong OT rules. (2011). *The HR Specialist, 9*(5, May): 1.

Strang, D., & Macy, M.W. (2001). In search of excellence: Fads, success stories, and adaptive emulation. *American Journal of Sociology, 107*: 147–182.

Straub, J.T. (1984). *Managing: An introduction.* Boston, MA: Kent.

Straubhaar, J. (1991). Beyond media imperialism: Asymmetrical interdependence and cultural proximity. *Critical Studies in Mass Communication, 8*: 1–11.

Strömback, J., & Karlsson, M. (2011). Who's got the power? Journalists' perceptions of changing influences over the news. *Journalism Practice, 5*(6): 643–656.

Strupp, J. (2000). Three-point play: Print, Web, and TV operations now live under the same roof in Tampa. Big Brother may not be watching, but everyone else is. *Editor and Publisher,* (August 21): 18–23.

Stuhlfaut, M.W. (2011). The creative code: An organisational influence on the creative process in advertising. *International Journal of Advertising, 30*(2): 282–304.

Sullivan, P. (2010). A dynamic analysis of educational attainment, occupational choices, and job search. *International Economic Review, 51*: 289–317.

Sylvie, G. (2011). The call and challenge for diversity. In W. Lowrey & P. Gade (Eds.), *Changing the news: The forces shaping journalism in uncertain times* (pp. 83–101). New York, NY: Routledge.

Sylvie, G., & Chyi, H.S. (2007). One product two markets: How geography differentiates online newspaper audiences. *Journalism & Mass Communication Quarterly, 84*(3): 562–581.

Sylvie, G., & Gade, P. (2009). Changes in news work: Implications for newsroom managers. *Journal of Media Business Studies, 6*(1): 113–148.

Sylvie, G., & Huang, J.S. (2006, May). Decision-making by newspaper editors: Understanding values and change. Presented at the meeting of the International Communication Association, Dresden, Germany.

Sylvie, G., & Huang, J.S. (2008a). Decision making by newspaper editors: Understanding values and change. In C. Dal Zotto & H. van Kranenburg (Eds.), *Management and innovation in the media industry* (pp. 215–240). Cheltenham, England: Edward Elgar.

Sylvie, G., & Huang, J. S. (2008b). Value systems and decision-making styles of newspaper front-line editors. *Journalism & Mass Communication Quarterly, 85*(1): 61–82.

Sylvie, G., & Moon, S. J. (2007). Framing change: Who's in charge in the newsroom. In L. Achtenhagen (Ed.), *Organizing media: Mastering the challenges of organizational change* (pp. 89–124). Jönköping, Sweden: Jönköping International Business School.

Sylvie, G., & Witherspoon, P. D. (2002). *Time, change, and the American newspaper.* Mahwah, NJ: Lawrence Erlbaum Associates.

Tajfel, H., & Turner, J. C. (1986). The social identity theory of intergroup behavior. In S. Worchel & W. G. Austin (Eds.), *Psychology of intergroup relations* (pp. 7–24). Chicago, IL: Nelson-Hall.

Thornton, L.-J., & Keith, S. M. (2009). From convergence to Webvergence: Tracking the evolution of broadcast-print partnerships through the lens of change theory. *Journalism and Mass Communication Quarterly, 86*(2): 257–276.

Time Warner, Inc. (2013). Annual Report. Retrieved from http://ir.timewarner.com/phoenix.zhtm l?c=70972&p=irol-reportsAnnual

Timmons, J. A. (2004). Opportunity recognition. In W. D. Bygrave & A. Zacharakis (Eds.), *The portable MBA in entrepreneurship* (pp. 29–70). Hoboken, NJ: John Wiley and Sons.

Title VII and the Courts: The legal basis for sexual discrimination lawsuits. (2011). *Supreme Court Debates, 14*(7, October): 7–8.

Torosyan, G., & Starck, K. (2006). Renegotiating media in the post-Soviet era: Western journalism practices in the Armenian radio program Aniv. *International Journal of Media and Cultural Politics, 2*(2): 201–218.

Track your traffic: Web analytics for journalists. (2010, December 9). Poynter's News University webinar. Retrieved from https://www.newsu.org/web-analytics-journalists

Tregoe, B. B., & Tobia, P. M. (1991). Strategy versus planning: Bridging the gap. *The Journal of Business Strategy, 12*: 14–19. Reprinted in P. Lorange (Ed.), *Strategic planning process,* (1994: pp. 79–84). Aldershot, England: Dartmouth.

Triandis, H. C., & Albert, R. D. (1987). Cross-cultural perspectives. In F. M. Jablin, L. L. Putnam, K. H. Roberts, & L. W. Porter (Eds.), *Handbook of Organizational Communication* (pp. 264–295). Newbury Park, NJ: Sage.

Tsotsis, A. (2011, November 6). Instagram's Kevin Systrom on international expansion, Instagram video, funding rumors and more. *TechCrunch.* Retrieved from http://techcrunch. com/2011/11/06/instagrams-kevin-systrom-on-international-expansion-instagram-video -funding-rumors-and-more/

U.S. Census Bureau. (2011, September 29). 2010 Census shows White population growth fueled by Hispanics. Retrieved from https://www.census.gov/newsroom/releases/archives/2010_ census/cb11-cn184.html

U.S. Census Bureau. (2014). Population. Retrieved from http://www.census.gov/topics/ population.html

U.S. Department of Labor. (2011a). Wages. Minimum wage. Retrieved from http://www.dol.gov/ dol/topic/wages/minimumwage.htm

U.S. Department of Labor. (2011b). Minimum wage laws in the States—January 1, 2011. WHD—Wage and Hour Division. Retrieved from http://www.dol.gov/whd/minwage/ america.htm

U.S. Government Printing Office. (2009, November). Fair Use. Retrieved from http://www. copyright.gov/fls/fl102.html

U.S. Government Printing Office. (2010, November). International copyright relations of the United States. Circular 38A. Retrieved from http://www.copyright.gov/circs/circ38a. pdf

Vaill, P. (1993). Visionary leadership. In Cohen, R. (Ed.), *The portable MBA in management* (pp. 12–37). New York, NY: Wiley.

*Valentine v. Chrestensen.* (1942). 316 U.S. 52.

Van Maanen, J., & Barley, S. R. (1984). Occupational communities: Culture and control in organizations. In B. M. Staw & L. L. Cummings (Eds.), *Research in organizational behavior* (pp. 287–365). Greenwich, CT: JAI Press.

Viacom Inc. (2013). Annual Report. Retrieved from http://ir.viacom.com/

Vroom, V. H. (1964). *Work and motivation.* New York, NY: Wiley.

Wakslag, J. (2008, March). Today's Media Landscape: Separating fact from fiction on today's media consumer. Presented to the conference on Advances in Audience and Consumer Marketing Research. Miami, FL.

Walsh, M.E. (2011). Life in the hyperlocal trenches. *Quill, 99*(1, January/February): 34.

Walt Disney Co. (2013). Annual Report. Author. Retrieved from http://cdn.media. ir.thewaltdisneycompany.com/2013/annual/10kwrap-2013.pdf

Wanberg, C.R., & Banas, J.T. (2000). Predictors and outcomes of openness to changes in a reorganizing workplace. *Journal of Applied Psychology, 85*: 132–142.

Weaver, D., Beam, R., Brownlee, B., Voakes, P., & Wilhoit, G.C. (2003). The face and mind of the American journalist. Retrieved from http://www.poynter.org/content/content_view. asp?id=28235

Weaver, D., Beam, R.A., Brownlee, B.J., Voakes, P.S., & Wilhoit, G.C. (2007). *The American journalist in the 21st century: U.S. news people at the dawn of a new millennium.* Mahwah, NJ: Erlbaum Associates.

Weaver, D.H., & Wilhoit, G.C. (1991). *The American journalist: A portrait of U.S. news people and their work* (2nd ed.). Bloomington, IN: Indiana University Press.

Weber, M.M., & Kirk, D.J. (2000). Teaching teachers to teach cases: It's not what you know, it's what you ask. *Marketing Education Review, 10*: 59–67.

Webster, F., & Knutson, J. (2011). What is project management? In P.C. Dinsmore & J. Cabanis-Brewin (Eds.), *The AMA handbook of project management* (3rd ed., pp. 1–12). New York, NY: AMACOM.

Weick, K.E. (1995). *Sensemaking in organizations.* Thousand Oaks, CA: Sage.

Weitekamp, R. & Pruitt, B. (2011, March 7). 'Jobless entrepreneurship' tarnishes steady rate of U.S. startup activity, Kauffman study shows. Kauffman Foundation. Retrieved from http://www.kauffman.org/newsroom/jobless-entrepreneurship-tarnishes-steady-rate -of-us-startup-activity.aspx

Wenger, E. (1998). *Communities of practice, learning, meaning, and identity.* Cambridge, England: Cambridge University Press.

Wertheim, E.G. (2006). A model for case analysis and problem solving. College of Business Administration, Northeastern University. Retrieved from http://www.ebah.com.br/content/ ABAAAAB_cAB/a-model-for-case-analysis-and-problem-solving

Who Makes the News? Highlights. (2010). Global Media Monitoring Project 2010. Retrieved from http://whomakesthenews.org/images/stories/restricted/ highlights/highlights_en.pdf

Wilson, B. (2012). How newspapers work. *Howstuffworks.* Retrieved from http://people. howstuffworks.com/newspaper4.htm

Wilson, I. (2003). *The subtle art of strategy: Organizational planning in uncertain times.* Westport, CT: Praeger.

Wimmer, R., & Dominick, J. (2011). *Mass media research: An introduction* (9th ed.). Boston, MA: Wadsworth.

Wirth, M.O. (2006). Issues in media convergence. In A.B. Albarran, S.M. Chan-Olmstead, & M.O. Wirth (Eds.), *Handbook of media management and Economics* (pp. 445–462). Mahwah, NJ: Erlbaum Associates.

Wirtz, B.W. (2001). Reconfiguration of value chains in converging media and communications markets. *Long Range Planning, 34*(4): 489–506.

Wirtz, B.W. (2011). *Media and Internet management.* Wiesbaden, Germany: Gabler.

Witschge, T., & Nygren, G. (2009). Journalistic work: A profession under pressure? *Journal of Media Business Studies, 6*(1): 37–59.

Wolfe, N. (2010, January 28). Strategic planning is obsolete. Quantum Thinking. Retrieved from http://quantumleadersblog.com/2010/01/28/strategic-planning-is-obsolete/

Wong, W. (2010, December 20). TV on the go ready to hit the small screen. *Chicago Tribune.* Retrieved from http://articles.chicagotribune.com/2010-12-20/business/ct-biz-1221-out look-technology-20101220_1_mobile-digital-tv-open-mobile-video-coalition-anne-schelle

Woods, K. (2005). *Looking inward, going forward.* McLean, VA: National Association of Minority Media Executives.

World Bank. (2012). South Asia overview. Retrieved from http://www.worldbank.org/en/ region/sar

Wu, D.W., & Izard, R. (2008). Representing the total community: Relationships between Asian American staff and Asian American coverage in nine U.S. newspapers. *Journalism and Mass Communication Quarterly, 85*(1): 99–112.

Zaccaro, S.J., Kemp, C., & Bader, P. (2004). Leader traits and attributes. In J. Antonakis, A.T. Cianciolo, & R.J. Sternberg (Eds.), *The nature of leadership* (pp. 101–124). Thousand Oaks, CA: Sage

Zacharakis, A. (2004). Building a business plan. In W.D. Bygrave & A. Zacharakis (Eds.), *The portable MBA in entrepreneurship* (pp. 107–139). Hoboken, NJ: John Wiley and Sons.

Zoch, L.M., & van Slyke Turk, U.J. (1998). Women making news: Gender as a variable in source selection and use. *Journalism & Mass Communication Quarterly, 75*: 776–788.

Zuckerman, L. (1982). Slaves to television. *Columbia Journalism Review, 20*(5, Jan/Feb): 11–12.

Zbylut, M.L., Brunner, J.M., Vowels, C.L., and Kim, J.M. (2007). Case method instruction: 25 minutes of discussion can make a difference. United States Army Research Institute for the Behavioral and Social Sciences Technical Report 1203—July 2007. Retrieved from http://www.dtic.mil/cgi-bin/GetTRDoc?AD=ADA472171

# AUTHOR INDEX

# SUBJECT INDEX

Note: figures are indicated by "*f*" and tables by "*t*".

inted in the United States
Bookmasters